Software Ecosystem

Software Ecosystem
Understanding an Indispensable Technology and Industry

David G. Messerschmitt and Clemens Szyperski

The MIT Press
Cambridge, Massachusetts
London, England

This book was set in Sabon by SNP Best-set Typesetter Ltd., Hong Kong
Printed and bound in the United States of America.

Library of Congress Cataloging-in-Publication Data

Messerschmitt, David G.
    Software ecosystem : understanding an indispensable technology and industry /
David G. Messerschmitt and Clemens Szyperski.
        p.   cm.
    Includes bibliographical references and index.
    ISBN 0-262-13432-2 (hc. : alk. paper)
    1. Computer software.   2. Computer software—Development.   3. Computer
software industry.   I. Szyperski, Clemens.   II. Title.

QA76.754.M47 2003
005.3—dc21   2002044404

10 9 8 7 6 5 4 3 2 1

To Dody and Laura
—D.G.M.

To Bianca, Leonie, Lennard, Amelie, and Luca
—C.A.S.

Contents

Preface

In this book, software technology and the myriad issues that surround its dissemination and use are examined from a number of relevant perspectives. This is especially timely as the importance of software in the overall industrial economy grows, and as the software industry undergoes important transformations. The tremendous success of the Internet is noteworthy in forever changing the structure of the industry, the applications of software, and software business models.

Most books on software focus on software technology or development methodologies. To be successful, software professionals need to appreciate the context of software in the real world. Other professionals like managers, lawyers, and economists with an interest in software and its uses and effects need to appreciate more deeply the technical aspects of software, at least those relevant to their own contexts. They need a vocabulary and a common frame of reference. This book addresses this need by explaining the characteristics of software in its context, emphasizing both technical and nontechnical issues, and relating the two.

The software industry cannot be fully appreciated outside the context of what precedes and what follows development. Conceptualizing what it does, the needs it serves, and its effects is an important prerequisite for understanding its development. Many issues follow software deployment, including provisioning, operations, use, maintenance and upgrade, customer service, and coordinated organizational changes and management challenges. Thus, an overall goal of this book is to integrate an explanation of pre- and post-development activities with a description of software development and technology.

The software industry is itself very complex, with many complementary products necessary to form a systems solution and complex alliances and standardization processes needed to meet the needs of numerous stakeholders. Together, the software suppliers, standardization bodies, content suppliers, service providers, and end-user organizations form a complex web of relationships. The "ecosystem" metaphor is truly descriptive.

The growing importance and special characteristics of software increasingly make it an area of activity for government and an interesting topic of study for the social sciences, law, and business. We capture the most important issues raised by the growing importance of software in the management, policy, and legal arenas, and relate them to the characteristics of software technology and business models.

The overarching theme of the book is that software is different. It is different from information goods in terms of its economic properties: although it shares some characteristics with information goods, with material goods, and even with services, it mixes these characteristics in unique ways. It requires a different legal perspective, as evidenced by the increasing attention given to software-specific issues in legislation and the courts, including patents, copyrights, civil liberties, and antitrust. It is distinctive among technologies and in its industrial and business challenges in numerous ways. The single most prominent objective of this book is to explain how software is different.

In summary, software touches many professional lives. This leads to many interrelated and overlapping perspectives on software, technical and nontechnical. Following introductory chapters, the book is organized around the perspectives of the user, software engineer, manager, industrialist, lawyer or policy expert, and economist as well as the overlaps and relationships among these perspectives. The objective of the book is to capture the key software issues and concerns of each profession, to describe the characteristics of software ecosystem as well as the relevant business relationships and processes that surround it, and then to explain these characteristics of software in a way that readers can understand even if they are not technologists.

Each chapter is not written primarily to address the needs of the associated professions; indeed, that chapter is likely to be rather superficial to an expert. Rather, the chapters are intended to convey a comprehensive view of the software ecosystem for the benefit of practitioners of each and every perspective. The book is primarily about software, so we make no attempt to be comprehensive in our treatment of the surrounding issues; rather, we explain them in sufficient detail to be able to relate them substantively to software. We do attempt to be reasonably comprehensive in explaining software itself, and in an accessible way, while avoiding numerous detailed technical issues of keen interest to technologists but less relevant from other perspectives.

The software industry has always undergone rapid change, but arguably this change has been never more swift than today, principally because of the Internet. We firmly believe that software would benefit from more in-depth research in economics, management, policy, and legal disciplines. For example, the opportunities surrounding the growing role of the service provider as an intermediary between software and the user are poorly understood but are nevertheless being very actively pursued. If you are a scholar interested in studying software-related issues, we aim to empower you by explaining arcane but relevant characteristics of technology and processes. As additional aids, a list of specific research and discussion issues is included at the end of each chapter and a glossary of the most important terms at the end of the book.

We are sensitive to the issue that since one co-author is an employee of Microsoft Corporation, the book may promulgate a Microsoft-centric view of the software world. As this is not our intention, we have given equal weight to numerous examples from across the software industry and have attempted to represent alternative viewpoints on many controversial issues rather than advocating a single viewpoint.

If you are a technical professional, you should also have a deeper appreciation and understanding of the many nontechnical processes, relationships, and issues that surround software. If you have an interest in molding the technology in ways that make it more useful and successful, enhance its positive outcomes, and mitigate its possible problems, you should find this book a helpful starting point.

This book is in part an outgrowth of a course taught at the University of California at Berkeley, "Strategic Computing and Communications Technology," to engineering, information management, and business administration students. It should prove useful in similar classes that examine the industrial and economic considerations of software: business, economics, and law courses, and courses for software professionals.

The book has an associated Web site, ⟨http://mitpress.mit.edu/softeco⟩, where supplementary materials like hyperlinks to resources referenced in the book, more detailed or analytical write-ups, and presentation slides are posted. This should be particularly valuable to instructors using this book.

This work was first published as a technical report (Messerschmitt and Szyperski 2001). Messerschmitt is indebted to Hal Varian, who co-taught the "Strategic Computing" course in 1997 and helped to refine and expand it in subsequent years, and to Carl Shapiro, who co-taught the course in 2001 and provided numerous helpful comments on the manuscript of this book. Others provided many useful comments on preliminary versions of the book, including Glenn Woroch of the University of

California at Berkeley, Leonard Cheng of the Hong Kong Institute of Science and Technology, Cuno Pfister of Oberon Microsystems, Zurich, and several anonymous reviewers. Messerschmitt has benefited from discussions with others with a deep and abiding interest in the software and communications industries, including Michael Katz and Joseph Farrell of Berkeley and Jean-Pierre Hubaux of the Swiss Federal Institute of Technology in Lausanne. Szyperski has benefited from discussions with Brad Cox, Ron Kay, and Norbert Szyperski.

Software Ecosystem

1
Introduction

[I want] minimum information given with maximum politeness.
Jacqueline Kennedy

Jacqueline Kennedy would likely be disappointed nowadays in her preference for receiving "minimum information." Information is proliferating wildly, and software is partly to blame. And sometimes the presentation of this vast information is none too polite, but hopefully this book is an exception.

The software industry has become crucial to the global economy. It is a large and rapidly growing industry in its own right, and its secondary impact on the remainder of the economy is disproportionate. In light of this, the software industry deserves much focus and attention by nontechnical professionals in fields such as management, economics, policy, and law. Obstacles to understanding include the often arcane and inaccessible nature of software technology, and a lack of visibility into the internal workings of the software industry and software in its context of uses. Individual productivity and Internet applications are familiar to us all, but the important role that software plays in organizations of all types is less visible though arguably far more influential. Controversial policy issues surrounding copyright enforcement and access to pornography by children are highly visible, but the public debate rarely takes adequate account of the opportunities and challenges afforded by the ubiquitous, embedded nature of today's software technologies.

This book seeks to explain to a broad technical and nontechnical audience the characteristics of software technology and of the business of software creation, and the context within which software is deployed, operated, and used. Given the growing importance of software and the rapid changes occurring in how it is developed, sold, and used, this is an opportune time for a comprehensive examination of the many facets of software.

1.1 What Makes Software Interesting?

Software has always been interesting to computer scientists, who appreciate its arcane details and deep technical challenges. But why should it be interesting to other professions? One reason has already been noted: It is the foundation of an important industry, and it is making an increasingly important contribution to the world's economy and raising a number of challenging policy and legal issues. Fortunately, there is much more to it than that—software is intellectually interesting from a wide variety of perspectives. The following are some interesting aspects of software; each is described here briefly and elaborated throughout the book.

1.1.1 Software Is Different

The software industry started from scratch only about fifty years ago, and has arguably become indispensable today, not only in its own economic effect but also in the efficient and effective management of many other industries. This journey from obscure to indispensable is by no means unique; for example, witness the earlier technological revolutions wrought by electrification or the automobile or communications. It is interesting to compare software to other industries, looking for parallels that might offer insights to the software industry. A basic thesis of the book is that software and the software industry are simply different; while such parallels are useful, they are inadequate to explain the many characteristics of the software industry.

Consider software as an economic good. It does have many characteristics that are individually familiar, but they are collected in unusual combinations. For example, like writing a novel, investment in software creation is risky, but unlike writing a novel, it requires collaboration with its users in defining its features. Like an organizational hierarchy, software applications are often essential to running a business, but unlike an organizational hierarchy, software is often designed by outside vendors with limited ability to adapt to special or changing needs. Although like many material goods and even human employees, software is valued for what it does, unlike material goods it has practically no unit manufacturing costs and is totally dependent on an infrastructure of equipment providing its execution environment. To a considerably greater degree than most material goods, a single software application and its supporting infrastructure are decomposed into many internal units, called modules (see chapter 4), which are often supplied by different vendors and with different ownership. Even the term *ownership* has somewhat different connotations than when used for material goods, because it is based on intellectual property laws rather than on title and physical possession. As with many other goods, the use of software includes an important operational side, but these operations are often split across a multitude of administrative domains with a limited opportunity for coordination. Like information, software is usually protected by copyright, but unlike information it can also incorporate patented inventions.

These examples, and others developed later, suggest that the software industry—as well as interested participants like the end-user, service provider, and regulatory authorities—confronts unique challenges. In addressing these challenges, it is important to appreciate the many facets of software and how it is created and used in the real world.

1.1.2   Software Is Ubiquitous

Software is everywhere! Many of us use computers and software on a daily basis, often many hours per day. Many material products that have a behavior, that do something, have software embedded within. Software has become a part of our lifestyle, but even more fundamentally it has become integral to the operation of organizations of all types, including industry, education, and government. The operations of most organizations are as dependent on software as they are on their human workers, and dependent as well on the smooth interworking of software with workers. This puts a burden on many professions and disciplines whose work bears on individuals or organizations to develop and incorporate a deeper understanding of software.

1.1.3   Software Makes Our Environment Interactive

One of software's primary effects is to change our environment in fundamental ways. In the past, our environment was mostly built; we were surrounded by largely passive objects and artifacts, and most of our interaction was with other people. Increasingly, software is creating an environment in which we interact with inanimate objects in increasingly sophisticated ways.

1.1.4   Software Is Important

In our information age and information society, information has become an important commodity. More and more workers are information workers, who manipulate and manage information as their primary job function, or knowledge workers, who create and use new knowledge based on assembling and assimilating large bodies of information. Software has become a primary vehicle by which the most mechanistic aspects of information acquisition, organization, manipulation, and access are realized, supplemented by the insights and actions of people. The growing importance of information and knowledge lead directly to the growing importance and role of software.

The addition of communication to the suite of information technologies (manifested primarily by the Internet) is dramatically increasing the importance of software to organizations and other social institutions. A primary distinguishing feature of groups, organizations, communities, and society is their patterns of discourse and communication, and software today joins mass transportation as a technology having a profound effect on those patterns. This is an evolution in its infancy, and software should only grow in significance over time.

1.1.5   Software Is about People

It is tempting to think of software in terms of instructions and bits and bytes, but fundamentally, from a user perspective, those technical constructs are largely irrelevant. Software is really the expression and representation of the wishes and actions of a human programmer in the context of an executing software program. As a useful thought model, consider a computer or material product with embedded software as having a person inside, that person responding to external stimulus and defining what actions to take next. In reality, that person is the programmer (or often a large team of software developers) who has anticipated all the possible external stimuli and expressed the resulting actions through the software she writes. Thus, software is really an expression of the behavior defined by a programmer in much the same way that a novel is the expression of plot and emotion.

Increasingly, software expresses and represents an information-based business process, along with a human organization and its participants. Software works in concert with a human organization, and the technological and social aspects of this combination are deeply interwoven.

1.1.6   Software Can Be Better

Software suffers from no significant practical physical limitations. Much more so than material goods, software can be molded pretty much as we choose. A lot of what we have today is the result of many arbitrary choices; the most significant limitation is conceptual bottlenecks and the remnants of history. We have an opportunity to make better choices in the future if we take account of the needs of users, end-user organizations, and societal needs. However, if this is to happen, we have to transcend the common perception of software as a manifestation of technology and think more deeply and clearly about software an important enabler of individuals, groups of individuals, organizations, communities, and society as a whole. We have to consider software a human artifact or tool, one that can be almost infinitely flexible and that could bring greater benefits if only it could be molded more appropriately.

1.1.7   The Software Industry Is Undergoing Radical Change

A number of factors are converging to radically change the software industry, and underlying many of them is the astounding success of the Internet. The Internet is not only opening up entirely new categories of applications. It is irrevocably changing the ways in which software is sold and entangling software technologies in contentious debates over many public policy issues, including national sovereignty, national security and law enforcement, and limitations to information access.

The fundamental structure of the software-related industries has undergone the change characteristic of an immature industry, but arguably never has that change been more rapid or fundamental than now. This creates interesting opportunities to consider different models for the industry, and their relative merits and challenges.

1.1.8   Creating Software Is Social

We are familiar with the "nerd" image of social isolation associated with programmers. Like many such prejudices, there is some truth to it but also a substantial falsehood and oversimplification. Most of the desirable properties that make software successful are not a result of technical prowess but of a deep understanding of what the users of a program need and want, and how they can be accommodated in an efficient, natural, and even enjoyable way. The creators of the best and most successful application software must think much more like managers, psychologists, and sociologists than technicians. Good software cannot be created without a strong connection to all the stakeholders, which includes not only users but also managers, administrators, operators, and others. Taken in its entire context, identifying and analyzing needs through operations and use, creating and managing software is ultimately a highly social activity.

On the other hand, the programming phase of creating software requires spending a lot of time in front of a computer. In this respect, creating software is no different than creative writing, not generally considered a "nerdy" activity. How does programming differ from creative writing? On the one hand, software is almost always undertaken by large teams, an inherently social enterprise, and writing isn't. But the perceptual gap probably arises from the programmer's focus on technical detail and the writer's greater attention to plot, to artistic expression, and emotional connections. This distinction is changing rapidly. Programming tools are reducing the technical content of application creation, especially as they allow the customization of existing applications. As software becomes more integral to the lifestyles of its users, and integral to the functioning of organizations, successful programmers form a strong emotional bond with the ultimate users. So, too, with expanding computer power, with software enabling good tools and rich graphics and sound, application programming assumes the flavor of an artistic rather than a technical endeavor.

1.1.9   Software Is Sophisticated and Complex

In contrast to every other economic good except information, software does not suffer from any important physical limits; it can be molded in almost any way we wish. For this reason, the limitations on what we can do with software are primarily social, economic, and conceptual, not physical. The sophistication and complexity of software grows to the point where it can no longer be managed because of conceptual limitations; no amount of money or resources can overcome these human limits. Understanding this unique aspect of software is essential to understanding the challenges faced by the software industry in moving forward.

If we think of an executing software program as a surrogate agent for its creators, one great challenge is that responsible actions must be predefined for all circumstances that may arise, not only the normal and expected but also the abnormal and exceptional. This makes accomplishing a complex task through software much more challenging than accomplishing the same task via a human organization because people can be counted on to react intelligently to exceptional circumstances.

Although it wasn't always true, post-Internet the software industry faces a monumental challenge in industry coordination. Infrastructure from many vendors must work together, and applications must work with infrastructure and work in complex ways across organizational boundaries. Other industries face coordination challenges—train locomotives have to fit with the tracks, and lubricants have to match the design of machinery—but arguably none face as wide-ranging and complex a coordination challenge as the software industry.

1.1.10   Software Can Be Tamed

Technologies are morally neutral; each can be used for good or for ill. We have a collective opportunity and responsibility to mold software in ways that give it higher utility and mitigate its possible negative effects. The potential deleterious effects of software are numerous and well publicized. They include increasing the social disadvantage of poor or handicapped citizens, curtailment of free speech and civil liberties, stifling of innovation through excessive reliance on intellectual property, an overabundance of information and communication, and many others. Addressing these challenges is largely the role of public advocates, policy experts, politicians and lawmakers, but to do the job properly they must understand more fully the capabilities and limitations of software and the industries that surround software.

1.2   Organization and Summary

In the real world, software touches the personal and professional lives of most individuals. Of course, for most people this is in the sense of being a user and beneficiary of software. For a smaller (but still very significant) number of people, their professional lives are directly involved in facilitating the creation and use of software, or understanding its effects on individuals, organizations, or society. This book is primarily dedicated to capturing the perspective of these professionals.

This book is organized around the perspectives of different professions regarding software. Following an introductory chapter on information technology (chapter 2), the remaining chapters are organized around six such perspectives, and each chapter also relates its own perspective to the others. Users (chapter 3) are affected by what software does on their behalf. Software engineers and other professionals involved in software creation (chapter 4) start with a good understanding of what users want to accomplish and end by creating software code. Throughout the software life-cycle, managers (chapter 5) must deal with a number of issues, such as acquiring the necessary infrastructure to run the software, organizing the people and business processes that surround the software, and operating the software applications and infrastructure. Industrialists (chapters 6 and 7) organize themselves into companies to create and manage software and are concerned about ownership and business relationships and bringing together the complementary infrastructure and functions that together make the benefits of software available to users. Policy experts and lawyers (chapter 8) are concerned with ensuring a healthy and innovative industry, mitigating possible negative effects of information technology, and resolving various conflicts among the industry participants. Economists (chapter 9) offer many useful insights into the workings of the software marketplace. The book concludes with a look into the future (chapter 10).

Many issues affect more than one of these perspectives. In each case, we locate that issue in the chapter that seems most relevant but also relate it to the other perspectives as well.

A greater appreciation for the variety of issues surrounding software and their interdependence can be facilitated by starting with an overview of the book. Software works in conjunction with information content and the information technologies, as described in chapter 2. All information, as well as software itself, can be represented by data (collections of bits), manipulated by a processor, stored for future access, and communicated over a network. Information is valued for how it teaches or influences us, whereas software is valued for what it does, that is, its behavior. Many legal, economic, and business considerations for information and software are influenced by the simplicity of creating perfect replicas of information and software. Software depends on a complementary material technological infrastructure for its execution, including both hardware (processor) and infrastructure software (e.g., operating system). The software industry has benefited from several decades of geometric advance in the performance per unit cost in processing, storage, and communication technologies, an observation known as Moore's law. To understand the future of software, it is important to understand among other things the driving forces behind Moore's law and how it may evolve in the future.

The primary value of software is in the features and capabilities it provides the end-user, as described in chapter 3. Historically, applications have been largely driven by the addition, one after the other, of processing, storage, and communication to the suite of information technologies. The major classes of applications include scientific modeling and simulation, databases and transaction processing, information publication and access, collaboration and coordination, and software embedded in larger systems. Today, many applications strongly exploit all three technologies. Many of the most valuable generic applications supporting large numbers of users have doubtless been invented and refined, so today applications are becoming increasingly specialized to meet the needs of particular vertical industries, types of organization, or organizational functions. Sociotechnical applications, one growth category, emphasize the integration of a human organization with information, information technology, and software. As a result of the deeper integration of software applications into human and organizational activities, the process of understanding user needs and how the features and capabilities of software applications can meet them has become an important design activity separate from technical software implementation.

A number of factors contribute value to the user of software, including specific features and capabilities, effects on an organization, amount of use, quality, performance, usability, flexibility, and extensibility. One consideration that recurs throughout the book is network effects, wherein the value to the user depends on the number of other adopters of particular software.

The process of creating software, and some of the technical characteristics of software most relevant to business models and economic properties of software, is considered in chapter 4. A major issue in creating software is the software development process, which deserves careful attention and must be highly principled because of the increasing size of investments in and the complexity of software. The development process has come to be focused on iterative refinement, agility to meet changing needs and requirements, and ways to bring the user experience more directly to bear. For some types of infrastructure software, the market is experimenting with community-based models in which multiple individuals and companies participate in advancing and maintaining the software.

Software architecture is the first stage of software implementation. It decomposes and partitions a software system into modules that can be dealt with somewhat independently. This modularity has significant business implications, including open interfaces and application programming interfaces (APIs), system integration, and the composition of different applications and infrastructure.

Program distribution and execution options bring to the fore many business and legal issues, including whether the customer is offered source code, whether the software is interpreted or compiled, and whether software is dynamically distributed as it is needed. Increasingly software applications are distributed across multiple computers and organizations.

The management of the entire software life cycle is considered in chapter 5. The major steps in its life cycle include analysis of user needs, development of the software (architecture design, programming, testing, integration, and other functions), provisioning of the equipment and software in the user environment (including user training and often organizational changes), operation and administration of the software, and use. These steps form a value chain, where each step depends upon the successful completion of previous steps and adds value to them. The entire cycle is typically repeated multiple times, and the software supplier faces interesting challenges in managing the process of maintenance and upgrade of coexisting versions of the software while it is in use. Distributed applications often cross organizational boundaries, and this leads to many management challenges and also increases the importance of standardization (discussed in chapter 7). The management of security and privacy is used as an example of the types of issues that arise in a distributed administrative environment.

The software industry past and present and how it is changing are discussed in chapters 6 and 7. The value chain in software can be partitioned into cooperative and competitive companies; some of the most common ways of doing this are discussed in chapter 6. There is a trend toward offering software as a service over a network, moving responsibility for provisioning and operations from end-user organizations to service providers.

One step in the value chain is software creation, and this is considered in depth in chapter 7. A typical software application draws upon equipment and software from at least a few, if not many, individual firms, leading to issues about business relationships within the software industry as well as between software and end-user firms. Coordination among firms is essential to getting operational software into the hands of the users. Standardization is one way in which software suppliers coordinate themselves, and it is growing in importance as distributed applications move across administrative and organizational boundaries.

Driven largely by the rapid success of the Internet and distributed applications and new requirements for mixing different information media within a single application, the industry organization has been moving from a vertical to a horizontal structure, the latter consonant with an architecture concept called layering. Layering provides a relatively flexible way to partition an infrastructure to provide a wealth of services, with the possibility of adding additional features and capabilities by building layers on top of an existing infrastructure.

There is growing interest in software reuse and component software as a way of improving the productivity of development organizations, addressing complexity, and improving quality. The idea is to assemble applications largely from existing components, which are modules created independently of any particular system context and constructed for multiple uses. To derive the full benefit, component software will require a marketplace for buying and selling components, which would in turn result in marked changes in the organization of the software industry. A related direction is Web services, in which applications are assembled from services made available over a network such as the Internet.

Government plays many roles in the software industry, as considered in chapter 8. A successful industry depends on government-sanctioned and -enforced intellectual property rights, but information and software present many special challenges that remain to be fully explored and settled. Software technologies can help in enforcing intellectual property rights, for example, through copy protection, although this presents some controversies. Some aspects of the software market are regulated by government, for better or worse. Security and privacy are areas of regulation, both to protect the rights of citizens and to enhance law enforcement and national security. Free speech and civil liberties are areas of controversy, and software plays multiple roles in potentially restricting access to offending materials, and collecting and amassing personal information that may potentially violate individual privacy. Government regulation attempts to insure a competitive software industry and fair business practices through antitrust laws. Government also plays a major role in ensuring an adequate workforce in the software industries through its direct support of education and publicly funded research and through immigration laws.

Some insights and perspectives on software from the economics profession are described in chapter 9. On both the supply and demand sides, software displays a number of characteristics that, while not unique to software, are mixed in unusual ways. Software shares characteristics with many other types of goods and services, including information, services, material goods, and even plans for a manufacturing factory. Insights that are relevant to understanding business strategies and relationships in the software industry include network effects, lock-in, economies of scale, and risk. Software is arguably the most flexible of any economic good in pricing options, and it can even be self-aware and autonomously initiate payment. The economic rationale for infrastructure includes sharing and economies of scale as well as some special characteristics in mitigating congestion.

Some trends in software use and markets that will have a marked effect on the future of the industry are discussed in chapter 10. These include information appliances, nomadic and mobile users and applications, and pervasive computing (software embedded in many everyday material products).

1.3   Research and Discussion Issues

In each chapter, some interesting and important issues that deserve further discussion and investigation are listed. These are not comprehensive but rather illustrate the possibilities for further study.

1. If we look at software as an economic good, it has some distinctive differences from other technologies. How does the evolution of the software industry compare to earlier technologies, such as mass transportation, electrification, and radio? Does it share a considerable number of similarities, or show major differences? Did it develop faster or slower?

2. How well do you think we are doing in providing an appropriate education in software at the primary, secondary, and postsecondary levels? What base level of understanding and specific skills should all students possess?

3. Starting with the observation that products of many types become increasingly interactive, in what ways does the design of these products and how they interact with their owners and users change?

4. If you were to compare computers and software to earlier technological advances like mass transportation, electrification, and radio/television, how would you compare the effects on individuals, organizations, and society in general? Has software been more or less important in changing everyday lives?

5. As you are using some of your favorite software applications, think about how your experience relates directly to the programmers who created them. Do you see the personality or culture of the programmer shining through? Or do you feel really isolated from them even when you try to connect? Why?

6. As you are using those same applications, step back and ask how they might be much better. Do you think they are about as good as they can be, or can they be significantly improved? What do we mean by "good"?

7. Consider how the Internet has changed the software applications you use. What very specific observations can you make?

8. As the software industry has matured, for example, evolving from back office functions to individual productivity to serving as the foundation of many organizational processes, consider how the challenges facing the creator of software have changed.

2

Information Technology

We have become a people unable to comprehend the technology we invent.
Association of American Colleges

Information technology is undergoing rapid advancement and change, and is having a profound effect on our civilization. This is one of the remarkable developments of our age. A theme of this book is that software can be more fully understood and appreciated by considering it in its broader context, including the full suite of information technologies described in this chapter. This chapter is merely a prelude to the focus on software and its broader contexts in subsequent chapters.

What is *technology*? A comprehensive definition is given by the National Research Council (2002):

In its broadest sense, technology is the process by which humans modify nature to meet their needs and wants. However, most people think of technology only in terms of its artifacts: computers and software, aircraft, pesticides, water-treatment plants, birth-control pills, and microwave ovens, to name a few. But technology is more than its tangible products. An equally important aspect of technology is the knowledge and processes necessary to create and operate those products, such as engineering know-how and design, manufacturing expertise, various technical skills, and so on. Technology also includes the entire infrastructure necessary for the design, manufacture, operation, and repair of technological artifacts, from corporate headquarters and engineering schools to manufacturing plants and maintenance facilities.

Information technology (IT) in particular is dedicated to capturing, manipulating, storing, communicating, retrieving, and presenting information represented in digital form on behalf of people, whom we call *users*. The elements of this technology embodied in the definition will be encountered throughout the remainder of the book. We are currently living in what many consider an information age, a period of time where IT is having a dramatic effect on our personal and professional lives, and on society generally.

IT encompasses three basic functions: the processing, storage, and communication of information. Each of these functions involves hardware and software, the software serving as the controlling element and the hardware responding to and carrying out the "wishes" of the software. Both software and the hardware required for its execution are examples of useful technological artifacts.

This chapter begins by clarifying what constitutes information and the complementary roles that hardware and software play in IT. The primary effect of the hardware on software is measured by its performance metrics, so the most relevant metrics and their effects on the software are discussed. Finally, the driving forces behind Moore's law, which models the dramatic advancement in IT hardware performance metrics over time, are discussed along with its relevance for software.

2.1   Information

What is *information*? We know it when we see it—text, documents, pictures, audio, video, and similar entities. We also know that its purpose is, roughly speaking, to inform us. What does that mean? Generally we are informed when we are affected in some concrete way—taking action, making a decision, seeking further information, or experiencing emotion are all examples. Or, as a result of acquiring information, we may simply develop knowledge—familiarity, awareness, or understanding.

This is a human perspective, and after all, the sole rationale for information is its relevance to people. Within IT a more arcane and technical definition of information is appropriate. Information consists of recognizable patterns, like text, drawings, pictures, audio, or video, normally patterns that are conveyed to our consciousness by our six senses (hearing, sight, smell, touch, taste, and equilibrium). Considering that our senses are physical in nature, conveying information to people requires a *physical medium*, such as sound (as a pressure wave in the air), an image (a two-dimensional light intensity field), or video (a sequence of images typically accompanied by audio). Inevitably, the interaction between IT and human users is through these physical media, in both directions (see figure 2.1). Acquiring information from the physical world requires a *sensor* (like a microphone or camera), and conveying information to people requires a *transducer*[1] (like an earphone, speaker, or monitor).

2.1.1   Digital Representations

Within IT information is represented in a way that it can be stored, communicated, and manipulated conveniently and cost effectively by available electronics and pho-

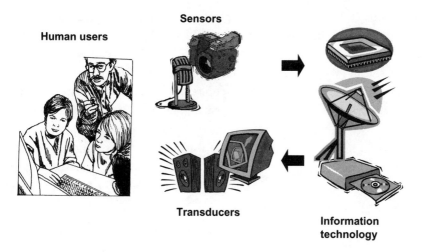

Figure 2.1
Information techology (IT) uses sensors and transducers to convey information to and from the material world.

tonics technologies. This internal representation is usually quite different from the original form of the information as created or sensed by people.

Example People experience sound as a pressure wave in the air, but there is no available technology to store sound in that same physical form. Thus, a different representation must be used within IT. This representation has changed over the years as technology has changed. For example, the storage of sound has migrated from vinyl records (the most immediate representation of a pressure wave), to magnetic tape (still analog), to compact disks (digital representation on a specialized medium), to MP3 files (digital representation on any storage medium) stored in a computer.

In IT now and for the foreseeable future, the dominant representation of all forms of information utilizes *bits* (short for "binary digits"). A bit assumes one of two values: 0 or 1. Bits are ideal because they can be stored simply by a switch ("off" or "on"). A collection of bits representing information is known as *data*.[2] It is remarkable, and perhaps not altogether obvious, that most forms of information that we commonly encounter can be represented in this way and thus can be captured in the IT infrastructure.[3] This includes documents, pictures, audio, and video.

Example A simple representation of an image is to define a square array of pixels, each pixel having a value representing the intensity of light in a small partition of the image (see figure 2.2). The value of the pixel can in turn be represented by n bits, where n is typically 8 (for monochrome) to 24 (for color). These n bits can represent 2^n distinct intensities ($2^8 = 256$ to $2^{24} = 16{,}777{,}216$). The image in figure 2.2 is 200 pixels tall by 300 pixels wide, and the intensity of each pixel is represented by 8 bits, so 480,000 bits total are required. The number of bits can be reduced using compression, which eliminates visually unimportant redundancies in the data.

We have used the term *representation* without defining it. In a representation, information is temporarily replaced by data for purposes of storage, manipulation, and communication, in such a manner that it can later be recovered in its original form, at least in an adequate approximation.

Example   Sound can be captured by an audio sensor (microphone), converted to an internal representation as an MP3 file (which contains a large collection of bits) for purposes of storage, and later recovered by a computer driving an audio transducer (speaker). MP3 is a specific representation, one that is particularly apropos for today's IT. Often (as in this example) the representation only yields an approximation to the original, hopefully good enough so that the user can't tell the difference. The more data used to represent, the more accurate the approximation.

The term *digital* is often used to describe this data representation of information. Actually *digital* describes a representation using any *discrete alphabet*, where bits are the specific case of a binary alphabet.

Example   Nature uses the DNA molecule as its representation for conveying information about the composition and processes of an organism from one generation to another. The information is conveyed by sequences of amino acids chosen from four possibilities: adenine (A), thymine (T), cytosine (C), and guanine (G). This representation is digital because it is discrete, but it uses an alphabet with four elements rather than two. Nature could have used bits, for example, 00 for A, 01 for T, 10 for C, 11 for G.

Digital representation is distinct from *analog* representation, in which information is represented by continuous quantities (like the pressure of a sound wave, which is continuous in both time and amplitude). A digital representation (which is always expressible using bits) is advantageous for several reasons. The processing, storage, and communication of bits are easily and cheaply realized by the available electronics and communication technologies. A uniform digital representation allows all forms of information to be freely mixed within a common

**Expansion reveals
representation by square
pixels**

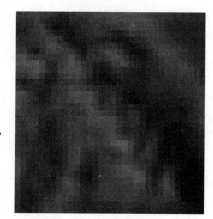

Original picture

Figure 2.2
An image can be represented by square pixels, the intensity of each represented by eight bits.

infrastructure.[4] Most of the infrastructure is not even concerned with what those bits represent.

Example In an operating system, a *file* is a collection of data. The representation of the data is preserved by some means (for example, a file extension like .doc or .jpg), so that an application can know how to interpret the file. The operating system itself ignores the representation as the file is stored and retrieved from disk and transported across the network. Files using different representations can be freely mixed in all these contexts.

Another advantage of a digital representation has profound implications for the economic properties of information, and even raises complex policy issues.

2.1.2 Copying and Replication

An important distinction is between the copying and replication of information. *Copying* can be approximate, while *replication* is exact. This is where analog and digital representations differ in a fundamental way.[5] Copying an analog representation inevitably adds noise and distortion, and once introduced, they cannot be removed. Physical media also introduce similar impairments to a digital representation, but because the representation is discrete it is usually possible to remove any impairment as long as the original bits can be detected accurately. On the other hand, the original conversion of an analog representation to digital involves some *quantization* impairment, although that can be rendered imperceptible.

Example When sound is captured and represented by an MP3 file, the audio that is later played back is a copy of the original: its pressure wave is a good enough approximation so that people cannot distinguish it from the original. That MP3 file can be replicated by simply copying the bits in the file to a new file. In that process, if the bits are detected accurately in the face of any noise and distortion, a representation results that is identical to the original. Each such replica, when converted back to sound, will be virtually identical. A replica can itself be replicated and still remain faithful to the original. In contrast, analog representations (like cassette magnetic tapes) can only be imperfectly copied—a copy of a copy of a copy begins to suffer increasingly significant impairments through accumulated noise and distortion.

Each time a replica is made of a replica, it is called a new *generation* (see figure 2.3), and it is identical to the first generation. In contrast, with an analog representation slightly imperfect copies will add imperfections to the previous generation, and later generations will be noticeably and increasingly impaired.

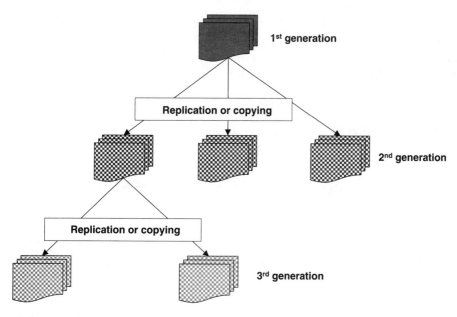

Figure 2.3
Successive generations result from replication or copying.

In principle, information can be accurately preserved over time—even very long periods of time, like thousands of years—by periodically making a replica of information stored on a physically deteriorating medium onto a new medium. This replication is called *regeneration*. However, there is an important caveat here. Regenerated replicas are only data—to recover the information requires knowledge of the representation.

Example A document authored in Microsoft Word (.doc file) can be preserved over time by periodic regeneration, but its interpretation (like viewing or printing) will require a compatible version of Word. Will Word 3000 be able to read Word 2000 .doc files? If we preserve a replica of Word 2000, also by periodic regeneration, will it run on Windows 3000? One response to these issues is the standardization of representations (see chapter 7).

Regeneration is a technical underpinning of networks. Communication over long distances is fundamentally noisy and unreliable, but the delivery of an accurate replica of data is still possible because of periodic regeneration.

Regeneration is a double-edged sword. It reduces the manufacturing and distribution costs for information suppliers relative to analog representations. It also enables piracy, the unauthorized mass replication and sale of information that violates its creator's intellectual property rights. This poses considerable challenges for policymakers, lawyers, and law enforcers (see chapter 8). This problem is considerably less acute for analog because successive generations are progressively more impaired.

2.1.3 Some Properties of Information

Important economic characteristics of digitally represented information follow from these technical characteristics (Shapiro and Varian 1999b). The replication, storage, and communication of data are inexpensive, so digital information has *supply economies of scale*: fixed creation costs that are typically much larger than the ongoing manufacturing and distribution costs. (Highly volatile information like stock prices is different.) Digital information is *nonrival in use*: an arbitrary number of users can be given replicas of the information, equivalent in every way, without interference. One user can create a replica and pass it to another user, absent technological obstacles (like copy protection; see chapter 8). This is in contrast to many material goods, where a user would have difficulty in creating replicas.

All information (digital or not) is an *experience good*: its quality and utility is best judged by experiencing it. This puts a premium on the *recommender*: someone who applies judgment or expertise to advise on the quality or utility of information. Alternative mechanisms can familiarize users with information, such as free trials or samples.

IT encourages the creation and dissemination of a prodigious account of information. Users can experience information overload, but fortunately IT also provides valuable tools to deal with this, including search engines and indexes that catalog the content of large information repositories. Creators of information can also assist with *indexes* (lists of available topics), *hyperlinks* (pointers to related information), and *metadata* (descriptions of information content). Information suppliers face commensurate challenges in attracting the attention of consumers in the face of the large mass of available information.

Social approaches involving users and enabled by the Internet can be helpful, too. Users can publish reviews on an information supplier's site, and other users can rate those reviewers. This is an example of a *recommender system* (Resnick and Varian 1997), a software application that aggregates and analyzes the recommendations of many users. A *viral approach* encourages users to notify other users of valuable information.

2.2   The Constituents of IT

As a preliminary to focusing on the software portion of IT, it is useful to appreciate its technological context. We largely ignore sensors and transducers, and focus on the core technologies that process, store, and communicate information. Examining the complementary role of these technologies, and the complementary and mutually dependent role of hardware and software, foreshadows the importance of cooperation and coordination in the industry (see chapter 7).

2.2.1   Material vs. Immaterial

It is useful to make a distinction between a material and an immaterial good. A *material good* has a physical manifestation; among other things, it is distinguished by physical properties (like mass, momentum, and temperature). An *immaterial good* is merely logical, like an idea or a stock price. Software and information are immaterial. A popular (although somewhat flawed)[6] metaphor for the material-immaterial distinction is atoms versus bits.

Information is the basic commodity that is captured, stored, manipulated, and retrieved by the information technologies. At its most basic level, software comprises the set of instructions created by a human programmer that controls all aspects of this process, specifying precisely what actions to take in each circumstance.[7]

While their roles are quite different, both software and information are immaterial but cannot exist or function without a material support infrastructure. Information uses a material medium for storing, conveying, and accessing its logical significance, such as paper, disk, or display. Software needs a computer *processor* to realize its intentions. Software is thus the immaterial sequence of instructions for a processor that controls its specific behaviors. Because software works only in concert with a material processor (and other material technologies like power supplies, network routers, communication links, and disks), in practice it assumes some properties similar both to immaterial information and material goods, which like software (but unlike information) are often valued for their behaviors and actions. The properties of software as an economic good are discussed in more detail in chapter 9. Information may also incorporate behavior (such as an animation), but that behavior is in reality a manifestation of software.

2.2.2   Three Underlying Technologies

Aside from sensors and transducers, the physical embodiment of IT has three constituents: *processing* modifies digital information under the direction of the software; *storage* conveys digital information from one time to another (by storing it and later retrieving it from storage); and *communication* conveys digital information from one place to another. Each constituent has suppliers that tend to specialize because the three technologies are distinctly different, and so the economies of scope (for example in controlling all three technologies) are relatively weak.

Example   Intel, Sun Microsystems, and Compaq (now Hewlett-Packard) focus most of their research and development energies on processing, EMC on storage, and CISCO on communication. In each case, vendors may wish to provide integrated products in which they get other necessary constituents from other manufacturers. IBM is an example of a large vertically integrated company that devotes considerable development effort to two constituents, processing and storage.[8]

2.2.3   Hardware and Software Are Interchangeable

Hardware is the material portion of IT based directly on physical laws, like electronics, magnetics, or optics. In principle, any IT system can be constructed exclusively from hardware. Given any external behavior, it is possible in principle to reproduce that behavior by building hardware, or software (with a supporting hardware processor, of course), or various combinations. Given this interchangeability, it is useful to view software as immaterial hardware. Over time, the boundary between hardware and software changes, largely as an effect of Moore's law (see section 2.3).

The hardware-software distinction is further blurred by the existence of hardware description languages (such as Verilog), which allow digital hardware to be specified through a computer language. This language can be directly executed on a processor (like any software language) to check if the hardware will work, or automatically translated into a form that can be fabricated as an integrated circuit (this is similar to the compilation of software source code into object code; see chapter 4). However, there are severe limits on the complexity of software that can be translated into hardware (see section 2.2.4).

An operating IT system conveys streams of bits through time and space. Bits flow through space via a communication link from a sender to one or more receivers. Storage conveys bits through time: a sender stores bits at one time and a recipient retrieves these bits at some later time.[9] Processing modifies bits at specific points in space-time. When controlled by software, processing is performed by hardware specialized for interpreting the bits representing that software. A fundamental requirement is for material hardware to underpin all bit-level operations: the material structure (including atoms, electrons, photons) brings the immaterial bits into existence and carries out the processing, storage and retrieval, and communication.

2.2.4 What Distinguishes Software

From the interchangeability of hardware and software one might conclude that hardware and software are simply implementation options, where choices can be relegated to the bowels of some development organization. This is incorrect, because in many characteristics that affect its business and economic properties, software profoundly differs from hardware.

Various forms of flexibility can be incorporated into products. Paper is manufactured without presupposing what will later be written or printed on it, and automobiles are manufactured without presupposing where they will be driven. The central idea behind the computer is *programmability*, a new and much more powerful form of flexibility. The computer was conceived as a product whose basic function is not determined at the time of manufacture but is defined later with the addition of software. Of course, many earlier products could be put to new uses (for instance, paper's becoming a paper airplane), and the computer's programmability has its limits (it cannot fly), but when it comes to capturing and manipulating information, the computer is completely flexible because most of its functionality is determined by the postmanufacture addition of software.

Software is a superior implementation for functionality that is highly complex, diverse, or irregular (as opposed to highly repetitive), because it makes economic sense to share a single processor over varied uses at different times. The only cost penalty is the storage to retain the diverse functionality and invoke it as needed, whereas it is usually necessary to duplicate hardware for each different function it serves. The whole IT infrastructure generalizes this concept of sharing (see chapter 9).

What is fundamentally different about software is that it is not manufactured into a product. It can be bundled with a product as it is sold initially, or it can be sold separately and deployed to hardware that is already in use. It can be installed initially, or it can be added later. It can be static, or it can be changed and upgraded later. These properties make the market for software irrevocably and profoundly different from the market for material products (including computer hardware).

The boundary between what is relegated to software and what is relegated to hardware changes with time, driven by issues of complexity, performance, and security. With advances in computer-aided design tools and hardware description languages, hardware design has come increasingly to resemble software programming, requiring similar skills but utilizing different languages and tools. A primary driver for the changing boundary between hardware and software is Moore's law (see section 2.3).

2.2.5   Layers of Technology

Like many industries, software and its supporting industries are layered, as a natural outcome of market forces (see figure 2.4). (Layering is also an important software architectural technique; see chapter 7.) The central idea is to build new capabilities not from scratch but rather by the addition of a new top layer that extends or specializes the capabilities of the layers below without modifying them.

Example   When a new business is started, it does not reproduce much existing infrastructure (post office and transportation systems, for example) but will subsume those capabilities into its business. It may extend those capabilities (extend postal delivery from the mailroom to individual offices) or specialize them (use the highway for a specific vehicle suitable for its purposes).

The bottom layer of IT is semiconductor and photonics devices. Devices may be discrete, like lasers and transistors, which have a single simply described function

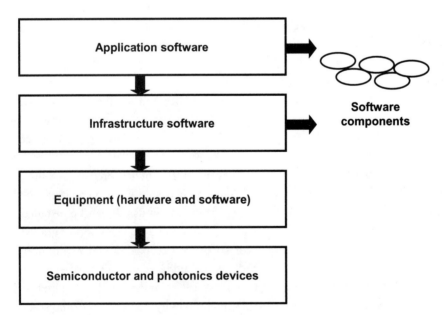

Figure 2.4
Layers of complementary supporting software. (The arrows mean "built on".)

and cannot be further decomposed. Or they may be *integrated devices* that combine large numbers of discrete devices into physically small (although often very complex) packages, such as integrated circuits (ICs) or integrated circuits and photonics. This is the hardware.

The next layer is IT *equipment* (like a computer or router), which comprises a complex system composed of hardware and bundled software. By *bundled*, we mean they are sold as a unit, and it is hard for the user to distinguish what is accomplished in hardware and what in software. Such software is often called *embedded*.

Example A personal computer as shipped has two types of software: the basic input-output system (BIOS) controls low-level functioning of the computer (for example, how it retrieves the operating system from disk as part of an initial boot) and is specific to a given computer design. The operating system is not an integral part of the computer. It is designed to run on multiple computer designs. Nevertheless, it is installed by the manufacturer.

Equipment with similar functionality from two suppliers may have a very different partitioning of software and hardware—this is another manifestation of the interchangeability of hardware and software.

The *infrastructure software* layer provides many services of value to a wide range of applications. This "pure software" layer includes the operating system and an expanding range of other useful capabilities as well (see chapters 4 and 6). One of its roles is to isolate application software from the particulars of the equipment. This allows the application software to offer a diversity of options at the equipment layer, and equipment and application software to largely evolve independently (innovations in each realm are minimally dependent and require minimal coordination). Infrastructure software also provides the commonality that allows applications to work together (a property of applications called composability; see chapter 4).

The top layer is *application software*, which provides capabilities specific to the context of the end-user or end-user organization. This software builds on capabilities of the infrastructure software, which in turn builds on capabilities of the equipment.

An application (and indeed infrastructure and other software) may incorporate *software components*, which are ready-to-use elements of functionality that can be purchased and incorporated into the application as is, without modification. Components create a software supply chain, in which one supplier builds on software acquired from others (see chapter 7).

2.2.6   Categories of Software

As discussed in section 2.2.5, there are at least four distinct types of software: embedded, infrastructure, component, and application. Embedded software is integral to and bundled into equipment or information appliances (see chapter 10) and is largely indistinguishable from the supporting hardware, from the user's perspective. The infrastructure software is separately available to the operator (for example, it can be replaced or upgraded) even if it is initially bundled with the equipment (see chapter 7). Components are bought and sold in the market and incorporated into applications, do not themselves constitute a complete application, and can be independently upgraded or replaced after deployment (see chapter 7). These four types of software have quite distinct value propositions and business challenges.

Example   The screen and keypad in a cell phone is controlled by embedded software. In a desktop computer, the operating system is infrastructure and an e-mail reader is an application. The e-mail reader may incorporate a text editor component; that same component is also incorporated into a number of other applications, such as word processors, presentation generators, and spreadsheets, to perform text editing.

Software is essential in all three areas of IT. While software always requires a processor to execute, embedded software (like the BIOS) may also be integral to the processor itself. Similarly, embedded software is an important part of all storage and communication equipment.

2.3   Moore's Law

A fundamental underpinning of the software industry is Moore's law, which observes a relentless and dramatic improvement in the performance per unit cost of the material information technologies and predicts similar future improvements. Moore's law is one of the central features of our industrial age, since it is a significant driver for economic growth and is behind the relentless changes wrought by IT. To understand the software industry, it is important to appreciate Moore's law and its ramifications. It is also instructive to delve into its underlying causes, particularly in extrapolating it into the future.

2.3.1   Metrics of Performance

Hardware performance metrics affect the software and ultimately the user in various ways. Three major classes of performance metrics are summarized in table 2.1.

Table 2.1
Performance Metrics Relevant to a Software Application

Performance Metric	Description	Examples
Capacity	The ideal throughput of a specific resource that is completely utilized, like a single processor, storage medium, or communication link.	Number of transactions per second for a processor, assuming it is performing only these transactions and assuming a new transaction is presented just as the previous transaction is completed.
Throughput	What is actually accomplished per unit time for a total system, typically consisting of multiple resources and a mixture of processing, storage, and communication. Greater throughput is desirable because it supports a higher level of activity.	The number of transactions per second on an e-commerce site that farms these transactions out to multiple processors depends on the rate the network can accommodate the requests and the processors can complete them.
Delay	Time elapsed while waiting for something expected to happen, taking into account all the resources involved. Less delay is desirable because it allows an application to respond more quickly to user actions or requests.	The delay between clicking a hyperlink and viewing the resulting page depends on the network and the remote Web server; delay between a live sporting event and its video representation on the screen depends on the network.

Capacity applies to a specific resource, like a processor and memory, and is where the characteristics of individual material technologies are most directly relevant. *Throughput* and delay apply to the entire system, software and hardware, taking into account all resource constraints, in the context of a specific application. *Delay* is the metric most evident to the user of an application. Throughput is usually of greatest concern to the operator of an application, because it relates to the aggregate level of activity that is supported across all users and ultimately the number of users.

While the equipment and application software can be largely functionally separated by appropriate intermediate infrastructure software, as shown in figure 2.4, the performance of application software inevitably depends on the performance characteristics of the hardware.

Example   The user cannot perform a given task on a Web server more quickly than the execution time of the software that realizes that task (that execution time depends in turn on the speed of the processor), plus any time required to transfer the request over the network and get the results back (which depends on the performance of the network).

Throughput and delay are dependent. At low throughput, delay is directly determined by the capacity constraints of individual resources, like the time to store a file on disk or the time to transfer a message on a communication link. As throughput increases, *congestion* occurs. Congestion is due to irregular requests of the system, causing at times a rate of requests that temporarily exceeds capacity constraints on individual resources, and these requests must wait for available resources, introducing a congestion delay.

Example In a Web server, during periods of congestion (high utilization), requests to view Web pages may temporarily exceed the ability of the server to satisfy those requests. The excess requests are queued up waiting until the completion of earlier-arriving requests. That waiting time is a congestion-induced delay.

Congestion thus causes excess delay at high throughput. The severity of congestion can be predicted from the *utilization* $u \leq 1$, a property of an individual resource (particularly a processor or communication link) defined as the actual average throughput as a fraction of the capacity. (As an example, a processor that is working half the time and idle the half the time on average has a utilization of 0.5.) According to one simple statistical model,[10] the average excess congestion-induced delay D_c is related to the utilization u by

$$D_c = \frac{u}{1-u} D_s,$$

where D_s is the average service time, defined as the average time to complete the incoming tasks. Thus, for small utilization, the congestion delay approaches zero, but as u approaches 1, the congestion delay gets arbitrarily large. The total (service plus congestion) average delay is the sum

$$D = D_c + D_s = \frac{1}{1-u} D_s.$$

Congestion plays a role in the economics of resource sharing; it can be controlled through pricing and other mechanisms (see chapter 9).

The delay and throughput performance parameters relate directly to the cost of the hardware required for a given application. To maintain acceptable delay, the utilization must be kept within bounds. This means that hardware resources cannot be fully utilized on average in order to account for the variation in load. If a larger throughput is required (e.g., the number of users has increased), the utilization can be increased (e.g., no hardware resources are added) but only at the expense of added delay. Alternatively, capital expenditures on additional hardware can increase capacity, keeping utilization and delay constant.[11]

2.3.2   Statement of Moore's Law

Economic historians will undoubtedly view the rapid advance in information technologies as a seminal and remarkable defining characteristic of the information age. This advance can be captured succinctly by Moore's law, which in its simplest form states that "the performance per unit cost of material information technologies increases exponentially with time." It applies to all three areas of IT, at least for the time being, although the law as originally stated by Gordon Moore (1965) applied specifically to integrated circuits. (Amusingly, Moore used the inelegant term *cramming* to describe the progress in getting more devices on each chip.) Engineers do not usually associate the appellation "Moore's law" with storage and communication, although the exponential improvement in both those technologies can be traced to similar underlying phenomena as in electronics (specifically scaling) and to the fact that both storage and communication incorporate electronics as well as other material technologies (such as magnetic or optical storage medium or fiber optics).

Economists are quite familiar with exponential advances. For example, the compounding of reinvested interest results in an exponential increase in principal, and similarly if the world economy grows at a fixed percentage rate, then its total size increases exponentially. However, an exponential improvement in the cost-effective performance of technology (in contrast to the diffusion of technology, which is related to the growth in the overall economy) was unknown to science and engineering prior to the information age, and is not an observed characteristic of earlier technologies such as transportation and electrification.

Example   An exponential increase in railroad tracks was observed during the first few decades of the railroad industry in the United States (Schaller 1997). However, this relates to the *diffusion* of the technology through the compounding of investments, not the *performance* of the technology. For trains, performance would be measured by speed or fuel consumption per unit distance or maximum load capacity. As *Time* magazine (January 3, 1983) wrote, "If the automobile business had developed like the computer business, a Rolls Royce would now cost $2.75 and run 3 million miles on a gallon of gas." Even those figures would be dwarfed in the two decades since that was written.

If one waits long enough, the cumulative effect of an exponential advance is dramatic. We have seen approximately three to four decades of the operation of Moore's law thus far, and it is expected to pertain some years into the future.

2.3.3   Incrementing Moore's Law

An exponential improvement requires a parameter to describe the speed of advance. Economists are accustomed to using the rate r, where the exponential advance in time t is described quantitatively as $(1 + r)^t$, and r can be interpreted as the fraction (usually expressed as a percentage) of increase in unit time ($\Delta t = 1$). Scientists and engineers, on the other hand, are accustomed to a different (albeit equally descriptive) parameter, the time d required for a doubling.

Example   Radioactive decay is typically characterized by its half-life, defined as the time for the intensity of the radioactive decay to decrease by a factor of 2.

These parameters are related by $(1 + r)^d = 2$ and shown in table 2.2 for the three areas of IT (based on published estimates). It is also useful to compare the accumulated performance improvement over an extended period of time; one decade is shown in table 2.2. Note that processing is improving more slowly than electronics because of implementation inefficiencies. Storage capacity (total bits that can be stored per unit cost) is improving as fast as electronics, while the storage through-

Table 2.2
Estimated Improvement in Performance per Unit Cost for the Information Technologies

Technology	Metric	Doubling Time (months)	Rate (%/year)	Multiplier (per 10 years)
Electronics throughput (CMOS)[a]	Data processed per unit time	18	59	102
Processing throughput (commercial computers)	Data processed per unit time	21	49	53
Storage capacity (magnetic disk)	Bits stored	18	59	102
Storage throughput (magnetic disk)	Bits written or read per unit time	36	26	10
Communication throughput (fiber optics)	Bits transported per unit time	12	100	1024

Sources: Bokerts (1969; 2000); Dray and Shenoy (2000).
a. CMOS stands for complementary metal oxide semiconductor.

put (rate at which bits can be written or read) is improving more slowly. Communication throughput for fiber optics is improving dramatically, but this is a recent and relatively short-term phenomenon.[12] Longer-term, fiber optics should follow a similar trend to electronics. Generally, these capacity improvements flow directly to the achievable throughput for a given application, if the application and its supporting hardware infrastructure are well designed.

2.3.4   Effect of Moore's Law on Software

The implications of Moore's law to the software industry are profound and expected to continue for some time. The role that electronics and photonics play in the software industry is analogous to the role of the aircraft industry from the perspective of the travel industry. However, contrary to aircraft, electronics and photonics performance characteristics per unit cost are improving exponentially with time, adding a dramatic "tail wind."

Historically the computer industry has evolved through four phases, listed in table 2.3. They are overlapping because none has disappeared; for example, the mainframe is still widely used for crucial enterprise applications. The evolution through these phases has been largely driven by the declining cost and improved performance of computing as well as (in the fourth phase) the declining cost and improved performance of communication. Computing power once affordable only to large organizations is now affordable to individual consumers, opening up entirely new business models for the software industry. The dramatic effect of the networked computing phase has just begun and is an important issue in this book.

Another result of the operation of Moore's law is to free developers to concentrate less on performance and more on features that enhance usability (e.g., graphic user interfaces and real-time video), reduced time to market, or added functionality. In earlier years, software developers spent lots of time and effort enhancing performance to achieve adequate interactive delays; this remains important but secondary to functionality. The operation of Moore's law has allowed advances in processing power for user interface enhancements through graphics and for incorporating new media like audio and video into applications. The sale of a sequence of upgrades of the same application is an important economic underpinning of the software industry, but this would be less feasible without the advances in processing power. A major technical challenge to software developers today is dealing with the inherent complexity of applications rather than achieving adequate performance. Many of the techniques for dealing with this complexity require added processing power (see chapter 4).

Table 2.3
The Four Historical Overlapping Phases of Computing

Phase	Description	Effect on software
Mainframe computer	All computing is done in batch mode on a large, expensive centralized computer.	Computers are affordable only to large organizations, and essentially all software applications serve back-office business needs or the computational needs of science and engineering.
Time-sharing computer	Multiple users can work interactively on the same (relatively large and expensive) centralized computer.	Software applications begin to focus on the needs of individuals as well as large organizations, enhancing their effectiveness and productivity.
Personal computer	Individual users have dedicated desktop computers. Individuals can acquire new applications directly from software vendors and install them.	A consumer market for software develops with distinctly different sales and distribution mechanisms.
Networked computer	All computers can communicate with one another. Applications can be distributed across different computers. For example, client-server computing is a mixture of the time-sharing and personal computer modes, in which shared applications on a server are presented to individual users on their personal computers.	Software applications become deeply ingrained in enterprise business processes, which are inherently distributed. Software applications become a basis for communication among individuals and groups, and for distributed information access. New challenges of interoperability and portability arise.

Source: Messerschmitt (1999c).

Advances in storage are also having a profound effect. It is estimated that the total information generated worldwide is growing at about 50 percent per year (Lyman and Varian 2000). Since this rate is comparable to Moore's law for storage, the cost of storing this information is not growing very fast, if at all. The pace of generation of information is profoundly influenced by IT, and the declining cost per unit storage is one enabler.

A final effect of Moore's law is its influence on the boundary between hardware and software. For any given application, with the declining cost of electronics, a software implementation becomes more attractive over time.

Example   At one time, dedicated hardware was required to process speech. Later, it became attractive to process speech using specialized programmable digital signal processing. Today most speech processing can be performed on a standard personal computer with the addition of software, eliminating the need for specialized hardware.

Software solutions leverage the greater manufacturing volumes and resulting economies of scale for programmable hardware devices, allow a given application to readily benefit from future technology advances, and allow a reduced time to market and greater flexibility to change and upgrade a design (often after manufacture and shipment). Software solutions benefit from the sharing of a single programmable device by multiple applications. Of course, customized hardware solutions are required for applications that stress the performance capabilities of today's electronics. A key predictor of the economic viability of a software solution is the gap between the intrinsic capabilities of electronics on the one hand and the application needs on the other—as this gap grows, software implementation on standard programmable devices becomes increasingly attractive.

2.3.5   System Bottlenecks

An IT *system* is a mixture of various hardware and software elements working together to achieve a single purpose. Practical systems mix all the technologies we have discussed. While they directly benefit from the operation of Moore's law, they also suffer from bottlenecks. A bottleneck is a capacity parameter that limits system performance; even increasing other aspects of the system capacity would not help. Moore's law translates into improved system performance only with skillful system design, in part to avoid or bypass bottlenecks. This is considered further in chapter 4.

Some important system bottlenecks are imposed by both technology and economics. The deployment of broadband communication technologies to individual residences is constrained by the high capital investments and risks of deploying fiber optics technology. Mobile applications require wireless communication technologies, which are inherently less capable than fiber optics.[13] The characteristics of battery technology also limit the amount of processing that can be performed within portable terminal devices.

One physical property that is not described by Moore's law is the speed of light, which remains fixed and ultimately becomes a bottleneck. Because of the finite speed of light, physically small systems are likely to outperform physically large ones.

2.3.6   Why Moore's Law?

The origins of Moore's law lie in observations of three material technology inventions at the beginning of the information age. The first was the transistor in the late

1940s, followed by the integrated circuit in the late 1950s. The second was magnetic storage using a rotating disk as a medium in the 1950s, which has similarly benefited from decades of incremental improvement. The third was communication by light using fiber optics as the medium in the 1970s, also followed by decades of incremental improvement.

Moore's law is an empirical observation, but what factors underlie it (Schaller 1997)? There seem to be three contributing factors: the physical law of scaling, the economics of internal investment, and the self-fulfillment of expectations. First, consider physical laws. Like other technologies, electronics and photonics have fundamental limits on performance defined by physical laws. Fortunately today's technologies are far from these physical limits, suggesting that the rate of improvement predicted by Moore's law may continue for some time (Keyes 2001).

Since previous technologies (like transportation or electrification) did not advance according to Moore's law, there must be something distinctive about the material information technologies. That is the *physical law of scaling*: as the physical dimensions of electronic and optical devices are miniaturized, *all* their important performance characteristics improve. This is a remarkable observation to engineers, who are accustomed to making trade-offs: as one performance measure is improved, others get worse.[14] The law of scaling can be stated as follows. Let $s < 1$ be a factor by which all the feature sizes of a given technology are scaled; that is, all physical dimensions of transistors are scaled by s, as are the widths of the wires connecting the transistors. Then physical laws predict the performance implications listed in table 2.4.

With material IT everything improves with scaling: device speed improves, the complexity (number of devices) can increase, and the power consumption per unit of complexity or speed is reduced. Technological improvements focus on scaling, making devices smaller and smaller and packing more devices on a chip. Similar phenomena occur in storage and communication.[15] There are other advances as well, such as the increasing total area of chips and improvements in materials.

How does scaling result in an exponential improvement over time? This seems a likely outcome of scaling (in the direction of miniaturization, not gigantism), using the following logic. Suppose the feature sizes for each generation of technology is scaled by the same scaling factor s. Then the feature size decreases as s, s^2, s^3, and so forth. Assuming these generations are equally spaced in time, the improvements in table 2.4 occur geometrically with time in accordance with Moore's law. Thus, with a couple of (perhaps bold) assumptions, we can predict Moore's law as a direct consequence of the law of scaling.

Table 2.4
Scaling Laws for MOS[a] Integrated Circuits with a Fixed Electric Field Intensity

Parameter	Interpretation	Numerical change	Reason
Complexity	Increase in the number of devices per unit area of a chip (or total number of devices on a chip with the same total area).	$\dfrac{1}{s^2}$	The area of each device is proportional to the square of its dimensions.
Speed	Rate at which operations can be performed by each device.	$\dfrac{1}{s}$	The velocity of electrons does not change, but the physical distance they must move is reduced by s.
Power	Power consumption per unit area (or total power consumption for a chip with the same total area).	1	Both supply voltage and the distance traveled by electrons drops, reducing Ohmic losses per device. This is offset by the larger number of devices.

Source: Firesmith and Henderson-Sellers (2001).
Notes: All these scaling predictions assume that the power supply voltage is reduced in proportion to s (so-called constant electric field scaling). In practice this voltage reduction is difficult because systems like to mix technologies and use a single supply voltage. For this reason, these scaling laws are somewhat optimistic, but they do capture trends.
a. MOS stands for metal oxide semiconductor.

While the law of scaling predicts the exponential improvement described by Moore's law, it provides no explanation of the observed rate of improvement. For this, we turn to the economics of internal investment. The doubling time is determined, to a large degree at least, by the investments that industrial firms and the government make in research and development (R&D) directed at incremental technology improvements (principally scaling). At every generation of technology, new obstacles are faced that require innovation, and new equipment and technologies have to be designed. Since the size of the improvements and the time required to make those improvements depends on the size of the investments, economics must intervene.

Consider industrial firms investing in a new generation of technology: they must make three dependent investment decisions. First, they determine the rate of investment in R&D. Second, they choose a scaling factor s to aim at with that investment. Third, they decide the time interval over which that scaling is to be achieved. Qualitatively, for a given rate of R&D investment, a larger s (a more modest scaling and a smaller performance payoff) can be achieved in a shorter time, therefore increasing the present value of that payoff,[16] and with lower risk.[17] The overall rate of investment in R&D depends on current revenues and profitability expectations, where revenues depend in turn on the outcomes of previous R&D investments and the success in defining new products based on previous generations of technology. Overall, firms must balance a large number of factors to achieve the ultimate goal of profitability, now and in the future. The point is that the rate of technological improvement depends in a complex way on a financial and economic model of R&D investment, and the law of scaling provides no clue in and of itself.

The situation is further complicated (in a delightful way) by the observation that scaling results in an ever-expanding suite of applications and products at lower cost, and therefore an increase in unit volumes. This expanding market results in a virtuous positive feedback cycle: scaling expands the market, and the market expansion creates increasing revenues for suppliers, which in turns allows ever expanding investments in R&D to fuel the next cycle of scaling (as well as capital equipment investments in the required new fabrication plants). This is fortunate, because empirically each cycle of scaling requires ever-larger R&D and capital investments.

The third factor behind Moore's law is the self-fulfillment of expectations, and this has to do with how the industry is organized and coordinated. The electronics industry as a whole must coordinate three complementary businesses: the supply of equipment required to fabricate integrated circuit chips, the construction and operation of factories to fabricate those chips, and the manufacture and assembly of equipment that incorporate those chips.[18] (Of course, a major point of this book is that the IT industry has spawned a fourth business, software. Industrial organization is discussed in greater depth in chapter 7.) These complementary investments must be coordinated and precede the need. Technology thus advances in discrete generations, where fabrication equipment suppliers supply each new generation of equipment, chip manufacturers construct factories to accept this equipment and produce salable chip designs to fabricate, and equipment manufacturers design new chips into their new generations of equipment. Coordination is considerably enhanced by a predictable road map that all can follow. The world's semiconductor manufacturers cooperate on just such a road map (International Technology Roadmap 2002). If this road map happens to be based on Moore's law, and this law is feasible in terms of the pace of innovation and internal investment, then the law becomes self-fulfilling. Firms that don't follow the road map lose out to competition.

See chapter 10 for discussion of the applicability of Moore's law in the future.

2.4   Research and Discussion Issues

1. Think about the definition of technology used in this chapter. Does this accurately reflect what it is, or does it capture everything that it is? Repeat this for information technology specifically.

2. In today's popular press, technology is often equated with information technology. What are some examples of technologies that don't fall into the category of information technology? Why does the popular press confuse this issue? Does this confusion lead to significant problems?

3. Consider the economic implications of representing information by a common form that can be supported in a common IT infrastructure. What if this were not possible and different infrastructures were required to support different information media (for example audio and video)?

4. While a digital representation of information can be precisely and cheaply replicated, it may not capture all aspects of the original creation. Consider for example, a musical concert as compared to a digital recording of that concert. What are the implications of this to the economic properties of information and the manner in which information is bought and sold?

5. Considering the last issue, software is represented in digital form even in its original creation. What are some significant differences between software and information as to their economic and business properties that flow from this observation?

6. What substantive differences are there, if any, in the mechanisms that overcome the "experience good" property that applies to both information and software? Consider all the mechanisms you can think of that are commonly used for either, such as metadata, hyperlinks, indexes, recommendations, and free trials.

7. Consider the atoms versus bits metaphor for material versus immaterial goods. Specifically, what constitutes these goods beyond atoms and bits?

8. Think about the ability of a single processor to support a plethora of software programs at different times. Are there analogies to this form of sharing elsewhere in the economy? What are all the ramifications you can think of to the economic

and business properties of hardware (both programmable and nonprogrammable) and software?

9. Reconsider the last question in light of the ability to change and upgrade software in the field even without replacing the programmable hardware it depends on.

10. Identify a few other examples of layering in industries outside information technology, and consider in depth what similarities and differences they display to IT.

11. Given that computers are increasingly able to recognize spoken speech and also generate speech, do you think that literacy (the ability to read and write) will be as important in the future as it has been in the past? What specific functions might benefit from or require literacy in spite of these speaking skills on the part of the computer?

12. Consider a software application that you are familiar with, one where performance issues are important. Discuss the relation between delay and throughput performance measures for processing and communication on the one hand, and the characteristics of the application as you observe them on the other.

13. Compare information technology and other situations (like transportation) where congestion is an important phenomenon. What differences can you discern in the effects of congestion on users or other people?

14. There is always some uncertainty as to how long Moore's law will apply. What if its observations no longer described actual progress accurately? What would be the lasting effect on the software industry? This is one way to approach the role that Moore's law has in continuing progress.

15. Discuss in more detail the considerations that an implementer would take into account in choosing between a customized hardware solution and writing software for a standard programmable device.

16. Discuss the detailed considerations that a manager of a semiconductor manufacturer must take into account in determining R&D and the capital equipment investments required for a new generation of electronics technology scaling.

17. Can you construct a financial model that predicts (or at least explains) the time interval for each generation of scaling in electronics, and the scaling factor, based on revenue and internal investment models? Alternatively, can you develop a model that quantifies the limits on R&D and capital expenditures that are consistent with responsible fiscal management?

18. Discuss some alternative mechanisms that could be used to coordinate semi-conductor equipment manufacturers, chip makers, equipment makers, and software suppliers as Moore's law plays out. What are their advantages and disadvantages? Why do you think the mechanisms currently in place have been chosen? Can you recommend improvements?

2.5   Further Reading

The early history of the computer is described in Allen (1971); a more recent source is Meyers (1993). A general reference on the convergence of computing and communications is Messerschmitt (1999a; 1999b). A recommended article on the history of Moore's law is Schaller (1997).

3

Users

It troubles me that we are so easily pressured by the purveyors of technology into permitting so-called "progress" to alter our lives without attempting to control it—as if technology were an irrepressible force of nature to which we must meekly submit.
Admiral Hyman G. Rickover

Admiral Rickover's words are particularly relevant to information technology (IT), which suffers from very little in the way of significant physical limits. If you think the technology too weak or too expensive today, just allow Moore's law (see chapter 2) to play out a bit longer. This implies that we are free to mold IT just about any way we choose, subject of course to limitations imposed by the installed infrastructure and past investments. Clearly, the desires and needs of end-users are (or should be) a dominant consideration. The greatest success (at least in a business or societal sense) will accrue to those who make people—individual users of IT as well as their social and industrial organizations—central to their thinking about software.

Application software is the subject of this chapter. Its primary purpose is to serve the needs of end-users, be they individuals, groups of individuals, organizations (e.g., companies, universities, government), groups of organizations (e.g., commerce), communities of interest, or society at large (e.g., entertainment, politics). Application software is distinct from infrastructure software, whose primary purpose is serving software application developers directly and users secondarily. A more complete definition of a *software application* is a set of functionalities and capabilities (also called features) that forms a cohesive whole, has integrating qualities (e.g., a common security model), and targets a characteristic domain of human activity. This domain may, at its extremes, be horizontal (serving a wide range of human activities, like word processing), or vertical (serving a specific range of human activity, like the administration of a medical practice).

It is important to note that the users are often not the customers of a software supplier. In some cases they are one and the same, as with an operating system and applications purchased for home use. In an organization there are usually intermediaries who acquire and deploy the software and operate it on behalf of users (see chapter 5), and they are the customers. The same would be true of an application accessed over the Web.

While software development has a reputation as an isolating and antisocial activity, this prejudice is increasingly outdated and inaccurate, particularly in the case of application software. Successful application software results when developers placing themselves in the contexts and mind-sets of the future users, and possess empathy for them. The application software developer needs to work closely with future users (or at least a representative sample) and not simply imagine and conceptualize their contexts. Imagine building or landscape architects or interior decorators who failed to interact extensively with future occupants, who must live with their decisions indefinitely. They won't succeed, and neither will application software developers who work in isolation.

3.1   Applications Present and Future

The past five decades of computing have been characterized by a continuing expansion in the scope of functionality of software applications. This is a direct result of the expanding range of technologies, the continuing performance advances observed by Moore's law, the ongoing progress in finding new and innovative ways to use the technology, and growing end-user comfort and experience with software products.

3.1.1   Application Traditions

Historically, the three areas of IT—processing, storage, and communication—arose in that order. This statement is an oversimplification, in that useful computer systems have always needed all three elements, at least in small measure.

Example   Even the earliest computer systems used paper tape or punched cards to store programs between executions, and communication channels to interact with peripherals like printers.

Nevertheless the introduction of mass storage systems based on magnetic media (tape and disk) and a global computer network (particularly the Internet) that allowed all computers to communicate with one another were critical demarcations in the development of software applications.

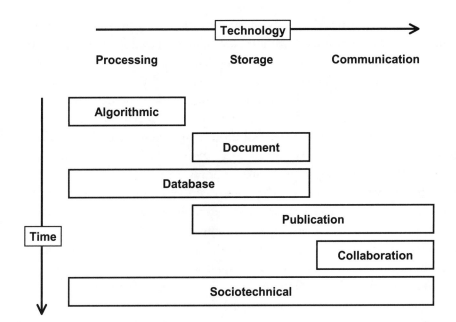

Figure 3.1
Classification of software applications in order of appearance and the primary technologies they leverage.

Each of these major areas of IT is associated with a period of innovative new applications relying heavily on the new technology. Associated with each technology is an identifiable application tradition, that is, a group of innovative new applications that draws heavily on the new technology or in many cases on both the new and the older technologies. In figure 3.1 major application groupings are classified in this manner, by order of appearance and by the technology or technologies they primarily leverage. On a cautionary note, no such classification could ever be perfectly accurate, complete, or defensible; rather, the goal is merely to capture and classify major trends.

The *algorithmic tradition* relies heavily on processing and is the basis for applications like signal processing (e.g., audio and video compression), financial engineering (e.g., pricing derivative instruments), modeling in scientific and engineering fields (e.g., weather forecasting), and design (e.g., computer-aided design of integrated circuits).

Following the invention of magnetic storage and the addition of vast information reservoirs, applications in the *document tradition* emphasized the storage and retrieval of documents. A document is information-as-thing, an artifact the primary purpose of which is to capture a body of information. A broad definition of the document (especially appropriate with the computer) includes pictures, video, and audio in addition to the printed document. The document tradition includes applications that support commerce (e.g., purchase and fulfillment), scholarship (e.g., the scholarly literature), and entertainment (e.g., movies on demand). While paper documents remain important, computer-mediated documents offer multi-media (audio and video as well as text and images) and automated searching and navigation aids.

It was natural as a next step to make use of heavy doses of processing together with mass storage, which enabled the *database tradition*. Like a static document in the print world, the database enables information to be stored and retrieved. However, it also relies on ample processing to allow information to be dynamic and volatile, and to allow documents relying on that database also to reflect these volatile changes. Although originally considered an application, today a database would rarely be used directly. Rather databases typically form an infrastructure foundation for various information management applications.

Example The database management system (DBMS) is an infrastructure software category (major vendors include IBM, Informix, Microsoft, Oracle, and Sybase) that underlies many business applications. It is used to maintain up-to-date customer identity and contact information, and to track purchase and order status. In online transaction processing (OTP), workers update a database based on volatile new information, such as that obtained over the telephone. Documents like management reports access a snapshot of current database information.

The introduction of even more massive doses of processing enables data mining, the extraction of often unexpected trends from databases.

Although the electronic communications industry dates to the nineteenth century (starting with radio and telephony), communications wasn't brought to mainstream computing until the 1980s (local-area networking) and 1990s (the Internet for wide-area networking). With the Internet, the document tradition expanded to encom-pass the *publication tradition*. Massive collections of information, whether stored in central repositories or distributed across many smaller repositories, could be made practically instantaneously available to users anywhere in the world. This quickly resulted in a new challenge: too much information and the need to narrow it down for particular uses. Building on processing combined with storage and communica-tion, modes of finding useful information based on searching and navigation evolved.

Example   Search engines such as AltaVista and Google focus on identifying documents that contain specified keywords. Navigation through masses of information on the Web can be accomplished by utilizing hyperlinks (a mechanism that allows one document to contain links to other relevant documents) and indexes (such as Netscape, MSN, and Yahoo).

The addition of communications to the IT mix enabled a new *collaboration tradition*, including applications that support groups of people working together (e.g., e-mail and video conferencing), playing together (e.g., multiparty games), or socializing (e.g., chat rooms). This tradition also supports coordination, which is an element of many human and technical activities, such as design collaboration and business or military logistics. This tradition began with e-mail, now encompasses a growing set of capabilities, and is the least mature of the traditions considered thus far.

Example   The use of computer-mediated collaboration tools is growing rapidly and becoming an important supplement to the face-to-face meeting or the simple telephone call. The computer-mediated meeting can supplement audio with other media such as video conferencing, drawings in scribbling, and so on. Perhaps in the future a remote conference will be considered as good as, or even better than, a face-to-face meeting.

Before considering the *sociotechnical tradition*, it is appropriate first to reflect on the types of end-users and the ways in which applications are integrating all the capabilities represented in the traditions mentioned thus far.

3.1.2   Type of End-User

Another way of classifying applications is by the type of user group they support (Messerschmitt 1999a; 1999c). *Individual applications* enhance the effectiveness or productivity of individuals and are the focus of the algorithmic, document, and publication traditions. *Group applications* serve a group of individuals and are emphasized by the database and collaboration traditions. Then there are applications that serve organizations (groups carrying out a long-term collective purpose.) A community application allows a large group of people sharing a common agenda or interest to interact or coordinate, even though they may not know one another or the membership is dynamically changing. *Enterprise applications* support an organizational mission (business, educational, or government) and the basic processes that occur within an organization. These come in two basic categories: business process applications that automate repetitive tasks, and managerial applications that support ad hoc decision making. *E-commerce applications* allow two or more organizations to carry out collective functions, especially where the sale of goods or services is involved. An e-commerce application is to the enterprise application what the group application is to the individual application.

3.1.3 Applications Are Increasingly Heterogeneous

As a new area of IT was added, new applications typically incorporated capabilities of both the new and the previous technologies (as illustrated by the database and publication traditions in figure 3.1). Thus, many applications today strongly combine processing, mass storage, and communication in various ways, and this will be increasingly true of applications in the future.

Example An automotive design project in a global firm may be conducted across several continents. It mixes modeling and simulation (the algorithmic tradition), coordination of concurrent design activities across time zones (the collaboration tradition), group meetings (the collaboration tradition), and a stored and updated design database capturing the current status of the design (the document tradition). While these activities could be supported by logically separate applications—where only the people and not software formed the linkages—there is great benefit to integrating these elements. For example, the design database can capture the complete history of the design and how it arose from collaboration, decisions made during collaboration can be automatically documented, and the implications of those decisions can be characterized by modeling and simulation as an integral part of the collaboration. Many engineering design activities fit a similar model.

What is the value of mixing the algorithmic, document, database, publication, and collaborative traditions? As examples, searching and data mining added to information access (document tradition) can assist users in locating useful information or even uncovering unexpected patterns is large data sets. The addition of communication allows users to publish information to a broad audience, and for users to aggregate, filter, and consolidate information from many sources. A recommender system observes the actions of many users (collaborative tradition) and extracts from them information about the preferences of those users (algorithmic tradition). The possibilities are limitless.

3.1.4 Sociotechnical Applications

The automotive design example illustrates a sociotechnical application (NRC 2001b). This tradition combines groups of people working on collective tasks (that is, an organization), IT (processing, storage, and communication), voluminous information and knowledge (the latter mostly the province of the people), and many physical elements (materials, goods, and shipping). All the application traditions are integrated in such applications, often in intricate ways. In a very real sense, this is the culmination of application traditions, at least as appreciated today.

In sociotechnical applications, IT is only a *part* of a sociotechnical system comprising people and their organizations, possibly large amounts of information, various organizational processes, and IT. The IT component cannot be meaningfully defined or studied in isolation from other elements; it is embedded as an integral part of the system, much as embedded software is integral to equipment (see section 2.2.6). The conceptualization of such applications requires the partitioning of functions between technology and people, the organization of the people as well as the technology, and the appropriate interface between technology, people, and organization. The design of sociotechnical applications should be—more than applications of the past—an interdisciplinary activity involving technologists with organizational specialists and social scientists (see chapter 4).

There are several increasingly ambitious approaches to defining sociotechnical applications:

• *Automation.* Take an existing process and automate it. Typically this involves moving steps of the process over from manual labor or paper shuffling to automated mechanisms but without any material change to the underlying processes.

• *Reengineering.* Without changing the fundamental goals or functionality, go back to basics, focus on the overarching goals, and ask how those goals would best be partitioned between people and their organizations and the IT, and what would be the best form of interaction among those elements. Consider and design all elements of the sociotechnical system from scratch without a material change to the overarching goals.

• *Innovation.* Reach out to new goals and functionality that were not feasible without IT.

The economic history of earlier technologies suggests strongly that the full benefit of new technologies does not accrue from automation alone.

Example   One eventual benefit of electrification was substantial productivity improvements, but only after manufacturing processes were completely reorganized to take advantage of the electric motor's ability to distribute rather than centralize mechanical power, not in the early stages where centralized turbine or water generation units were simply replaced by electric motors (David 1990).

While understanding the needs of users is a primary issue, and users can play a primary role in defining opportunities for automation, users often don't have sufficient understanding of the opportunities and potential of technology to fully exploit reengineering and innovation opportunities. Technologists may also have insufficient domain knowledge to fully appreciate how best to leverage IT. Again, this suggests close collaboration between end-users or domain experts and technologists (see chapter 4).

3.1.5   Applications Are Increasingly Diverse

Another distinctive characteristic of modern applications, and especially sociotechnical applications, is their specialization and diversity. Whereas the horizontal applications of the past (such as telephony, e-mail video distribution, word processing, video conferencing, instant messaging) had wide generic appeal across a wide spectrum of organizations, sociotechnical applications are specialized, because their capabilities are specific to an organizational mission.

This has profound implications for the processes of conceptualizing and developing new applications (see chapter 4). As applications become more diverse, each with a smaller user base, either development costs must be reduced or users must be willing to pay more for specific value added (see section 3.2). Users with domain-specific knowledge must participate more deeply throughout the application conceptualization and development.

One way to reduce development costs is exploit the reuse of existing software or to build applications from components (see chapter 7). Another approach is to expand the scope of infrastructure software (see chapters 4 and 7). Even specialized applications tend to incorporate many similar capabilities, and these can be captured in the infrastructure.

Example   The Web was originally conceptualized as an application, a way for scientists to publish information for colleagues. More recently, the Web has expanded to serve as a foundation for many networked applications, particularly in providing standardized capabilities for presenting and capturing information. As developments incorporate Web technologies, they reduce development effort and eliminate special software on users' computers.

This is a general trend: The new builds on the old rather than replacing it, and some applications form the basis for new applications; in other words, they gradually morph into infrastructure (see chapter 7).

3.1.6   Conceptualizing New Applications

An effective way to identify compelling new applications is to try out many ideas with users, leverage that experience to refine and further develop ideas, or abandon

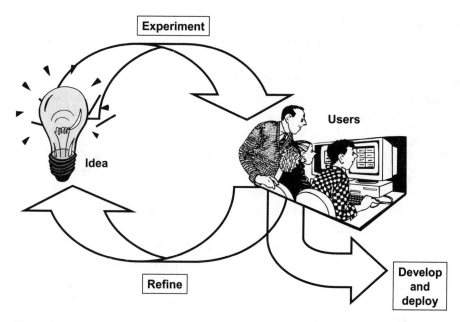

Figure 3.2
Methodology for iterative refinement of application ideas involving end-users.

ideas that don't add value (see figure 3.2). This suggests an iterative stepwise refinement approach to software development, the close cooperation of users and developers, and inexpensive ways to try out ideas (for example, rapid prototyping of user interfaces). These needs are strongly influencing software development (see chapter 4).

Figure 3.2 captures a process for integrating group and individual contributions into application development, but sociotechnical (enterprise and commerce) applications are much more complicated and challenging. The application software is integrally tied into the various processes that organizations use to formalize their repetitive tasks and capabilities, and processes, organizations, and software must be designed as an integral unit.

3.2 User Value

An important issue for application software suppliers is the *value* offered to a customer (individual or organization). Value can be quantified economically by users' willingness to pay (see chapter 9), but there are many constituents to this value. No explicit distinction is made between individuals and end-user organizations, although this will obviously change the equation substantially. Of course, suppliers may have other goals in addition to maximizing value, such as excluding competitors by creating switching costs for their customers (see chapter 9) or gaining competitive advantages through lower costs or higher volume sales.

The customer is assessed various costs associated with acquiring, provisioning, and operating software, including payments to software suppliers, acquiring supporting hardware, and salaries for operational and support staff (see chapter 5). To the user, these costs and their relation to value is an important issue. A supplier will also work to maximize the value (and hence the price that can be charged).

Willingness to pay is difficult to quantify during the conceptualization and development of an application. Value is derived from the behavior the software invokes; that is, what it causes a computer to do on behalf of a user (or group, community, or organization), and how well it does those things. Although the specific context of the user is important, there are also generic characteristics of value that transcend the specific context. We discuss some of these now—how they affect value and how they affect the supplier's business model. Business issues relating to the sale of software are discussed more extensively in chapter 6.

3.2.1 Productivity

One source of value is the tangible and intangible effects of an application in making a user (or group or organization) more productive, effective, or successful. An application may improve productivity, decrease the time to complete tasks, enhance collaboration among workers, better manage and exploit knowledge assets, or improve the quality of outcomes. Often, productivity enhancements can be quantified by financial metrics, such as increased revenue or reduced costs. Other types of effects (e.g., the effectiveness of an organization in customer service and greater customer satisfaction) are less quantifiable but no less real. When reengineering of processes and reorganization accompany application deployment, it is difficult to assess what portion of the benefit accrues to the software directly, but that artificial separation is arguably unnecessary because those benefits may be unattainable without the software.

Applications can sometimes enable outcomes that are otherwise not achievable, such as movie special effects or design simulation. In this case, the effect is not to improve but rather to extend the range of the feasible.

Examples   While auctions are sometimes used in the physical world for selling high-value goods that are unique and whose price is therefore difficult to set (like artwork), auctions have become more common in e-commerce. The network cir-

cumvents one obstacle, getting bidders physically together. Many remote collaboration applications allow interaction at distances that would otherwise not be possible. The online tracking of inventories has allowed businesses to greatly reduce
business interruptions for manual inventory accounting. Searching the content of
all Web sites is enabled by the global Internet.

Software suppliers may try to adjust pricing based on an application's usefulness,
or value, to a specific organization, since that is one of the biggest variables for different customers in the willingness to pay (this is an example of price discrimination; see chapter 9). How well the application fills an organization's needs varies
widely; for example, is the organization already using a competitive application, or
is it stuck with a manual process? Negotiation of price, with usefulness to a particular organization as a prime consideration, is especially common for custom-
developed applications. For off-the-shelf applications, it is common to publish a
standard catalog price but offer discounts based on value to the particular organization and willingness to pay or number of licenses bought. Another strategy is to
offer different variants at different prices and allow customers to self-select (this is
called versioning by economists; see chapter 9).

3.2.2 Meeting Needs

Software features do not always exactly match the needs of users, but a better match
offers greater value. This is clearly true for off-the-shelf applications, where different adopters usually have differentiated needs that may be partially (but not totally)
met by configuration options, but it is true even for custom-designed software.
Unfortunately there is an inevitable mismatch between what is built and what is
needed. It is relatively easy to provide many configuration and customization
options in software, but this is insufficient. It is difficult enough to capture precisely
the requirements of any individual user at any one point in time. Most software
targets a large number of users (to share development and maintenance costs or to
meet the needs of an organization) and also serves users over an extended period
of time, during which needs change. Needs of large numbers of users over extended
time can be approximated at best.

The matching of needs is a significant factor in make versus buy decisions in software acquisition. One argument for internal development of software in a large
organization is a more precise match to specific needs and more control over future
evolution to match changing needs. This is balanced against a higher cost of development (not amortized over multiple organizations) and often an increased time to
deployment and higher risk of budget or time overrun or outright failure. On the

other hand, an independent software supplier that achieves a closer match to needs offers higher value. For this reason, capturing user needs and requirements is always an important part of the application software development process (see chapter 4). Software acquisition is discussed further in chapters 5 and 6.

3.2.3   Network Effects

For much software, the value depends not only on intrinsic features and capabilities of the software itself but also on the number of other adopters of the same or compatible solutions: the more adopters, the higher the value. This is called a *network effect* or *network externality* (Church and Gaudal 1992; Katz and Shapiro 1985; 1986b; Shapiro and Varian 1999b), and it plays an important role in some software markets.

An externality is a situation where the actions of one party affect another without a compensating payment (e.g., air pollution). Network externalities can be either positive (the form of primary concern here) or negative. In a negative externality, value actually decreases rather than increases with more adopters.

Example   Congestion of a communication network (or highway system) is a negative externality in the absence of congestion-based pricing. As more users generate traffic and as throughput increases, the delay for information traversing the network increases for other users (see section 2.3.1), decreasing the value to them.

Positive network externalities in technology products come in two distinct forms (Messerschmitt 1999a; 1999c), as illustrated in figure 3.3. Assume that there are multiple instances (copies) of a product in the hands of different adopters. When these instances have no relationship, there is no network and *no network effect*. When they are dependent in some way, a network results. (This does not imply that there is an actual communication network connecting them but rather merely a network of complementary dependencies.) In the stronger *direct network effect*, the different instances of the product are directly complementary to one another, and the value to each individual adopter typically increases with the size of the network. In particular, the first adopter may derive no value at all.

Example   A facsimile machine's value increases as the number of owners of facsimile machines increases, because this creates more opportunities to send a fax. The first purchaser of a facsimile machine derives no value. A similar software example would be a remote conferencing or group meeting application for a desktop computer.

It is important to realize that there are two distinct sources of value in the presence of direct network effects. First, there is the intrinsic value of the software: what

**Direct network effect: instances of
product are directly dependent**

**No network:
instances of
product are
independent**

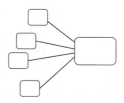

**Indirect network effect: mutual
dependence on a complementary
commodity**

Figure 3.3
Network effects on instances of a software product.

it does, how well it does it, and its effect on users when it is used. Second, there is the network effect: how many opportunities there are to use the software, the size of the network.

Example   Once a remote conference begins, its value will depend on various features and performance characteristics that determine effectiveness and user experience. This is distinct from the direct network effect, which flows from the number of opportunities to conference.

In the weaker *indirect network effect*, the instances of the product have no direct dependence, but their value is collectively dependent on some complementary commodity, like available information content or trained staff, technical assistance, or complementary applications. (In the economics literature, direct and indirect network effects are sometimes associated with "real" or "virtual" networks, respectively.) In this case, a larger network typically stimulates more investment in this complementary commodity and thus indirectly affects value.

Example   The Web exhibits an indirect network effect based on the amount of content it attracts. With more adopters of Web browsers, information suppliers have more incentive to provide information content (for example, they are likely to derive more revenue from advertisers, paying for more content). As another example, the value of a software development toolkit (languages, compilers, and other tools; see chapter 4) to a software development organization depends on the total number of adopters. With a larger base, there are more prospective workers who can work with that toolkit, and a richer set of complementary products, like training materials.

There are, of course, intermediate cases. These examples illustrate that the relative importance of intrinsic capabilities and network size in affecting user value can vary widely. This can be true even for a single software product.

Example A word-processing application offers intrinsic value to a solitary user (increasing effectiveness in authoring documents), but a larger network also gives more opportunities to share documents in a compatible format or to author a document collaboratively. For some users, the ability to share or collaborate is paramount, whereas it may be a marginal benefit to others.

Chapter 9 gives a simple quantitative model of network effects and discusses the dynamics of software markets influenced by network effects.

Network effects are common in software and have a couple of practical results. First, they make it more difficult to establish a market if the initial demand is diminished by a dearth of adopters. The early product cycle is precisely when the supplier is most concerned with recovering the high fixed (and often sunk) costs of creation. Second, if a substantial market is established, network effects create a positive feedback in which "success breeds success." An incremental increase in adoptions makes the product appear more valuable to the remaining population.

Example The Linux operating system is benefiting from this cycle (as did Mac OS, UNIX, and Windows before it). As the number of adopters increases, more software suppliers choose to offer applications on Linux. The availability of applications is one of the prime motivators for adoption. More adopters in turn encourage application development.

There are a number of measures that suppliers can take to help establish a market in the presence of network effects (Shapiro and Varian 1999b). One is to offer backward compatibility with established products.

Example Voiceband data modems have followed Moore's law for years, introducing new generations of product with increasing speed and more (but still affordable) processing power. If each new generation communicated only with its own generation, early adoptions would be stifled. This was avoided by allowing each new generation to communicate with the older generations (at their lower speed). Since the communication algorithms are implemented in embedded software, the incremental manufacturing cost (the cost of storage for the older software) is low.

Another approach is to develop an industry standard that allows all suppliers to offer compatible products, and thus expand the collective market (see chapter 7).

Example The Digital Versatile Disk (DVD) illustrates the role of standardization for a representation of information (entertainment video). Initially two groups of manufacturers formed alliances to share research and development (R&D) costs. Eventually, the two groups felt the need to cooperate to bring a single format to market, in part to satisfy content suppliers worried about consumer confusion. The DVD Forum is an association of 230 companies cooperating on DVD standards. Such efforts are always fragile: periodically companies dissatisfied with the forum consensus choose to develop incompatible technologies; the forum explicitly states that members are free to do so.

3.2.4 Usage

Generally speaking, software that is used more offers more value. *Usage* comprises two factors. First is the number of users, which in an organizational context often relates to the overall value of the software to the organization. Second is the amount of time each user spends with the application; a user who invokes an application only occasionally may derive less value than one using it the entire working day. Of course, if greater usage is a side effect of poor usability (see section 3.2.7), this could represent lower, not higher, value. Also, the value varies among different activities within an organization, so usage is at best an approximation of value.

Software licensing and pricing often take usage into account (see chapter 9), usually by fairly crude but easily formulated and enforced mechanisms.

Example Price may be coupled to the number of computers on which an application runs or to the speed of those computers. A *floating license* allows a certain number of concurrent users while allowing the software to be installed on a greater number of computers. Another usage approach is to couple pricing to the number of transactions; this makes sense for certain types of applications (like e-commerce). Selling software as a service (rather than licensing software code; see chapter 6) makes it easier to couple pricing directly to usage.

Software licensing is discussed further in chapter 8.

3.2.5 Functionality and Fidelity

Software functionality and fidelity speak primarily to the perceptual experience of the user (Slaughter, Harter, and Krishnan 1998): how accurately and expeditiously an application completes user directives. *Functionality* refers to whether the software does what is asked or expected, from the user perspective. *Fidelity* refers to the accuracy with which the software achieves that functionality. Observed *defects* in the software (both their number and severity) contribute to a perception of lack of fidelity.

With respect to defects (sometimes colloquially called "bugs"), *observed* is an important qualifier. The actual number of defects may be either higher or lower than the number observed. Some defects won't be observed under typical use (the defective behaviors are not exercised). On the other hand, a perceived defect may actually be a misunderstanding as to how the software is supposed to work. The latter case could be reinterpreted as an actual defect in the intuitiveness of the usage model, the help/training material, or the certification process used to determine whether a user is qualified to use the application. Some perceived defects represent legitimate disagreement between the software developer and the user about what an application should do, reflected in the old joke "it's not a bug, it's a feature."

Perceived and real defects cannot be avoided completely. Perceived defects are defined relative to specific requirements, which can't be captured fully and accurately (see section 3.2.2). While a similar dilemma is faced by all engineering disciplines, many benefit from relatively slow change and much longer historical experience, allowing them to deliver close-to-perfect products from this perspective. IT as well as user requirements have always changed rapidly, and any stabilization in requirements is accurately interpreted today as a leading indicator of obsolescence. Of course, this has been generally true of all relatively immature technologies.

Example   The automobile in its early days was perceived as cranky and hard to keep running, requiring a great deal of technical knowledge on the part of its drivers.

A second reason defects can't be eliminated is the impracticality of detecting all design flaws in software during testing (see chapter 4). As pointed out in chapter 2, software is subject to little in the way of physical limits in the hardware, and therefore software complexity tends to balloon to whatever level its human designers think they can cope with. The resulting complexity results in an astronomical set of states and outcomes, astronomically more than can be exercised during testing. Thus, the reduction of defects focuses on development testing, on making software correct by construction, and inevitably on the maintenance of the software to remove latent defects observed by users (see chapter 5).

There are important gradations of defects that determine their perceptual and quantifiable severity. A defect consuming considerable invested time and effort is more severe than a defect that, for example, temporarily disturbs the resolution of a display.

3.2.6 Performance

Performance refers to how fast and expeditiously software achieves its delegated tasks. As discussed in section 2.3.1, there are several types of performance attributes of interest, some of which are of interest to users and some of which are of primary concern to operators. *Delay metrics* are of greatest importance to the user, such as interactive delay, playback delay for audio or video sources, or the delay introduced in an audio or video conference. Other types of delay are of importance to organizations, such as added delays in propagating work flow tasks through an organization.

Example Consider an application performing real-time control of an electric power network. Individual workers will notice interactive delays when they request information about the network status. The power company will be affected by delays between entering control actions and achieving resulting actions, since this may reduce the control accuracy and effectiveness.

Throughput metrics interest operators because they affect the number of users supported more than the perceptual experience of each individual user. There is a connection between utilization (throughput as a fraction of capacity) and interactive delay that should be taken into account (see section 2.3.1).

Observed performance is not strictly objective. For example, poor interactivity in one activity can be masked by a multitude of attention-diverting activities. For this reason Web browsers display animated graphics while waiting for the arrival of requested Web content. When the "observer" is actually another piece of software rather than a human user, then objective measures apply.[1]

Example In Web services, one application makes use of the services of a second application made visible on the Web (see chapter 7). The effect of the performance attributes of the second application on the first application can usually be defined and measured objectively.

The most immediate determinant of performance is the capital expenditures that the operator chooses to make in hardware resources, which is not under the control of the software supplier. The architecture of an application does have a great deal to do with whether or not performance can be maintained under all operational conditions (e.g., as the number of users increases).

3.2.7 Learnability and Usability

Other aspects of quality are *learnability* (ease with which the user can become facile with the application) and *usability* (the user's perception of how easy or difficult it is to accomplish a desired task once an application has been learned) (Nielsen 2000; Usability Professionals Association). These are hard to quantify and vary dramatically from one user to another, even for the same application. Education, background, skill level, preferred mode of interaction, experience in general or with the particular application, and other factors are influential. There is often a trade-off as well, because features that make an application easier to learn often make it more cumbersome to use.

Example   Novice users of an application will find it easier to get going if the user interface relies heavily on pull-down menus. An experienced user may prefer keyboard shortcuts for the same functions because they don't require taking the fingers off the keyboard. Experienced users may prefer an online help system with searching and hyperlinks, whereas a novice user may prefer a printed manual.

Thus learnability and usability, like needs, vary widely among users, and usability varies over time for the same user (Nielsen 1993). Offering alternatives in each user-interface function is one way to enhance usability across all users and to combine ease of learning with ease of using.

Example   An application may allow the same function to be invoked by mouse or keyboard, offer visual and audio cues, or offer context-free and context-based operations.

Another useful technique is adaptation to the user's desires or sophistication.

Example   An application may allow a "discovery" of features via several likely paths, while later repetitive use of certain features can be fine-tuned to minimize the required number of manipulative steps. Examples include the reconfiguration of user interface elements or the association of common functions with command keys.

3.2.8 Security

Security recognizes that there are inevitably individuals who, for whatever reason, will try to penetrate or disrupt an application or steal information. In the popular press, these individuals are frequently called hackers, but among computer aficionados the term *hacker* has a much more positive connotation as a person who has "technical adeptness and a delight in solving problems and overcoming limits" (Raymond 1996), adeptness that can be channeled in various ways positive and negative (but overwhelmingly positive). The preferred term for those whose goal is

breaking into systems for nefarious purposes (such as theft of information or vandalism) is *cracker*.[2]

Security strives to exclude unauthorized attacks that aim to unveil secrets or inflict
damage to software and information (Howard 1997; Pfleeqer 1997). Damage can
come in many forms, such as rendering services unavailable, or compromising the
authenticity, integrity, or confidentiality of information. The user (or end-user organization) of a software application is most directly affected by security breaches,
and therefore software that is less susceptible to cracking offers greater value. Secure
software is, however, insufficient; good security requires vigilance and conscientious
action on the part of both the users and operators of the software and in extreme
cases involves law enforcement agencies who investigate and prosecute illegal cracking activities (see chapter 5).

There is a natural trade-off between security and usability. Introducing security
measures within software as well as organizations operating and using the software
frequently makes the software harder to use.

Example   Requiring a password is annoying to some users, but it is an important
security measure for limiting who gains access. Requiring different passwords for
multiple applications is doubly annoying. This can be mitigated by allowing a single
password for multiple applications, but this weakens security because a single
successful cracking of one password allows the cracker access to all applications.
However, allowing a single password may improve security if it obviates the user's
need to write down the password.

3.2.9   Privacy

Another issue of concern to the user of a software application is *privacy*, which
relates to how much information is available about a user, or a user's location or
activities, and to whom that information is disclosed. Privacy is compromised, from
the user perspective, when other parties learn too much about his or her persona
or activities by virtue of using a software application.

Example   Users often disclose personal information like e-mail address and credit
card number to e-commerce applications. A site may track which products a user
purchases as well as the products a user examines without purchasing. A wireless
network must know (and thus can track and record) the geographic location of a user
over time. Potentially this personal information can be shared with third parties.

There are considerable variations in privacy concerns depending on circumstances. Users are considerably more sensitive about financial, health, and

employment information than they are about shopping habits, for example. Sensitivity may also vary depending on the nature of the organization gathering the information, for example, private firm or government.

Example   Seeking a compromise between the privacy requirements of users and the interests of marketers in the United States, the Financial Services Modernization Act of 1999 (also known as Gramm-Leach-Bliley, or GLB) introduced the user's right to opt out of the collection of personal information. That is, everyone has the right to request nonuse of their contact information for marketing and other purposes, on a provider-by-provider basis. From the perspective of maximizing privacy, requiring users to opt in instead (where the default would be nonuse) would be preferable.

Users may be deterred from using applications that they perceive as violating privacy, whether this is real or not. Software can help by allowing user control over which personal information is disclosed. The primary issue is not the software, however, but the ways in which organizations operating an application treat information that is gathered. In the normal course of using an application, personal information often must be legitimately revealed, and the user may be concerned that this information not be passed to third parties. Organizations can respond to these concerns by setting and posting privacy policies providing users with sufficient information to make an informed choice about which information to reveal; they may also provide the user some control over how the information is used by offering policy options. Common options are opt out, in which the user must explicitly specify that the personal information should not be shared with third parties, or opt in, in which the user must explicitly give permission before information can be shared. Organizational and management issues surrounding privacy are discussed in chapter 5, and government roles are discussed in chapter 8.

3.2.10   Flexibility and Extensibility

Business changes at a rapid rate, including organizational changes, mergers and divestment, updates to existing products and services, and the introduction of new products and services. The ability to rapidly change or introduce new products and services is a competitive advantage.

Many enterprise applications are the product of a long evolution. Often they are custom developed by starting with existing departmental applications using obsolete technology (called *legacy applications*), modifying them, and adding translators so they work together to automate enterprise business processes (this is called a *federation of applications*). This level of flexibility is achieved by handcrafting, and is not as structured and systematic as one would like. It is time-consuming and expensive, and creates high maintenance costs in the long run.

Another approach is to purchase an off-the-shelf enterprise application and mold the business processes around it. Although more disruptive, this course of action may yield a more cost-effective and higher-value solution in the long run. Suppliers of enterprise software solutions try to make them more flexible in meeting differing and changing needs in a couple of ways. One is to offer, instead of a monolithic solution, a set of modules that can be mixed and matched at will (see chapter 4 for a description of modularity and chapter 7 for a description of the related concept of frameworks). Another is to offer many configuration options to allow customization.

End-user organizations often make large investments in acquiring and deploying an application, especially where reorganization of business processes is required. The cost of licensing software is usually a small portion of that investment. Organizations thus hope for staying power, both of the solution and its suppliers. Software suppliers that articulate a well-defined road map for future evolution provide reassurance.

Flexibility is hardly a strength of most business and enterprise software applications today, especially in an environment heavily infused with legacy applications. In an ideal world, IT would be a great enabler of change, or at least not a hindrance. Instead, it is sadly the case that bringing along information systems to match changing business needs is often perceived as one of the greatest obstacles. Redressing this problem is a big challenge for the software industry (NRC 2000b).

3.2.11   Satisfaction

Functionality and fidelity, performance, usability, flexibility, and extensibility compose user satisfaction. In fact, two distinct criteria can be identified for judging the alignment of a software program with its requirements (Lehman et al. 1997). *Specification-driven programs* are judged by how well they satisfy an objective specification. *Satisfaction-driven programs*, on the other hand, are judged by the perception, judgment, and degree of satisfaction of various stakeholders.[3] This generalizes the notion of user satisfaction, since the stakeholders may include many parties other than end-users, including operators and managers of software development and end-user organizations (see chapters 4 and 5).

Specification-driven programs can be adequately evaluated through objective testing procedures in the laboratory, whereas satisfaction-driven programs can only be assessed by actual users. Although there is no hard dividing line, applications tend to be satisfaction-driven, whereas some types of infrastructure software may be specification-driven. Lehman et al. (1997) make some useful observations about satisfaction-driven programs:

- They must be continually adapted else they become progressively less satisfactory.
- Unless rigorously adapted to take into account changes in the operational environment, quality will appear to be declining.
- Functional capability must be continually increased to maintain user satisfaction.
- Over time complexity increases unless explicit effort is made to contain or reduce it.

These observations have profound implications for the software development process (see chapter 4).

3.2.12   Operational Costs

The user is concerned with value provided, but also with the total *cost* associated with using an application. The user is not concerned with value alone but rather with value less costs. Costs include direct payments to a software supplier, but also any other costs incurred by the user or intermediaries acting on behalf of the user. For example, whether an application and its supporting infrastructure are operated by the user or by a separate organization, a significant portion of the cost of use is in the operational support (see chapter 5). Suppliers thus have control over the user's costs directly through the price charged for the software and indirectly by controlling other costs of ownership. This is especially significant given that software acquisition decisions are often made by operational rather than end-user organizations.

3.2.13   Composability

A single closed software solution offers less value than one that can be combined with other solutions to achieve greater functionality. This is called the *composability* of complementary software solutions.

Example   The office suite (e.g., ClarisWorks, Lotus Smart Suite, Microsoft Office, StarOffice, and WordPerfect Office) illustrates composability. It allows sharing of information and formatting among individual applications (like a word processor and a spreadsheet), and objects created in one application can be embedded in documents managed by another application (such as embedding a spreadsheet in a word-processing document). A more challenging example is the ability to compose distinct business applications to realize a new product or service by the federation of existing departmental applications, as described in section 3.2.10. A third example is Web services, in which applications are built up by composing multiple application services on the Web (see chapter 7).

Composability is most valuable when it is easy and automatic. Less valuable (but more practical in complex situations) is composability by manual configuration, or *handcrafting*. Composability is one of the motivations behind many major standardization initiatives in the software industry (see chapter 7). The Internet has greatly magnified the opportunities for composability, but also its inherent challenge, because of its ability to mix solutions from different suppliers running on different platforms (see chapter 4).

3.3   Research and Discussion Issues

1. Project the application traditions of figure 3.1 onto the following user contexts: individuals, enterprises, educational institutions, communities, society. What specific applications can you identity for each context from each of the traditions? What trends do you expect in the future?

2. As the application mix has changed historically, what is the changing effect on society? In particular, can you identity any technological development that has had an especially remarkable effect?

3. Do you think that ways of remotely interacting in groups making use of information technology can ever completely match the perceptual experience of a face-to-face interaction? To the extent that it is less satisfactory today, what aspects of this will disappear with technology advances (see section 2.3), and what limitations may be more fundamental? What are some opportunities to make a computer-mediated conference superior to a face-to-face meeting?

4. To what extent does lack of appreciation or understanding of information technology inhibit innovative new uses? How much understanding is really necessary to conceptualize uses?

5. What factors can explain whatever variance may exist across regions and countries in the use of information technology? Is a strong supply industry correlated with more innovation in usage, and if so which is cause and which is effect?

6. What types of insights might psychology, sociology, and anthropology have that could contribute to the more effective use of information technology?

7. To what extent are organizational design and the design of supporting information systems intertwined, or can they be separated?

8. Compare the effect on society, organizations, and individuals of IT and earlier technological revolutions, like mass transportation and electrification.

9. Have any important elements of the user value proposition been missed in this chapter? If so, what?

10. Continuing the last question, rank the relative importance of the elements of value considered, and justify your ranking. Identify those elements that are more generally important versus those that are highly context-specific.

11. Consider specific instances you have encountered of software behavior that you considered anomalous. Do you think these were defects or a mismatch of intended features with your needs?

12. As technology advances continue to follow Moore's law, in the context of any specific type of application performance issues become less and less prominent. What are the results of this for the businesses of hardware supply and software supply? Contrast the two.

13. Choose a specific instance from your experience where you believe security features of software interfered with usability. Why did they interfere, and how did they improve security? Analyze how even tighter security might further harm usability.

14. Exactly what is privacy? This is the first question to address before the right combinations of policy, laws, and technology can provide more assured privacy. This is a difficult question because it is so context-dependent and because it attempts to set a boundary between legitimate and undesirable behavior. Also, there is a strong interaction of perceived privacy issues and culture, making privacy that much harder to define on a *worldwide* Web.

15. To what extent are legacy applications an obstacle to changes in business, such as new products or services, reorganization, or mergers and acquisitions? What application characteristics would enable change instead of blocking it?

16. To what extent do you believe that user satisfaction can or cannot be captured by objective specifications? Consider this issue for some specific applications.

17. Compare the relative importance of the elements of user value identified in this chapter. Which are overall more important, and which less important? Why?

3.4   Further Reading

A National Research Council report (2000b) discusses sociotechnical applications and opportunities for research in this area, and software support for business processes is described in Berztiss (1996). A full description of different application types is beyond the scope of this chapter, but Messerschmitt (1999a; 1999b) gives a more comprehensive discussion for the specific area of networked applications. Shapiro and Varian (1999b) have a much more extensive discussion of network effects and strategies surrounding them, and Shy (2001) gives a rigorous survey on network effects. David (1990) gives a useful historical perspective on how the full potential of technology is not realized until the environment is rethought to take full advantage of it.

4

Creating Software

Whatever creativity is, it is in part a solution to a problem.
Brian Aldiss

Creating software is a multifaceted activity. A common perception is that software creation is synonymous with programming. This is roughly analogous to saying that creating movies is synonymous with cinematography and audio and film editing. Like creating movies, creating software involves many complementary activities, such as evaluating the opportunity and making an investment decision (analogous to the movie producer), working out the details of what features and capabilities to provide (the screenwriter), qualifying and refining the ideas with real users (focus groups), creating an architecture (the storyboard), managing a large group of programmers (the director), implementing the software through programming (cinematography and editing), testing (prescreening), and maintenance (making versions for foreign markets, videotape, DVD media, and so on).

As stated by Brian Aldiss, the goal of all this activity is to satisfy users' needs or solve their problems, although users are themselves not always able to represent or express the opportunity in advance. Creativity in software is manifested through the identification of novel opportunity as much as through novel realization of that opportunity, and accomplishing both requires understanding of the capabilities and limitations of the information technologies, empathy for users and a deep understanding of their context, and an understanding of how the market in software works.

The movie-making analogy suggests parallels with software creation, but there are major differences as well. Compared to cinematography and editing, programming requires considerably deeper technical skills (at least with the current state of technology), represents a much larger fraction of the total investment, and requires larger groups, with the attendant coordination and management issues. As compared with the relatively standardized movie media and projection systems (e.g., 35 mm film), software development must deal with a greater diversity of environments (e.g., Mac, UNIX, Windows). Compared with the relatively passive act of movie watching, users interact more deeply and in more complex ways with software, and often have to deal with installation and administrative issues, introducing many issues of user learnability and usability (see section 3.2.7) to the creation process.

A comprehensive treatment of software creation—indeed just the programming phase—would fill many books, so aspects that are especially relevant to nontechnical perspectives on software are emphasized in this chapter. Some other technological issues are discussed in other chapters, notably an overview of information technology (IT) in chapter 2 and security technologies in chapter 5. Meeting the needs of users was discussed in chapter 3, the needs of other stakeholders (such as operators) are described in chapter 5, and the working of the market in software is a primary topic of chapters 6–9.

The first step is to review general issues that strongly affect ultimate success in creating software. Following this, the overall organization of the software creation process is examined, including sequential, iterative, and community-based approaches. The remainder of the chapter examines technical issues highly relevant to the industrial, social, and economic properties of software, including alternatives for software distribution and execution in the Internet era.

4.1 Elements of Success

As emphasized in section 2.3, the remarkable advances in underlying electronics, magnetic storage, and fiber optics technologies are rapidly removing any physical barriers to what can be accomplished by software. Software development is increasingly free to focus on maximizing the benefits of software to people, organizations, and society. This includes, of course, the economic interests of the software supplier, but there are many other considerations and opportunities as well.

Staying on top of the latest development in software technology—and indeed driving those developments—is essential for a supplier; that much is clear. But beyond this, in light of the empowerment observed by Moore's law, the success of software development requires a focus on four issues:

• *Keeping in mind the user and the operator.* Software offering more value to end-users will yield greater economic rewards for the supplier and more benefits for users and society (see chapter 3). Offering value to operators as well as users is also crucial to success (see chapter 5).

• *Taking into account what already exists.*   In practice, progress must be made largely by adding to rather than replacing legacy technologies or applications. Wholesale replacement of an infrastructure or application (or both) is often not an option because of the higher risk, the greater disruption, and the customer's desire to make productive use of previous investments. Software suppliers must therefore offer solutions that are viable *in the user's context*, which may mean compatibility with legacy equipment and software. Change must be incremental, moving things forward without forcing excessive capital and development investments or arbitrarily overthrowing the status quo.

• *Taking into account the workings of the marketplace.*   The workings of the marketplace in software and complementary products (like equipment and networks) as well as suppliers' responses substantially affect outcomes. Close attention and response to competitors is always wise. For reasons outlined in chapter 7, close attention to complementary firms as well as competitors is important because one supplier can rarely offer a complete solution. Other important workings of the marketplace include distribution in the Internet age (this chapter), standardization (chapter 7), the industrial organization and how it is changing (chapter 7), intellectual property portfolios and rights management (chapter 8), and various factors arising from economics (chapter 9).

• *Paying attention to the collective welfare.*   Developers should recognize the possible positive (as well as negative) effects of software on our collective welfare—on society as a whole—and work to accentuate the positive and mitigate the negative. Issues with societal scope, such as privacy, law enforcement, national security, intellectual property rights, and maintaining a competitive marketplace, are discussed in chapter 8. This is virtuous and demonstrates good citizenship, but it is also good business. Inattention to these issues can do direct economic harm to suppliers, negatively affect the public perception of the software industry, and provoke actions by politicians that may not benefit the industry.

4.2   Organizing Software Creation

The creation of a new software product often involves large teams of specialists applying complementary skills with a high overhead for coordination. Especially with application software, achieving a successful product requires close coordination with users and eventual customers (including managers and operators) and the effective management of large teams of programmers. Effective software creation is thus an organizational and management challenge as much as a technical challenge.

Example An individual productivity application like a word processor or spreadsheet may require a team of roughly one hundred team members turning out a new version every couple of years. A large infrastructure project like an operating system would require the coordinated efforts of one thousand to a few thousand team members creating an upgrade every couple of years. Of these workers, a typical breakdown would be 30 percent developers (who actually write software programs), 30 percent testers, 30 percent program managers (who generate the specifications and drive the process forward), and 10 percent workers ensuring a variety of functions (usability, accessibility, internationalization, localization) and architecture design.

Software projects today have reached an order of size and complexity that warrants careful consideration of this process. A significant differentiator among software suppliers is their development process, which can affect added value (see section 3.2), productivity, costs, and time to market. Success, in the sense of creating software that is viable, deployed, and used, is not even assured. A significant number of large software developments fail, often because the development organization lacks the requisite skills and experience.[1]

Since physical limits such as processing power and storage capacity are decreasing in importance (see section 2.3), the most significant constraints on software creation relate to managing complexity, managing development, meeting windows of opportunity, and limited financial and human resources.

The aspect of creating software most closely associated with technology is software *development*, which refers to the range of activities (including design, implementation, testing, maintenance, and upgrade) surrounding the creation of working software programs (Pressman 2000). Software development processes warrant their own complete books, so the goal here is simply to convey the range of options and some of their strengths and weaknesses. Specifically, we now discuss three distinct but overlapping approaches: sequential, iterative, and community-based development, followed recently by the family of agile development processes.

4.2.1 Sequential Development

The most obvious approach to defining a software process is to decompose its distinct functions into individual phases that can be performed sequentially, each phase building on the previous one. The resulting model of software development is called a *waterfall model* (Royce 1970). While there can be different classifications, table 4.1 shows a typical list. While the waterfall model is useful for identifying some distinct development activities, it is oversimplified because it does not recognize that most software today is built on an existing code base, because these phases must be overlapping rather than sequential, because there are numerous stakeholders to satisfy (not simply users), and because the model fails to recognize that requirements change throughout a software life cycle. Thus, it is a useful categorization of required functions that provides little clue as to the actual organization of the development process.

As the software industry matures, most software is created from an established repertoire of source code available to and mastered by the development organization. The impracticality of wholesale modification or replacement of existing code must be taken into account throughout development, even (at the extreme) in the setting of requirements. Testing, integration, and user feedback should occur early and throughout the implementation. A given project must compete for resources within a larger organization and be coordinated with other projects competing for those resources. The internal and external (user and competitive) environments change, and the process must be flexible to be effective.

In addition, there is increasing emphasis on software reuse and software components (see chapter 7). The idea is to enhance productivity and quality by using software code from other projects or purchased from the outside, and conversely, each project should attempt to generate code that can be reused elsewhere in the organization. Thus, even new projects can use existing software modules, and all projects should take into account the needs of an entire development organization.

The assumption that requirements are static, defined once and for all at the beginning of the project, has several shortcomings. Users' needs and market conditions evolve over time. If the requirements tend to be satisfaction-driven rather than specification-driven (see section 3.2.11), there is significant advantage to refining these requirements based on real-world experience with users. The best way to do this is to involve users throughout the project, not just at the beginning or end. Testing should be conducted with users and should look for compliance with all the value indicators described in section 3.2, not simply uncover defects or match specifications.

Another problem with the waterfall model is the top-down style of development it fosters. Whenever a development effort needs to take into account existing code or components, it needs be bottom-up rather than top-down. Bottom-up development proceeds from what is already available and constructs new software step-by-step by building on existing software.

Example A "divide and conquer" approach to software architecture attempts to find modules that cater to requirements known from the beginning. However, it

Table 4.1
Typical Phases in a Waterfall Model of Software Development

Development phase	Description	Outcome
Conceptualization	Develops a vision for what the software is to accomplish, and why it is a good opportunity.	A story that convinces executives the project is worth pursuing and secures a financial commitment to the next phase.
Analysis	Qualifies the opportunity in sufficient depth and scope to justify a major investment in the remaining phases. Includes defining in more detail the features and capabilities of the software with the assistance of eventual users.	A business plan, including estimates of development, maintenance, upgrade resources and costs. For software sold externally, customer willingness to pay, assessment of competition, description of market window. A commitment to pursue the development, with a detailed development plan.
Requirements	Develops a detailed definition of features and capabilities, and other characteristics such as performance and usability.	A requirements document, which guides programmers as they implement individual features and helps coordinate their efforts.
Architecture	A "divide and conquer" plan in which the overall software is decomposed into pieces called modules that can be implemented (mostly) independently.	A plan identifying modules that can be assigned to development teams, requirements imposed on each module, and how the modules interact and will later be integrated.
Implementation	Programs individual modules in accordance with the architectural plan.	Working software programs representing each module.
Integration	Brings all modules together and makes them work together to realize the overall system functionality. Often involves integration with other software acquired rather than developed.	A working software system in its entirety.
Testing and evaluation	Runs the software through its paces, establishing that it works in accordance with the requirements document or the needs of end-users.	A software system ready to be deployed and moved into operation.

Table 4.1 (continued)

Development phase	Description	Outcome
	(depending on whether it is specification- or satisfaction-driven).	
Maintenance	Gathers reports of defects or performance issues from operators and users, and makes repairs and improvements (without changing the features and capabilities).	A service release (replacement for the software code) that can be distributed to operators and users.
Upgrade	Based in part on feedback from the field, adds significant new features and capabilities that track changes in user needs or maintain competitive advantage.	A version release that can be sold to new or existing customers.

is extremely unlikely that any modules identified this way will coincide precisely with existing code.

The waterfall model can be adjusted to follow a bottom-up approach. However, just as top-down approaches fail to build well on existing code, bottom-up approaches fail to meet user requirements fully. Somehow an intermediate ground must be established.

4.2.2 Iterative Development

In rethinking the waterfall model, development processes should emphasize characteristics of the resulting software that matter—productivity, quality, usability, value, and so on. Then iterative processes involving rapid prototyping, experimentation, and refinement can lead to successive refinements of the software by repeating more than once some or all of the functions identified in the waterfall model. (We can think of these as eddies in the waterfall.)

An early attempt at adapting the waterfall process introduced "back edges" between the stages of the waterfall. Instead of emphasizing a downstream flow of results from one stage of the waterfall to the next, an upstream flow of feedback to previous stages was introduced. In other words, problems discovered at a later stage resulted in corrections to a previous stage's outcomes. Taken to the extreme, the back-propagation of severe problems discovered in very late stages (such as integration testing) can result in redoing early stages (such as analysis). While theoretically complete, this refined process does not provide much guidance about practical execution and can lead to dramatic cost and schedule overruns.

Example   Suppose that testing during the integration phase uncovers a mistake in the architectural design. The overall decomposition then needs to be redone, and then all subsequent steps may need to be fully redone for affected portions of the architecture. Assuming that such a catastrophic mistake isn't anticipated in the original plan, the project is likely to fail completely because its resources may be exhausted or its market window of opportunity may close.

The *spiral model* of software development (Boehm 1988; Software Productivity Consortium 1994) was an early attempt at fundamentally modifying the waterfall model to be iterative in the large. The basic idea was to allow the outcomes of the integration and testing stages to flow back to the requirements and analysis stages. An appropriate model is not information flowing upstream, but a spiral that explicitly repeats the stages of the waterfall, adding more specificity and substance in each iteration. Geometrically, this can be considered a spiral that grows outwards, each 360-degree rotation of the spiral corresponding to a complete cycle through the waterfall model. Since the waterfall stages are repeated, they are more appropriately seen as *phases*. The four major phases of each cycle of the spiral model are the following:

• Capture and define objectives, constraints, and alternatives for this cycle. The emphasis is on identifying action alternatives and constraints rather than on achieving full specificity. One goal is to consciously preserve as much flexibility as possible later, while explicitly recognizing practical limitations on that flexibility.
• Evaluate the alternatives with respect to the objectives and constraints. Identify and resolve major sources of risk.
• Define the product and process. This is the phase where the architecture defined in the previous cycle is refined, and the code from that cycle is refined and appended.
• Plan the next cycle and update the life cycle plan, including partitioning of the system into subsystems to be addressed in future cycles. This includes a plan to terminate the project if it is too risky or proves to be infeasible. Obtain management's commitment to implement the plan through the next cycle.

In essence, the first phase corresponds to the conceptualization, analysis, and requirements stages of the waterfall model. The third phase corresponds to the remaining waterfall stages, except for the final maintenance phase, which is not included in the spiral model. The second and fourth phases provide risk management, cycle planning, and the assessment of relative success or failure. These are crucial, since the spiral model could easily lead to an open-ended sequence of cycles without converging to a useful product. The spiral model has been applied successfully in numerous projects (Frazier and Bailey 1996; Royce 1990).

The spiral model provides little guidance as to where to begin and how to augment the project in each cycle, or how many full cycles should be expected. Unlike the waterfall model, the spiral model is best described as a philosophy rather than a complete process. Rather than planning and executing the entire project at once, the philosophy is to start with incomplete prototypes, learn as much as possible from the experience, and refine and extend the implementation in subsequent cycles.

The *WinWin spiral model* (Boehm and Bose 1994), refines the spiral model by offering guidance on the identification of objectives, alternatives, and constraints. This is a critical improvement, needed to establish cycles that are productive and that converge on a good outcome. As figure 4.1 illustrates, the WinWin spiral model adds three new phases to the beginning of each cycle:

• Identify the system or subsystem's key stakeholders. These include finance, marketing, product management, developers, testers, users, and anybody else who has a stake in the outcomes of the following cycle.

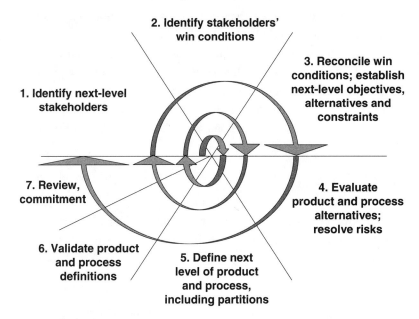

Figure 4.1
WinWin spiral model of software development.

• Identify the stakeholders' win conditions—outcomes that will benefit or satisfy those stakeholders—for each system or subsystem. Often these win conditions will conflict—a win for one stakeholder or subsystem may be a loss for another.

• Negotiate win-win reconciliation of the stakeholders' win conditions across subsystems, trying to arrive at a set of conditions that satisfies as many stakeholders as possible and justifies any resulting stakeholder losses. There are software tools to help organize this negotiation.

While the spiral model and its refinements (such as WinWin) move toward a principled iterative software development process, they leave open many issues such as scheduling and cost estimates for individual phases. While it would take us too far afield to delve more deeply into complete and principled processes, especially since many alternatives have been proposed and used, a couple of examples illustrate some possibilities.

Example   The Rational Unified Process (RUP) (Kruchten 2000) aims to be a single universal process for software development. While RUP can be configured and customized to adapt to specific organization and project needs, it focuses on one process. An alternative approach, illustrated by the OPEN process framework (Firesmith and Henderson-Sellevs 2001), is to avoid a single (even customizable) process but construct a framework and toolkit of process and method ingredients, accompanied by guidelines and recipes that can be used to construct custom processes and methods. Both RUP and OPEN provide process-level guidance: team structure; costing, scheduling and resourcing; quality assurance; client involvement; and so on. RUP takes a best-practice approach to establishing a single overall process. OPEN identifies many process modules and acknowledges that organizations of different sizes, skills, experience levels, ambitions, and so on, will want to custom create their processes from such modules, guided but not dictated by OPEN rules and principles.

4.2.3   Organizational vs. Project Efficiency

A principled process for a single software project does not address the real problem in most development organizations, which must manage a few or even many projects overlapping in time and sharing skilled personnel. Meeting schedules and achieving overall productivity for the organization as a whole must be balanced against quality and cost-effective outcomes for specific projects.

Principled processes such as RUP and OPEN explicitly allow for the concurrent and overlapping execution of development activities, with clear definitions of work flow.

Example   As soon as the architectural design of a subsystem has stabilized, detailed design within that subsystem can proceed. While software architects are still working on other subsystems, implementers can concurrently drive forward their contributions on subsystems with stable architectures.

Keep in mind that different phases require distinct skill sets and different specialists. The waterfall model embodies another development process weakness: if all activities are done sequentially, most specialists have nothing to do most of the time. Controlling top-level system partitioning and enabling concurrent progress in separate phases of the overall process can yield higher organizational productivity.

Keeping all development specialists engaged is a matter of *organizational efficiency*. One option is to stagger the order of multiple independent projects, so that later phases of one project proceed concurrently with earlier phases of another project but utilize different specialists. However, this leads to inefficiency in another way—a specialist moving from one project to another expends valuable effort in the context switch.

Minimizing the time to delivery is a matter of *project efficiency*. If an organization runs at maximum efficiency by overlapping projects, the tendency is for deep sequential activity chains to lead to long completion times per project. This creates several problems:

• The market window of opportunity can be missed. The longer a project's completion time, the larger the likely variation in completion time and the greater the opportunity to miss deadlines. A window of opportunity is closed when competitors move more quickly, technology becomes obsolete, market conditions change, or user needs or requirements change.

• The efficiency of specialists suffers if there is no stable context over extended time. As the project completion time extends, more specialists must enter and leave and spend time reconstructing problems and solutions encountered earlier. Departing team members, even if documentation is performed conscientiously, take tacit knowledge with them, setting back the project. New team members need time to adjust to team culture as well as to understand objectives and project status. Greater completion time increases these inefficiencies.

For most projects and organizations it is best to optimize project rather than organizational efficiency, since software development projects require substantial creativity and highly qualified people, are front-loaded in investments, and thus carry both high sunk costs and risks.

Example   It is usually better to assign a specialist to one project (or a small number of projects) rather than to aim for full utilization of his or her time. Creative work is usually characterized by particularly high context-switching cost for individuals, suggesting that it is actually more efficient for project and organization to not aim for full utilization. Productive use can often be made of project dead time, such as professional development or project tool building.

As projects get larger, it becomes easier to balance project and organizational efficiency because there are more opportunities for specialists to contribute productively to different aspects of the same project. One important source of organizational efficiency is software reuse (see chapter 7).

4.2.4   Community-Based Development

A third and distinctively different model for software development is community-based development. In this model, a loosely knit group of software developers collaborate on a software project utilizing the Internet and online collaboration tools. Often these developers do not belong to a common organization or even get paid—they're simply volunteers.

The foundation of community-based development is making source code available to the community; indeed, it is usually made available to anybody who is interested. Most commercial software suppliers do not make source code available to anyone outside the organization—it is a closely held trade secret (see chapter 8). Making source code available is a radical departure from traditional commercial practice.

The term *open source* describes a particular type of community-based development and associated licensing terms as trademarked by the Open Source Initiative (OSI), which enthusiastically describes open source as follows: "The basic idea behind open source is very simple. When programmers can read, redistribute, and modify the source code for a piece of software, the software evolves. People improve it, people adapt it, and people fix bugs. And this can happen at a speed that, if one is used to the slow pace of conventional software development, seems astonishing." There are many possible licensing terms as well as different motivations for making source code available (see chapter 8).

What benefits can accrue from making source code publicly available? What issues and problems can arise? What would motivate programmers to volunteer their time and effort? Successful community-based development projects can shed light on these questions.

Example   The most famous open source software project is Linux. This UNIX-like operating system was originally developed by Linus Torvalds, and he made source code available to the community. Subsequently, a dedicated band of programmers upgraded the software, while Torvalds maintained control. Companies such as Red Hat Software and Caldera Systems distributed versions with support, and vendors such as Dell and IBM offer Linux installed on computers they sell.

Example FreeBSD is another UNIX operating system based on a version of UNIX developed at the University of California at Berkeley in the 1970s and 1980s. Sendmail is a widely used application for handling and forwarding e-mail. Both FreeBSD and sendmail are widely used by Internet service providers. IBM offers another open source e-mail program, Secure Mailer. Apache Web Server is a widely used open source program and has been adopted in IBM's WebSphere product. Apple Computer made the core of its newest operating system, Mac OS X, open source and called it Darwin. Netscape created an open source version of its Web browser and called it Mozilla. This partial list properly conveys the impression that open source is gaining popularity.

The open source licensing terms (O'Reilly 1999; Open Source Initiative) require that source code be available without charge and redistribution be unrestricted. Although open source software typically has a license that restricts its use (licenses are associated with ownership under the copyright laws; see chapter 8), it must permit modifications and derivative works and must allow derivatives to be redistributed under the same terms as the original work. The essence of these restrictions is to create software that is not only available free (although the user may want to pay for support services) but will always remain free even after modification and incorporation into other works. Other types of licenses are discussed in chapter 8.

Community-based development has not yet proven that it can contribute to the conceptualization through architecture phases of the waterfall model. It may be that these phases inherently require a single individual or close-knit group. Today's community-based development projects have focused on the incremental advancement and maintenance of an existing piece of software. This also addresses the issue of who owns the software and who can place licensing restrictions on it. The answer to date is whoever contributed the first working software to the community. Community-based development can greatly extend the reach of such a person by bringing in a whole community of programmers to extend and maintain his or her original vision.

What organizational structure is imposed on the community to avoid anarchy? One manifestation of anarchy would be n different variations of the software for each of the n participants without any mechanism to merge results. The most successful projects have maintained the discipline of a sequence of versions resulting from a merging of collective efforts, with a governance mechanism to decide which changes are accepted. (See chapter 5 for discussion of how a software project must be managed through multiple releases.) A prime goal of the governance is to preclude "forking" of two or more coexisting variants of the software, which would result in duplication of effort and, through market fragmentation, reduce the network effect component of user value (see section 3.2.3).

Example   The arbiter for Linux is its originator, Torvalds, who has always controlled what went into each successive version. If the software is managed by a commercial firm (like Apple's OS X or IBM's Secure Mailer), it is that firm that arbitrates, merges, and integrates all changes.

What would motivate programmers to donate their time to a project? The commercial interests of large corporations have not proven to be a strong motivator for donated efforts, and as a result, community-based development projects started by companies have been noticeably less successful than projects originated by individuals or originating in academe. A viable community-based development project must have a fairly large community of interested programmers from the perspectives of need (the programmers are themselves users) and interest (they find it intellectually challenging and interesting). Most such projects involve infrastructure software, since the community of users is large and the technical challenges interesting. In fact, this kind of development seems the most appropriate methodology for a certain type of infrastructure that is, by nature, a commodity (see chapter 7). Programmers are motivated by a technical challenge (much like solving mathematical or crossword puzzles, which is usually also an unpaid activity) and by the recognition conferred by the community. The latter should not be underestimated, since peer recognition of technical merit and innovation are powerful motivators.

Community-based development can also be appropriate for developing and maintaining an application that for practical reasons cannot be made commercially available.

Example   Many scientific communities maintain a collective body of software for modeling or simulation. In this case, rather than technical challenge or peer recognition, the motivation comprises the division of effort and sharing of scientific results. The software is more than an enabler, it is itself a research outcome. Again, the developer community and the end-users are one and the same.

What would motivate a user to adopt community-based development software? For one thing, it is free, although this is probably a secondary benefit (as discussed in chapter 5, the cost of licensing software is often dwarfed by the operational expenses). Because of the scrutiny that it receives from many programmers, much community-based development software has a reputation for quality. Similarly, security is generally enhanced by scrutiny of the code (although there is also a danger that crackers could insert their own back-door security holes). Some users appreciate software not associated with any commercial vendor, believing it less likely to enhance the interests of that vendor and free from constraints imposed by the vendor.

The most powerful reason for adopting community-based development software is the possibility of modifying it to specific needs (although doing so makes it more difficult to benefit from future enhancements). One such modification is to remove unwanted capabilities, which can save resources and enhance security (Neumann 1999). Modification of commercial software distributed only in object code is at best difficult and usually violates the software license.

An observed weakness is (at least thus far) the lack of a methodology for systematically gathering user needs and requirements, and perpetuating the usability of the software. As a result, successful community-based development projects have a user community that is one and the same as the developer community—participants work most effectively when they are focused on satisfying their personal needs. The methodology also violates some of the basic tenets of modularity, as discussed later in this chapter.

While community-based software development appears to have its limitations, it is an interesting phenomenon, one that teaches us about the software development process and hacker culture. Commercial software suppliers have been struggling to understand and accommodate this movement, both in terms of its potential for competition with their interests and understanding how the movement might benefit their commercial interests.

Example   Microsoft's shared source model makes source code available to support learning processes by enabling the study of the source code and its experimental modification. However, shared source excludes the right to redistribute or to derive commercial products. Shared source can allow the community to examine code for security loopholes and also precludes the introduction of new loopholes by crackers. However, just as with open source, crackers could also discover existing loopholes and use such knowledge to mount attacks.

4.2.5   Agile Development
Since the ultimate goal of software development is to achieve high satisfaction on the part of all stakeholders—there are many, and their relative importance and number changes over time—development processes should be flexible. Another of

the laws of satisfaction-driven systems (see table 3.1) is "satisfaction-driven evolution processes constitute multi-level, multi-loop, multi-agent feedback systems and must be treated as such to achieve significant improvement over any reasonable time" (Lenman et al. 1997). A recent advance is families of lightweight development processes called *agile processes*[2] (Fowler and Highsmith 2001). Agile processes are really frameworks for the creation and customization of processes, for every project cycle and over multiple cycles. Thus the property of agility: a process found lacking is immediately adjusted.

Agile processes emphasize a tight interaction with the user or customer, including operators, at all stages. Rapid prototyping is an important enabler of user interaction, since user feedback can be gathered and assessed early and often. Rather than assuming that requirements can be captured ahead of time (or even at all), agile processes assume that a dialogue with the user is maintained continuously throughout the entire software life cycle.

Agile processes are not really about rapid development, an approach favored in the early 1990s that aimed for very rapid development and delivery of solutions. Rapid development, as practiced then, is now viewed as more of a "hack" than a principled approach: accelerating the stages of production without embedding an appropriately agile process probably cannot deliver much value. Agile processes emphasize speed, but indirectly, by insisting on small incremental steps (much smaller than in traditional incremental processes) that provide feedback and assessment early and often.

Arguably some small and large software companies had adopted forms of agile processes even before they were identified and named.

Example   Microsoft introduced the job classification "program manager" in the early days of its Excel spreadsheet application. This professional represents users, since mass-marketed software has no individual user or customer to benchmark. The development process validated and corrected course with feedback from program managers early and often. For instance, a program manager performed competitive analyses to continually understand and size the target market and its complementing and competing players, thus influencing development decisions. The delivery of beta releases and release candidates for testing with representative customers gathered direct input at less frequent intervals.

4.2.6   Beyond Computer Science and Engineering
Significant differences in orientation, culture, and methodology exist between the programming phases of a software project (implementation, testing, repair, and

maintenance) and the earlier design phases (requirements, architecture). Historically much application software has been weak in its ability to provide natural and forgiving interfaces, especially for naive users. This is accentuated as applications become more pervasive, diverse, and sophisticated. For this reason, new professions are emerging (Gerlach and Kuo 1991) that focus on this aspect of software creation, as distinct from programming.

Example These professions are analogous to the relation of building architecture to civil engineering: the architect is primarily concerned with the needs of the building occupant, the aesthetics of the building, how it relates to its environment, and various policy issues (like handicapped access). The civil engineer is primarily concerned with the structural integrity of the building and the functionality of its various subsystems, and with managing the actual construction.

In software at least three largely separate professions already exist or are emerging:

• *Industrial design* is concerned with the physical appearance of physical products and how appearance relates to functionality. It is applicable to many products, including computers and information appliances.
• *Graphics design* is concerned with the artistic representation of concepts and ideas through pictures rendered by computer programs and is most relevant to the graphical user interfaces of programs.
• *Interaction design* addresses the interaction between people and complex systems, analyzing that interaction and finding ways to decompose it to make it more intuitive and functional.

The sophisticated programmers emerging from undergraduate computer science programs are highly technical, and as a result they are often less well equipped by training and orientation to deal with these human-centered design issues. Industrial and graphics design benefit from artistic training and are considered to be aspects of the design arts. Interaction design is an emerging discipline that draws heavily on the liberal arts and social sciences (particularly psychology and cognitive science). All these activities benefit from ethnography, a branch of the social sciences that focuses, from a human perspective, on the interaction between people and a rich environment.

4.2.7 End-user Contributions

A significant contribution to software functionality can occur after software is licensed to a customer. Many software products specifically offer opportunities to configure, customize, and extend. This is a good way to accommodate the increasing specialization of applications, trying to achieve a reasonable trade-off between accommodating the differing and changing needs of users and the benefits of an off-the-shelf application (see chapter 6). In the future we can expect improvements in tools enabling a significantly greater involvement of users in defining the functionality of the software they use. In their more sophisticated forms, end-user activities resemble programming more than merely adjusting a configuration.

The central idea behind computing is to define the functionality of a product after it is in the hands of the customer rather than at the time of manufacture. Software applications that offer no user configurability or programmability essentially move the definition of functionality to a second entity in the supply chain, the software supplier. Leaving increasingly rich and sophisticated configuration and programmability options to the user is in the best computing tradition.

Programming-like activities performed by users can be traced back to the earliest interactive applications.

Example   Spreadsheets come to life through models defined by users, models that may include complex mathematical formulas, decision logic, and a customized user interface. Client-side database applications such as FileMaker Pro or Microsoft Access allow complex queries (a form of programming) and the design of custom user interfaces. Word processors support style sheets and templates, which allow users to define document formatting. Most applications support macros, the automatic execution of common sequences of actions recorded or authored by a user.

End-user programming is sometimes taken to a level close to sophisticated programming. Such capabilities are not intended for the ordinary user, but rather enable an aftermarket of independent or captive software developers to add value based on local needs.

Example   Visual Basic for Applications (VBA), as integrated into the Microsoft Office suite, is a powerful development environment, rich and featured enough so that many users quickly reach the limits of their own programming skills. Microsoft Office is also a software development platform, commonly used by enterprise information systems departments to create custom applications. A variant called Office Developer addresses this derivative market.

4.3   Software Architecture

Architecture is an early phase of software design, following requirements gathering and preceding implementation (see section 4.2.1). Architecture is particularly important because it is closely tied to industrial organization (see chapter 7) and project development organization. The industry layering described in section 2.2.5 is an example of a system architecture, one that hierarchically builds up capability, starting with devices incorporated into equipment, and equipment supporting software. Here the focus is on the software portion of the system.

4.3.1 Why Software Architecture Is Needed

Rather than physical, the constraints on what can be done with software are financial and human. Software design often stretches the capability of its human designers to absorb and manage complexity and to organize large collaborative efforts to create ever more complex systems, including architecture and tools.

One challenge is containing the communication and coordination costs among members of a large development team (what economists call transaction costs). An early attempt to characterize this issue was *Brooks' law* (1975). If we assign programmers to a software project, we might expect on the order of n times faster results. Unfortunately, there are potentially $n(n - 1)/2$ distinct interactions among pairs of these programmers,[3] so Brooks pessimistically asserted that the transaction costs increase on the order of n^2. A pragmatic statement of Brooks' law is, "If a software project is behind schedule, adding more people will push it even more behind schedule." In this worst-case scenario, transaction costs consume a growing fraction of each individual's effort (growing on the order of n), so in economics terms there are diminishing returns to scale. While Brooks' law is grossly pessimistic, a diminishing returns to scale in software projects is observed.

This same problem is encountered when considering the economy as a whole. The economy is partitioned into individual industrial firms that operate as independently as possible, engaging in commercial transactions where appropriate. The most efficient size of the firms depends on the trade-off between external and internal transaction costs—the effect (if not the explicit goal) is to group in one firm activities that have a high dependence and would create excessive transaction costs if performed externally.

The software industry encounters these same issues of the appropriate size of firms and minimizing transaction costs (see chapter 7). Similar issues arise at a smaller granularity in the development of a single piece of software or a set of complementary pieces of software. Should this software be developed by a single firm, or should multiple firms arise to contribute composable pieces? These issues are largely resolved by market forces.

Organizational theory has much to offer and in particular would assert that transaction costs can be reduced through mechanisms like hierarchical management structures and shadow pricing. Nevertheless, the effectiveness of these modern management techniques still depends on the nature of the task being undertaken: if it really is true (in the extreme) that the activities of project team members are deeply intertwined, then in that case organizational techniques will be less effective than if the overall project can be broken into largely independent pieces. This a role of *software architecture*, which imposes a 'divide and conquer' methodology in which the overall software system is divided into manageable pieces, and each developed independently. This can be viewed at different granularities, such as (in the small) within a software development group and (in the large) among companies in the software industry. In software (as in other branches of engineering) these pieces are called *modules*, and the act of breaking the system into modules is called *decomposition* or *modularization*. Architectural decomposition is the first step leading to an effective project's organizational structure that can tame Brooks' law.

The term *architecture* in software can create some confusion when compared to the use of that term elsewhere.

Example   One of the roles of the building architect is to decompose a building into functional units (rooms, hallways), to meet the eventual occupants' needs. This is the general sense in which architecture is used in software as well. However, another role of the building architect is to address usability and aesthetics, which is not a role of an architect in software. In fact, decomposition in building architecture is driven in no small part by the needs of future building occupants, whereas software architecture is primarily for purpose of organizing the development process and has a minimal relation to user needs. For software that is required to be extensible or evolvable after being deployed by users, this distinction is fuzzier. For such software, the architectural decomposition is guided by what parts might need to be added or changed after deployment, and it puts rules in place that enables safe extension and evolution.

There is a strong relation between architecture and the organization of the software development teams. Since only one implementation team is assigned to each module, the boundaries of team responsibility generally follow the boundaries of modules. This leads to *Conway's law* (named after Melvin Conway, an early programmer), which states that the organization of software will be congruent to the organization of its development team. In Conway's day the organization of the team preceded and largely determined the organization of the software; today, the opposite is typically true: architecture precedes organization.

A capable architect is necessary to complete a software project successfully. The architect has global knowledge of the project and its pieces, and how they fit together. Most other participants purposely have only local knowledge of the piece within their domain of responsibility.

Software from different companies frequently must compose, and the boundary of modules in cross-firm composition has to follow the boundaries of the firms: shared responsibility for a module isn't viable. An interesting question is how market forces determine these module boundaries (see chapter 7). The primary mechanism by which companies coordinate their efforts at achieving the composability of modules across firm boundaries is either standardization or through permitting documented extensions. Large corporations may intentionally relax central control and allow for degrees of redundancy and competition among suborganizations. The resulting software boundaries are somewhere between architected ones and those driven by market forces.

As mentioned earlier, most software projects don't start from scratch but must build on available assets. Where existing code is incorporated, architecture can provide a structured and principled approach to coordinating subsequent and earlier efforts. Instead of relying on developers to "discover" that some available code or component may be reused in new situations, software systems are designed to be related by construction. Architecture is the level of design that emphasizes such relations (Bass, Clewents, and Kazman 1998; Bosch 2000; Szyperski 1998).

4.3.2   The Role of Software Architecture
The primary role of software architecture is to address systemwide properties by providing an overall design framework for a family of software systems. Systemwide properties can be compared to those established by the load-bearing walls and super-structure of a building. Concrete designs then follow the architecture's guidelines, complementing it with concrete local design decisions. Architecture decomposes systems into well-identified modules, describes their mutual dependencies and inter-actions, and specifies the parameters that determine the architecture's degrees of configurability. As illustrated in figure 4.2, architecture has three facets: the *decomposition* of the system into modules, the *functionality* of each module, and the *interaction* among modules. *Global system properties* (also known as *system qualities*), such as performance, maintainability, extensibility, and usability, emerge from the concrete composition of modules (Thompson 1998).[4]

4.3.3   Modularity
Modular is a term describing architectures with desirable properties with respect to supporting a good development methodology and containing complexity (Baker and

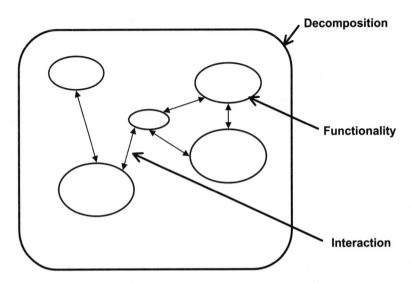

Figure 4.2
A simple software architecture.

Zweben 1979; Jung and Choi 1999; Parmar 1972). While *modularity* originally implied nothing more than "an implementation broken down into pieces," over time the term has assumed more connotations as experience has taught us what properties are most effective in taming Brooks' law. Today, the following properties are considered most important for a modular architecture:

• *Strong cohesion.* The modules have strong internal dependencies, requiring a high degree of communication and coordination (transaction costs, as an economist would say). A module not having this property is a candidate to be further decomposed. This is precisely the role of hierarchical decomposition.

• *Weak coupling.* There should be weak dependencies across module boundaries, so teams implementing different modules have minimal need for coordination. This is the most important property.

• *Interface abstraction.* Abstraction is a difficult concept to convey precisely, especially without displaying examples, but roughly it means that the external view of a module should be as simple as possible, displaying essential properties and hiding unnecessary details. Abstraction makes module functionality easier to understand and use, and also contributes to modules that are more general and thus more likely to be reused.

• *Encapsulation.* Internal implementation details are invisible and untouchable from the outside of a module. This precludes inadvertent dependencies among modules created by exploiting implementation details, where such dependencies

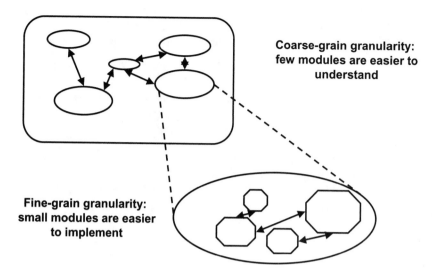

**Coarse-grain granularity:
few modules are easier to
understand**

**Fine-grain granularity:
small modules are easier
to implement**

Figure 4.3
Hierarchical decomposition.

would cause changes in implementation to unnecessarily affect other modules or cause system defects. A first line of defense in encapsulation is to distribute module object code only, because source code makes implementation details more visible. (Encapsulation is thus compromised for source code–available software, a weakness in that methodology.) Fully effective encapsulation also requires support from languages and tools.[5]

These four properties are primarily aimed at taming Brooks' law. Encapsulation has significant implications for the business model of software (and other products) as well (see chapter 7). Modularity is critical to decomposing a large software system into distinct vendor efforts that are later composed. Commercial software firms do not want their customers modifying software because support of a customer-modified program would be difficult or impossible, and support contributes to customer satisfaction and repeat sales. Encapsulation is familiar in many manufactured products for similar reasons ("your warranty is voided if the cabinet is opened").

As illustrated in figure 4.3, modular architectures are usually constructed *hierarchically*, with modules themselves composed of finer-grain modules. The *granularity* refers roughly to the scope of functionality comprising one module, from course granularity (lots of functionality) to fine granularity (limited functionality). *Hierarchical decomposition* enables the same system to be viewed at different granularities, addressing the tension between a coarse-grain view (the interaction of relatively few modules is easier to understand) and a fine-grain view (small modules are easier to implement). Of course, the cohesion of modules is inevitably stronger at the bottom of the hierarchy than at the top; otherwise, further decomposition would be self-defeating. The coarse-grain modularity at the top is a concession to human understanding and to industrial organization, whereas the fine-grain modularity at the bottom is a concession to ease of implementation. The possibility of hierarchical decomposition makes strong cohesion a less important property of modularity than weak coupling.

As suggested by this discussion, software architecture has interesting parallels in the design of human organizations (Baldwin and Clark 1997; Langlois and Robertson 1992; Langelaar, Setyawan, and Lagendijk 2000; Sánehez and Mahoney 1996). Similar principles of modularity are applied there.

4.3.4   Interfaces and APIs

The interaction among modules focuses on *interfaces*. A module interface roughly speaking, tells other modules all they need to know to use this module. Interfaces are a key mechanism for coordinating different development groups (or companies) that build composable modules. Interfaces are a frequent target for standardization (see chapter 7).

More precisely, an interface specifies a collection of atomic *actions* (with associated data parameters and data returns). By *atomic*, we mean an action that cannot be decomposed for other purposes—it must be invoked as a whole or not at all—although it can often be customized by parameterization.

Example   Consider the user interface of a four-function calculator as a module interface. (The idea of module interface is applicable to the user interface as well, if one unromantically characterizes a user as a "module.") Actions for this interface are functions like "add this number to the display register," where a parameter is a number punched into the keyboard and the action is invoked by the plus key.

The interface also specifies *protocols*, which are compositions of actions required to accomplish more functionality than offered by individual actions. A protocol typically coordinates a sequence of back-and-forth operations between two or more modules that can't be realized as a single action. Multiple protocols may reuse a given action; making actions elementary and building more complex functionality with protocols contributes to software reuse (see chapter 7). By design, protocols are not atomic, and actions can be reused in different protocols.

Example For the calculator example, adding two numbers cannot be accomplished by a single action but requires a protocol consisting of two actions: "punch first operand and enter to display register, enter second operand and punch add." The result of the addition will appear in the display register. The "punch operand and enter" action could be reused by other protocols, for example, a protocol that multiplies two numbers. Most protocols are far more complicated than this example would suggest; in fact, protocol design is a complex specialty in its own right.

The second purpose of an interface is to tell a module developer what to implement. Each action is implemented as an operation on internal data and often requires invoking actions on third-party modules. Thus, in a typical scenario one module invokes an action on another, which as a result invokes an action on a third, and so on. Through encapsulation, an interface should hide irrelevant internal implementation details and preclude bypassing the interface to expose implementation details.[6]

An interface is *open* when it is available, well documented, and unencumbered by intellectual property restrictions (see chapter 8). Interfaces remain an important manifestation of modularity within proprietary software, but open interfaces are nonproprietary and are intended to be invoked by customers or by software from other vendors. There are different degrees of openness; for example, an interface may be encumbered by patents that are licensed freely to all comers; or there may be moderate license fees, the same for all, and the interface might still be considered open.

Example Modem manufacturers provide an open interface that allows other software to send and receive data over a communication link. This open interface can be used by various vendors of communication software to make use of that communication link. From a user perspective, the ability to use many communication software packages with a modem is valuable, which in turn encourages the modem manufacturer to ensure the availability of many complementary software packages.

An open interface designed to accept a broad class of extensions is called an *application programming interface* (API). By *extension*, we mean a module or modules added later, not only following development but following deployment. The API terminology arose because the interface between an application and an operating system was its first instance: applications can be considered extensions of infrastructure (operating system). Today, the acronym API is used more generally: API may allow one application to extend another or one piece of infrastructure to extend another. It helps that the acronym has largely replaced the words it represents in the common vernacular.

Example   A Web browser accommodates plug-ins, which can extend its function-ality. For example, Shockwave supports animated objects in Web presentations. Web developers must purchase Shockwave development tools to embed these animated objects, and users must download and install the free Shockwave plug-in to view them. The Web browser provides an API that accommodates various plug-ins including Shockwave; some of the plug-ins may not have existed at the time the API was defined, the browser was programmed, or the browser was distributed to the user.

A firm that provides and documents an API is opening up its software to exten-sion by other firms, much as a TV manufacturer opens up its display device to a variety of video sources. This is a serious strategic business decision, and it may be irreversible as both a matter of business (customers will be upset if software prod-ucts suddenly fail to compose) and law (in some circumstances this may be con-sidered an unfair business practice; see chapter 8). APIs form the basis of *open systems*—software systems with ample APIs, giving customers rich possibilities for extension and allowing them to mix and match solutions from different suppliers, thus reducing switching costs and lock-in (see chapter 9). The growing popularity of open systems is one of the most dramatic trends in the software industry over the past few decades (see chapter 7).

4.3.5   Emergence

Architecture and development focus on defining and implementing modules that can later be composed (see section 3.2.12). The act of composing modules and doing whatever it takes to make them work properly together (including modifying the modules themselves as well as configuring and extending them) is called *integration*. A single module in isolation does not normally provide self-contained capability useful to a user; it must be composed with other modules. Any additional func-tionality that arises from the composition of modules is called *emergence:* if avail-able, the integrated whole is more than the sum of its modular parts.[7]

Example   A classic example of emergence in the material world is the airplane, which is able to fly even though each of its subsystems (wings, engines, wheels) cannot. The flying behavior is said to emerge from the composition of those sub-systems. In a computer system, neither a computer nor a printer can print out a document; that emerges from the composition of the computer and printer.

Note that emergence is different from extension. Emergence arises from the com-position of existing modules, whereas extension proceeds from full knowledge of an existing module and adds new capabilities to it. This distinction is crucial to the understanding of components (see chapter 7).

Emergence is a source of value in the development process. Module composition and the emergent behavior it triggers are a source of value. (Firms called *system integrators* specialize in module integration: the value they add is emergence; see chapter 6).

4.3.6   Achieving Composability

In many instances, modules must be composed even if they weren't implemented within the same development project or organization, or designed explicitly to work together. Examples include two applications purchased from different suppliers that must work together (see section 3.2.13) or software components (see chapter 7). This leads to two fundamentally different approaches to architecture: decomposition from system requirements and composition from available components.

Composability of modules is actually difficult to achieve, especially for modules not designed and developed in the same project. It requires two properties: interoperability and complementarity.

For two modules to communicate in a meaningful way, three requirements must be met. First, some communication infrastructure must enable the physical transfer of bits.[8] Second, the two modules need to agree on a protocol that can be used to request communication, signal completion, and so on. Finally, the actual messages communicated must be encoded in a mutually understood way. Modules meeting these three requirements are said to be *interoperable*.

Mere interoperability says nothing about the meaningfulness of communication. To enable useful communication, the modules need to *complement* each other in terms of what functions and capabilities they provide and how they provide them.

Example   Imagine a facsimile machine that calls an answering machine, which then answers and stores the representation of the facsimile in its memory.[9] Anyone observing either the facsimile or answering machine would conclude that they were interoperable, but in fact no image has been conveyed because the functionalities aren't complementary. The answering machine has no capability to display or print the stored facsimile, and the facsimile machine can't create an audible message to communicate something meaningful to the user.

Modules that are interoperable *and* complementary (with respect to some specific opportunity) are said to be *composable* (with respect to that opportunity). Composable modules offer additional value through the emergence resulting from composition.

Example The Web browser (on a user's desktop computes) and the complementary Web server (an information supplier), together provide an example of interoperability and complementarity. The browser and server must be interoperable to exchange and display document pages. In a more complicated scenario, Web pages contain interactive elements like forms that accept information, implemented by splitting functionality between the browser and the server, which complement one other with respect to this opportunity. The browser and server compose to provide capabilities that neither provides individually. In a more involved scenario, the browser provides an API for plug-in modules downloaded from the server, enabled by rich composition (interoperability and complementarity) standards between plug-in and browser.

Usability (see section 3.2.7) can be considered a form of composability of a user and a software application.

4.4   Program Distribution and Execution

A software program embodies the actions required in the processing, storage, and communication of information content. It consists of instructions authored by a programmer and executed by a computer that specify the detailed actions in response to each possible circumstance and input. These actions are embodied in an *algorithm*, which prescribes those actions and the sequence in which they must be taken.

Software in isolation is useless; it must be executed, which requires a *processor*. A program captures an algorithm in a form that the processor can understand and act upon. A processor has a fixed set of available instructions; a program specifies a sequence of these instructions. There are a number of different processors with distinctive instruction sets, including several that are widely used.

A challenge in the software business is *distribution*: How does software get from where it is produced to where it is executed, that is, on a processor available to a user? Software is represented digitally and can thus be replicated cheaply, stored on the same media as information, and transferred over a network. This leaves unanswered some questions, however. In what form is the software distributed? In what manner are the replicas conveyed from supplier to user? These questions have profound implications to the business model of software suppliers.

This section deals with the technical aspects of this problem. Later, in chapters 5 and 6, some related business issues are discussed. There is also much more involved in getting an application up and running for the benefit of users than just distributing the software (see chapter 5).

4.4.1   Application and Infrastructure

After software is distributed, it typically doesn't execute in isolation. Rather, its execution requires a context incorporating a substantial amount of infrastructure software, making use of capabilities provided by that infrastructure through its APIs. The prevalence and market share of a given infrastructure largely define the available market for software making use of that infrastructure; this creates obstacles to the commercialization of infrastructural innovations (see chapter 7).

As defined in section 2.2.6, infrastructure software provides capabilities that support a variety of applications, while application software is focused on needs specific to end-users. The application developer's attention focuses on user needs, whereas the infrastructure developer is more concerned with providing useful capabilities to a variety of application developers and operators. Infrastructure software comes closer to being purely technical. Although applications are becoming more specialized (see section 3.1), even specialized applications have much in common, and this creates an opportunity for expanding infrastructure (see chapter 7).

As applications become more specialized, market size decreases, but the value to each user may be higher. Can a higher revenue from each user compensate for the smaller user base? To make it more likely that answer will be yes, an important trend is reducing the cost of application development. One method is software reuse, using an existing solution rather than creating something from scratch (see chapter 7). Another is software components (see chapter 7), which are modules designed for multiple uses, software tools, and user programming (see section 4.2.7). Another is expanding the capabilities of the infrastructure by observing what is reimplemented in various applications and capturing it in a general and configurable way.

Example   Although some applications don't restrict access, many applications require access control, the ability to specify who has permission to use them, means of identifying users trying to gain access, and means of denying access to users not having permission. It makes sense to capture this access control in the infrastructure. An alternative is reusable software components implementing these functions that can be incorporated as is into many applications.

The software category where this infrastructure expansion is occurring is often called middleware. *Middleware* is something added to the existing infrastructure, just below the application, to expand its capabilities.

Example   Message-oriented middleware (MOM) provides a set of capabilities surrounding the generation, storage, and retrieval of messages (packages of information, such as documents, packaged up for communication). Work flow applications, where documents flow through an organization and are acted upon, can make use of MOM capabilities.

Infrastructure software faces many industry and economic challenges, among them overcoming issues of network effects (see chapters 6 and 9).

4.4.2   Platform and Environment

There are many software execution models, which lead directly to different forms in which software can be distributed, as well as distinct business models.

Consider a specific software program (it could be an application, or part of the infrastructure, or a component), which we call here the *software distribution*. As described in the last subsection, the distribution likely relies on complementary software, and other software may rely on it. One instance is where the distribution is an application that depends on an infrastructure.

Example   An application program always requires an operating system (OS) (e.g., Apple OS, Linux, Mac OS, Microsoft Windows, Sun Solaris). The OS is infrastructure software providing many functions.

Another instance is where the software distribution is an application that depends on other applications.

Example   Each of the programs in an office suite (word processor, spreadsheet, and presentation) needs the ability to create and edit drawings. Rather than implementing separate drawing editors, these individual programs will likely share a common drawing editor.

A *platform* is the aggregate of all hardware and software that is assumed available and static from the perspective of the software distribution. Sometimes there is other optional software, neither part of the platform nor under control of the platform or the distribution. The aggregation of platform and this other software is the *environment* for the distribution. These concepts are illustrated in figure 4.4.

Example   The Web browser has become part of a platform for many applications that make use of its presentation capabilities. An application can add an executable program to a browser, for example, a program written in JavaScript that is embedded in a Web page. The Netscape browser can be extended by adding plug-ins, software capabilities that extend the browser's capabilities. Where an application

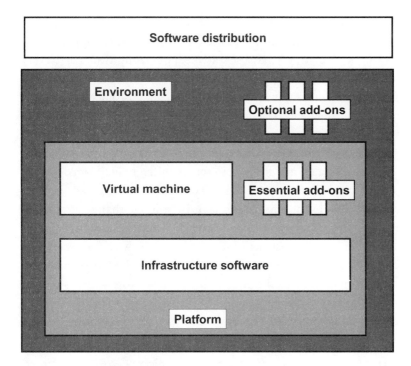

Figure 4.4
Architecture of a platform and environment for a software distribution.

program depends on a capability to function at all, that capability becomes part of its platform requirements. If it is not essential for the functioning of the software distribution, but if present can be used, it becomes part of the environment. For example, a plug-in may enhance the looks of the user interface but not be necessary for proper functioning of the browser.

Other software may come to rely on the software distribution's being available and static, in which case the distribution becomes a part of that program's platform. Thus, the platform is defined relative to a particular software distribution and will typically be different (but overlapping) for different distributions.

Usually, although not always, the platform is infrastructure software and the distribution is an application.

Example   An office suite is an application that may use a particular operating system as its platform. Middleware is infrastructure software that uses an operating system platform; this illustrates that infrastructure software can also be a distribution.

4.4.3 Portability

The market reality is that potential customers use different software suppliers, and thus a software distribution's platform may use software not readily available to every potential customer. There are several approaches a supplier might take. It can address only one platform, thereby limiting market share or forcing customers to adopt a different platform and imposing added switching costs (see chapter 9 for a discussion of lock-in). The supplier can produce a variation on the distribution for more than one platform, increasing development and distribution costs. Or the distribution can be made *portable*, allowing a single software code to run on different platforms.

The first (but not only) obstacle to portability is distinct microprocessor instruction sets. Regardless of portability considerations, it is desirable that programming not be too closely tied to a particular processor instruction set. Because of the primitive nature of individual processor instructions, programs directly tied to an instruction set are difficult to write, read, and understand. *Portable execution*—the ability of a program to execute without modification on different microprocessors—is the first step to portability.

Portable execution falls far short of portability because a distribution makes use of many capabilities provided by its environment.

Example   An executing distribution may need to communicate across the Internet, store and retrieve files from storage, and display interactive features on its screen. To be portable, the distribution would have to perform these functions in equivalent ways on different platforms and without modification.

A given software distribution is portable with respect to a specific set of platforms if full functionality and behavior are preserved when executing on those platforms. Besides portable execution, portability requires that each platform provide the distribution with an environment on that platform that *appears* to be identical *from the distribution's perspective*. The word *appear* is important here; the environments on different microprocessors need not actually be identical (and in fact cannot *be* identical if they incorporate different platforms). What is required is that the differences be encapsulated and hidden from the distribution, at the API.

Example   If a software distribution is to run on both an Apple Macintosh and a Windows PC, the environments will necessarily incorporate different microprocessors (a PowerPC and an Intel-86 compatible processor, respectively) and different operating systems, since Mac OS doesn't run on a PC and Windows doesn't run on a Macintosh[10]. If we succeed in this, the distribution will have a larger potential market, including both PC and Mac users.

A way to achieve portability was already illustrated in figure 4.4. First, the distribution software is developed using an abstract execution model, divorced from the instruction set of a particular processor. Second, a *virtual machine* is added to each platform that realizes the abstract execution model by building on the native instruction set of the platform. This achieves execution portability, inevitably at some expense in performance. Third, an environment is created that appears to the distribution to be the same on each platform. This environment provides means to access operating system services, access the network and display, and so on, that appear identical across all platforms. That environment provides standard APIs, with equivalent functionality and behavior behind those APIs.

Example Java from Sun Microsystems defines an environment for portable execution that is available for a number of platforms (Apple OS, Microsoft Windows, Linux, and others). Java provides a virtual machine (called the Java virtual machine) that executes a program represented by so-called bytecode, as well as uniform ways to access operating system services, the network, and display. For example, a Java virtual machine is embedded in Web browsers so that Web servers can download programs represented as Java bytecode for execution in the browser environment, without regard to the platform and in a uniform environment provided by the browser. Similarly, Microsoft .NET introduces the Common Language Runtime (CLR), a virtual machine that supports multiple programming languages and portable execution. Although different in technical detail, it is comparable to a Java virtual machine. Portability is achieved by the portable subset of the .NET Framework. The underlying specifications for the runtime, for the new programming language C# (pronounced "C sharp"), and for several of the frameworks have been standardized by an industry standards group, the European Computer Manufacturers Association in Geneva (ECMA 2001a; 2001b). As with Java, there are variants on CLR for other platforms and for small devices.

Portability is valuable to both users and software suppliers. For suppliers, it allows a single software distribution to be developed for two or more platforms, reducing development, maintenance, and distribution costs. For users, it decouples decisions about platform from decisions about application software and allows them to replace one without the other. The most compelling advantages arise in a networked environment, as discussed later.

Having said this, the goal of universal portability—*all* software distributions execute identically on *all* platforms—is probably not an attainable goal and arguably not even desirable. Universal portability can be accomplished in one of two ways. First, all platforms offer essentially the same capabilities and thus are undifferentiated and commoditized. At that point, there is little incentive or opportunity to invest in new capabilities that differentiate one platform from another. Alternatively, all distributions take advantage only of capabilities common to all platforms, what might be called "lowest common denominator" capabilities. Here again, the differentiating benefits that one platform might offer are neutralized, since the other platforms do not offer this capability. In either case, innovation in the platform is largely thwarted. Thus, portability is most reasonably ascribed to a single software distribution regarding its execution on a specific set of platforms.

4.4.4   Compilation and Interpretation

The virtual machine illustrates that software programs can have different representations that preserve the same functionality, just as information can have different representations that preserve its content or meaning (see Section 2.1). In the case of programs, equivalent functionality can be preserved even while executing on microprocessors with different instruction sets, but only if the necessary software infrastructure is in place to translate from the assumed instruction set (the virtual machine) to the physical microprocessor instruction set. This idea put into practice is an essential underpinning to software distribution with a diversity of platforms in the hands of users.

The program format manipulated directly by the software developer is called *source code*. Source code is designed to enhance its descriptive abilities in the application context, and also to be a natural representation for human programmers. Source code is inappropriate for direct execution on a processor—the microprocessor and the human have very different capabilities and needs. The processor executes *object code*, expressed directly in the processor instruction set. Source code is for people to write and understand, object code is for machines to execute, and is generally not very accessible to people.[11]

Example   Source code to add up the first *n* integers would look something like:

sum = 0;

For {i = 1 to n} sum = sum + i;

When translated to object code, this small program would consist of a sequence of instructions having specific meaning to the microprocessor in terms of its primitive instructions. The processor typically has a set of registers to store data values and a set of primitive instructions operating on the values currently stored in these registers. The object code does primitive operations like resetting a register value, adding the values in two registers, jumping through the instructions back to the beginning, and checking if the index *i* (stored in one register) has yet reached *n* (stored in another register). While a person could figure out what this object code was accomplishing, it would be tedious.

There are many specialized source code languages in use, for general purposes the holdovers from early days of computing are COBOL and FORTRAN, and more modern widely used languages include C, C++, and Java.[12] There are strong indirect network effects in languages. While software written in different languages can be composable, source code is an important means of documentation and communication among programmers, so more widely used languages prove more valuable. In addition, development organizations tend to choose a language familiar to a large number of prospective employees.

The form of object code that is directly executed on the microprocessor is called *native code*. Native code is expressed in terms of instructions implemented directly by the microprocessor. A software tool can automatically translate the source code to object code, including native code. However, it is not necessary to translate directly from source to native code. Instead, a series of transformations can be used to achieve that goal—these transformations can even be *staged* to happen at different times and places (Lee and Leone 1996). This adds a needed degree of flexibility in business and operational models for software, especially in the Internet age, when software is often distributed over a network.

Specifically, three approaches to distribution software are prominent today (see figure 4.5). The two single-stage approaches dominated before the Internet:

• *Native code distribution.* Once development is complete, a single automatic translation from source to native code creates a native code representation of the program that can be distributed to customers.[13] This translation is called compilation and is performed by a *compiler*.

• *Source code distribution.* Source code is distributed to the customer, and the translation to native code occurs on the fly, during the execution of the program. This translation is called interpretation and is performed by an *interpreter*. The interpreter must be included in the platform; often it is added to the native platform to create an environment for interpreted programs. Special source code languages are designed[14] to be particularly appropriate for interpretation, including the widely used JavaScript and Visual Basic Script.

A compiler is analogous to a German-to-English language human translator who waits until the end of the speech and then translates the entire speech. A software interpreter is analogous to a human interpreter who translates the speech as it is spoken.

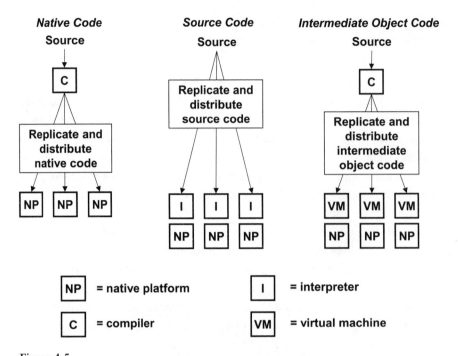

Figure 4.5
Three common approaches to distributing software: native code, source code, and intermediate object code.

Example   ECMAScript (ECMA 1999), sometimes called JavaScript or Jscript, is an interpreted language in which small programs can be written and the source code embedded in Web pages. When the Web browser encounters a JavaScript program, it interprets and executes it, providing an environment and APIs for this program to do various things. JavaScript is used to enhance the richness of functionality of Web pages, extending the native capabilities of HTML, where the programmer must not be sensitive to making source code available.

Each of these first two approaches has strengths and weakness—this problem is addressed by the additional stage of translation shown in figure 4.5, intermediate object code. The advantages and disadvantages of single-stage compilation and interpretation are listed in table 4.2. The choice of one or the other method has considerable business implications.

A multistage transformation with more than one object code representation—the native code and also one or more intermediate object codes—can overcome these disadvantages. Each intermediate object code is not native code—it requires at least

Table 4.2
Considerations in Choosing Single-Stage Compilation vs. Interpretation

	Advantages	Disadvantages
Compilation	Compilation to native code avoids the distribution of source code, contributing to maintaining trade secrets and enhancing encapsulation. The execution time interpreter overhead is avoided.	Execution portability is lost, because a different native code version must be generated for each platform. Different environments on the different platforms necessitate different variants of the source code, not simply a recompilation for each platform.
Interpretation	Execution portability can be achieved if a set of platforms include an interpreter for the source language and provide an equivalent environment for a set of software distributions.	Source code is distributed to user, compromising trade secrets and the benefits of encapsulation. Interpretation during execution adds processing overhead. Portable execution depends on a compatible environment provided on the host platform, reducing market size.

one stage of transformation to native code—but it is low-level object code, helping to preserve trade secrets and encapsulation, and reducing the runtime overhead in the final stage of interpretation.

In this case, compilation and interpretation can be combined in a two-stage process, gaining the advantages of both. One stage of compilation to an intermediate object code is followed by a stage of interpretation by a virtual machine (see figures 4.4 and 4.5). The intermediate object code is the program representation replicated and distributed to the customer. Portability to all platforms hosting the intermediate object code is preserved, while retaining the advantages of distributing object rather than source code. An added advantage is that the source code language need not be designed with interpretation in mind.

Example Java can be compiled into intermediate object code called *bytecode*. Identical bytecode can be distributed to and executed on different platforms, as long as each includes a Java virtual machine (bytecode interpreter). Java can also be compiled directly into native object code for a given platform.

For a software distribution executed multiple times on the same processor, the repetitive overhead of interpretation can be avoided by *just-in-time* (JIT) *compilation*, in which a compiler is invoked within the interpreter to compile some of the intermediate object code to native code. Compilation includes optimization, tuning the output object code to minimize execution time. JIT compilation's online optimization actually improves efficiency by observing the local execution.[15]

Example Current implementations of Java illustrate this (Suganuma et al. 2000; Sun Microsystems 1999a). All current Java virtual machine implementations use JIT compilation, often including online optimization, to achieve good performance.

There are many variations on this theme. Interpretation can be avoided entirely without losing portability by always applying install-time or JIT compilation (as is the case with the CLR virtual machine of the Microsoft .NET Framework). In a narrower definition of portability, interpretation and JIT compilation can allow any software designed for one platform to be run on another specific platform, enhancing the latter with a new suite of applications.

Example Digital Equipment Corporation (absorbed into Compaq, then into Hewlett-Packard) included interpretation and compilation in its Alpha platform that allow Microsoft Windows applications to execute.[16]

4.4.5 Trust in Execution

An important security issue to users is the implicit trust that a user places in an executing program (Devanbu, Fong, and Stubblebine 1998). An untrustworthy program could damage stored data, violate privacy, or do other invasive or damaging things (see section 3.2.8 and chapter 5). This is a consideration in the choice of an intermediate object code format and the design of the interpreter.

Two different models are currently in use. Users or operators acquiring software from what they consider a reputable software supplier may trust the code based on that fact alone. Software sold in shrink-wrap form in retail stores can use physical techniques like unique holograms to help establish trust. However, today much software is distributed over a network, where approaches based on physical security are not feasible. Fortunately, security technologies provide an even more trustworthy approach, the *digital signature* (see chapter 6), which verifies that code originated from a specific supplier and has not been tampered with since it left the supplier. This does not affect the choice of intermediate object code or program functionality.

Example Java applets, Microsoft's Authenticode technology for ActiveX controls, bytecode, and Microsoft's .NET Framework assemblies use digital signatures. The .NET assemblies are unusual in that two signatures are used. The standard signature protects against tampering. An optional additional signature establishes the authenticated originator of the assembly.

The second approach is policy-based, as many security systems are. A set of policies as to what the intermediate object code is allowed and not allowed to do is established, and the virtual machine is responsible for enforcing these policies.[17] There may be user-set configuration options, allowing the user some control over the trade-off between functionality, usability, and security.

Example   A strict policy might preclude the executing program from reading and writing files in storage, or from communicating over a network. This might be appropriate for some programs but not for others. For example, if the user knows a program needs to legitimately write to a file on disk, she can relax that policy.

Security always requires qualifiers. Both the techniques described require the user to place implicit trust in the platform and environment to enforce security policies or properly check digital signatures. A piece of hardware, software, or hardware/software combination that is relied upon to enforce security policies is called a *trusted system*.[18]

Example   The software environment that checks signatures or enforces execution policies is also acquired from a software supplier. The user is thus placing implicit trust in that supplier. Even assuming the supplier is trustworthy (as is normally the case), security can still be compromised by tampering with that software after it leaves the supplier. That vendor can add a digital signature, but how can that signature be checked in a trustworthy manner?

4.4.6   Operating System

A universal software infrastructure is the *operating system*. It provides core infrastructure capabilities that virtually all applications rely upon. Among its functions are to provide an abstract execution environment serving to isolate the program from unnecessary hardware details (e.g., the particulars of how data is stored on disk), hide the reality that multiple programs are executing concurrently on the same computer (called *multitasking*), allocate shared resources (e.g., memory and processor cycles) to programs, and provide useful services (e.g., network communication). The operating system is thus an essential part of any platform, along with the hardware. Two platforms can differ because they have different operating systems, different hardware, or both.

Example   The Intel 86–compatible PC has two commonly used operating systems, Microsoft Windows and Linux, and thus supports two platforms. Linux runs on other hardware and hence provides similar platforms on different hardware foundations. However, these Linux platforms are not identical; for example, they provide software distributions with different processor instruction sets.

Some users appreciate the ability to mix and match solutions from different equipment and software vendors, and this contributes to competition.

4.4.7 Development Tools

Development *tools* help programmers' productivity and enhance their ability to manage complexity. These software tools automate tasks that would otherwise be time-consuming and do a number of other functions like keeping track of and merging changes. Sophisticated toolkits are necessary for the management and long-term success of large projects involving hundreds or thousands of programmers. Today, most developments employ an *integrated development environment* (IDE) that combines many tools in an integrated package.

Example   Traditionally, the two most important tools of a software developer were source code editors and compilers. In IDEs the toolkit has grown to include functional and performance debuggers, collectors of statistics, defect trackers, and so on. However, facing the substantial complexity of many current software systems, *build systems* have become one of the most important sets of tools.[19] They coordinate the largely independent efforts of different software teams, allowing them to merge their efforts into a single software distribution while providing audit trails and automating retrenchment as necessary.

In terms of the categories of software (see section 2.2.6), these tools can be considered either applications (serving a developer organization) or infrastructure (aiding the development of many applications).

4.5   Distributed Software

Before the Internet, computer systems mostly ran in isolation, and applications executed on a single computer. With local-area networks, and later the Internet, it is now common for applications and infrastructure programs to be partitioned across different *hosts* (Internet terminology for computing systems that operate at the edge of the network). As discussed in section 3.1, these distributed or *networked computing* applications have added communication, collaboration, and coordination as new application categories and as feature extensions in other applications.

If an application is distributed over hosts, the issue arises as to how to partition it, and why. Merely distributing an application does not by itself enable additional functionality—any functionality in a distributed environment can also be accomplished centrally. There are nevertheless some compelling reasons for distributing an application. First, performance may be improved when multiple hosts execute concurrently (see sections 2.3.1 and 3.2.6). Second, a centralized application must be administered centrally, whereas the administration and control of a distributed application can be partitioned. This is crucial for applications that span organizational boundaries, where close coordination is not feasible (see chapter 5), for example business-to-business e-commerce. Third, the security of an application is affected by its distribution (see section 3.2.8). For example, if an application must access crucial data assets of two organizations, each organization can exercise better control if each maintains its own data. Similarly, distributed data management can address privacy (see section 3.2.9) and ownership issues.

Because communication is a key differentiator of organizations and the society from the individual, the Internet has dramatically expanded the effect of computing on organizations, communities, society, and the economy (see section 3.1.4). It has also irrevocably changed software technology and the organization of the software industry (see chapter 7).

4.5.1 Network Effects in Distributed Applications

Distributed computing is substantially bringing forward direct network effects (see section 3.2.3) as a consideration and constraint on the software industry. Software has always been influenced by indirect network effects: the greatest information content and application availability flow to the most widely adopted application, and software developers flow to the most popular languages.

Direct network effects have a quantitatively greater reach and effect, however. The reality (pre- and post-Internet) is that the market provides a diversity of technologies and platforms; that is what we want to encourage. Previously, the major categories of computing (see table 2.3) coexisted largely as independent marketplaces, serving their own distinct needs and user communities. In addition, different organizations established their own procurement and administrative organizations and procedures. Before the Internet, the market was segmented for computing across platforms and organizations. Each supplier and each platform emphasized its own differentiated group of uses and functions. Indirect network effects favored technologies and platforms that gained larger acceptance, but the suppliers offering these differentiated solutions could otherwise mostly ignore one another.

With the Internet, users want to participate in applications that are distributed, like e-mail, information access and sharing, and coordination. Many of these applications exhibit a direct network effect: the value of the application depends on its intrinsic capabilities and also on the number of adopters available to participate. Users want these applications to work transparently with many technologies and platforms, and across organizational and administrative boundaries. Distributed computing applications that targeted a single platform were put at a disadvantage. Fragmented and independent markets became dependent, and users who once cared little about other users' computing platforms and applications now want shared applications.

Example   The telecommunications industry has always dealt with direct network effects. Users in one organization want to converse with users in other organizations even if they have chosen different phone suppliers. With the Internet, the software industry was put in a similar situation.

One approach to meeting this new requirement would be to simply start over from scratch. This clearly isn't practical with sunk costs that are huge for both suppliers and customers, as well as switching costs that are substantial for both. Ways had to be found to incrementally modify and extend the existing hardware and software infrastructure to meet the new requirements. Fortunately, the flexibility of software and the declining importance of efficiency observed by Moore's law were enablers.

Example   A virtual machine can be added to existing platforms, turning them into compatible environments. The added runtime processing of the virtual machine, while a consideration, may be far outweighed by the benefits and mitigated by the increasing performance observed by Moore's law (see section 2.3).

The transition to an infrastructure that meets these modern needs is not complete, but good progress has been made.

4.5.2   Internet Interoperability

The inspired vision of the Internet inventors was to connect heterogeneous computing platforms, allowing them to communicate with one another in common applications. They certainly could not have anticipated the results we see today, but they were confident that this capability would lead to interesting research opportunities and new distributed applications. Allowing communication falls far short of what is needed to achieve distributed computing over heterogeneous platforms, but it is a necessary first step. How the Internet pioneers approached this problem is instructive because it suggests solutions to larger problems. They conceptualized an hourglass architecture (see figure 4.6) that had only one waist at the time; we have added a second based on hindsight.

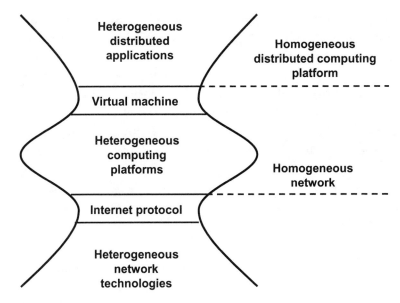

Figure 4.6
Internet hourglass architecture extended to processing.

The bottom waist of the hourglass is the *internet protocol* (IP). Before the Internet, there were distinct local-area networking (LAN) technologies. These existing LANs could have been replaced with new wide-area-network–compatible LANs. Instead, the Internet inventors defined a standard way to interconnect these existing (and future new) LANs by a new wide-area backbone network. Building on existing LANs was a major market success.[20]

Example The major competitors at the time were Ethernet and the IBM Token Ring. Since then, there has been continuing innovation, including a succession of faster and faster Ethernets, Ethernet switching, and several wireless networking solutions, including the IEEE 802.11b wireless LAN standard. These innovations are consistent with the requirement of Internet compatibility.

IP was the standard way for LANs to be concatenated through the Internet backbone, allowing hosts on different hosts to communicate. The solution required a piece of equipment connected to the LAN (called a gateway) that translates from internal LAN data and addressing formats to and from the common representation used in IP, and similar translation equipment added to each of the host operating systems. To avoid impeding technological progress in networking, the IP designers tried to be forward-looking to capture capabilities needed by future LAN technologies.

The virtual machine infrastructure described in section 4.4.3 can be interpreted in a similar light. It provides a common representation for programs (rather than data traversing the network) that allows them equal access to heterogeneous platforms. It is a second waist in the hourglass shown in figure 4.6, allowing heterogeneous platforms to interact with application programs (whereas the IP waist allows them to communicate with one another) in a standard way.

The hourglass approach does have a couple of drawbacks. It introduces processing overhead and sometimes added equipment cost (e.g., for gateways). Most important, if the designers of the waist are not sufficiently forward-looking in anticipating future needs, there is a danger that the waist may become a bottleneck, introducing restrictions that cannot be bypassed other than by replacement. *Extensions* to the waist (sometimes a sign of middle age) are no problem, but *changes* to the waist have ramifications that spread far and wide.

Example   The original designers of IP, not anticipating how successful the Internet would become, gave it too few distinct host addresses (about four billion).[21] The latest version of IP (version six) dramatically increases the number of addresses (unfortunately this is a change rather than an extension) along with a number of extensions. Since it is impractical to deploy a new version of IP instantaneously over the many nodes in an operational network, the design of a new version is greatly complicated by the need for backward compatibility and version coexistence.

4.5.3   Client-Server and Peer-to-Peer Architectures

One basic architectural question in distributed computing is why and how to partition an application across hosts. There are a number of considerations here (Messerschmitt 1999c), representative examples being performance, administration, and security:

• *Performance.* Today most users access applications using a dedicated desktop host: a personal computer or workstation. Often the part of the application that interacts directly with the user is allocated to this dedicated computer so that the delay performance characteristics are improved (see section 2.3.1). Many applications support multiple users, and scalability is a concern for the operator. Scalability refers for the feasibility of expanding the number of users by adding equipment at a cost that grows no more than linearly (increasing returns to scale, in economics terms). Scalability usually requires more hosts and associated networking resources, so that the application becomes distributed.

• *Administration.* Many applications have administrative responsibility shared across organizations (e.g., business-to-business e-commerce). The application will be partitioned according to administrative responsibility. Today recurring salary costs are the major consideration, so it often makes sense to provision more hosts according to administrative convenience.

• *Security*. This is an important consideration in the partitioning of applications (see section 3.2.8 and chapter 5). Where data are sensitive or constitute an important organizational asset, they must be isolated from threats and protected against loss. A dedicated host (often a mainframe), isolated from the other hosts and the public network, will improve security.

Two distributed computing architectures that predominate today, sometimes in combination, are client-server and peer-to-peer (see figure 4.7). In client-server there is an asymmetry of function: the server specializes in satisfying requests, and the client specializes in initiating requests. The application communicates in a star-shaped topology of communication, with each client communicating with the server and the server communicating with all clients. In a peer-to-peer architecture, there is a symmetry of function, with all hosts both initiating and satisfying requests for one another. (In effect, each host acts as both a client and a server.)

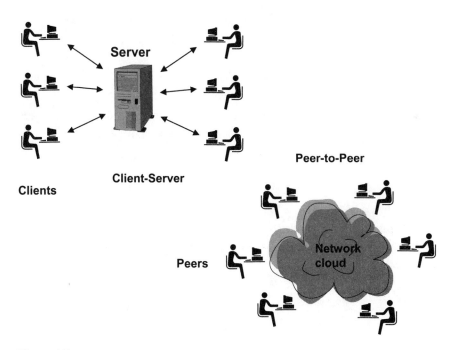

Figure 4.7
Client-server and peer-to-peer architectures are distinguished by their symmetry or asymmetry of function and by their interconnection topology.

Communication many occur between any pair of hosts, so the communication topology is fully connected. (Often reality is more complex than depicted here; for example, an application may involve multiple servers, or a peer-to-peer architecture may also incorporate a server.)

Example   The Web emphasizes a client-server architecture, with the Web server satisfying requests for Web pages initiated by clients (desktop computers in the hands of users). Napster, a popular music-sharing service that was shut down by the courts because of copyright law violations, emphasized a peer-to-peer architecture. The users' computers communicated directly with one another to share music files, and at any give time a computer might have been sending (acting as a server) or receiving (acting as a client). In these examples, aspects of the architecture violate the "pure" architectural model: Web servers may communicate with one another in a peer-to-peer fashion (this predominates in: Web services; see chapter 7), and some file-sharing applications like Napster and Groove include a centralized directory of all the files stored on users' PCs.

Client-server and peer-to-peer architectures are associated with very different business models. It is important to distinguish between the business model of the operators of an application and the business model of the software suppliers (see chapters 5 and 6).

There is a direct correspondence between these two architectures and indirect and direct network effects (see figure 3.3). The operator of a client-server application will typically put up a server with valuable services and content and hope that users will come. The intrinsic value of the services and content will attract the early users, who are not directly affected by the lack of other users. (A notable exception is community features, like discussion forums and e-mail, where the number of other users is an issue.) As the number of clients grows, more investment can be made in upgrading the services or adding content. Also, a large number of users can create congestion (a negative externality), and as a result scalability is an important issue in the management of the application. Within a single organization, coordinated decisions can be made about investing in client and servers, the number of users can be better anticipated, and investments in content can be made accordingly. Hence, network effects are less an issue.

The challenges for suppliers of a client-server application are different. For a public application they will typically distribute client software directly to users. A common business model is to distribute client software free, resulting in more clients, which encourages operators to pay for the server software. One can imagine two related business models for complementary products in the material world: "giving away the razor to sell razor blades" and "giving away razor blades to sell the razor." In the material world, giving away razor blades doesn't make much sense because the aggregate blades consumed by a given razor cost the supplier much more than the razor. In the world of software, giving away client software (analogous to giving away blades) is sensible because of low replication and distribution costs.[22]

Example   RealNetworks distributes basic client software (its RealPlayer for playing streaming audio media) free but charges for complementary server software (compressing and streaming audio media) and for premium client software with additional features. By enlarging its user base through free distribution and advertising, it encourages the sale of its server and premium software. Adobe follows a similar strategy with its Acrobat document format, distributing a reader free but selling authoring tools. Microsoft provides free readers for its Excel, Word, and Power-Point formats as well as a free media player.

An obstacle in distributed applications that must work across administrative domains (a public market with individual consumers each administering their own computers is an extreme example) is the distribution of the necessary software. If the users have to install special software, even if it is free, this is an obstacle to overcome. There is the time and trouble of going through the installation process, the disk space consumed, and so on. One innovation of the Web was to establish a single client software (the Web browser) incorporated into a number of client-server applications. This software can even be extended using mobile code (see section 4.5.5). Operators of Web servers benefit from a ready supply of users able to access their server applications without special software installation.

An additional factor favoring client-server is centralized administration of the application on the server. Especially if the client software is standard (like a Web browser), many users prefer to place the administrative responsibility on someone else. This is also a driver for the application service provider model that outsources operations of an application to a service provider (see chapter 6).

Peer-to-peer establishes itself in a public market in a very different manner. Since each peer includes full application functionality, not merely the user interface elements, users always have to install special software (unless mobile code is used). If the supplier chooses to charge for the software, users bear this cost, and suppliers have no opportunity for revenue from complementary server software. Early adopters are deterred by the lack of other users. These direct network effects and adoption costs largely explain the preponderance of the client-server model today, even for applications (like community-based applications) that could be realized using peer-to-peer.[23]

4.5.4   Network Software Distribution

Since software programs are represented by data, they can be distributed over a network. A network is an attractive distribution channel, with low cost (no physical media to manufacture and transport) and low delay (low transport delay relative to physical media). This significantly affects the business model, transcending even the cost advantages:

• One of the greatest advantages of network software distribution is psychological: the power of instant gratification. Experience has shown that purchase is encouraged by avoiding the delay between purchase and use. This was a significant factor in the popularity of the personal computer (which reduced the delay in acquiring and using applications relative to some earlier mainframe and time-sharing models) (see table 2.3).

• By reducing adoption cost and delay, the startup obstacle of direct network effects is somewhat mitigated. For example, a peer-to-peer architecture becomes easier to establish in spite of its requirement for special software. Not surprisingly, peer-to-peer applications were rare before network distribution.

• Software service releases (fixing defects but not adding new features; see chapter 5) can be distributed easily and quickly, and even automated. Before network distribution, service releases were rare in consumer applications and, some would say, have reduced the number of defects in earlier releases.

• Similarly, upgrades (adding new features and fixing defects) are easier and cheaper to distribute. This is especially valuable for distributed software, where interoperability must be maintained across different hosts—an obstacle to upgrades, which may require simultaneous upgrade to two or more hosts to provide full feature flexibility. Network distribution mitigates these problems.

Today, it is common to make the first sale of consumer software by physical media, in part for rights management reasons and in part because of long download times over the network. As discussed in section 2.1.2, information and software distributed in digital form are subject to low-cost replication and redistribution. Rights management techniques (deterring distribution to other users that violates a copyright; see chapter 8) like copy protection are more effective on physical media. This is less an issue with upgrades, which need a successfully installed application as a starting point.

4.5.5 Mobile Code

Traditionally software is semipermanently installed on each computer, available to be executed on demand. With *mobile code*, the idea is to opportunistically transport a program to a computer and execute it there, ideally transparently to the user and without explicit software installation. This can mitigate adoption costs and network effects by transporting and executing applications in a single step. One advantage in distributed applications is that mobile code can ensure a single version of the code everywhere, bypassing interversion interoperability problems. Mobile code can dynamically move execution to the most advantageous host, for example, near the user (enhancing responsiveness) or to available processing resources (enhancing scalability).

Mobile code must overcome some challenges (see section 4.4). One is portable execution and providing a preinstalled platform that allows mobile code to access resources such as files and to display in the same way on different machines. Another is enforcing a set of (usually configurable) security policies that allow legitimate access to resources while preventing rogue code from causing damage. A final one is protecting the mobile code (and the user it serves) from rogue hosting environments. (Today, this last issue is an open research problem.)

In some circumstances, it is advantageous for a program to actually move between processors during the course of its execution. This is called a *mobile agent* and requires that the program carry both data[24] and code along from host to host. Mobile agents have applications in information access and in negotiation but also pose even more security and privacy challenges.

4.5.6 The Network Cloud and Its Future

Today's infrastructure for distributed applications includes three primary elements:

• *Processing resources* to support the execution of applications and storage resources for retaining data over time.

• *Infrastructure software* providing various processing-based services to the application. This includes the operating system as well as possibly a virtual machine and other middleware.

• *The network*, which allows hosts to communicate with one another by sending packets of data. The network is thought of as a cloud in that what goes on within the network to realize the communication services it provides is largely irrelevant to applications: they care about the reliability of delivery and delay in the arrival of packets and nothing else.

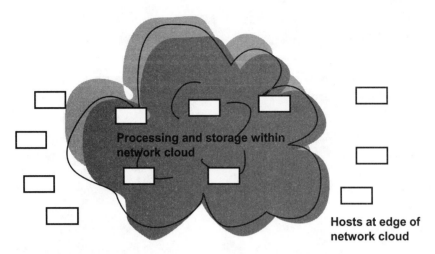

Figure 4.8
The future network cloud will include processing and storage as well as connection services made available to applications.

As illustrated in figure 4.8, infrastructure is evolving toward making available to applications the processing and storage resources within the cloud.[25] This moves in the direction of a *utility model* for infrastructure, in which applications can draw upon the full suite of processing, storage, and communication capabilities shared among many users and applications (see chapter 9). This more readily accommodates uncertainties or irregularities in the required resources.

Why is this useful? First, as discussed in section 4.4.1, infrastructure is expanding to provide many useful capabilities to applications, some of which require processing and storage resources within the cloud.

Example Inktomi and Akamai offer a distributed caching service for the Web. Their servers are placed within the cloud in strategic locations close to users, and they temporarily store Web content that is accessed repeatedly by those users. The two companies pursue very different business models. Inktomi sells these caches to Internet service providers, who can then reduce the delay of frequently accessed Web pages (giving them competitive advantage over other providers) and reduce network traffic (lowering costs). Akamai deploys these caches around the world and then sells caching services to information providers, who gain competitive advantage over other information providers through lower delay accesses to users.

There are many capabilities like caching that would be useful to some or all applications; a partial list is given in table 4.3.

Table 4.3
Examples of Middleware Services That Would Extend the Infrastructure Utility Model

Capability	Description
Security	Support common security needs of applications, like identification, authentication, confidentiality, authorization and access control.
Performance	Enhance the performance and scalability of applications, such as caching or adaptive and distributed resource management.
Location	Help applications find needed resources, through directory, naming, and location services.
New networking services	Support services, such as multicast or global event notification, not currently provided by the network.
Reliability	Help applications achieve reliability and availability, for example, by supporting fault detection and reconfiguration.
Quality of service	Support end-to-end quality-of-service objectives and guarantees not currently available from the network.
Mobile code	Support mobile code dynamic downloading and security.
Mobility	Support mobility of devices and users, for example, allowing applications to be location transparent.
Information representations	Support standard structured data types (XML, audio, video) widely needed by applications.
Accounting	Support scalable usage accounting for processing, storage, and communication.

Source: NSF (National Science Foundation) (2001).

Another reason for including processing and storage within the network cloud is that this opens up alternative business models for the operation of applications. For example, the operator of an application may want to make use of processing and storage resources provided by a utility rather than buying or leasing and operating them itself. This has long been the dominant business model for networking services,[26] and it is conceptually a small step to extend this to processing and storage.

Example The Microsoft .NET MyServices project (formerly code-named Hailstorm) aims to deliver a variety of Web services that provide services within the cloud, including authentication (Passport service) and storage.

4.6   Research and Discussion Issues

1. How is the profession of software programming changing?

2. Compare the professions of writing, building architecture, and software programming. What are some similarities and differences?

3. Consider the overall project of constructing a large building, and compare the steps required to accomplish that with the phases in a waterfall model of software development. Where and why are there significant variations, and what are the implications?

4. Carrying forward the last question, in what manner might a spiral model of development apply to the design of a building, or not?

5. Considering all the elements necessary to create a successful application, what is their relative value? That is, what is their relative importance in terms of contributing to the overall value?

6. Consider in more depth the differences in the term *maintenance* as applied to software (matching changing environment and needs) and to material goods (wearing out or breaking). What substantive economic and business issues flow from this difference?

7. Understand in more depth the relation between project and organizational efficiency, and extend this further to quality of outcomes. Can analytical project management tools or models be built that assist in optimizing this trade-off? Does this relate to project management tools in the construction industry?

8. What are the advantages and disadvantages of grouping different software development projects within a common organization rather than keeping them separated?

9. How are iterative and community-based development methodologies related? Should community-based development also be iterated, and if so, what is a good process for making that happen?

10. Given that the profitability of a software project depends on many factors besides the effectiveness or efficiency of a development organization, what are the best metrics to apply in evaluating the performance of a software development organization?

11. What specific insights does organizational theory have on the software development process? In particular, does it offer insights into the role of architecture or how architectural design should be carried out?

12. List several different ways that a software project can fail to meet expectations. What are some likely or possible causes of these failures, and how can they be avoided?

13. Understand and discuss in more depth how user needs and requirements definition (see chapter 3) should be integrated into the software development process. How are they formulated, and where are they plugged in?

14. Discuss how the education of computer scientists and other professionals might be improved to emphasize user satisfaction (see section 3.2.11)?

15. How can commercial software companies best apply the lessons or even the methodology of community-based development successes?

16. As applications become more numerous and diverse, consider the opportunity to combine more generic but highly configurable applications with configuration and customization by end-user organizations. Is this a good way to proceed? How does this compare to the outsourcing of software development to meet specialized needs?

17. Consider the desirable properties of modularity as applied to a human organization. Are they important properties? Are there other properties of organizations that are even more important?

18. What strategic considerations come into the business decision to provide an API in a software product?

19. Is the concept of platform and environment (or close analogies) common in other goods and services, or unique to software? Give specific examples. What effect does this complementarity have on business strategies for the suppliers of both the platforms and the software depending on the platforms?

20. Delve more deeply into the issue of software portability and its benefits and disadvantages. How does it affect strategies for both platform and application software suppliers?

21. As discussed, the introduction of a virtual machine on top of physical processors helps make software run on different processors without modification. In an attempt to counter piracy, a software vendor could request a unique key from the target machine and then try to make the distributed software run only on that target machine. Discuss how these two approaches could complement each other to the benefit of the vendor; also discuss any disadvantages for the vendor. Discuss advantages and disadvantages of both approaches as seen by the client or customer using the software.

22. A compiler is an example of a tool that aids software developers. How do the strategies and challenges of tool suppliers differ from those of application and infrastructure suppliers?

23. Understand and discuss in greater depth the strategic business considerations underlying the choice of distributing software in intermediate or native object code.

24. Given some interactive applications' need for responsive user interaction at the client side and massive data processing at the server side, consider various strategies for distributing such an application. Discuss the main application characteristics you would expect such distribution strategies to cause.

25. Understand and discuss in greater depth the strategic business decision to develop a distributed application using a client-server or peer-to-peer model. Can you distinguish the application characteristics that make one model or the other more advantageous?

26. Trust is transitive: if a user trusts an application supplier, who in turn trusts a service employed by the application, then the user (perhaps unknowingly) trusts that service as well, though this trust may be unwarranted. Discuss how trustworthiness and transitive dependencies (including security, privacy, and reliability) interfere.

4.7   Further Reading

This book does not emphasize the nature of innovation in software, a topic discussed in other books (Torrisi 1998). A classic but still recommended discussion of the software development process is Brooks (1975). A comprehensive though somewhat dated treatment of the economics of software development is Boehm (1981), and a more modern treatment is Gulledge and Hutzler (1993). For an excellent discussion of the issues attendant to community-based development software, see the April 1999 issue of the *Communications of the ACM*, which includes an article by O'Reilly (1999). Bass, Clements, and Kazman (1998) and Bosch (2000) provide comprehensive discussions on software architecture.

5

Management

Technology makes it possible for people to gain control over everything, except over technology.
John Tudor

Some management challenges encountered in creating software were discussed in section 4.2, but software creation is only one of several stages required before a software application can be made available to users. The software must be marketed and sold, a process that is closely intertwined with its creation. Management has to oversee the planning, deployment, and testing of equipment and infrastructure software required to run an application, and the application software must be installed and tested. Users have to be trained, and in the case of organizational applications the organizational and business processes often have to be revamped to match the assumptions of the software. Once the application is successfully up and running, someone has to keep it operating, including reporting and repairing defects, maintaining vigilance for security breaches, and providing support to users. Software administrative and management tools can assist in all this, but people are the key players. It is an ongoing challenge to gain and maintain control over a software application and the technology that underlies it.

This chapter discusses this management challenge in more depth. We begin with a model for the stages in the supply chain from creator to user of software, and discuss the differing roles within these stages. This sets the stage for considering the industry structure that supports these diverse roles (see chapter 6). We then consider the total cost of these activities, known as the total cost of ownership, a major consideration for both managers and suppliers. Finally, we delve into the issues raised when an application spans multiple management domains (like autonomous end-user organizations), using security to provide an in-depth illustration.

5.1   Value Chains

There are two *value chains* in software, in which participants in one chain add value sequentially to the others. The *supply value chain* applies to the execution phase, starts with the software vendor, and ends by providing valuable functionality and capability to the user. The *requirements value chain* applies to the software implementation phase, starts with business and application ideas, gathers and adds functional and performance objectives from users, and finally ends with a detailed set of requirements for implementation. Many innovations start with software developers, who can better appreciate the technical possibilities but nevertheless require end-user involvement for their validation and refinement (see section 4.2).

The interrelation of these chains is shown in figure 5.1, where infrastructure and application software are separated into distinct supply chains. The requirements chain starts with *analysis* of user needs and requirements, and *design* of the concrete approaches for realizing those needs and requirements, the results of which define the detailed requirements for *implementation* of application software. The needs and requirements of application developers similarly must be analyzed to define the requirements for the implementation of infrastructure software. For most application software and virtually all infrastructure software, the analysis takes into

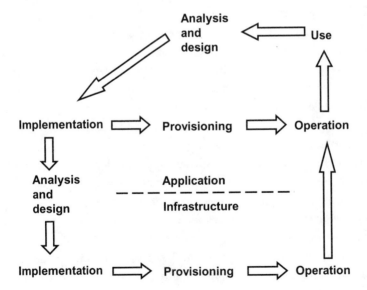

Figure 5.1
Value chains in the software industry.

account the needs of many users or developers, not a single user or organization. At the other end of the supply chain, the use of the application software is supported by the *operation* stage, where everything required to keep the software running and give users appropriate access to it is performed. Similarly, the operation of the application is supported by the operation of the infrastructure, which includes both infrastructure software and equipment (like networks and processors). Between implementation and operation is *provisioning*, which includes all steps necessary to plan, install, and test the software and required infrastructure to prepare it for operation.

The requirements chain was discussed at some length in section 4.2, so here we focus on the supply chain. The supply chain has four primary stages (see table 5.1): implementation, provisioning, operation, and use. There are, of course, other standard business functions like sales, not specifically discussed here.

The *implementation* stage includes detailed requirements, architecture, and programming, as described in chapter 4. In addition, it includes testing of the software in a laboratory environment and with actual end-users. An outcome is a working software product that can be sold, distributed, and used. Responsibility does not end there, however. All software that is still used requires ongoing maintenance and in most cases upgrades and extensions over time.

In the *provisioning* stage, the facilities (network, servers, desktop computers) are procured and deployed, depending in large part on the unique performance requirements of the organization, and the software is installed, integrated, and tested in this environment. Frequently, an important role is the integration (installation and testing) of software from different suppliers. An outcome is an application that is ready for use. But provisioning is not just about software and technology. The organizational and business process changes necessary to accommodate the application in the organizational context must also be planned and implemented, including training of workers. Neither does provisioning end when the application becomes operational. System throughput and growth needs must be forecast, and facilities and accompanying software installations must be added to maintain performance attributes in spite of (for example) a growing user population.

In the *operation* stage, an application and its supporting infrastructure are kept running reliably and securely. In addition, users are supported, and problems arising from defects or changing needs are reported back to suppliers. Note that the operation and the use of a software application and supporting infrastructure are separate roles, usually involving different people. Many of us are accustomed to combining these roles in our everyday experience with desktop computers, but

Table 5.1
Stages of the Software Supply Value Chain and Their Generic Tasks

Stage	Planning	Deployment	Facilitation	Maintenance	Evolution
Implementation	Architecture; performance and scalability objectives	Build systems	Software tools support	Repair defects, performance tuning	Service and upgrade releases
Provisioning	Organizational design; performance and scalability requirements	Installation, integration, configuration, and testing	Procurement, finance		Installation, integration, configuration, and testing
Operation	Adjustment to changing security threats	Facilities growth to accommodate increasing throughput	System administration	Patching, configuration to counter security threats	
Use	End-user organization	Organizational adjustments, user training	Help and trouble desk	Reorganization and user retraining	

Note: The table cells are examples not meant to be comprehensive.

outside this environment, there are invariably operators (often not also users) taking responsibility.

At the *use* stage, the application functionality provides direct value to users and end-user organizations (see chapter 3). Just as the implementation stage overlaps provisioning and operation in time, provisioning overlaps operation, and operation overlaps use.

This summary of supply chain stages should make clear that there are many roles and management issues. Organizations taking responsibility for their own provisioning and operation as well as development require a range of skills. This can be problematic for small organizations, and as a result the outsourcing of provisioning or operation is common (see chapter 6).

The stages in the supply and requirements value chains are now discussed in greater detail.

5.1.1 Analysis and Design

Analysis and design are closely linked phases of the software chain. Analysis decides what is to be accomplished in the software context and how, and design takes the results of analysis as a starting point and turns them into a concrete plan and organization for the software.

Analysis starts with a conceptualization of what is to be accomplished, and considers in depth the features and capabilities of the software as they relate to the context of its uses. It is important to involve representative users through focus groups or interviews. For organizational or e-commerce applications, significant issues of business processes and organizational structures assumed by the application must also be addressed. In the spirit of modularity, the analysis and design phases interface through specifications and requirements (typically formalized as documents), which provide specific and detailed guidance to designers as to what the software is to ultimately accomplish. Requirements include capabilities and functionality, as well as the many characteristics listed in section 3.2, such as performance, reliability, security, and privacy.

The design phase seeks a concrete and detailed plan that can be followed through implementation. Elements of the design phase include determining aesthetic and human use characteristics (such as the user interface, including interaction, industrial, and graphics design; see section 4.2.6) as well as the internal details of the software itself (software design).

Analysis and implementation are not actually sequential (see section 4.2), but are ideally integrated through the development process (like iterative development).

From a managerial perspective, it is useful to separate them in the value chain, as we have done in figure 5.1, because the core skills and orientation of the two activities are quite different, and it is increasingly common for them to be separated organizationally (at least in part). For example, the analysis may be assigned to a product marketing organization distinct from the software development organization, or employ outside industry consultants (see chapter 6). Of course, even separate organizations must maintain an ongoing and close collaboration.

5.1.2 Implementation

The creation of software was discussed at some length in chapter 4. Software design is often considered a part of implementation and includes the definition of architecture and a plan and requirements for individual modules. Thus, software design realizes a recursive application of the analysis design process, often at different granularities of architectural decomposition and over time (as in the spiral model). At each stage of analysis, design, and implementation, organizational issues and budgets must be worked out and approved. The processes discussed in chapter 4 ideally lead to software that meets its requirements with acceptable performance and with an acceptable level of defects within the user environment.

Before implementation is complete, the software must be extensively tested. This testing occurs at all phases—on individual modules, during the integration of modules, and in simulated and real user environments. Normally the developer solicits the assistance of cooperative end-users to try out the software during the later phases of testing. The first operational test, called an alpha trial, is the first trial in a real operational environment, usually at a limited number of customer sites. Depending on circumstances, these alpha sites may receive compensation in various forms, such as influence on the product features, free support, or outright payments. A later operational test, the beta trial, occurs at multiple customer sites. In some cases, anybody may download and try a beta version free, with structured feedback mechanisms. Depending on the company and its processes, additional test versions may be tried in the market before the software is finalized for sale. For custom software, there are factory acceptance tests (FAT, typically most demanding with customer representatives present) and site acceptance tests (SAT) to check the system in its operational environment. These testing vehicles are all included in the normal development investment.

The responsibilities of a development organization continue throughout the software's life cycle, that is, as long as the software is used and supported. The next stages of the value chain, provisioning and operation, require customer support from the software supplier. The supplier must assist in the configuration, installation, and testing of the software in the end-user environment, respond to inquiries, and assist in overcoming problems that arise in the operational phase. As part of this, the software supplier has an ongoing maintenance role, a function closely tied to customer support and feedback.

A *software release* is a collection of software code that is ready for deployment and installation on customers' hosts. A release follows a cycle of development and testing, and requires a number of coordinated actions, such as training of customer support personnel, priming appropriate distribution channels, and (in some cases) a marketing campaign. There are distinct types of releases, depending on the reasons for releasing the new code to customers, which illustrate logistical and business issues software suppliers face (see table 5.2).

The term *version* is used somewhat differently in software engineering and economics. In the parlance of economics, different versions are offered for sale simultaneously, offering different cost/capability points for a buyer to choose (see chapter 9). In software, only a single version is offered for sale at any time (although older versions may continue to be supported). Thus, a variant in table 5.2 is called a version in economics. The software industry commonly uses a numbering scheme of the form Version x.y.z, where x.y. identifies the version (major and minor revision) and z the service release.[1] Patches may be identified by more complicated numbering extensions.

Release types differ in terms of some important characteristics (see table 5.3). As defects in the software are reported during both provisioning and operation, repairs are undertaken and revised code is distributed to all the operators in subsequent service releases. These support and service functions are a cost to the supplier, which may be recovered through explicit support and maintenance contracts, or considered a normal cost of business recovered in licensing the software. These functions may be motivated by the desire for general customer satisfaction and repeat business, or laid out in specific warranty terms and conditions, or both.

As discussed in section 3.2.2, a typical application serves users with differing and changing requirements, so new versions to match changing requirements are necessary as long as there is a viable user base. Although software does not wear out like material goods, without upgrade it does inevitably deteriorate over time in the sense that changing user requirements and changes to complementary products render it less suitable. A new version entails some risks: it may prompt discontinued support for older data representations (alienating some customers), or suddenly fail to interoperate with complementary software or require new training. Operators are

Table 5.2
Generic Types of Software Releases

Type	Description	Purpose
Patch	Replacement code that repairs a defect or shortcoming, usually in a small portion of the deployed code.	The supplier wants to correct defects that may affect the stability or security of the software as quickly as practical.
Service	A cohesive, synchronized release of a whole collection of patches, many of which were never made available separately.	The supplier not only wants to correct defects but also to ensure that all customers have deployed the same set of patches, simplifying customer service. This is also an opportunity to deploy patches that interact with one another. Often, patches require prior installation of the most recent service release.
Version	A replacement of all or most of the code embodying new features and capabilities or removing or modifying undesirable characteristics of the previous version.	The latest version release (incorporating also the most recent service release) is sold to new customers. Charging existing customers for a new version release (usually voluntarily and at a price discounted relative to new sales) as well as new sales provides a revenue stream to pay for the ongoing development cost of keeping the software competitive.
Variant	A variation on the same software differing in features or capabilities that is offered to the customer as an alternative.	Offering variant releases that differ in features or capabilities is one basis for price discrimination, allowing customers to self-select the price they are willing to pay. Thus, all variants are offered for sale at the same time.

cautious where these are possibilities, and for this reason they are normally granted discretion as to whether or when to adopt a new version, which necessitates continuing customer support for at least one older version. In some business models for selling software, a primary source of ongoing revenue to support a development organization is from the sale of maintenance contracts or of new versions to existing customers. These business relationships and pricing issues are discussed further in chapters 6 and 9.

An important issue for software suppliers is how long to officially support older versions no longer being sold. Since adopting a new version is optional for the customer (without specific contractual terms to the contrary), different customers may operate and use different versions at the same time. The unseemliness of abandoning support and maintenance of older versions has to be balanced against the added maintenance and support costs. Suppliers have various ways to encourage customers to move to (and pay for) the latest version, including terminating support and maintenance of older versions (perhaps a couple of generations older). Another incentive to upgrade is maintaining compatibility with complementary software assets or compatibility across user communities.

Example When users who are making independent version decisions need to share files, or interoperate with the same application or other users across the network, or compose the software with other software (e.g., the composition of application with infrastructure), the issue of incompatible versions arises. Software suppliers usually attempt to maintain some level of compatibility across different versions, often with some loss of functionality (e.g., features in the newest version) and some loss of usability (e.g., forcing users to perform explicit conversions). Eventually abandoning this interversion compatibility can help to straighten out functionality and usability and is another way that suppliers can provide incentives for users to upgrade. Shapiro and Varian (1999b) discuss strategies surrounding this at some length.

5.1.3 Provisioning

Before software can be used, a number of steps must be taken to acquire the necessary infrastructure equipment and software, and install, integrate, and test it. The value added at the provisioning stage includes capabilities arising from emergence in integration (see section 4.3.5), the expectation that the application will meet performance, availability, and security goals during operation, and that the application can be smoothly administered.

The first step in provisioning is planning and designing the facilities and the software configuration. At this step, both the characteristics of the equipment and software and the end-user needs must be taken into account. In planning, several issues must be addressed in depth:

• *Performance.* What use patterns are expected? The ultimate performance depends on both the software itself and on the configuration and sizing of the processing, storage, and communication facilities. Performance must be addressed at both the development and provisioning stages. Developers focus on ensuring a range of performance through the appropriate sizing of facilities (scalability). At the provisioning stage, the focus is on minimizing the facilities and costs needed to meet end-user requirements within the range anticipated by the developers. A maximum credible user and usage base must be established, and a plan must be in place to incrementally add facilities as use increases.

Table 5.3
Characteristics Ascribed to Different Types of Releases

Characteristic	Possibilities	Considerations
Coverage	A release may replace a single module (typical of a patch), many or most modules (typical of a version), or everything.	Replacing more modules is an opportunity to make changes that affect the interaction among modules but also increases development and testing.
Frequency	Typically patches are made available daily or weekly, service releases every few months, and versions every couple of years.	The primary consideration in patches is making crucial changes, for example, correcting a security flaw that may be exploited by crackers. Other releases involve considerable development effort and testing and thus take time. Operators are encouraged to install patches and service releases as soon as they are available, whereas installation of a version release is optional.
Architecture	A release may change the modularity or simply replace existing modules.	A change in modularity has widespread consequences, so is typically undertaken only in a major version release and only for compelling reasons (for example, major new features).
Features	A release may add new features and capabilities, simply correct defects, or make existing features work more smoothly.	Changes from a user perspective are generally avoided in patches and service releases because user training and experience is disrupted and there is no revenue to compensate for development costs. Version releases are sold primarily on the basis of user value derived from new features and capabilities or improvements to existing ones.
Installation	A release may involve an upgrade or overlay (replacing portions of the installed code), or it may be clean (removing the existing installation and starting from scratch).	Patches and service releases do not replace all the code and thus are installed as an overlay. This removes a source of piracy (because the release is not self-contained) and reduces download and installation time. A clean installation ensures that possible corruption in an existing installation will not propagate to the new installation, and is often employed for version releases. Existing user configuration options can still be preserved if they are kept separate.

Table 5.3 (continued)

Characteristic	Possibilities	Considerations
Coexistence	Different releases may or may not coexist in customer installations.	The coexistence of different releases complicates customer support. To minimize this, the first step in problem solving is typically to install the latest service release and all subsequent patches. The supplier may terminate support of older versions, reducing costs and providing incentives to customers to adopt the latest version. Variants are explicitly designed to coexist in different customer installations, and the resulting support costs must be balanced against added revenue.

• *Availability*.   Objectives must be established for the availability of the application, which means the fraction of time it is operational and ready to be used. Nonoperational time, often called *downtime*, can be due to software defects or equipment failure, or to administrative procedures that require bringing the application to a halt (like maintenance or installation of patches or upgrades). Detailed characteristics of downtime, such as when it occurs, its frequency, and its duration, are important. Like performance, availability must be addressed at both the creation and provisioning stages. Tighter availability requirements require more extreme planning and measures like redundant equipment and software.

• *Administration*.   The provisioning stage is the time to put an operational administration plan in place. The goal is to minimize administrative burdens and costs while achieving adequate availability and support for end-users. Processes need to be defined, personnel and job requirements established, and personnel hired or reassigned.

• *Security*.   Potential security threats must be identified and characterized insofar as possible (see section 5.3.1). Procedures, processes, and policies must be designed for preventing or dealing with these threats as they become reality. The types of operational vigilance necessary to identify unanticipated threats also have to be established, as do plans for dealing with these in a timely fashion.

• *Privacy*.   Privacy policies for an application must be designed, and procedures and processes planned for enforcement of those policies (see section 5.3.2).

All these elements must be addressed in both development and provisioning. Typically, developers try to anticipate general end-user needs while allowing flexibility to meet the specific needs of a particular user in the provisioning phase. Thus, developers emphasize meeting the range of needs across different user groups, whereas provisioners focus on the needs of a specific user group. The developers want to provide sufficient configurability so that the provisioners can adjust to specific requirements while minimizing capital and recurring costs. In provisioning, concrete decisions must be made, usually involving trade-offs between cost and performance, availability, and support, and between security and usability, and so forth.

Provisioners must make concrete decisions on equipment, software vendors, and versioning options. Often the marketplace offers opportunities to mix and match different vendors and options. Considerations include not only the features, performance, and cost of the options but also their composability. The latter is a particularly difficult issue that rests on the credibility of suppliers' representations and evaluation of their support services and on the willingness of different suppliers to work together to resolve interoperability problems that arise. The greatest comfort is achieved when concrete demonstrations of composability can be identified, either in the laboratory or (most credibly) in similar customer environments. Typically, suppliers identify existing or previous satisfied customers as references that can be contacted and questioned as to their experience and outcomes.

Once planning is complete, the necessary equipment and software must be procured, installed, integrated, and tested. The integration of equipment and software procured from different vendors is the most difficult phase, not too different from module integration in development that sometimes requires maintenance actions on the part of suppliers as problems arise. The installation and testing of the resulting equipment and software usually have acceptance criteria based on functionality, performance, and composability criteria, and those criteria may be specified in procurement contracts.

Departmental and enterprise applications require coordinated redesign of organization and business processes to match the assumptions of application creators. Configuration options provide some flexibility but certainly never complete flexibility to address these issues independently. If an end-user organization is dogmatic about how it wants to organize itself, it may have to develop all or part of the application itself in accordance with local requirements. There are two schools of thought on this. One says that acquiring an application and its associated business processes is a way to spread best practice and avoid the time and expense of designing processes from scratch. The other says that internal development minimizes the disruption of process and organizational changes, and that customization allows differentiation and competitive advantage. The best answer depends on the objectives and constraints of the specific context.

Detailed transition planning is also required. How will the transition from the old processes and organization to the new processes and organization be managed? When and how will users be trained to use the new application? If problems or flaws arise, how will the organization retrench to the old system, or what backup procedures are in place?

It is common for an end-user firm to engage the services of outside firms— consultants and system integrators—in the procurement stage (see chapter 6). Consultants bring direct experience with the configuration and process issues for similar applications in other end-user organizations, and system integrators bring knowledge of equipment and software options, experience in integration (which has some commonality with development), and an ongoing working relationship with suppliers.

The provisioning stage does not end when an application becomes operational. As use grows or use patterns change, commensurate reconfiguration, and equipment and software upgrades, must be planned and executed. This phase of provisioning overlapping operations is called *systems management*.

5.1.4   Operation

The daily operation of most software systems requires human attention. For example, with organizational and personnel changes, authorization levels need to be adjusted. Security is another issue that requires vigilant attention: security breaches must be identified, and patches fixing security holes or flaws must be installed. Together, these functions are called *system administration*. System administration and systems management together strongly influence how well an application meets user and organizational needs.

One major administrative responsibility is the installation of new software releases (see table 5.2): Who must install them and ensure compatibility with complementary software and user training? To ease the burden somewhat, the installation of releases is increasingly automated.

In the operation phase, user support (commonly called a *helpdesk*) assists users with difficulties they may encounter and sometimes identifies defects in the software or its configuration, which are reported to system administrators and perhaps to software suppliers. The operational organization is thus typically split into two groups: one focused on end-users and one focused on the technology and suppliers. The skills and orientations of these groups are distinct, mirroring a similar division in software development (see section 4.2).

5.2 Total Cost of Ownership

An important consideration to managers is the *total cost of ownership* (TCO) (Ellram 1994; Ellram and Siferd 1998), including provisioning and operation, facilities and personnel. In addition, TCO may include costs for an application wholly or partly developed and maintained internally. Where users perform administrative functions (like administering their own desktop computers) or provide training or help to other users, the imputed costs of these responsibilities should be included.

It is difficult to estimate TCO accurately because so many roles are included, some intangible. For facilities, the TCO includes the cost of equipment and services (like network access), consumables, maintenance contracts and repair costs, service fees, and electricity (Griffith 1998). Personnel costs include technical support and administration, user support and administration, systems management, and training and retooling (Emigh 1999).

As software applications become more widely embedded in organizations, the TCO is an increasing portion of a typical organization's budget. Estimating and minimizing the TCO has become a significant issue to managers and to suppliers sensitive to these concerns. The quest to lower the TCO has resulted in pressure on vendors to provide streamlined and automated administration and management of applications and infrastructure as well as improved usability with simplified training and helpdesk requirements (Petreley 1999).

The observation that the administration of desktop computers is costly has resulted in a trend toward greater centralization of administrative and management functions. This can be accomplished in two complementary ways: partitioning more processing and storage functions on the servers, and introducing tools that centralize the distributed administrative functions. In a sense, this harks back to the days of centralized mainframes, albeit with considerable enhancements. One enhancement is the graphical user interface of desktop computers, even where many functions are partitioned to the server. Another is that today's server software is more likely to be off-the-shelf rather than internally developed, providing greater application diversity and user choice. The application service provider model enhances this further (see chapter 6). Neither have mainframes disappeared, particularly as repositories of mission-critical information assets.

An extreme case is *thin clients*, where the desktop computer executes no application-specific code except that which can be dynamically loaded as mobile code (see section 4.4). An alternative is *rich clients* (rich in local customizability and functionality) supported by improved centralized administration and management tools. Most organizations deploy a mixture of thin and rich clients, reflecting the varying job profiles supported by the clients.

Clearly, we have a long way to go in minimizing TCO. Because of Moore's law and the increasing complexity of software, personnel costs are growing in relation to facilities cost and the cost of software acquisition. Thus, increasing effort will be devoted to reducing personnel costs, even at the expense of increased facilities or software costs. Tools that support distributed management and administration are a major opportunity for the software industry, emphasizing again that operators as well as users are important customers.

5.3   Social Issues in Software Management

Software applications often have a social context. The features a software supplier includes in an application or infrastructure software often has implications for people other than its own customers. Conversely, others' actions may affect an application and its users. This is an economic externality, in that the actions of others can profoundly influence the operators and users of an application, often without compensatory payments. Two specific issues in this category are security and privacy, and both raise significant management challenges. In section 5.4, a security example is used to illustrate some management challenges in distributed applications.

5.3.1   Security

Ensuring good security—preventing cracking if possible, and cleaning up in its wake when it does occur—is a major function in operation (see section 3.2.8). Crackers can operate inside or outside an organization, but the problem has certainly become more acute with the connection of most computer systems to the public Internet, opening them up to attack from anywhere in the world. While security may focus on crackers coming from the Internet, it is important to realize that attacks may originate within an organization as well. Outside contractors or even employees of good standing have an opportunity to access, destroy, or change unauthorized information.

Security technologies, operational vigilance and measures, and laws and law enforcement all work in concert as essential components of an overall security system (see figure 5.2). The party most directly affected by security lapses is the user, but the user is largely dependent on the other three players—software suppliers, operators of the application and infrastructure, and law enforcement—to prevent

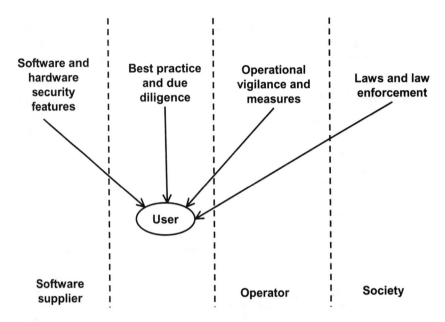

Figure 5.2
Dependence of the user on other players in an overall security system.

and contain losses. Users have responsibility also, for example, in maintaining the secrecy of passwords.[2] Security requires a systems approach, and its effectiveness tends to be only as strong as its weakest link. Often that weakest link is the user: even with training, it cannot be assumed that individual users will always take proper care. Thus, the management of the end-user organization, not just the software creators and operators, must be sensitive to and act upon these concerns (Keliher 1980).

Some cracking activities depend on security defects in application or infrastructure software. Software offering tighter security provides greater value but also increases development costs and typically reduces usability.

Example   Many large organizations manage mission-critical information, such as customer and employee lists, inventory, and orders using a database management system (DBMS). Major vendors include IBM, Informix, Microsoft, Oracle, and Sybase. The DBMS is a software infrastructure that provides structured storing and retrieval of information. Because many users are sensitive to the opportunities for theft and vandalism of this crucial information, commercial vendors compete partly on the security features. For example, a DBMS can capture authorization lists of

Table 5.4
Four Major Threats to Information as It Crosses a Network

Threat	Description	Example
Interruption	The delivery of information is prevented.	An employee precludes his manager from submitting a poor performance evaluation.
Interception	An unauthorized party views the information.	An employee improperly views the performance evaluation of another employee as a manager submits it.
Modification	The information is modified before it reaches the recipient.	An employee modifies her performance evaluation to remove unfavorable comments before it is submitted.
Fabrication	False information is created by an unauthorized source.	An employee submits a false (and presumably positive) performance evaluation, pretending it came from his manager.

Source: Stawlings (1999).

who may access or modify which information and enforce access policies based on these lists.

Many security issues arise in all aspects of an application.

Example   It is common for information to be communicated across a network, sometimes among applications, and in that context there are at least four major security threats (see table 5.4).

The composition of applications raises security issues as well. This makes improved security a natural aim of infrastructure software developers and equipment manufacturers as well as application software creators.

Example   A *firewall* is specialized equipment[3] installed on all connections between a protected enclave (like a company's internal network) and the public network, and it protects applications within the enclave or operating through the firewall from certain attacks. The virtual private network (VPN) is offered by some networking service providers, or it can be provisioned by an end-user organization using software added at the network boundaries (usually within firewalls) that provides secure transfer of information between sites. When provisioned as a service, it often includes other features like guaranteed performance characteristics.

Where cracking depends on a security defect or weakness in software, the larger the market share for that software, the greater the collective vulnerability. Thus, greater diversity in deployed software can improve security. On the other hand, widely used software may economically justify more maintenance and testing resources and receive more attention from benign hacking activities, reducing its vulnerability.

Organizations systematize and control security by defining *security policies*, which define what actions should and should not be allowed.

Example Access control illustrates policy-driven security. For some protected resource like a database or a protected enclave, access control establishes a list of user identities and associates with each individual attributes of access, such as no access, full access, access to examine and not change, and so forth. Alternatively, access control may be based on roles (manager, administrator, clerk) rather than on user identities. Security mechanisms built into the software enforce these policies (see section 5.4).

Policies are difficult to establish and enforce because they attempt to distinguish between legitimate actions by users and illegitimate actions by others, something that is often not easy to distinguish (for people, let alone software) by observing impersonal actions over the Internet. We say impersonal because Internet actions lack physical proximity, which would provide many clues to legitimacy or intent beyond simply observing actions.

Returning to figure 5.2, how do different parties interact to provide security, and what incentives encourage them to contribute to overall security in a cost-effective way? From an economics perspective, the private costs (penalties or liabilities) of security lapses should accrue to those in a position to prevent them and approximate the social costs. Accomplishing this, voluntary actions tend to efficiently balance threats against the costs of measures to counter those threats. Both software suppliers and operators are in a similar position vis-à-vis the user. Their actions can mitigate security threats, but they are less likely to directly suffer a loss, and they are motivated primarily by user desire for security and willingness to pay for that security. As a rule, security policies should be defined by the user or end-user organization and, to the extent possible, enforced by the software and hardware. There is a trade-off between what can be accomplished by operational vigilance or by software and hardware means, but generally the latter is more cost-effective because it avoids recurring labor costs.

Thus, a software supplier will view security protections as important but also offer configurability options that allow the user to adjust security policies to local needs. Technological mechanisms to support security policies can range from simple declarations or warnings at entry points to total physical containment and separation. The ability of software by itself to enforce security policies is limited; stronger security measures can be achieved in the hardware as well as by separation of physical location.

Example   A cracker who gains access to a user account on a computer is in a much stronger position to cause harm than one who relies on access to applications (such as a Web server) running on that computer over the network. A cracker who has physical access to a computer is in an especially strong position. For example, he may be able to reboot the computer from an operating system on a removable medium and gain complete control.

As shown in figure 5.2, laws and law enforcement play a role, particularly in dealing with serious breaches of security policies. Laws and associated sanctions are appropriate for situations where direct harm is inflicted on the user, such as information stolen for commercial gain or vandalism that causes economic loss, where the user has taken reasonable precautions to prevent such loss. It is arguably not society's responsibility to compensate software suppliers and users for the cost of security measures—this is the price of joining an open society like the Internet—but it can help in several other ways. First, legal remedies help deter crackers, thereby reducing the scale of the problem and preventing it from inflicting great harm on society as a whole. Second, one role of society generally is to step in when one person harms another. Third, society might compensate victims for their losses, although this creates a moral hazard because economic incentives to invoke appropriate security measures or demand them from suppliers and operators are removed. An alternative approach is insurance. Although still creating a moral hazard by diluting incentives, the insurance underwriting process adjusts premiums in accordance with the credibility of the security measures taken.

There is also a trade-off between technology and laws in enforcing security. At one extreme, Draconian security policies may be able to reduce the role of laws and the importance of law enforcement but may unduly harm usability. At the other extreme, relying heavily on laws can encourage lax technological security and is not advisable, given the high costs and uncertainty of law enforcement. Further, law and law enforcement are relatively ineffective when tackling a global threat, because of jurisdictional issues, and cracking over the Internet is truly a global issue. International agreements and collaborative enforcement help but are even more costly and less certain.

Example   The 1986 Computer Fraud and Abuse Act makes unauthorized access and theft of data or services from financial institution computers, federal government computers, or computers used in interstate commerce a crime (Marsh

1987). To prosecute offenders, their actions must be documented, and thus companies must maintain complete audit trails of both authorized and unauthorized data accesses. This is an illustration of how the software application and laws must work in concert to facilitate law enforcement and appropriate remedies.

Specific capabilities that are available in software to enhance security are described in the next section, and law enforcement challenges are discussed further in chapter 8.

5.3.2 Privacy

Privacy is another example of a social issue that raises significant management issues (see section 3.2.9). As a user invokes the features of an application, there is an opportunity for the operator of that application to capture user *profile information* (see figure 5.3). That profile can include personal information directly provided by the user as well as other information inferred from the user's actions.

Example   The discussion forums a user visits, as well as the messages the user reads and posts, could suggest hobbies, interests, or political views. The Yellow Pages

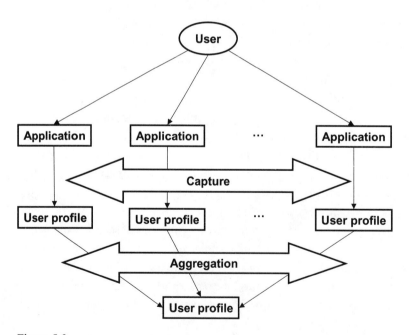

Figure 5.3
Operators can capture user profiles and potentially aggregate that information over multiple applications.

entries and maps and driving directions accessed by a user could suggest her physical locality over time. The products viewed in an e-commerce catalog could suggest products the user may be susceptible to buying.

Customization based on personal profile information can make applications more usable and valuable to the user. However, this depends heavily on what information is collected, how it is used, and whether it is disseminated to third parties. Particularly disturbing to privacy advocates is the ability to trace and correlate multiple activities. This can occur in at least a couple of ways. First, the user profile for a user's visit to one application can be aggregated over multiple visits to that application. Second, the user profile can potentially be aggregated over multiple applications (see figure 5.3). Over time, there is the potential to learn a lot about an individual's activities, perhaps more than she has perceived or would assent to.

Example   If an individual's accesses to automatic teller and vending machines can be traced and captured, information can be gathered about location and activities. The more of those traces that can be aggregated, the more comprehensive the picture. Similarly, aggregated traces of an individual's activity across multiple e-commerce sites are more comprehensive and revealing than a single trace. Already there are specialized firms (such as DoubleClick) that offer such aggregation services, usually in the context of targeted Web advertising.

These examples illustrate that, as with security, the popularity of the Internet raises new privacy issues and makes privacy a more serious issue for software suppliers, operators, service providers, application providers, and users. There are several legitimate tensions in privacy rights. Many users demand a right to privacy but also derive legitimate benefits from sharing information with applications. Application providers have the potential to derive significant revenues from utilizing user profiles to aim advertising at certain consumers or to sell that information. Government has a need to gather personal information in law enforcement investigations and in national security (see chapter 8).

Given the importance of these issues, it is useful to see how software applications and infrastructure might enable invasions of privacy or prevent or defeat them. Two elements of an application determine the level of privacy: *anonymity* and *control*.

The best way to ensure complete privacy is to ensure the anonymity of the user. In this regard, there are two forms of identity. *Personal identity* includes information associated with an individual, such as name, address, e-mail address, or credit card number. *Anonymous identity* uniquely distinguishes one individual from all other individuals but doesn't reveal personal identity.

Example   When visiting a delicatessen, a customer may be asked to "take a number." This number uniquely identifies that individual among all customers in the deli (in order to serve customers in order of arrival) but in and of itself offers no hint of personal identity.

In this context, there are three levels of anonymity:

• *Complete anonymity.*   No identity information (personal or anonymous) is available to applications or service providers. There is no feasible way to capture traces of user activity over time or across applications.

• *Anonymous identification.*   While no personal identity information is available, it can be inferred when the same user revisits an application or provider (using an anonymous identifier, as in the deli example). Traces can be captured of a single user's activity, but those traces cannot be matched to personal identity.

• *Personal identification.*   Applications or providers are aware of at least some personal identity information. Often, even with incomplete information, it is possible to correlate across distinctive sets of personal information if there is some commonality (e.g., an e-mail address).

There are also intermediate cases.

Example   Anonymous identification of a network access point or a computer used to access an application is common, for example, the network address used for access. This may approximate the anonymous identification of a user over relatively short periods of time, when the user is at a single computer and network access point, but not over longer times if the user switches computers or network access points (this is called nomadic access; see chapter 10). In addition, multiple users sharing a single computer will be identified erroneously as a single user. This form of anonymous identification would be more complete and accurate for mobile terminals like personal digital assistants (PDAs) or cell phones, which are less commonly shared.

Anonymous identification is relatively benign and offers many possibilities to application and information providers, for example, in collecting anonymous but comprehensive statistical profiles of customers so as to better position products or services. The direct benefit to users is more questionable, although in many cases they may not mind anonymous identification provided they are certain it is not associated with personal identification. On the other hand, in many situations anonymity is not the right answer.

Example   It is necessary to identify buyers and sellers in an e-commerce application in order to enforce the terms and conditions of a sale and for fulfillment (shipping the goods or providing the service). A user may appreciate a Web site that automatically personalizes its screen (this requires at least anonymous identification) or sends e-mail notifications (this requires personal information, e.g., e-mail address). In practice, most Web sites demand personal information (which can be fabricated by the user) for personalization because this is in their business interest.

Privacy rights and policies allow the user some control over the types of personal information collected and to whom that information can be disseminated. Or, at minimum, they require disclosure of collection and dissemination, so that the user can make an informed choice to use the application or not.

What does software technology offer in the way of privacy protection? It can enable some control over what information is shared with an application provider in the first place. Once personal information is shared, however, software cannot unilaterally determine whether and how information is further disseminated, because in the process of legitimate collection and use of personal information it is inherently revealed. If the application provider chooses to restrict further dissemination (because of self-imposed policies or legal requirements) certain security technologies can help (see section 5.4). In fact, this is no different from any other situation when confidential information is to be protected from disclosure. A similar issue arises in rights management (see chapter 8): to legitimately use information is to disclose it, rendering most direct technological limitations ineffective.

What does technology offer in relation to anonymous or personal identity? Some technologies offer full anonymity if that is what the user desires. Whether these technologies are reliable or can be defeated depends on the strength of the security and the integrity of a service provider.

Example   An anonymous remailer is a service that accepts e-mail messages, strips off all identity information, and forwards those messages to their intended destination. By keeping track of identity for each message, the remailer can support replies to the anonymous sender. However, the preservation of anonymity depends on the integrity of the remailer and the effectiveness of security measures. The sender is not anonymous to the remailer and must trust the remailer to preserve anonymity. Laws that force the retention and disclosure of personal information by the remailer may intervene in some circumstances.

Anonymous identity can be insidious because it has the potential to allow violations of privacy without the user's knowledge or permission, since the user has not provided explicit information. Later, if the user does reveal personal information, this can potentially be coupled with all the information collected under the anonymous identity. Some technology companies have been blindsided by being oblivious to privacy issues connected with anonymous identity. Fortunately, there is a growing awareness of these issues, and they are increasingly being addressed in advance by software and hardware suppliers.

Example   In 1999, Intel proposed to add a unique serial number to each of its Pentium microprocessor chips, not in the time-honored way of stamping it on the outside but embedded electronically, so that applications could potentially access this serial number and anonymously identify a computer participating in an application. Intel relented when privacy advocates pointed to the potential for abuse (Markoff 1999a). Yet, telephone companies have long retained unique personal identity information for each telephone and have collected detailed records of telephone calls. A U.S. law even mandates that cell phones must capture accurate location information by 2002 so that emergency services can be dispatched more reliably and expeditiously (Romero 2001). Not all users may be aware when anonymous identity information is collected and disseminated. A significant difference between these cases is that telephone companies are subject to specific legal restrictions on revealing information.

Technology can help limit the ability of applications to correlate users' activities across multiple visits or applications. The key issue is what personal identity information is disclosed to operators or service providers by an application.

Example   Each time a credit card is used for a purchase in the physical world, the merchant obtains personal identity information (e.g., the person is physically present and could be photographed by a security camera). This isn't necessary if a user provides a credit card number to a merchant on an e-commerce site, because it is the merchant's bank, not the merchant, that needs this personal information (the credit and number) to secure payment, and the merchant bank doesn't need to know anything about what was purchased other than payment information. A standard for Secure Electronic Transactions (SET) promulgated by credit card companies provides this enhanced privacy by allowing merchants to authorize a sales transaction without access to the credit card number, and passes no information about the transaction other than payment to the merchant bank. The credit card number is hidden from the merchant using encryption technologies (see section 5.4).

Example   The World Wide Web Consortium's P3P standard (Platform for Privacy Preferences) allows software and services to explicitly support a user's privacy preferences. Version 6 of Microsoft's Internet Explorer added several features based on P3P that help users understand and control the privacy implications of their browsing. One feature allows selective blocking of cookies from third-party sites; this information is typically deposited by aggregating advertising firms. Another feature

Table 5.5
Issues to be Addressed in Privacy Policies

Issue	Description
Disclosure	Does the application abide by a comprehensive privacy policy, and is that policy disclosed to the user?
Anonymity	Is the personal identity of the user known or included in the user profile?
Control	Is the user allowed some degree of control over attributes of the policy, what information is collected, and how it is used?
Default	If there are user-selected options, what are the defaults if the user makes no explicit choice? Extreme cases are "opt in," where no information is collected unless the user explicitly so chooses, or "opt out," where all information is collected unless the user explicitly says no.
Ownership	Who owns and exercises control over information that is captured?
Sharing	With whom is a user's personal information shared, and how may they disseminate it further? What happens if a company merges or is acquired?
Persistence	Over what period of time is personal information captured, and how long is it retained?

reveals the privacy policies of visited Web sites, and users can configure the browser to make decisions based on the absence or presence of a standard policy document.[4]

Personal identity information is the most complicated case because there are many options on how trace information as well as personal information might be captured and aggregated. As with security, the technological, operational, and legal responses to privacy concerns require the establishment and enforcement of privacy policies on the collection and dissemination of personal information. Some issues that such a privacy policy should address are listed in table 5.5. Another issue is whether users must rely on voluntary compliance with privacy policies, or whether there are legal constraints (see chapter 8).

In summary, ensuring appropriate levels of privacy requires a combination of policies, security technologies, operations, law enforcement, and legal remedies. The essence of achieving privacy is offering the user control over what kind of information is gathered and how it is disseminated, and providing technological and nontechnological means to enforce privacy policies (see section 5.4).

5.4 Security as a Distributed Management Example

The discussion in section 5.1 presumed that an application exists in a monolithic administrative domain with control over an application-global scope. Increasingly prominent are *distributed management* applications whose scope can include multiple autonomous organizations with an arms-length relationship as well as individual networked users.

Example E-commerce displays a rich set of distributed management applications. An example is supply chain management, in which suppliers and customers (autonomous companies) coordinate production and inventories, schedule shipments, and make payments through a distributed application. E-commerce also enables individual consumers to participate in a distributed application to purchase goods and services from online merchants.

Such distributed management applications are also distributed software systems, and hence all the issues discussed in section 4.5 arise. Distributed management, however, introduces many new challenges arising from the lack of centralized control, administration, and authority.

Example The public telephone network is a distributed management sociotechnical system. It is global in extent and spans virtually all national boundaries. It is also jointly owned and operated by a number of private and government-owned telephone companies. These companies cooperate to support phone calls between any two citizens, to ensure adequate quality, and to collect revenue and distribute it to the participating companies. Although this is challenging enough, some aspects of this example make it less challenging than many distributed management software applications. Telephone companies exist for the primary purpose of operating this network and selling a single telephone service, whereas a distributed software application is often operated by heterogeneous firms whose primary businesses have little to do with software. The interaction of individuals with distributed management applications is often complicated and intricate compared to a telephone (number dialing and talking).

As this example illustrates, the challenges of distributed management are not unique to distributed networked applications. Society has established many mechanisms and processes directly applicable to distributed management. These include a wealth of experience and best practices, an existing infrastructure for commercial transactions (e.g., insurance, escrow services, funds transfer), and an extensive legal infrastructure (laws, courts, law enforcement). Thus, the challenge for the software industry is at least threefold:

• The technology must support and complement existing mechanisms and processes that organizations use to coordinate and manage distributed decision making and responsibility, accommodating heterogeneity in the management styles and processes of participating organizations.

• The technology should accommodate different styles and practices in the administration within a common distributed application. In particular, the management tools mentioned in section 5.2 must work adequately in an environment of distributed decision making and responsibility.

• The technology should allow different organizations some autonomy in their software acquisitions—including choosing different vendors for infrastructure and application software—and still allow them to participate jointly in applications (see chapter 7).

The challenges inherent in distributed management are diverse and extensive, so we use security (see section 5.3.1) to illustrate some representative challenges (Anderson 2001). Security serves as a good illustration because it brings in both technical and organizational issues and demonstrates their interdependence, and it is strongly affected by distributed management. Some specific security technologies described here also point to the potential and limitations of technological remedies for social issues like privacy (see section 5.3.2) and intellectual property rights management (see chapter 8).

The general participants in a security system and their roles were described in section 5.3.1, where it was emphasized that security technologies are only one pillar of a sociotechnical system that also incorporates individuals (both users and administrators) and end-user organizations. Technology cannot be fully effective by itself—the human element of the sociotechnical security system is critically important as well. A discussion of some specific security issues follows. Afterwards, we return to reflect on the general challenges facing distributed management applications.

5.4.1 The Security Challenge

A distributed management security system must address at least two challenges. The first is preventing deliberate attacks from crackers (who usually aren't legitimate users of the application). The second is determining a framework to manage the activities of legitimate users. The latter is actually more difficult because legitimate users have *conditional* rights, rather than *no* rights, within the application context. Security must deal with many nuances, such as a user who resides in one management domain and has limited (rather than no) rights within another.

What distinguishes a potential cracker from a legitimate user? Among the legitimate users, what distinguishes their different roles (such as administrator, user, customer, and supplier), and how do those roles lend them distinct privileges within the application?

Example A firm using a consumer e-commerce application allows all network citizens to examine the merchandise catalogs (it wants to advertise goods for sale very broadly) but allows only those who present valid credentials (like a verifiable credit card number) to submit a purchase order (because it wants to be paid for goods shipped). It trusts only its own workers to change prices in the catalog (because otherwise users could lower the prices before submitting a purchase order); in fact, it trusts only *authorized* workers to do so (others may have no understanding of its pricing policies).

Again, these issues are not unique to software. The challenge is to realize mechanisms in distributed applications similar to those in the physical world.

Example A bank branch is established specifically to allow bank customers access to their money and various other banking services. However, the customers must deal with the bank only through tellers at the window; access to the vaults where the money is stored is prohibited. Similarly, access to the vaults is restricted only to employees who need access to meet a legitimate job function. Meticulous audits of vault access are kept in case any question arises.

These examples illustrate that privileges are typically not ascribed to all individuals or to organizations as a whole, but rather are tied to specific actions or information in relation to specific roles in the organization. A general principle is to restrict users' privileges to actions and information legitimately ascribed to their roles.

Thus, the security framework focuses on three concerns: need, trust, and privileges. Each user is prescribed privileges, and the security system must prohibit access to anyone not explicitly possessing those privileges. Privileges are based on the following concerns: What does a particular user need to do, or what information does he need to see, as part of his prescribed role? If we want to expand privileges beyond explicitly anticipated needs (for example, to encourage individual initiative or enable response to an emergency), what level of trust are we willing to place in a user? Usually, trust of individuals comes in gradations, not extremes (an exception is a cracker, in whom we place no trust). Privileges are usually not generalized but pertain to specific actions or information.

At the level of technology, privileges are translated into *access*. Based on the privileges assigned to an individual and referenced to a specific action or content, restrictions are placed on his access to actions and information. Access itself is nuanced: in the case of information, it may be divided into access to see, or access to see and to change, or access to replicate and distribute, and so on.

5.4.2 Access Control: Enforcing Privileges

A key element of security in a distributed application is enforcing access policies, which is the role of *access control*. The scope, specifics, and configurability of available access policies are determined during application development, and the enforcement of those policies is implemented by access control mechanisms within an application, within the infrastructure, or both. The specific access restrictions placed on an individual user can be configured (within the policy limits afforded by the developers) by a system administrator (who is given the privilege of controlling access policies and the responsibility to maintain security), or they may be determined dynamically by the application itself.

Example In a consumer e-commerce application, a system administrator will configure a worker's permanent access privileges to change the catalog information if that is the worker's intended role. On the other hand, the right of a consumer to submit a purchase order will be determined by the application itself, based on credit information it acquires from external bank or credit-rating agencies.

An important design issue is the granularity at which access is restricted. This issue comes up at both ends of the access: the people doing the access, and the information or application functionality being accessed. Considering first the people, access policies may be established for each individual, but more likely access will be role-based, that is, classes of individuals with similar roles are granted the same access privileges. Introducing roles leads to enhanced flexibility: an individual may play multiple roles and roles may be reassigned.

Example While she is on vacation, an employee may delegate some of her roles to a co-worker. Or to rebalance workload, a manager may reassign roles or assign more people to a demanding role. Any such change in a system directly associating individual users with access rights would be tedious: all access control lists on all relevant resources would have to be inspected and, if necessary, changed. This is costly, and opportunities for mistakes abound. In a role-based approach such complications only arise when it becomes necessary to redefine the roles themselves, not their association with access control lists or their assignment to individuals.

Regarding the information being accessed, distinct access control policies might be implemented for each elemental action or data item (fine granularity), or a common access control policy might be enforced across broad classes of actions or data (coarse granularity).

Example In the e-commerce example, the granularity may range from all sales employees' being granted the right to change all prices in the catalog (coarse granularity) to granting a particular individual the right to change prices in a particular category of merchandise (fine granularity). A customer may be granted the right to purchase any merchandise in the catalog, or only merchandise below a specific maximum price based upon his credit rating.

The form of access control policies appropriate to a particular application context would typically be established and configured during provisioning, and configuration of those policies applied to individual users would be configured (and occasionally updated) during operation.

In recognition of their importance, access control mechanisms are a standard feature of most infrastructures, although the Internet itself is a notable exception[5] that has been addressed by some add-on technologies (such as the firewall and the virtual private network; see section 5.3.1). Some major access control capabilities provided by the infrastructure are listed in table 5.6.

The ability of the infrastructure to meet the special access control (and other security) needs of individual applications is limited because by design the infrastructure can know nothing of the internal workings of an application (see chapter 7). Thus, an application typically configures generic infrastructure capabilities to its needs and may add its own access control capabilities.

The access control mechanisms of table 5.6 actually predate the rising prevalence of distributed management applications. There remains much for research and development to do to arrive at solutions that meet emerging needs.

Example   The intranet and extranet concepts do not, by themselves, restrict access to users within the protected enclave they create. This is too coarse a granularity, because of the need to maintain role-based gradations of trust within a protected enclave. Worse, firewalls do not provide sufficiently nuanced control over access for workers while traveling or at home (leading to some well-publicized security leaks) nor take sufficient account of the need to accommodate conditional access policies for business partners or customers.

5.4.3   Authentication: Establishing Identity

A fundamental issue in access control is verifying the identity of a user (or alternatively a host or an organization) across the Internet—this is called *authentication*. In the absence of the ability to authenticate reliably, access control can be circumvented by an imposter. In contrast to the physical world, authentication cannot rely on normal physical clues like sight, hearing, and smell. It is not sufficient to substitute electronic sensors for our senses, because an impostor can often defeat them,

Table 5.6
Examples of Access Control Mechanisms Enforced in the Infrastructure

Infrastructure Context	Name	Description
Operating systems	File system permissions	Each file has a set of attributes, one of which lists the permissions of specific users to read, or to read and change, that file.
Network	Intranet	Firewalls can create a protected enclave based on the topological point of connection to the network. Only users accessing the network from within that enclave can fully participate in the application. The firewall enforces security policies such as which applications can or cannot be accessed from outside the enclave. Finer-grain restrictions on how applications are used are not the province of a firewall, which may know of an application but not about it.
	Extranet	Creates a protected enclave that incorporates the public Internet. This is typically done by connecting intranets through the public Internet via secure links or by subscribing to virtual private networking (VPN) service from a networking service provider.
Database management	User access control	Permissions to read, or to read and change, individual tables in the database can be set for individual users. Finer-granularity access control within tables is also available.[a]

a. Column-based access control is usually available, and some databases support predicative access control, e.g., a user can see all records of employees with salaries below some limit. One way to achieve both is to create a "view" that only displays the allowed rows and columns and then limit access to the view, not to the underlying tables.

for example, by substituting a picture from storage for a picture captured in real time by a camera.

This challenge is not unique to networked computing—business has been conducted by mail for years. Some of the mechanisms that have been developed in the postal system, such as envelopes, permanent ink, and signatures, have direct analogies in digital security systems. Similar challenges and mechanisms arise in the physical world, such as identity badges.

Authentication of an individual, on the network or in person, can be based on something he *knows* (and only he knows, i.e., a secret), an artifact he *possesses* (and only he possesses), or something only he *is*. The third option—some physical characteristic that distinguishes one person from another—is known as *biometric authentication.*

Examples   A password or a codeword (reputedly used by spies) is a distinguishing secret. A door key or a credit card is a unique artifact possessed by one person only. A person's face or fingerprint is a unique physical characteristic. A signature in handwriting is unique because it depends on physiological characteristics and experience unique to an individual. All these are used for authentication in the physical world.

Authentication across the network can leverage similar ideas. A secret is usually a *password* chosen by the user, or a collection of random-looking bits, called a *cryptographic key*, provided to the user. (The larger the number of bits in the key, the less easily guessed it is or the more keys would have to be exhaustively tried. Keys on the order of 56 to 1,024 bits are common.)

A common artifact used for authentication is a *smartcard*, which looks much like a credit card but contains an encapsulated microprocessor and storage. One smartcard can be distinguished from all others because of a unique secret cryptographic key encapsulated within it. Thus, the smartcard is merely a variation on the secrets approach, a convenient way for a user (particularly one who needs to travel and doesn't always have a computer around) to carry a cryptographic key and use it for authentication. (Smartcards can do much more than this, of course, like store medical or financial information.) Authentication based on possession of an artifact like a smartcard is reliable only if it is not easily replicated or forged. In the case of a smartcard, this means that the unique secret it harbors must be encapsulated so that it cannot be extracted (or is at least very difficult to extract).

How would you actually exploit a secret for authentication (including a secret in a smartcard)? Your first inclination might be to check whether the entity being authenticated can produce the secret. Seems simple enough, but there is a fatal flaw in this simplistic protocol. It requires that you know the secret, in which case it isn't secret. Woops! It also requires that the secret be sent over the network, where it could be intercepted by a cracker. These are weaknesses of most password authentication protocols.[6]

A solution to this conundrum is a *challenge-response protocol*. A challenge is issued that requires the entity being authenticated to respond in a way that confirms it possesses the secret while not revealing that secret. Verification requires enough information to conclude an entity possesses the secret. For our purposes, call this the *corroboration information* for the secret (although this is not standard terminology). The secret and its corroboration information must be coordinated, that is, they must effectively originate from the same source. The secret is given to the entity that wants to be authenticated in the future, and the corroboration information is given to everybody who wants to authenticate that entity. It must not be feasible to infer the secret from its corroboration information.

The core technology that accomplishes this is *cryptography*, which consists of an *encryption* algorithm applied to an original message (the *plaintext*) based on a cryptographic key that yields a gibberish version of the message (the *ciphertext*). A coordinated *decryption* algorithm (based on another cryptographic key) can recover the original plaintext. When the encryption and decryption algorithms use identical keys, the algorithm is symmetric; otherwise, it is asymmetric (see figure 5.4).

Example   A standard challenge-response protocol can be based on the asymmetric encryption algorithm shown in figure 5.4. This workhorse uses two coordinated keys, key-1 and key-2. The algorithm and keys have the properties that (1) the plaintext cannot be recovered from the ciphertext without knowledge of key-2, and (2) key-1 and key-2 are coordinated so that the plaintext is recovered, and key-1 cannot be determined from knowledge of key-2, or vice versa. All these statements must be prefaced by the qualification "within a reasonable time using the fastest available computers."

With these properties in mind, the asymmetric encryption algorithm shown in figure 5.4 can be used in a challenge-response authentication protocol as follows. Key-1 is the secret held by the entity being authenticated, and key-2 is the corroboration information for that secret, which can be made public so that anybody can do an authentication. To authenticate that entity, you issue the following challenge: "Here is a random plaintext, and you must calculate the resulting ciphertext and return the result to me." You can verify that the entity possesses the secret key-1 by applying decryption to the returned ciphertext using key-2. If the result is the original random plaintext, authentication is successful. Note that the secret, key-1, is not revealed and cannot be determined from the corroboration information, key-2, or the encrypted ciphertext.

Important management issues arise in using a secret for authentication. How is a secret to be kept secret? There are two ways a secret could be improperly divulged. First, it can be lost or stolen. Means must be taken to prevent this (like encapsulating the secret in a smartcard). As in all areas of security, human issues loom large. Many security breaches result from deliberate actions on the part of people, like the theft of a secret by an unscrupulous employee or inadvertent revealing of a secret through carelessness. Second, the holder of a secret might deliberately divulge it for

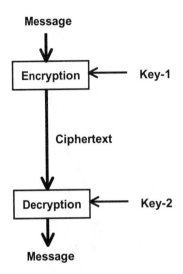

Figure 5.4
An asymmetric encryption algorithm uses two coordinated encryption keys.

economic gain or other advantage. This is unlikely in the case of secrets used for authentication, since rarely is there a motivation or incentive to deliberately empower an imposter. The situation is entirely different in other cases, like rights management (see chapter 8).

Authentication by biometric identification requires a sensor to gather the biometric information, like a fingerprint or a retinal scan. This has the inherent problem mentioned earlier, namely, biometric information can be faked, although sophisticated sensors measure dynamic information that is difficult to take. This can be overcome to some degree by using a trusted system (see section 4.4.5) to gather the biometric data. A trusted system is relied upon to enforce certain security policies, in this case gather information from a sensor (like fingerprint scanner or camera) that is encapsulated in the trusted system and transmit that over the network without modification. Biometric authentication also requires corroboration information to interpret the biometric information that is gathered.

All these means of authentication have serious obstacles to being widely adopted, among them network effects (see section 3.2.3). How do we ensure that everybody who needs to be authenticated is supplied the needed secret (or trusted system) and that everybody else is supplied corroboration information they can trust. We can appreciate these obstacles further by examining some additional issues in authentication.

5.4.4   Secrets and Credentials: the Digital Certificate

Cryptography, smartcards, and challenge-response protocols are impressive technologies, but technologies alone cannot solve the access control and authentication problem. A social system or organization must back up the technology by establishing the level of trust to be placed in each individual (or host or organization) and verifying identities for the benefit of authentication. There must be someone or something to whom we grant the authority to tell us whom to trust. Not surprisingly, this entity is called a *trusted authority*.

An immediate need for a trusted authority arises in authentication. Suppose you are to authenticate an entity using a secret and its corroboration information. Where is the corroboration information obtained? Clearly it has to come from a trusted authority, not from the entity being authenticated; otherwise, you could easily be fooled.

Example   Consider the security associated with entering a country. If Eve could manufacture her own passport, she could fool the immigration authorities by manufacturing a forged passport. That passport might associate the identity of someone else (say Alice) with Eve's picture, and Eve could then enter the country as Alice. The immigration authority accepts Alice's passport only because it is manufactured by a trusted authority (e.g., the U.S. State Department), and it trusts that this authority has taken appropriate precautions to ensure that Alice's (and not Eve's) picture appears in Alice's passport and to ensure that the passport cannot be easily modified.

Thus, authentication is fundamentally a social phenomenon arising from two or more entities (people, organizations, hosts, smartcards) participating in some application over the network with the assistance of one or more trusted authorities. The role of a trusted authority is (1) to establish to its own satisfaction the identity of and trust to be placed in some entity, (2) to provide that entity with a secret (one that the authority creates, for example, by generating a large random number) to be used to authenticate the entity in the future, and (3) to assist others in authenticating that entity by providing corroboration information for that secret.[7] The authority is legally responsible for negligence in any of these roles.

Example   In a closed administrative domain (like a corporate intranet), the system administrator may serve as a trusted authority. In a distributed management (but sensitive and closed) application like an electronic funds network or credit card verification network, the operator of the network may serve as a trusted authority. In Internet e-commerce today, a *certificate authority* is a company that specializes in serving as a trusted authority for merchants and other providers, and the acquirer bank who supplies a credit card to an individual acts as the trusted authority for that individual. Serving as a trusted authority is potentially a role for government as well, as in other contexts (driver's license, passport). For a trusted system, its manufacturer is a trusted authority.

There are several methods of distributing and utilizing secrets and using them for authentication (see figure 5.5). These different methods are appropriate in different circumstances, illustrating how technology can be molded to social needs. Specifically, the three methods shown can apply to a closed environment (e.g., a departmental application where the trusted authority is a local system administrator), to a proprietary public environment (e.g., where a set of users subscribe to an authentication service), and to an open public environment (e.g., where there is a desire for any network citizen to be authenticated, as in e-commerce).

In the closed environment it is feasible for the authority to create and distribute secrets to all entities needing to be authenticated (see figure 5.5a). In this case, the challenge-response protocol can be based on a single *shared secret*, shared between

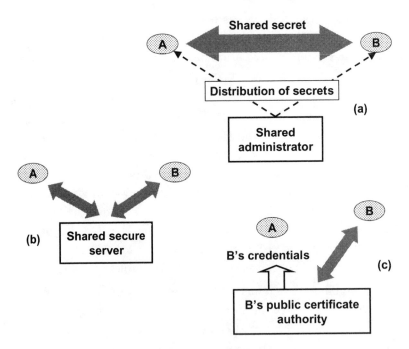

Figure 5.5
Three methods of secret distribution in security systems.

the entity being authenticated and the entity doing the authentication (the secret is its own corroboration information in this case).

Example If entity A needs to authenticate entity B, a trusted authority anticipating this need could create and distribute a single secret to be shared between entity A and entity B. The secret might be distributed by physically visiting each party rather than communicating it over the network, where it could be intercepted. Entity A can then authenticate entity B by issuing a challenge (such as "encrypt this plaintext using our shared secret" or "decrypt this ciphertext using our shared secret"), thereby avoiding sending the secret over the network.

A shared secret approach does not scale to large numbers of users because of the proliferation of secrets to distribute and manage. If there are n entities, then each entity has to store $n - 1$ secrets (one it shares with each of the other entities) and the authority has to create and distribute $n \cdot (n - 1)$ secrets total (roughly a trillion secrets for a million entities, for example). The number of secrets can be dramatically reduced by the shared secure server approach (see figure 5.5b). (This is used in a popular public domain protocol called Kerberos.) Here, a trusted authority creates a secret shared between itself and each entity (n secrets for n entities) and operates a secure server to help any two entities authenticate one another. (The server becomes a single point of security vulnerability, which is why it must be "secure.") If entity A wants to authenticate entity B, then A can first authenticate the secure server (using the secret shared between the secure server and entity A) and then ask the secure server to authenticate entity B (using the secret shared between the secure server and entity B).[8]

The shared secure server approach is not practical when the community of entities to be authenticated is very large or dynamic. An extreme case is the public Internet, where it would be desirable for any network citizen to be able to authenticate any other citizen, or at a minimum, any application or service to be able to authenticate any citizen. It is hard to believe that the entire citizenry could agree on a single trusted authority, unless such an authority were imposed (say, by some global government), and use a single trusted server to assist in every authentication. There is also the question of a business model: How does an authentication service recover its costs? On the other hand, authentication is affected by direct network effects (see section 3.2.3), which reduce the value of any fragmented solution that prevents users or applications employing one authentication service from authenticating entities employing a different service. Desirable is a solution that appears uniform to users (any entity can authenticate any other entity) but that allows distributed trusted authorities (each dealing with a local population with which it is familiar), competition among competing solutions, and the flexibility for technology and capability to advance. The first two objectives are described as *federation* of a distributed system, the idea being that the federated system appears uniform and homogeneous to the user, but without imposing centralized control or requirements. Successful federation must be based on interoperability standards (see section 4.3 and chapter 7) that allow heterogeneous technical solutions and competitive options to work in concert toward a common goal through standardized interfaces and network protocols.

It must also be recognized that authentication does not exist in isolation; it is tied to the more general issue of personal identity and privacy (see section 5.3.2). A service that not only allows users to enter identity information once and only once (rather than at every application and every site), allows users and applications to validate their mutual identity through authentication, and deals with privacy concerns by giving users control over which personal information is disclosed to applications and sites, is desirable. Services with most of these characteristics based on a secure server have been offered for some time.

Example AOL's Magic Carpet, Microsoft's Passport, and Yahoo!Wallet are services that allow individuals to provide personal identity information (including credit card information) to a secure server. Today the servers use a password provided by the user as a shared secret for authentication. The user can then access a number of partner e-commerce sites without entering the information again, and the secure server assists the site in authenticating the user without her reentering the password. The trusted authority (from the perspective of validating the user identity) is the credit card company, which checks the consistency of personal identity information against its records and authorizes the use of the credit card. These services compete on the basis of the quantity and quality of partner e-commerce sites, and each brings a natural user community to the table, giving them natural advantages in competing for merchant partners. However, they are unnecessarily fragmented, and recognizing the importance of direct network effects, initiatives are under way to create federated solutions. Sun Microsystems initiated the Liberty Alliance, an industry standards group dedicated to creating open standards, which includes AOL/Time Warner (as well as other software companies), online merchants, and banks. Microsoft, while not participating in an industry standards group, has created its own open standards that allow other services to federate with Passport. Thus, there are at present two major federated alliances forming, and individual users will have the option of joining one or both.

A third technical solution to the authentication challenge is the credentialing approach (see figure 5.5c), which eliminates the need for a secure server's participating in every authentication. In this approach, each entity is associated with its own trusted authority. In the case of entity B, this authority is B's certificate authority (CA). This CA must be public, meaning that all entities wishing to authenticate B (potentially all network citizens) must recognize this CA's judgment as to the level of trust to be placed in entity B, The CA initially establishes the identity of entity B to its satisfaction, and also establishes a level of trust to be placed in entity B, taking necessary measures that account for its legal responsibility. The CA then creates a secret that it supplies to B, as well as corroboration information it is prepared to provide to anyone wishing to authenticate B.

Example A merchant who wishes to sell items on the Internet will seek out a CA that is widely known and whose authority is respected by the potential customers of this firm. To establish the legitimacy and responsibility of this merchant, the CA will likely take a number of actions. It will inspect its physical premises, talk to executives, and check the reputation and financial resources of the firm with ratings sources (such as Dun and Bradstreet). Having convinced itself that its own reputation (or pocketbook) will not be harmed by its endorsement of this merchant to potential customers, the CA will create a secret and physically convey this secret to the firm. It is the solemn responsibility of the firm to preserve secrecy because any other party obtaining this secret could masquerade as this merchant, potentially defrauding customers and sullying its reputation.

Once B has established a relationship with this CA, the CA assists other entities in authenticating B. Entity A, acknowledging the authority of the CA, requests the assistance of this CA in authenticating entity B. The CA might provide the necessary information in the form: "Here is the corroboration information necessary to authenticate B, and here is the protocol you should use to issue a challenge to B. If B's response conforms to this, then you can be sure that B possesses the secret I gave it." In practice, this direct CA involvement in every authentication is avoided by *credentialing*. The CA issues a credential for entity B (analogous to a government passport) that can be used by anybody that respects the authority of the CA to authenticate entity B. This credential (called a *digital certificate*; hence "certificate authority") includes identity information for entity B, the level of trust that can be placed in B, and corroboration information for entity B's secret. This digital certificate, together with a challenge-response protocol that the CA makes publicly available, can be used to authenticate B. In practice, entity B provides its own certificate as a credential to whomever wishes to authenticate it.

Example The Netscape Communicator and Microsoft Internet Explorer Web browsers implement an authentication protocol within the *secure socket layer* (SSL), originally developed by Netscape. SSL allows any browser to authenticate (and communicate confidentially with) secure Web servers that implement SSL. A secure Web server must obtain a secret and a digital certificate from a public certificate authority. Which CAs are recognized as authoritative by the browser? Today the browser suppliers largely make this determination by building a list of CAs whose authority is recognized in the browser software distributed to users. (Internet Explorer allows for the addition of new CA root certificates, typically distributed through a trusted channel such as the Windows Update mechanism.)

The public infrastructure of certificate authorities and digital certificates is called a *public key infrastructure* (PKI). Unlike the shared server approach, credentialing requires special software in the user's client, in this example incorporated into a Web browser. It combines authentication with secure personal identity information; the latter can be included in the certificate. However, it is relatively inflexible in that any change to this information must pass through the CA, and it is also relatively cumbersome to incorporate privacy features into this protocol. One detail: if entity B is to provide its own certificate, there must be a reliable way to establish that the certificate was created by the CA, not by entity B, and that the certificate has not been modified. This is the question of accountability (see section 5.4.6).

5.4.5 Confidentiality: Encryption

Confidentiality makes it possible to share information with someone or something without making it available (in usable form at least) to unauthorized third parties. Technologies can help ensure confidentiality, but legal restrictions (laws and contracts) play an important role also, particularly in ensuring that the recipients of confidential information do not voluntarily distribute it to third parties. The primary role of technological measures is preventing third parties from benefiting from information that is stored or communicated in a public place, or as a second line of defense against unauthorized access to information.

Example A consumer may need to transmit a credit card number to an online merchant over the Internet to pay for merchandise. The conversation of a user talking on a cell phone can be monitored or recorded with appropriate radio equipment. A cracker may gain unauthorized access to an intranet and view information stored on servers there. In all these cases, confidentiality technologies can prevent that cracker from using or gaining any benefit from the information.

Confidentiality is important to *digital rights management*. As discussed in section 2.1.1, information in digital form is easily replicated. This creates difficulties in enforcing the privileges of ownership to information, as conveyed by the copyright laws (see chapter 8). The owners of information often use confidentiality technologies (as well as the laws) to restrict information to paid subscribers.

Example   A provider wanting to sell subscriptions to music or movies downloaded or streamed over the network faces two challenges. First, this information may be stolen while it traverses the network, and second, the legitimate subscriber may replicate it and provide it to others (this is termed "second use" in the copyright laws). The provider can attempt to prevent both these actions by using confidentiality technologies.

Confidentiality can help enforce privacy policies.

Example   An online merchant maintains a repository of information about customers, including their purchases and credit card numbers. The merchant may have privacy policies that restrict the dissemination of this information, or government laws may impose some restrictions. Employee training will hopefully prevent the unauthorized divulging of this information, but it cannot preclude a cracker from gaining unauthorized access. Access control will defend against crackers, but should information be stolen in spite of this, confidentiality technologies can prevent the use of the stolen information.

Like authentication, confidentiality is based on secrets. Suppose that information is to be sent from entity A to entity B (users, hosts, or organizations). We can allow entity B to use the information while preventing the use by any other entity if entity B possesses a secret not available to anybody else.

Example   A plaintext can be sent confidentially to an entity possessing key-2, which is presumed to be secret (see figure 5.4). Anybody else possessing key-1, which can be public information, can encrypt the message using key-1 to yield the ciphertext, and only the entity possessing key-2 can recover the plaintext from the ciphertext.

The use of asymmetric encryption for confidentiality does not require knowledge of entity B's secret to encrypt the information. The same secret that is distributed to entity B to aid in authentication can be used by entity B for decryption, and the same form of corroboration information that is used for authentication can be used for encryption. Entity B's digital certificate serves the double purpose of enabling authentication and allowing information to be conveyed confidentially to entity B.

Another form of cryptography (called *symmetric encryption*) requires a shared secret for confidentiality: the same secret cryptographic key is used for encryption and decryption. An advantage of symmetric cryptography is that it requires much less (roughly a thousandfold less) processing power. Thus, a common form of confidentiality is for one entity to create a random key for temporary use (called a *session key*) and convey it confidentially to another entity using asymmetric cryptography. Subsequently the session key can be used for symmetric encryption until it is discarded when no longer needed.

Example   The secure socket layer (SSL) (see section 5.4.4) can maintain confidentiality (in both directions) throughout a session with a secure Web server. After authentication of the server by the client using the server's digital certificate, the client generates a random session key and sends it confidentially to the client. Subsequently, this session key is used to ensure confidentiality for information sent in both directions using this shared secret session key with symmetric encryption. Note that SSL does not assume that the client possesses a secret initially or a digital certificate, and authenticates the server but not the client. This is a pragmatic concession—only the relatively few secure Web servers need to possess secrets and certificates.

The authentication and confidentiality protocol of this example is often combined with password authentication of the user of a client, as in the Magic Carpet and Microsoft Passport example (see section 5.4.4). This addresses two issues: equipping all users with digital certificates is a daunting problem, and passwords serve to authenticate a user rather than a computer, a desirable feature because two or more users may share a computer.

5.4.6   Accountability: Nonrepudiation and the Digital Signature

Another important social issue in distributed management applications is *accountability*. When entities (users, organizations, or hosts) initiate actions, trust by itself is sometimes inadequate, and it is important to hold users accountable. Society sanctions mechanisms to enforce accountability, like contracts, laws, and courts, but they work only if the technology can produce credible evidence. *Nonrepudiation* is a security technology that provides evidence preventing an entity from repudiating an action or information that it originated.

Example   In a consumer marketplace, a merchant needs to enforce the terms and conditions of a sale, including promises of payment once goods have been shipped. If the purchaser tries to repudiate the order ("somebody else must have ordered and downloaded this software"), then the merchant can produce proof (satisfactory to a court) to collect payment.

There are two issues in nonrepudiation. First, credible evidence must be gathered that an action or information originated from an accountable entity (user, organization, or host), and not an impostor, and that there has been no modification of that action or information beyond the control of the accountable entity. (Otherwise, repudiation would be as simple as claiming that something was changed elsewhere.)

Nonrepudiation depends on a secret available only to the accountable entity. The accountable entity produces a *digital signature* that can only be produced by someone possessing that secret. To complete the protocol, the digital signature must be checked for validity, using corroboration information for the secret. If it is valid, this provides lasting evidence that the action or information was generated by the entity possessing the secret. Repudiation is still possible by claiming that the secret was lost or stolen. This requires a policy that lost or stolen secrets be reported, and in the absence of such a report the presumption is that the secret was not lost.

Example The situation is similar with credit card purchases. The purchaser can later repudiate a purchase by claiming that his or her credit card number had been stolen. If the theft had not previously been reported, then this form of repudiation may not be accepted by the credit card issuer. (Of course, credit card issuers may be required to pay even if a lost or stolen card is not reported, but that is a separate issue.)

The digital signature works much like a paper signature. Given a piece of information, the signature is a piece of data determined by a calculation performed on the information and the signing entity's secret. The same secret can be used for authentication, confidentiality, and a digital signature. The signature is validated using corroboration information for the secret included in the signer's digital certificate. The signature can be retained along with the digital certificate, as evidence that the information originated with the entity possessing the secret associated with corroboration information in the digital certificate. The credibility of this evidence depends on the credibility of the certificate authority.

Example A digital signature algorithm can be based on an asymmetric encryption algorithm (see figure 5.4). The entity that wishes to sign a plaintext is assumed to possess a secret key-1. The signature is simply the ciphertext resulting from the encryption of the plaintext. Then the plaintext, the signature, and the digital certificate are sent to the recipient, who verifies the signature by decrypting it using key-2 (obtained from the digital certificate) and comparing the result to the plaintext. If they agree, the signature must have been created by an entity possessing key-1.

A digital signature also establishes that the signed information has not been modified since it was created. Lacking the secret, no other entity could have modified the information and signature in such a way that the latter would still validate the former.

The digital signature solves another problem: How do we verify that a digital certificate came from the certificate authority it claims, and that the certificate has not been modified since it left the authority? The certificate includes a body of information together with a digital signature created by the authority. The authenticity and integrity of the certificate can be verified by validating the signature, requiring the corroborating information for the authority's secret. Ultimately there has to be a root authority that is trusted but not substantiated by any other authority.

Example As explained earlier, the Web browser recognizes a set of certificate authorities. Provided in the browser software distribution is corroboration information for each of those certificate authorities recognized by the browser's supplier. Another approach is a hierarchy of trust, in which one authority's certificate is signed by another (higher) authority, and its certificate is signed by another (even higher) authority, and so on. In this manner, all authority can be referenced back to a root authority, such as an agency of the United Nations. Corroboration information for the root authority must be known to the user.

5.4.7   A Security System

Security is a sociotechnical system (see section 3.1.4), and all the elements of a security system must work in concert. Trusted authorities are an essential element of this system, together with *all* the security technologies that have been described.

Example Suppose that a customer Alice wants to purchase a book from Bob's Bookstore, which has set up a store on the Internet. Bob's supplies Alice with a credential, its digital certificate issued by Cleo's Certificates. (Cleo's had previously checked out Bob's business and finances and convinced itself that Bob's was a legitimate and trustworthy bookseller.) Alice validates Cleo's digital signature attached to Bob's certificate, convincing herself that Bob's certificate is genuine Cleo's. Second, Alice decides that she accepts Cleo's as an authority she can rely on to vouch for Bob's trustworthiness as a merchant. Alice extracts the corroboration information from Bob's certificate necessary to authenticate Bob's. She initiates a challenge-response authentication protocol with Bob's, and it passes the test with flying colors—its response matches against the corroboration information in its certificate. (Without this authentication, somebody else could easily masquerade as Bob's in order to defraud Alice, for example, by stealing her credit card number and failing to ship the merchandise.) Next, Alice generates a random secret session key and communicates it confidentially to Bob's using asymmetric encryption based on information from his certificate. Alice and Bob's now use this secret session key to confidentially communicate bidirectionally, so that Alice can be sure her privacy is not violated (for example, her credit card number is not stolen as it crosses the network to Bob's). (Of course, this doesn't prevent Bob's from releasing information about Alice's activities or giving out her credit card number. However, Bob's has posted a privacy policy acceptable to Alice, and takes various organizational and technological measures to enforce that policy.)

After browsing the catalog awhile, Alice finds a book she wants to buy and submits her order to Bob's confidentially. However, before Bob's will accept this order, it imposes two requirements. First, it authenticates Alice using information obtained from a certificate she supplies to Bob's. (That certificate was issued by Demon's Authoritative Certificates, which Bob's accepts as a trusted authority, and Bob's of course first validates Demon's signature on that certificate.) Second, Bob's requires that Alice attach a digital signature to her order, and validates that signature using corroboration information obtained from her certificate. Bob's permanently stores the order, Alice's signature, and her certificate so that Bob's can later produce them as credible evidence that the order originated from Alice in the unlikely event that she later tries to repudiate it. Finally, Bob's ships the book and charges Alice's credit card through Bob's acquiring bank.

It may appear from this example that security places a great burden on users. In fact, these detailed protocols are encapsulated in application software and are thus largely transparent to users. Of course, users do have a solemn responsibility to avoid the accidental or deliberate divulgence of their respective secrets.

5.4.8 Other Issues

Security is only one issue distinguishing a distributed management application from one that is closed or centralized. However, security does illustrate the types of issues arising, and in particular the strong influence of distributed management on software requirements. Trust, access, administration, laws, and commercial relationships are all issues. The analysis leading to software requirements must recognize and take into account these and many other issues.

In provisioning, the opportunities for coordination of technology choices may be limited by the participation of multiple autonomous end-user organizations. New end-user organizations may even join an application during operation. Even where end-users acquire technology from the same supplier, it is difficult to avoid distinct versions of that software (see section 5.1.2). This places an additional composability burden on the participating suppliers, and is also an opportunity to expand the role of infrastructure to facilitate this composability (see chapter 7). Testing becomes much more complex in both development and provisioning, because it potentially involves multiple customers and suppliers.

At the operational stage, differences in procedures and processes across autonomous end-user organizations must be accommodated. Where administrative functions cross organizational boundaries, as with establishing and enforcing trust and access, arms-length coordination mechanisms must be supported by the application. Distributed administration may be made easier and more effective through improved tools.

Distributed management applications offer an opportunity for the software industry, because they force it to reconceptualize software in a way that is much more distributed and decentralized, administered and provisioned by multiple autonomous or semiautonomous agents, coordinated through arms-length compromise, adaptation, and negotiation rather than by centralized planning and administration. Like an evolution from a centrally planned to a market economy would, these techniques penetrate and benefit all large-scale software systems, allowing software to move to a scale of scope and complexity that can only be imagined today.

5.5   Research and Discussion Issues

1. Understand and discuss how success at each phase of the software value chain affects the success of following stages. What are the metrics of success, and how are they affected by earlier stages?

2. What is the relation between the software value chain and interactive development processes (see section 4.2.2)? Should the value chain be considered iterative?

3. Qualitatively compare the four phases of computing of listed in table 2.3 for the following characteristics, important to organizations using information technology to support their business processes: levels of staffing, staff expertise, availability,

responsiveness to changing business needs, user training, security, total cost of ownership.

4. How is the software development process (see section 4.2) intertwined with the software value chain? Discuss how provisioning, operation, and use are related to development.

5. What is the customer value proposition associated with each type of software release listed in table 5.2?

6. Consider in more detail the strategy issues a software supplier faces in deciding which past versions to continue supporting?

7. What are some alternative strategies for deriving revenue to a software supplier from investments in maintenance?

8. Understand and discuss the effect of network software distribution on provisioning and operation (see section 4.5.4). What new capabilities does this invoke?

9. Repeat the last question for mobile code (see section 4.5.5).

10. How can organizations most effectively integrate human organization and business process design with software configuration and integration in the provisioning phase?

11. What are the relative merits and strategies surrounding the make vs. buy decision in acquiring a software application, especially from the perspective of organization and business process design and effectiveness?

12. What cost accounting measures have to be in place to accurately estimate the total cost of ownership for a software application or infrastructure?

13. What is the appropriate trade-off between government laws and user and operator measures to ensure security? That is, to what extent should laws demand appropriate measures and actions on the part of users and operators as necessary to defend against lawbreaking? Without this, to what extent do laws against cracking reduce the incentive for preventive action?

14. To what extent is the detrimental effect of security on usability unavoidable? To what extent are laws as deterrence to crackers justified by the collective usability gains?

15. How can the harm inflicted in security breaches be quantified? How can risk be assessed in advance? Do you think it feasible to sell insurance against security breaches?

16. How should any laws seeking to preserve privacy distinguish between anonymous identification and personal identification?

17. Who has responsibility to ensure privacy? Is the onus on infrastructure service providers, on the operators of applications, on government, or on users? Presuming the answer is all of these, how should responsibility be partitioned? Does responsibility flow from the responsibility to exercise control, the ability to exercise control, the economic incentive to exercise control, or benevolence? What are the relative responsibilities of the participants, the marketplace, communities, or regulation? What is the trade-off between ethics and laws?

18. Assuming privacy can be adequately defined, to what extent can technology aid in achieving it, and what limitations are there on what technology can accomplish? What is the appropriate partitioning between technology and other means (like laws) for ensuring privacy? Should laws mandate that available technologies be employed to the maximum?

19. What is the trade-off (if any) between privacy and usability? Between security and privacy?

20. What fundamental differences (if any) exist between computer-mediated conditional access to information and physical access?

21. What differences are appropriate in laws protecting an entity that relies on the three methods for authentication and an entity that relies on only one of these?

22. What mechanisms (technical and legal) should be built into a public key infrastructure to account for the possibility of an accidentally or deliberately compromised secret?

23. Smartcards can encapsulate a secret, providing a way for a user to securely carry that secret even in the absence of a computer. A smartcard can help authenticate a user even if the device the smartcard is inserted into is not trusted. A personal identification (PIN) code (a secret memorized by the user and provided on request) further protects a smartcard from being used in case it is lost or stolen. (Note that smartcards normally cannot accept the pin code directly—they don't have a keypad embedded.) To further increase security, a smartcard's validity can be revoked. Based on the techniques described in section 5.4, explain how all these measures can be realized, and discuss the various risks involved.

24. A federation of certificate authorities raises the question of transitivity of trust. Should a CA-1 that trusts a CA-2 also trust a CA-3, provided CA-3 can demon-

strate that it is trusted by CA-2? Discuss potential risks and possible solutions by drawing on the techniques described in section 5.4.

5.6 Further Reading

An excellent treatise on security that discusses many of its social and policy effects has been published by the National Research Council (1996). Anderson (2001) discusses many practical considerations in security technologies.

6
Software Supply Industry

Specialization is a feature of every complex organization, be it social or natural, a school system, garden, book, or mammalian body.
Catharine R. Stimpson

While the managerial perspective of chapter 5 defines the steps and functions necessary before users can benefit from software, this does not by itself define how industry is organized to provide these functions. At one extreme, an end-user organization may undertake the creation, provisioning, and operation of an application on its own behalf, although it would invariably incorporate software products and tools from software suppliers. At another extreme, all these functions may be undertaken by different companies. The actual organization influences how effectively the user is served, as well as efficiency and costs.

In this chapter, the industrial organization surrounding the creation (including analysis and implementation), provisioning, operation, and use of software is considered. Primary goals are to understand the rationale behind current organizational approaches observed in the industry as well as the range of possible alternatives and some forces that may be driving the industry toward alternative organizations. Industrial organization is also an interesting and changing picture within the software creation industry (see chapter 7).

6.1 Industrial Organization and Software Architecture

Industrial organization closely parallels software architecture (see section 4.3). As with software architecture, there are three issues that must be addressed: the decomposition of the industry into cooperating and competing firms (analogous to software decomposition), the separate and overlapping responsibilities of the individual firms (analogous to the functionality of software modules), and the business relationships among firms (analogous to the interaction among software modules). Organization and architecture influence one other because organizational efficiency increases if organizational and architectural structures can be reasonably aligned. Conway's law (see section 4.2) made this observation early on: "Organizations which design systems are constrained to produce systems which are copies of the communication structures of these organizations" (Conway 1968). The recent view suggests it is advantageous for organization to follow architecture (Coplien 1995).

There are also strong indications that the most successful software suppliers (and computer suppliers) over the long term are those that take the lead in defining an architecture and then position themselves strategically within this framework (Ferguson and Morris 1994). Such firms have many more strategic options and opportunities to manage the relationships with competitive and complementary firms than those focused on "point products" that serve a specific need independently of other products.

Example   With its System/360, introduced in 1964, IBM offered for the first time an architectural framework for mainframes that supported a range of needs from small and inexpensive to very advanced, all with compatible software and allowing its customers to migrate gracefully as their needs grew. By defining and controlling this architecture, it set the basic ground rules for competitors' adding components and applications to a system. Intel has followed a similar path with its 286 microprocessor architecture; it has sought to define and promulgate an architecture for all the functions surrounding the microprocessor, the bus for expansion cards, and the interfaces to peripherals. In software, successful operating system suppliers (Digital, Hewlett-Packard, IBM, Microsoft, Sun Microsystems, and others) all define and promulgate an architecture that allows applications to access system resources and enables application composability.

From this perspective, choosing the industrial organization is choosing the modularity of an industry, as well as the modularity of the software produced by that industry. (Of course, the industrial organization is determined to a large degree by market forces rather than the invisible hand of an architect.) To emphasize these parallels, this chapter uses the terminology and perspective of software engineering to describe industrial organization. What modularity would be natural in terms of natural business functions and core competencies and the relationships among those functions? These insights are then compared to the observed industry structure.

Relative to software, decomposition arises in two contexts. This chapter examines the decomposition of the overall supply chain functions that were discussed in chapter 5: software creation, provisioning, operation, and use, in which the software itself is considered monolithic, an economic good that is acquired as a prelude to the other steps in the supply chain. The division of labor between traditional software companies and other types of firms is fluid and ever-changing. The supply chain perspective best captures the issues faced by end-user organizations, and the software industry perspective best captures the issues of software creation. The intermediate ground between these perspectives harbors many organizational possibilities, in theory and in practice.

Individual firms have responsibility for complementary functions, for example, software development and maintenance, user support, provisioning, administration, and management. A goal is to address how these responsibilities can be naturally divided among firms, how this partitioning of function is changing, and what factors drive this change.

Another issue is business relationships among firms. In this regard, one driver is ownership. A software application and its supporting infrastructure typically incorporate a number of modules and underlying hardware technologies that may be owned and supplied by different firms. Boundaries of company responsibility must align with interfaces among software modules, and interface design and specification form an important means of coordination and separation of responsibility. Since software is freely replicated and nonrival in use, it is not sold in the traditional sense but is licensed for replication and use under specified terms and conditions. Ownership takes the form of intellectual property, a form of government-sanctioned and enforced property rights (see chapter 8).

6.2   Organization of the Software Value Chain

The software value chain captures the major functions that must be brought together to put a working software application in the hands of users. In this section some natural alternatives for the industrial organization of this chain are discussed.

6.2.1   Decomposition of Natural Business Functions

The value chain of figure 5.1 displays a natural partitioning of business functions from software creation to use. Companies tend to form around individual units of value that enhance internal synergies and exploit common competencies and expertise, so the organization (Langlois 1992; Robertson and Langlois 1995) of the industry itself is a partitioning of this value chain. In these terms, natural business functions represent distinct sources of value (see figure 6.1). This partitioning displays the desired characteristics of modularity: strong cohesion of function within

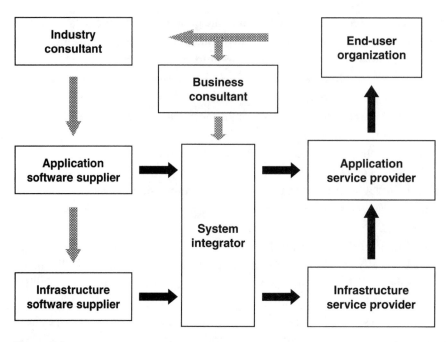

Figure 6.1
Natural business partitioning of the value chain.

modules and weak coupling of function among different modules. Of course, there *is* coupling, which forms natural boundaries for business relationships within the industry.

Recall that weak coupling is a much more important property of modularity than strong cohesion because a hierarchical decomposition of a module lacking strong cohesion into submodules possessing stronger cohesion is possible. This phenomenon is also observed in industrial organization. For example, while software creation is a natural unit of decomposition, it is also an impractically large activity for any one company to encompass in its entirety, and thus further decomposition of the industry into more specialized areas, such as application, infrastructure, embedded, and component software, is observed. Some companies pursue and exploit synergies among two or more of these areas. Chapter 7 considers the internal organization of the software creation industry in more detail.

Consider some natural business functions (see figure 6.1) and the argument for why it displays weak coupling to the other functions. The *industry consultant* analyzes and conveys the needs of a vertical industry segment (e.g., medical care) or horizontal business function common to all businesses (e.g., accounting), and how they can be expressed in application software features and capabilities (see chapter 3). The *application software supplier* develops the application, maximizing market share by attempting to meet the needs of multiple end-user organizations, and emphasizing core competencies like technical and project management skills in software development (see chapter 4). The industry consultant need only study representative end-users to achieve an effective requirements definition; this sharing of effort and costs over multiple end-user organizations contributes to economical application creation.

The end-users for infrastructure software are both application developers and operators. The *infrastructure software supplier* must be cognizant of the requirements imposed by a wide range of applications and the needs of application developers. Like the industry consultant, this supplier benefits from economies of scale in studying only a representative set of applications. Infrastructure software that attracts many applications offers more value to its end-users, a form of indirect network effects (see section 3.2.3). For both these reasons, a many-to-one coupling of application suppliers to a single infrastructure supplier is beneficial. (For further economic justification for infrastructure, see chapter 9.)

The *system integrator* specializes in provisioning. This role takes responsibility for acquiring software from application and infrastructure suppliers (in the latter case, usually more than one), makes all this software work together and with the supporting infrastructure equipment, and installs and tests the software. The value added by the system integrator is the emergent capabilities arising from this integration. In the course of interoperability testing, required modifications to modules are sometimes identified, and normally it is the original supplier (in a maintenance role) who implements any such modifications. In addition, there is often a need to create custom modules to integrate with acquired modules, or even to aid in the composition of those modules, so some implementation may be required.

The important role of the system integrator in making the application and infrastructure work together is the primary argument for grouping the provisioning of application and infrastructure. The many-to-many relationship between application and infrastructure suppliers (including, in the latter case, both software and equipment) is an argument for having an independent system integrator.

To meet the needs of multiple end-user organizations, application software suppliers provide configuration options and often leave flexibility to mix and match modules to end-users. In a given end-user environment, different compositions of applications may meet specific needs. Making use of these options is an important component of provisioning, one that is closely tied to the needs, processes, and structure of the end-user organization. An important aspect of provisioning is thus making adaptations for the end-user organization and training its workers. Understanding a specific end-user context is the role of a *business consultant*, who can draw on past experience in applying the same or similar applications in other companies. Thus, system integration emphasizes the technical aspects, and business consulting emphasizes the organizational and needs issues. The industry consultant focuses on the needs of all firms, and the business consultant focuses on adapting applications for use in particular firms.

Example   The largest accounting firms, such as KPMG, Price Waterhouse Coopers, Deloitte and Touche, and Ernst and Young, have consultant organizations that assist end-user organizations in acquiring and adapting software applications to their needs. Often these consultants perform all the provisioning functions: needs assessment, organizational changes, configuration, and training. Large computer suppliers, such as Compaq, IBM, and Hewlett-Packard, also offer similar services. An increasing trend in the accounting industry is to spin off consulting arms as separate companies, for example, Accenture, which was spun off from Andersen Consulting, which was spun off from Andersen. These firms also provide system integration services, so they have two types of skilled employees who work closely together: systems analysts and business analysts.

Operations are the specialty of a *service provider*. An *application service provider* licenses and operates the application, and an *infrastructure service provider*[1] purchases or licenses and operates the hardware and software infrastructure (computers, storage, network, operating system). The primary argument for separating application and infrastructure operations is economies of scale in sharing a common infrastructure over multiple applications (see chapter 9). There are three distinct specialties in infrastructure service provision, corresponding to the three areas of information technology (see section 2.2.2): processing, storage, and communication. Communication and networking service provision is almost always separate from the others, especially in the wide area, since it requires the acquisition and management of radio spectrum or cable rights of way, a specialty in its own right. Processing and storage have similar needs for interior floor space for hosts and storage subsystems, but stored data often constitute an important corporate asset that requires special nurturing and protection (e.g., mirroring and backup), whereas processing has no similar durability requirement. For this and other reasons, the three-tier client-server architecture decomposes server functions into application logic and storage (see section 4.5.3).

Operation requires special skills to keep things running (availability) with high performance, to protect assets from threats (security), and to meet the operational needs of end-users (e.g., setting up and configuring accounts), functions that can often be shared over multiple applications. Application software suppliers and consultants focus on the functional needs of the user population as a class, and service providers focus on meeting individual day-to-day needs. Customer care by an application supplier helps users benefit from application features and capabilities, whereas customer care in operation includes functions like configuring authorization and authentication for access to the application.

Not shown in figure 6.1 is the *information content supplier*. One focus of many applications is the manipulation and presentation of information, which may come from an independent source (e.g., a stock analyst discloses company prospects to the users of a stock brokerage application). Such an information intermediary can aggregate, consolidate, and filter information in beneficial ways and supply similar information to multiple customers.

6.2.2 Composition of Business Functions

The argument that strong coherence is not an essential characteristic of good modularity cuts two ways, both down and up the hierarchy. It can suggest a hierarchical decomposition of the major business functions into ever more specialized firms, and also allow for composition of business functions into horizontally or vertically integrated firms. Any hierarchical decomposition extends the supply chain, where one firm incorporates products and services from its own suppliers into a finished product or service. We now discuss some common compositions of the natural business functions.

Functionally, as emphasized in section 4.2, end-user needs are not static, and thus requirements must be manipulated and refined throughout a software life cycle, including initial development, maintenance, and upgrade. There is a natural give-and-take between being excessively focused on changing requirements, on the one hand, and compromising schedules and even deployment by imposing too many changes, on the other hand. The industry consultant role is commonly subsumed within a product marketing function of the application software supplier, but we argue later that this and related expertise (like interaction and graphics design; see section 4.2.6) are distinct skills that will increasingly be sought from the outside.

Where an end-user organization has distinct requirements or wishes to emphasize competitive advantage through unique capabilities, it will typically pursue internal software development or directly contract for development.

The phases of computing (see table 2.3) and the resulting shifts in industrial organization illustrate the interdependence of business models and technology (although cause-and-effect is not always so clear). In the mainframe era, applications ran on a centralized mainframe computer commonly owned and operated (and often even developed) by the end-user organization's internal information systems department. Only the infrastructure equipment and software were acquired from the outside. This model composes every business function except infrastructure equipment and software (see figure 6.2).

Later in the mainframe era, and especially today, applications were increasingly acquired from software companies rather than developed internally, creating a new business sometimes called the *independent software vendor*. An early example was the financial or accounting application. This trend was encouraged by time-sharing, which for the first time brought individual workers directly into contact with their organization's computers. Their direct needs, such as presenting structured

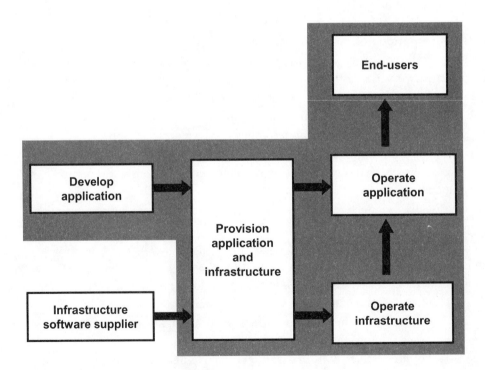

Figure 6.2
Composition of all business functions except infrastructure was common in the mainframe era, as represented by the shaded block.

information and authoring documents, tend to be generic—less specific to the organizational mission—than many mission-oriented mainframe applications.

Example An early popular application was the database management system (DBMS), which supports the acquisition, management, and retrieval of business data, such as character strings and numerical values (see section 3.1.1). The DBMS was often used in raw form, allowing workers to directly enter and access data, although today it is usually built into a larger application. Early word processors (crude by today's standards) appeared on time-sharing computers.

The decentralized desktop computer era greatly expanded individual productivity application offerings. Much of the personal computer's early popularity and rapid penetration followed the individual user's ability to directly acquire and install applications without depending on a centralized information systems organization that often imposed delays or achieved a poor match to changing needs. On the other hand, the early desktop computers shifted the burden of provisioning and operation to the individual user, affecting the total cost of ownership (see section 5.2), including the opportunity cost of distracting workers from other duties. This also resulted in chaotic management of information resources, creating inconsistent copies and making backups unreliable.

The networked computer era brought remarkable opportunities and changes. The desktop computer and the time-sharing computer were networked, and applications were partitioned across them in a client-server architecture (see section 4.5). The desktop computer both supported individual productivity applications and at the same time participated in server applications. The most immediate effect was to recentralize operational responsibility, as the information systems organization provisioned and operated server-based applications and administered the individual computers over the network using administrative tools from infrastructure software suppliers.

The networking era also brought the network service provider into the picture. Rarely would it make sense for an organization to provision and operate a wide-area network, and many organizations have outsourced their local-area networks as well.

Client-server applications serve specialized departmental functions in organizations, but a recent trend has been toward enterprise applications supporting a complete business process (from acquiring parts and material to shipping finished goods) spanning multiple departments. These applications often incorporate and federate existing departmental applications by setting up peer-to-peer communication and storage links among their servers, allowing them to share information. In this model, the enterprise application is developed essentially from scratch by an internal information systems organization.

An increasingly popular alternative is to acquire an enterprise application from an independent software supplier, including categories called (for example) enterprise resource planning (ERP), enterprise asset management (EAM), and customer relationship management (CRM). These off-the-shelf solutions generally require the end-user organization to start from scratch, designing and deploying new processes and organizations along with the software during provisioning.

Example   The largest ERP suppliers are SAP, Oracle, PeopleSoft, and Baan. Lately they have extended their applications to connect suppliers and customers, turning them into business-to-business e-commerce solutions. These supply chain applications illustrate the challenges of distributed management (see section 5.4). The largest supplier of CRM applications is Siebel, followed by the ERP suppliers growing into this market segment and many smaller companies.

End-user organizations installing ERP applications frequently contract to consultants who have experience in provisioning the same ERP solution in other organizations to aid in configuration, redefinition of processes, reorganization, and training.

Example   To accommodate a variation in needs, ERP applications offer many configuration parameters and options. The configuration of the ERP application suite R/3 from SAP (the largest ERP supplier) is daunting without the aid of experienced consultants. The independent consultant Ploenzke grew in parallel with SAP; now a subsidiary of CSC, CSC Ploenzke has multibillion dollar revenues from the installation of R/3 for large enterprises.

The industrial organization represented by ERP and other enterprise applications (see figure 6.3) moves another step toward the natural business decomposition shown in figure 6.1 by separating all functions except operation and use.

The ubiquity and performance of the Internet makes possible an alternative model (see figure 6.4) in which end-users access and invoke application features over a wide-area network. The firm providing the application is called an *application service provider* (ASP), although in practice such a firm typically composes both provisioning and infrastructure service provider functions. The ASP Industry Consortium defines an ASP as a firm that "manages and delivers application capabilities to multiple entities from a data center across a wide-area network

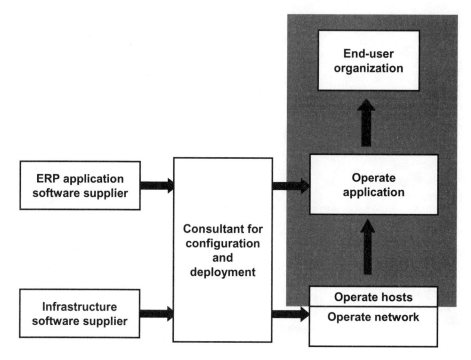

Figure 6.3
The enterprise application model leaves application software development and provisioning to specialized firms while retaining most operations in the end-user organization.

(WAN)." It is implicitly assumed that the ASP operates a portion of the infrastructure (the data center) and hence is also an infrastructure service provider by our terminology.

Example A historical example of an ASP is the telephone service provider. Telephony is an application[2] supporting voice conversations, with auxiliary software-based features such as switching, conferencing, call waiting, calling number identification, and so on. The telephony application is based on an equipment infrastructure originally custom-designed for telephony, but more recently similar capabilities have been based on the Internet and dedicated call-processing hosts. The application software suppliers include Cisco, Ericsson, Lucent, Motorola, and Nortel Networks, doubling as infrastructure software and equipment suppliers. Examples of telephony service providers that are ASPs include AT&T, British Telecom, Deutsche Telekom (which owns VoiceStream), SBC (which owns a majority interest in Cingular), Sprint, and WorldCom/MCI.

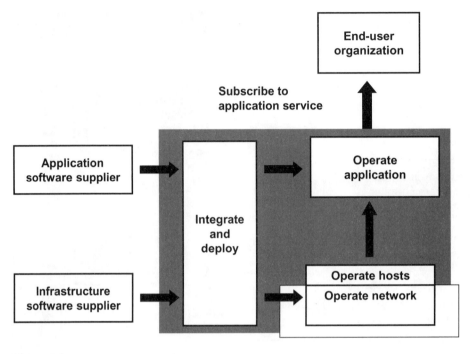

Figure 6.4
The application service provider (ASP) provisions and operates an application, offering it for use over a wide-area network.

The ASP can be viewed in two complementary ways. It decomposes provisioning and operation from use, or in more conventional terminology, it allows the end-user organization to outsource provisioning and operation. It is also sometimes viewed as a different way to sell software: instead of licensing software to the end-user organization to provision and operate, the software is licensed to an intermediary who manages the provisioning and operation. The software supplier may become an ASP itself, in which case it becomes a service provider with its own internal application software development.

Example   Borland was historically a software supplier but moved into the ASP market by acquiring Bedouin. With its "TeamSource Development Services Platform," Borland offers its rapid application development environment as a service, supplementing its traditional software licensing model. Nightfire is a startup business-to-business e-commerce company that serves as an intermediary between customers who want to subscribe to high-speed Internet access using digital subscriber loop (DSL) technology, firms providing that access as a service, and local telephone companies that lease their lines for that purpose. The subscription pricing is based on transactions: the service providers pay a fixed fee for each processed customer order.

The ASP model is often described as selling software by rental rather than licensing, but its essential business feature is outsourcing provisioning and operation. While the ASP model often leverages the wide-area network to offer similar application services to multiple end-user organizations from a common server infrastructure, despite the definition favored by the ASP Industry Consortium an ASP can also provision and operate applications on site, for instance, to address performance or security concerns. In this light, EDS and Perot Systems are precursors to the ASP idea, and big players in the over-the-network ASP field as well.

The ASP has significant advantages to both the user and the application software developer. To the end-user organization, this sheds one business function not directly related to its core business and expertise. Because of the economies of scale and specialization the ASP enjoys, the ASP model has proven cost-effective. Another major advantage is scalability to growing throughput requirements. Especially for applications that deal directly or indirectly with individual consumers, throughput requirements can grow dramatically in a short time, and the ASP's scale allows it to adapt more easily. Contractual relationships can hold an outside firm accountable for quality and performance in a way that internal organizations cannot, in effect shifting risk from end-user to service provider. On the other hand, users can be reluctant to share their proprietary data with an outside organization.

To the application software supplier, the ASP infrastructure environment is more homogeneous than the end-user environment, significantly easing the technical challenges. For example, the user doesn't care what kind of equipment and operating system platform is used to host an application accessed over the network, whereas different end-user organizations specify platforms based on supplier relationships and employee expertise. A software supplier may target a single platform for ASP hosting (especially where it acts as an ASP itself) but may need to support multiple platforms for applications licensed directly to end-user organizations. The ASP model also makes some pricing and revenue models easier to implement, such as third-party advertising revenue or use-based pricing (see chapter 9).

A significant ASP enabler is a Web browser incorporating scripting languages and mobile code. Although satisfactory only for fairly simple user interfaces (specially designed client software can provide much richer capabilities), it circumvents the obstacle of installing a proprietary client application. The ASP can use the Web browser for presentation and also dynamically download application-specific code to be executed in the client browser. Where this is inadequate, installing application-specific client software moves toward a hybrid model, where part of the application is provisioned and operated in the end-user environment. An additional advantage of custom client software is that it can, unlike a browser, make use of multiple mutually unaware providers while not divulging private information. This is a major element of Web services (see chapter 7).

The evolution of industry structure reflects a natural maturation of the software industry. In the early stages of any new software application area, end-user organizations view their software as a way to differentiate themselves and gain competitive advantage. This, plus the lack of competitive options, leads them to develop applications internally. As the industry matures, the spread of best practices reduces competitive advantage obtained in this way, and a given application domain settles on fairly consistent capabilities and features. At this point, effectiveness and efficiency are enhanced by outsourcing functions no longer a direct source of competitive advantage, including, in the extreme, application development, provisioning, and operation. There always remains a "bleeding edge" where innovation and competitive advantage are gained by custom software development.

6.2.3   Unnatural Decomposition of Business Functions

Sometimes external factors intervene to prevent a natural decomposition of business functions such as that shown in figure 6.1. An example is the distributed management of an application spanning organizational boundaries (see section 5.4). Regardless of the strong coherence inherent in operating a single application, responsibility must sometimes be unnaturally partitioned. Some would argue that this creates an opportunity for the independent ASP, who can centralize operations while accommodating users from various organizations, but in fact distributed management issues always remain.

Example   Several industries have established independent online public exchanges for the procurement of goods and services, and there are even more private exchanges that allow suppliers to conduct e-commerce with a large firm. In such exchanges, customers post requests for bids, and potential suppliers respond with bids. The participants in such an exchange include employees of autonomous organizations, whether the exchange application is a centralized ASP or is distributed across the organizations. Thus, the issues of trust and access discussed in section 5.4 cannot be entirely circumvented regardless of application architecture.

6.3   Business Relationships in the Software Value Chain

Whatever the decomposition of the software value chain, there are a number of business relationships among the participating firms. A discussion of some important issues follows.

6.3.1   Types of Customers

Today, virtually every organization and most individuals are customers of software suppliers. It is important to recognize that the primary customer is whoever does provisioning and operation, which may or may not be the same entity as the end-user. Customers come in five distinct categories. First, individuals license applications for their own purposes, such as personal productivity, collaboration, information access, and entertainment. Second, organizations acquire (license, purchase, or develop internally) applications that support their internal business and external business relationships.[3] Third, service providers acquire software that they embed and bundle into services provided over the network. Fourth, equipment manufacturers embed and bundle software into equipment that they manufacture and sell. (The last two are similar in many ways.) Fifth, the "customer" of a piece of software can be another software application.

Example   When one entity exports a service over the wide-area network, other software may be constructed to specifically invoke that service. An example is the meta-search engine (Ixquick and SurfWax are two of many), which consolidates the results of a query it presented to a number of other search engines on the Web. A more general example is the portal, a Web site that allows a user to customize her view into a number of other Web sites. One economic driver for meta-search engines and portals is to attract and retain the user's attention, deriving revenue from advertisers. Higher-quality portals and aggregation services require subscription revenue. These are instances of the general concept of Web services (see chapter 7), which emphasizes servers' making use of data and application logic services derived elsewhere.

The primary distinctions are in the related areas of customer sophistication, support, and value. Individuals normally install, administer, and use the software and may be relatively unsophisticated in technology, requiring more automation of installation and upgrade and a strong customer support operation. While the ultimate value of software is in what it does for users, a customer who is not the end-user may be more sensitive to the technical features, configuration options, and operational support and tools.

6.3.2 Software Distribution

There are several ways to get software to a customer. Software is normally distributed as object code represented by data and distributed on magnetic or optical media or downloaded over a network (see section 4.4). The object code may be native code for a target processor or intermediate code intended to be executed by an interpreter or just-in-time compiler.

The technical means of distribution has considerable influence on the business model for selling software. Physical media require traditional inventory, warehousing, and transportation, functions avoided by network distribution. Distribution is complicated by multiple platforms, although software portability may eliminate this while introducing execution overhead and dependence on an interpreter or virtual machine infrastructure.

A consideration in distribution is digital rights management to protect against further distribution without payment (see chapter 8). The security of physical media is greater, so it is common to distribute on a physical medium but allow upgrades (which depend on prior installation of the original) over the network. Network distribution is also impractical with slow Internet access rates (such as voiceband modems), so an optional physical medium is usually offered.

Network distribution is less expensive and timelier. These properties make it valuable for the frequent distribution of service releases and upgrade versions, giving more freedom to change with less fear of incompatibilities. Many modern applications check for a network connection, automatically notify the operator of service releases, and automate downloading and installation, reducing the total cost of ownership (see section 5.1.4). This capability should be contrasted with hardware, which can be updated after deployment only with difficulty.

Example With partitioning of application functionality between server and client (see section 4.5.3) the server can be upgraded more freely knowing that timely upgrade of clients can follow. For example, with RealAudio (an audio streaming application) the server capabilities can be upgraded with relative impunity (even in ways that make it incompatible with the client) knowing that the client can be easily and quickly upgraded. A similar example is Adobe Acrobat Reader (downloadable free) and the matching Acrobat Distiller authoring application. Version 5 added new encryption technology to Distiller knowing that Readers would have to be upgraded. Downloading is especially powerful for peer-to-peer architectures because network effects place a premium on rapid adoption. Arguably, peer-to-peer applications such as Napster and Groove Networks could not be successful without simple downloading and installation.

Although network distribution eliminates some intermediaries, intermediary functions remain useful where there are alternative suppliers to consider, or where integration and bundling of different products are needed.

Example Many organizations (especially universities) have a fragmented administrative structure for computers but also want site licenses for commonly used applications. They typically make the licensed applications available for network download and installation internally to the organization, using access control (see section 5.4.2) to enforce licensing terms and conditions.

What has to happen before a customer can execute software? There are at least four possibilities. First, the software may be embedded in a piece of equipment distributed through conventional material distribution channels.

Example Many common products such as microwave ovens and automobiles use embedded software to control the complex features and a user interface. For example, software allows the microwave oven to be programmed by the user, and controls the cooking time and microwave power level.

Such equipment, when sold to an end-user, is called an *appliance*. When predominately based on information technology (processing, storage, and communication), it is an *information appliance*.

Example The personal video recorder (vendors include Microsoft, ReplayTV, and TiVo) allows users to easily schedule the recording of television programs and play them back at their convenience. They download TV schedules over the network, and provide a user interface on the TV screen to program the information appliance using a remote control. Internally, the PVR includes custom hardware, a processor, operating system, database management system, and large disk drive for storing video.

A variation on embedded software relies on *preinstalled software*. This model is commonly used to make generic hardware, such as desktop computers or personal digital assistants (PDAs), ready to use "out of the box." Preinstalled software always includes an operating system and typically also a set of applications and even demos for products that could be ordered separately.

Second, the customer may have to install the software herself, which requires conspicuous action. This *user self-provisioning* is typical of desktop applications.

Third, *mobile code* may be automatically downloaded over the network and executed without an explicit installation (see section 4.4.3).

Example Many Web-based applications download ECMAScript or Java code to the Web browser for local execution. This code requires no installation, is deleted once the user finishes the application, and can provide much less delay for animations and interaction than server implementation, particularly for slow Internet access connections. Further, it can implement user interface features not intrinsic to the browser.

Fourth, the user may utilize software executing remotely, which is operated by an application service provider (see section 6.2.2). This is often combined with mobile code that realizes user presentation and interface functions in the client. From the user perspective, all these options differ primarily in terms of performance.

Example   Mobile code may incur a noticeable delay while the code is downloaded, especially on slow connections. Remote execution suffers from round-trip network delay, precluding some capabilities like immediate rotation and redisplay of a manipulated complex graphical object, but it may offer more processing power. Local installation or mobile code offers scalability, as the processing resources grow in proportion to users.

For user-installed or mobile software, a traditional business model of production and marketing is appropriate. For embedded and service provider–operated software, the original equipment manufacturer or service provider acquires, provisions, and operates the software. Embedded software executes in a controlled and static environment, and hence operational support can be minimized or eliminated; where problems arise, they are handled through customer support. The key difference from the perspective of the supplier is one of scale and sophistication: Do the customers comprise a small number of technically sophisticated manufacturers or service providers, or a large number of relatively unsophisticated end-users? The decision process is also different. With a manufacturer or service provider or mobile code, a third party makes decisions to install an upgrade version or move to a competitive offering. With user self-provisioning, the user consciously initiates such actions, although the software itself may inform the user of the availability of service releases or an upgrade.

Mixtures of these distribution models are common. Appliances may fetch and automatically install upgrades from the network. An application service provider may use mobile code to move a portion of the execution closer to the end-user and improve interactivity. Mobile code may leverage desktop processing power, reducing server capacity and improving scalability, or a service provider may require complementary user-installed client software.

6.3.3   Software Pricing

There are many alternatives and issues in designing pricing models (see chapter 9). However, there are also standard practices observed in the industry today, often tied to a specific distribution model and recovering creation, maintenance, and upgrading costs. Software that is not maintained wears out fairly quickly (see section 3.2).

User-installed software is typically sold for a fixed price with unlimited use, as are many other information and material products. Upgrade versions are also offered at a fixed price, creating a revenue stream. This places a premium on selling upgrade versions to support ongoing maintenance and upgrading costs, although sales to new adopters also provide ongoing revenue. The biggest competition for upgrades is the installed base of older versions, unless customers are under contractual obligation to upgrade. To best this competition, suppliers offer new or enhanced features and often a favorable upgrade price. Some have asserted that this revenue model results in "feature bloat," with a negative effect on usability. Other strategies include upgrading complementary products in a way that encourages users to upgrade.

Example Suppliers of an operating system are pleased when applications exploit capabilities and features from the latest operating system version, and encourage this by offering advance technical information and assistance. Customers attracted by the latest application upgrade may want to upgrade the operating system.

Embedded and service provider distribution mechanisms place an intermediary in the supply chain, the supplier of an information appliance or a service provider. (In some cases, these entities may internally develop the software.) This requires two pricing strategies (software supplier to intermediary, and intermediary to end-user). From the supplier perspective, a common approach is to approximate the user-installed pricing model by basing price on the rate of end-user adoption (such as a fixed royalty per appliance sold or end-user served).[4] Another option is direct usage metrics, such as the total number of transactions completed. A third approach is to base pricing on the number and speed of servers on which the software is installed rather than on usage or users.

An information appliance bundles the hardware with embedded software for an all-inclusive price. Since the customer (especially an individual consumer) has little awareness that the appliance includes substantial software, pricing models typical of material goods are common. A fixed price is common, with no possibility of later upgrade and an established warranty period during which product defects or failures will be repaired. Whatever pricing model is adopted, the embedded software is sold under the same terms and conditions.

Historically suppliers of appliances considered the embedded software a cost of implementation, necessary to sell the product, rather than a separate source of value and revenue. As the software content of appliances has increased, most suppliers have come to realize that the embedded software is a source of substantial development costs as well as value. The flexibility to replace software in the customer's hands is not only a maintenance opportunity but also an opportunity to derive additional revenue by adding features and capabilities. The business model sometimes unbundles embedded software from hardware to maximize revenue. The supplier may even create a platform and application programming interfaces (APIs) that allow other suppliers to add application software, enhancing the value of the appliance but forgoing some possible revenue.

Example Suppliers of telephone switches (such as Lucent, Nortel Networks, Erickson, and Siemens) traditionally bundled call-processing software. As software development costs grew, they sold and upgraded the software separately, realizing significant revenues from upgrades. However, this highlighted to the customers the lack of competitive suppliers for this embedded software; they were locked into a software supplier with their original equipment purchase. The suppliers were eventually prodded into open APIs, allowing other software vendors to add application feature packages (this was called the "intelligent network").

Increasingly, information appliance suppliers are adopting an unbundled software pricing model, although this cannot be considered conventional as yet.

Example TiVo developed a personal video recorder but, rather than manufacturing this equipment, licensed the design to consumer electronics manufacturers Philips and Sony. Each customer purchasing a TiVo must separately purchase an embedded software license. TiVo derives revenue from both equipment royalties and a subscription to periodic TV scheduling information and software upgrades. This gives TiVo more opportunities to offer pricing and service variants (see chapter 9). This pricing is an interesting hybrid between what is typical of material goods and software. Competitor ReplayTV adopted a bundle including both software upgrades and schedule information in the original appliance price.

Like embedded software, the application service provider model adds an intermediary between software supplier and user. The service provider pricing to its customer (the end-user) often uses models commonly found in traditional service (rather than product) industries, such as subscription, pay-per-use, and cross-subsidy. A *subscription* offers the service for capacity-limited or unlimited use over a contracted time period with recurring payments. *Pay-per-use* requires metering and billing on a per-use basis, requiring (depending on the approach taken) significant infrastructure. For example, to support irregular uses (similar to Web browsing) at a fine granularity, an effective micropayment system may accommodate very low prices with acceptably low transaction costs. *Cross-subsidy* recovers the cost by attaching a technically unrelated service, such as advertising, or bundling it with another paid service.

Software's unique characteristics lend themselves to innovative pricing mechanisms. One of these is self-awareness, the ability of an executing software module to monitor its own use and communicate with a payment service.

Example The *superdistribution* model (Cox 1996) encourages operators and users to further distribute software modules to others (with the permission and blessing of the software supplier). The supplier can enforce a software license with payments by including within the module the awareness that it is executing and the functionality to convey a payment for use, again assuming a payment infrastructure. The model is transitive in that a module incorporating or using a module from a third-party supplier causes an indirect payment to compensate that third party. Superdistribution can be viewed as bundling of viral marketing (Ward 2000) with distribution and sale.

Superdistribution illustrates one important characteristic of software. It is unique among goods in its flexibility to decouple pricing from the distribution model and from the industrial organization. The difference between selling software for user installation and operation and selling it as a service is the responsibility for provisioning and operation, not pricing, and all pricing options are technically feasible for both organizational models. An application service provider can offer a product-like pricing model, such as single upfront payment. It can even simultaneously offer variants of the software at different prices, and offer different versions with the option for a paid upgrade. Similarly, software distributed to a user for self-provisioning can be priced based on use, as in superdistribution. This is more cumbersome for material goods, where the customer takes physical possession and the supplier must gain physical access to a meter that monitors use (unless, of course, that material good has embedded software and network access). It is not feasible for information goods (unless accompanied by software), which lack the dynamic behavior necessary for monitoring and billing.[5]

6.3.4 Acquiring Industry-Specific Applications

The business of selling generic and widely used software applications or infrastructure to a mass market is quite different from selling applications that meet specialized organizational needs. In the former, the large creation costs can be recovered through volume sales at moderate prices. In the latter, the price must be higher, commensurate with the smaller sales volume, and this will invoke considerable competitive evaluation and case-by-case negotiation by the customer. The customer will often consider internal development of the software, so the application software supplier competes directly with an internal information systems organization. These challenges are offset by the opportunity to substantially differentiate the application and derive significant revenue on the basis of unique and identifiable value to the user, assuming that pricing can be based in part on this value (see chapter 9).

An end-user organization acquiring software for specific internal purposes has several options: make, buy, license, and subscribe. Each has its advantages and disadvantages. In the *make option*, all four stages in the software value chain (creation through use) are kept in-house (see section 6.2.2). This offers the greatest potential to differentiate from competitors but also may foreclose or at least make difficult future interoperability with competitors (who may turn into partners through alliance, merger, or acquisition). It cannot spread the high development costs over multiple uses and has considerable risk of delay, budget overruns, or even failure. Budgeting must take into account not only creation costs but also ongoing maintenance and upgrade costs and their burden for years to come. These costs, too, will not be spread over multiple uses. Operational costs may be higher because of the reduced economies of scale and the inability to hire existing expertise. A "make" decision entails considerable opportunity costs, given the shortage of skilled software developers (see chapter 8); allocating development resources to one project denies resources to other projects.

The *buy option* is to outsource development to a firm specializing in contract software development. In this case, the source code will likely be owned by the end-user, and ongoing maintenance and upgrade may be the responsibility of developer or user. Like the make option, buying offers the opportunity to mold business processes, organizations, and software as a unit, gaining efficiency and competitive advantage but also incurring higher costs of development, maintenance, and operation. Negotiations (and associated transaction costs) with contracted software developers are often protracted and difficult because of the complexity of the issues involved. A developer will seek ownership or joint ownership of the software in order to be free to reuse modules in other projects or to use the code base as the starting point for future projects. The buyer will seek at least joint ownership so as to be free to take over future maintenance and upgrade and to avoid lock-in to the developer. If the buyer cedes ownership, the buyer will want a lower price in return or possibly royalties in return for use of the code in other projects. The buyer may seek to exclude direct competitors as future customers of the developer, preserving competitive advantage.

In the *license option*, an end-user licenses an off-the-shelf software product from a software supplier. Finally, in the *subscription option*, the application services are purchased directly from an application service provider. In practical terms, the subscription option offers less opportunity than the license option to deeply integrate the software with other applications in the organization (although Web services technology have a significant impact).

In choosing a software application and a supplier, many considerations come into play (see table 6.1). Usually applications are sold as a monolith, and the internal architecture is of little concern. External architecture assumptions, like which information formats are exported and which APIs are provided for extension or composition, are important considerations. Some acquirers value an internal architecture that includes open APIs because this enables internal or outsourced developers to add capability or more easily compose with other applications.

Table 6.1
Considerations in Choosing an Application and Its Supplier

Property	Description
Capability and functionality	What does the application do, and how well does that meet needs?
Quality, usability, performance	How well does the application do what it does?
Reengineering	What organizational or process changes, worker training, and so on, will be necessary?
Architecture	What interfaces are assumed to the infrastructure or to other applications? What APIs are provided, and what information formats are supported? How easy will it be to integrate the application into the end-user environment, and what flexibility is there for application composition in the future?
Customer service	How good are user and technical support and maintenance?
Road map	Can the supplier provide visibility into future plans for evolution of capabilities and functionality?
Viability	Is the supplier financially sound and will it be in business to support the application? Does the application itself have sufficient market acceptance and momentums so that future upgrades and support can be expected?

6.3.5 Acquiring Infrastructure

Acquiring a new application may also entail new infrastructure equipment and software to support that application. Usually the application supplier will specify a specific platform that is needed to run the application, but sometimes there is more than one option.

Example An application created for a Windows platform will usually not run on a UNIX platform, and there are several similar but not identical UNIX platforms, including HP-UX, IBM AIX, Sun Solaris, and Linux. A supplier of an application for one of these platforms may choose to port the applications to other UNIX platforms or not; this is a trade-off between development cost and market opportunity.

Where new infrastructure must be acquired to run an application, there are significant administrative costs in acquiring the expertise or training workers, adding acquisition or switching cost. This frequently makes infrastructure as a service more attractive than self-provisioning. Wide-area networking and communication in particular are often obtained from a service provider, because it is largely impractical for end-user organizations to provision wide-area communication links and because a public network offers rich connectivity. There are indications that infrastructure service offerings will grow in both features and popularity.

Example Caching improves the performance of information distribution by locating temporary information storage nearer to consumers of that information. Providers offering this service illustrate alternative business models. Inktomi targets Internet service providers, providing all their customers with enhanced information access. Akamai, in contrast, sells to information suppliers, offering them a global caching infrastructure that offers better performance to their customers.

Although infrastructure is rarely developed by an end-user organization, there are exceptions. One important role of infrastructure is to enable the composability of applications (see section 3.2.12).

Example Operating systems and their networking services offer standard mechanisms for applications to communicate, on the same or different host. One factor in the success of the Internet was allowing applications on different platforms to share data, although this is only the first step; it falls far short of composability (see section 4.3.6), which requires interoperability through application-level protocols and complementarity of function.

A need for custom infrastructure arises because many organizations find it impractical to replace legacy applications because of time, cost, and risk constraints, especially if they can be successfully composed with other applications. This issue arises in assembling enterprise applications by composing legacy departmental applications, and often requires significant development effort in creating a custom infrastructure. In this area, the boundary between application and infrastructure is hazy, as this infrastructure is actually an extension of the existing applications.

6.3.6 Accounting Issues

Investments in acquiring or developing software are substantially influenced by accounting standards and rules, which determine how investments affect income and the balance sheet. Financial and accounting practices for software have been a contentious issue for some time, again because of the distinctive nature of software. In particular, accountants have traditionally viewed software as an intangible asset, in contrast to, for example, tangible assets like a building, machinery, or equipment. Because tangible assets provide future ongoing returns, they can usually be *capitalized*, that is, their first cost is treated as an asset depreciated over time as their benefits accrue. One view of software development costs is simply as a labor *expense*, which flows directly to the income statement as that expense is incurred. The ability to capitalize software encourages greater investment in development, since the depreciation affects income over time rather than immediately. The argument (Munter 1999) in favor of capitalization is that software development is not essentially different from the development of tangible goods in that the benefits of the software do accrue over time as the software is operational, and indeed embedded software is integral to many tangible goods. The argument against capitalization is that software development is risky and that future benefits are difficult to estimate. Accounting standards have gradually relaxed the circumstances under which software development costs can be capitalized.

Example   Recent U.S. accounting standards identify three stages in the acquisition of internal-use software:[6] the preliminary project stage, the application development stage, and the postimplementation operational stage. Using our terminology, costs incurred during the preliminary project stage and the provisioning and operation phases (including preparing data, testing, training, maintenance, and administration) should be expensed. Costs associated with development of application software may be capitalized. Where software is acquired rather than developed, the amount paid should be apportioned over these same categories and treated similarly for accounting purposes.

Another issue is the rate of depreciation, which assumes a lifetime for the software. Contrary to clear evidence (see section 3.2.11), many view software as something that doesn't deteriorate and that has an indefinite lifetime. This view can lead to catastrophic management decisions that defer or seek to avoid investment into new software development, placing excessive reliance on large past investments. Assuming a realistic rate of deprecation brings software investments appropriately in line with investments in tangible goods with a finite lifetime and distinguishes software from both pure intellectual property and real property.

6.4   Research and Discussion Issues

1. Understand in some depth the relation between industrial organization and software architecture. What are typical circumstances in which organization precedes architecture or architecture precedes organization, and both are determined by market forces beyond the direct control of industrialist and architect?

2. Discuss in some depth how a firm that defines and promulgates a software architecture maintains control over it and how that firm gains competitive advantage.

3. Discuss the observed evolution in industrial organization surrounding the capturing of user needs and software requirements, and speculate on how that organization may change in the future. Is this an area where the world will look much different?

4. Discuss in some depth the different business challenges faced by application, infrastructure, embedded, and component software suppliers.

5. Discuss the level of configurability required of off-the-shelf software products to meet the needs of multiple end-user organizations. What is the likely trend in this area: toward more customization of software, toward more configurability, or toward greater standardization of business needs and processes around standard software solutions?

6. If software suppliers are effectively defining the organization and processes of their customers, how can that relationship be made more effective?

7. The term *system integrator* is a bit of a misnomer because more functions than integration of software modules and equipment are required. Discuss in detail the range of functions required in software provisioning. Also, discuss the relation between the business consultant and system integration functions.

8. The systems management function in operation has some similarity to the functions of provisioning. Discuss the similarities and differences.

9. Describe in some depth the distinct challenges faced by departmental, enterprise, and commerce applications.

10. What issues and challenges have application service providers encountered in practice? Why have there been some notable business failures? Are these fundamental problems, or can they be addressed by changes in strategy?

11. In terms of the advantages and disadvantages of the ASP model of provisioning and operation, discuss any differences that may exist between infrastructure software, application software, and software tools.

12. Are there any essential differences between the conventional and ASP models in terms of pricing strategies for the software supplier? Consider the cases where the software supplier is also the service provider, and the case where they are different firms.

13. Consider the relation between the means of distribution for a series of releases of the same application and customer value. As part of this, consider the effect on software provisioning, operation, and use.

14. Consider in some depth the relation between the various pricing models (section 6.3.3) and user value and willingness to pay (section 3.2). Do some pricing models come closer than others to matching pricing and value?

15. Consider in some depth the make, buy, license, and subscribe models for software acquisition for an end-user organization with specific needs. Under what circumstances is each likely to better match needs? How do the models compare in cost effectiveness and matching of cost versus value?

16. Speculate on future trends for end-user organizations' outsourcing of infrastructure (including facilities, equipment, and software) provisioning and operation. Do you believe this will become increasingly common, and if so, for which types of infrastructure, and why?

17. Discuss the capitalization of all expenditures in the software value chain. Under what circumstances do you believe this is justified?

6.5 Further Reading

Acquiring and managing software in an organization is the subject of many textbooks on "management information systems"; Laudon and Laudon (2001) is typical. Many issues are discussed beyond those considered here. Regarding the pricing of software and information, Shapiro and Varian (1999) is recommended.

7

Software Creation Industry

Competition has been shown to be useful up to a certain point and no further, but cooperation . . . begins where competition leaves off.

Franklin Delano Roosevelt

Chapter 6 addressed the industrial organization of the software value chain from software creation to use. Software creation, one of the more important links of the chain, starts with a set of requirements and culminates in a software distribution that can be provisioned, including analysis of user needs, development, maintenance, customer support, and upgrades (see section 5.1).

This chapter addresses the internal structure of the software creation industry. It is common for a total solution to be composed of software products from multiple firms, whether the integration is performed by a system integrator or by a software supplier who licenses modules from other suppliers. Thus, cooperation (as well as competition) among firms in the software industry is crucially important. Interesting issues addressed in this chapter include how the organization of this production industry arises, how and why it is changing, and how firms coordinate themselves to arrive at composable solutions meeting user needs. This chapter first discusses the industrial organization, then the ways in which firms coordinate themselves, and finally the supply chain arising within the industry based on software components.

7.1 Industrial Organization of the Software Industry

A relation between software architecture and industrial organization was pointed out in section 6.1; industry responsibility must follow interfaces of software modules at the top level of architectural decomposition. Is the architecture determined by the marketplace, or is industrial organization determined by architecture? What is the industrial organization of the software creation industry, and how is it changing, and why? These issues are dealt with in this chapter.

7.1.1   Applications and Infrastructure

The most fundamental architectural concept in software is the decomposition into application and infrastructure. With some notable exceptions, firms in the industry generally specialize in one or the other.

Example   There are three major types of exceptions. One is firms that combine the businesses of infrastructure supplier and application software supplier, for instance, Apple (particularly historically) and Microsoft. They strongly encourage independent application software suppliers to use their platforms but also supply their own applications. Another exception is firms that combine the business of infrastructure software supply and consulting services, the latter focused on helping end-user organizations acquire and provision new applications. Examples are IBM and Compaq, the latter a merger (Compaq and Digital) specifically designed to combine these businesses. A third exception is firms that combine infrastructure software with contract development of applications, for instance, IBM.

While both applications and infrastructure require technical development skills, the core competencies are different. Applications focus the value proposition on end-users, and infrastructure provides value primarily to application developers and to operators. Applications are valued most of all for functionality and usability; their performance and technical characteristics are more dependent on infrastructure. It is advantageous to move as much technical capability to the infrastructure as possible, so application developers can focus on user needs. This leads to a natural maturation process whereby novel technical functionality is first pioneered in leading-edge applications and then migrates to enrich infrastructure, or applications evolve (at least partially) into infrastructural platforms for other applications.

Example   The playing of audio and video media was originally built into specialized applications. Today much of the required support is found in common infrastructure, usually at the level of operating systems. Individual productivity applications (such as office suites) have been augmented with ever richer user programmability support, so many interesting specialized applications now build on them (see section 4.2.7).

From a business perspective, application software has the advantage over infrastructure of providing value directly to the end-user, who ultimately pays for everything in the software value chain. This direct relationship provides rich opportunities to differentiate from competitors and to leverage it for selling complementary products. Ceding this valuable direct relationship between supplier and user is a disadvantage of the application service provider model (from the supplier perspective) and also a motivation to become a service provider as well as a software supplier.

In some cases there are considerable marketplace obstacles to application adoption that make business difficult for application suppliers, such as lock-in and network effects (see chapter 9), but in other cases these are less important. Application software suppliers who provide variations on competitive applications find lock-in a greater obstacle but also benefit from a moderation of network effects, for instance, through providing backward compatibility or translations (Shapiro and Varian 1999b). There are many opportunities to pursue entirely new application categories, as illustrated by the recent explosion of Internet e-commerce.

As observed in section 3.1, applications are becoming increasingly numerous, diverse, and specialized. This is especially true of sociotechnical applications, which are often specific to the group or organizational mission they serve. This has several implications for industrial organization. First, a strong separation of applications and infrastructure reduces the barriers to entry to new application ideas. Where applications and infrastructure are supplied by separate firms, the latter find it advantageous to define open and well-documented application programming interfaces (APIs) that make it easier to develop applications, which in turn attracts application ideas from more sources and provides more diversity and competitive options to users. A good test of the application infrastructure separation is whether an application can be developed and deployed without the knowledge or cooperation of the infrastructure supplier or operator.

Second, application diversity is enhanced by doing whatever is necessary to make it faster, cheaper, and requiring less development skill. This includes incorporating more needed functionality in the infrastructure. Making use of software components (see section 7.3), and rapid prototyping and end-user programming methodologies (see section 4.2).

Third, application diversity is enhanced by an experimental approach seeking inexpensive ways to try out and refine new application ideas (see section 3.1.6). Applications should be a target for industrial and academic research, because a research environment is well suited to low-cost experiments and the refinement of ideas unfettered by the immediate goal of a commercially viable product (NRC 2000b) (see chapter 8). In reality, applications have traditionally not been an emphasis of the information technology (IT) research community for many reasons, including the importance of nontechnical considerations, the need for specific end-user domain knowledge, the difficulty of gaining access to users for experimentation, and the inherent difficulty in assessing experimental outcomes.

Fourth, innovative new applications are a good target for venture capital funding and startup companies. The funding of competing startups is a good mechanism for the market to explore alternative application approaches. Venture capitalists specialize in managing the high risks of new applications and have effective mechanisms to abandon as well as start new businesses. This should not rule out large company initiatives, but large companies are usually not attracted by the limited revenue potential of a specialized application, put off by the financial risks involved, and sensitive to the opportunity costs of tying up scarce development resources.

Returning to the separation of application and infrastructure, the successes here also build on the economics underlying infrastructure (see chapter 9). If a new application requires a new infrastructure, then the required investment (as well as investment risk) is much larger than if the application is built on existing infrastructure. Thus, the separation of applications from infrastructure reduces barriers to entry and encourages small companies.

Example   The history of the telephone industry illustrates these factors. Telephone companies are historically application service providers with one primary application—telephony. They are also infrastructure service providers, providing not only the infrastructure supporting telephony but also data communications (e.g., the Internet) and video (e.g., broadcast television distribution). They have shown interest in expanding their application offerings, primarily in directions with mass market appeal. In the United States, the telephone industry has launched three major application initiatives of this character: video telephony (extending telephony to include video), videotext (an early proprietary version of the Web), and video-on-demand. In all three cases, the financial risk in deploying an expensive capital infrastructure to support a new application with uncertain market potential proved too great, and the efforts were abandoned. The telephone industry also illustrates numerous successes in deploying applications building on the existing telephony infrastructure, including products from independent suppliers like the facsimile machine and voice-band data modem.

The telecommunications industry strategy addresses one serious challenge following from the complementarity of applications and infrastructure and from indirect network effects: an infrastructure supporting a diversity of available applications offers more value to users, and an application utilizing a widely available infrastructure enjoys an inherently larger market. Industry thus faces the chicken-and-egg conundrum that a new infrastructure cannot be marketed without supported applications, and an application without a supporting infrastructure has no market. The telephone industry strategy has been to define a compelling application with mass market appeal and then to coordinate the investment in application and infrastructure, while making the infrastructure fairly specialized to support that application.[1]

The computer industry has generally followed the different strategy of deploying a generic infrastructure that supports a diversity of applications. In part this can be attributed to the culture of the industry, flowing from the original idea of programmable equipment whose application functionality is not determined at the time of manufacture. The Internet (a computer industry contribution to communication) followed a similar strategy; the core design philosophy for Internet technologies always valued low barriers to entry for new applications and a diversity of applications.

However, a pure strategy of deploying a generic infrastructure and waiting for applications to arrive is flawed because it does not address the issue of how to get infrastructure into the hands of enough users to create a market for applications that build on that infrastructure. The computer industry has found numerous ways to deal with this challenge (and has also suffered notable setbacks), all focused on making one or more compelling applications available to justify investment in infrastructure. An approach for totally new infrastructure is to initially bundle a set of applications with it, even while keeping the infrastructure generic and encouraging other application suppliers (e.g., the IBM PC and the Apple Macintosh were both bundled initially with a set of applications, and the Internet initially offered file transfer and e-mail). For infrastructure that has similar functionality to existing infrastructure, interoperability with older applications and offering higher performance characteristics for those older applications is another approach (e.g., layering; see section 7.1.3). Related to this, it is common for infrastructure to be incrementally expanded while maintaining backward compatibility for older applications. Application and infrastructure suppliers can explicitly coordinate themselves (e.g., by sharing product road maps; see section 7.2). Yet another approach is for applications to evolve into infrastructure by offering APIs or open internal interfaces (e.g., the Web; see section 7.1.2).

Another difference between the computer and telecommunications industries is the long-standing role of a service provider in telecommunications. Selling applications as a service bundled with a supporting infrastructure is advantageous in providing a single integrated solution to customers and freeing them of responsibility for provisioning and operation. The software industry is moving in this direction with the application service provider model.

The goal should be to combine the most desirable features of these models, and indeed the separation of application and infrastructure at the technological level is not inconsistent with a service provider model and a bundling of application and infrastructure as sold to the user. One of the trade-offs involved in these strategies is summarized in the fundamental relationship (Shapiro and Varian 1999b):

Revenue = Market share × Market size.

An infrastructure that encourages and supports a diversity of applications exchanges market share (by ceding many applications to other suppliers or service providers) for an increase in total market size (by providing more diversity and value to users). Just as software suppliers must decide on their degree of application/infrastructure separation, service providers face similar issues. They can offer only applications bundled with infrastructure, or enhance the diversity of application offerings while ceding revenues and part of the customer relationship by giving third-party application providers access to their infrastructure. To maximize revenues in the latter case, use-based infrastructure pricing models can maximize the financial return from application diversity. These issues will become more prominent with the emerging Web services (see section 7.3).

7.1.2 Expanding Infrastructure

The growing cost of software development and the shortage of programming professionals concerns software development organizations. This is exacerbated by the increasing specialization and diversity of applications (see section 3.1.5); specialized applications may be economically feasible only if development costs can be contained. Several trends reduce developments costs, including improved tools, rapid development methodologies (see section 4.2), greater use of software components and frameworks (see section 7.3.6), and expanding infrastructure to make it cheaper and faster to develop and deploy applications.

The idea behind expanding infrastructure is to observe what kind of functionalities application developers reimplement over and over, and to capture those functionalities in a generic and flexible way within the infrastructure. It is important to capture these capabilities in a generic and general way so that they can meet the needs of a wide range of present and future applications. End-users for infrastructure software include application developers and operators.

Example   Many applications need authentication and access control for the end-user (see section 5.4). Many aspects of this capability are generic and separated from the specific needs of each application. If authentication and access control are included within the infrastructure to be invoked by each application for its own purposes, reimplementation is avoided and users benefit directly by being authenticated only once for access to multiple applications.

These economic realities create an opportunity for the infrastructure to expand in capability over time. This may happen directly, or sometimes software developed as part of an application can be made available to other software and subsequently serve as infrastructure.

Example   Early applications had to manage much of the graphical user interface on their own, but later this capability was moved to the operating system (initially in the Apple Macintosh). Software to format screen documents based on the Web markup language (HTML) was first developed in the Web browser but was also potentially useful to other applications (like e-mail, which frequently uses HTML to format message bodies). For example, Microsoft made this HTML display formatting available to other applications in its Windows operating system and to the system itself in displaying help screens. The company provided an API to HTML formatting within the Internet Explorer browser and included the Internet Explorer in the Windows software distribution.

Sometimes, an entire application that becomes ubiquitous and is frequently composed into other applications effectively moves into the infrastructure category.

Example   The Web was originally conceived as an information access application for scholarly communities (World Wide Web Consortium 2002) but has evolved into an infrastructure supporting e-commerce and other applications. Many new distributed applications today incorporate the Web server and browser to present application-specific information to the user without requiring application-specific client software. Office suites are commonly used as a basis for custom applications serving vertical industry markets.

Valued-added infrastructure adds additional capability to an existing infrastructure.

Example   A major area for innovation in infrastructure is *middleware*, defined roughly as infrastructure software that builds on and adds value to the existing network and operating system services. Middleware sits between the existing infrastructure and applications, calling upon existing infrastructure services to provide enhanced or extended services to applications. An example is *message-oriented* *middleware*, which adds numerous message queuing and prioritization services valuable to work flow applications.

Market forces encourage these additions because of the smaller incremental investments compared to starting anew and because of the ability to support legacy applications utilizing the earlier infrastructure. From a longer-term perspective, this is problematic in that it tends to set in stone decisions made earlier and to introduce unnecessary limitations, unless designers are unusually visionary. Economists call these *path-dependent effects*.

Example Early Internet research did not anticipate streaming audio and video services. The core Internet infrastructure therefore does not include mechanisms to ensure bounded delay for transported packets, a capability that would be useful for delay-sensitive applications like telephony or video conferencing.[2] While acceptable quality can be achieved without these delay guarantees, better quality could be achieved with them. Unfortunately, once a packet is delayed too much, there is no way to make up for this, as time moves in only one direction. Hence, no value-added infrastructure built on the existing Internet technologies can offer delay guarantees—a modification to the existing infrastructure is required. Value-added infrastructure lacks complete freedom to overcome earlier design choices, particularly in performance dimensions.

The chicken-and-egg conundrum—which comes first, the applications or the infrastructure they depend on—is a significant obstacle to establishing new infrastructure capability. One successful strategy has been to move infrastructure with a compelling suite of applications into the market simultaneously, presuming that even more applications will come later.

Example The Internet illustrates this, as it benefited from a couple of decades of refinement in the academic research community before commercialization. A key was developing and refining a suite of "killer apps" (e.g., file transfer, e-mail, Web browsing). This, plus an established substantial community of users, allowed the Internet to reach commercial viability and success quickly once it was made commercially available. This is an oft-cited example of the important role of government-funded research (see chapter 8), subsidizing experimentation and refinement of infrastructure and allowing a suite of compelling applications to be developed. Such externally funded experimental infrastructure is called a test bed for the new space to be populated.

Middleware illustrates another strategy. Applications and (future) infrastructure can be developed and sold as a bundle while maintaining strict modularity so that the infrastructure can later be unbundled and sold separately. A variation is to establish APIs to allow independent use of capabilities within an application.

Example   A way to establish a message-oriented middleware (MOM) product might be to develop and bundle it with an enterprise work flow application, such as a purchase order and accounts payable application. By providing open APIs to the MOM capabilities, other application suppliers are encouraged to add application enhancements or new application capabilities that depend on the MOM. If this strategy is successful, eventually the MOM assumes a life of its own and can be unbundled and sold separately as infrastructure.

7.1.3   Vertical Heterogeneity: Layering

The modularity of infrastructure is changing in fundamental ways, driven primarily by the convergence of the computing (processing and storage) and telecommunications industries. By *convergence*, we mean two industries that were formerly independent becoming competitive, complementary, or both. This convergence is manifested primarily by the Internet's enabling of globally distributed software (see section 4.5), leading to applications that emphasize communication using distributed software (see section 3.1). This led to competing data networking solutions from the telecommunications and computer industries[3] and made networking complementary to processing and storage.

The top-level vertical architecture of both the telecommunications and computer industries prior to this convergence resembled a *stovepipe* (see figure 7.1). This architecture is based on market segmentation, defining different platforms for different application regimes. In the case of computing, mainframes, servers (originally minicomputers and later microprocessor-based) and desktop computers were introduced into distinct market segments (see table 2.3), each segment offering typically two or three major competitive platforms. Each segment and platform within that segment formed a separate marketplace, with its own applications and customers. Mainframes served back-office functions like accounting and payroll, servers supported client-server departmental functions like customer service, and desktop computers served individual productivity applications.

Similarly, the telecommunications industry segmented the market by application or information medium into telephony, video, and data. Each of these media was viewed as a largely independent marketplace, with mostly separate infrastructure sharing some common facilities.

Example   Telecommunications firms have always shared right-of-way for different applications and media, and also defined a digital multiplexing hierarchy (a recent

Telecommunications   **Computing**

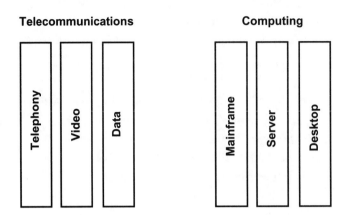

Figure 7.1
Historically, the telecommunications and computing industry both used an architecture resembling a stovepipe.

example is SONET, or synchronous optical network) that supported a mixture of voice, data, and video services.

While the telecommunications and computer architectures look superficially similar, historically the approach has been different, primarily arising out of the importance of the service provider in telecommunications but not in computing. With notable exceptions, in telecommunications the infrastructure and application suppliers sold to service providers, who did the provisioning and operation, and the service providers sold application services (and occasionally infrastructure services) to users. In computing, it was common for infrastructure suppliers to sell directly to users or end-user organizations, who acquire (or develop themselves) applications and do their own provisioning and operation. This is partly due to the different cultures and the relative weakness of data networking technologies (necessary to sell application services based on processing and storage) in the early phases of the computer industry.

These distinct industry structures led to fundamental differences in business models. Firms in the telecommunications industry historically saw themselves as application service providers, viewed the application (like telephony or television-video distribution) as their business opportunity, and constructed a dedicated infrastructure for their application offerings. Infrastructure was a necessary cost of business to support applications, the primary business opportunity. Further, service providers viewed alternative applications and application suppliers as a competitive threat.

In contrast, the relatively minor role of a service provider in the computer industry and the cultural influence of the technical genesis of computing (programmability, and the separation of application from infrastructure) resulted in a strikingly different business model. Infrastructure and application suppliers sold independently to end-user organizations, and the users integrated the two. As a result, neither the application supplier nor the user perceived much freedom to define new infrastructure but focused on exploiting existing infrastructure technologies and products. The infrastructure supplier encouraged a diversity of complementary applications and application suppliers to increase the value of its infrastructure and simultaneously provide customers better price, quality, and performance through application competition.

To summarize the difference in the telecommunications and computing business strategies, in telecommunications the infrastructure chased the applications, whereas in computing the applications chased the infrastructure. While there are many necessary qualifications and notable exceptions to this statement, for the most part it rings true. In a sense, the telecommunications business model formed a clearer path to dealing with the indirect chicken-and-egg network effects mentioned earlier. Regardless of whether applications chase infrastructure or the reverse, investments in new infrastructure technologies have to proceed on faith that there will be successful applications to exploit new infrastructure. In the telecommunications industry this was accomplished by directly coordinated investments, and in the computer industry an initial suite of applications was viewed as the cost of establishing a new infrastructure.

Example   To complement its PC, IBM initially supplied a suite of personal productivity applications, as did Apple Computer with the Macintosh. In both cases, open APIs in the operating system encouraged outside application developers, and it was not long before other application software suppliers supplanted the original infrastructure supplier's offerings (particularly for the PC).

This is all historical perspective, and not an accurate view of the situation today, in part because of the convergence of these two industries. The infrastructure has shifted away from a stovepipe form and toward a horizontal architecture called *layering*. The layered architecture organizes functionality as horizontal layers (see figure 7.2), each layer elaborating or specializing the functionality of the layer below. Each layer focuses on supporting a broad class of applications and users rather than attempting to segment the market. A natural way to enhance and extend the infrastructure is to add a new layer on top of existing layers. If applications are permitted to directly access services from lower layers, the addition of a new layer does

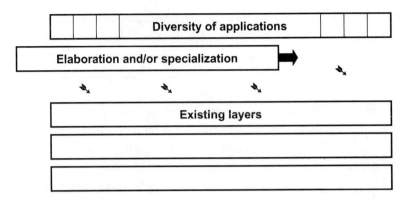

Figure 7.2
The layered architecture for infrastructure modularizes it into homogeneous horizontal layers.

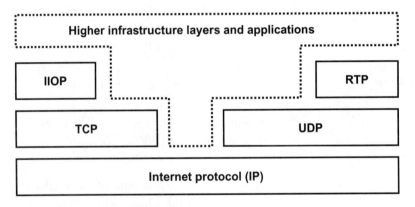

Figure 7.3
A simplified architecture of the Internet illustrates how new layers are added while future layers and applications can still invoke services of previous layers.

not disrupt existing applications but creates opportunities for new applications. While applications are allowed to access any layer, each layer is usually restricted to invoke only the services of the layer immediately below. This restriction can be eased by allowing two or more layers in parallel, at the same level.

Example   As illustrated in figure 7.3, the Internet is built on a foundation layer called the internet protocol (IP) and on top of that two widely used layers, transmission control protocol (TCP) and user datagram protocol (UDP). IP offers a service that conveys packets from one host to another with no guarantee of delivery order or reliability (analogous to sending postcards through the postal system).

TCP and UDP invoke the services of IP to direct packets to a specific application running on the host. TCP also offers reliability and guaranteed ordering of delivery, achieved by detecting lost (or excessively delayed) packets and resending them. Later, the internet inter-ORB protocol (IIOP) and the real-time protocol (RTP) layers were added on top of TCP and UDP, respectively, to support distributed object-oriented applications and streaming audio and video. HTTP (hypertext transfer protocol) is an important protocol layered on TCP, the main protocol underlying the Web and easily recognized in Web addresses (http://). In the future, more layers may be added; future layers and applications are permitted to access lower layers. Applications can even invoke IP services directly, although this would be unusual.

Since the layered architecture dominates the converged computing and telecommunications industries, it largely displaces the stovepipe architecture historically characteristic of both industries. There are several forces driving this shift and accompanying implications for industrial structure. The first is the effect of the Internet on the computer industry. By enabling distributed applications to communicate across platforms, it creates a new technical and commercial complementarity among them. End-users do not want to uniformly adopt a single platform to use a particular distributed application, nor do they want to participate in an application with only a subset of other users, reducing value because of network effects. Suppliers of new distributed applications don't want to limit their market to a subset of users on a given platform, or take specific measures to support different platforms. For applications to be easy to develop, deploy, and operate in an environment with heterogeneous platforms, application suppliers want to see homogeneity across those platforms. Horizontal homogeneity can potentially be achieved in a layered architecture by adding layers above the existing heterogeneous platforms, those new layers hiding the heterogeneity below. Because of path-dependent effects, this results in a hybrid stovepipe-layered architecture.

Example The virtual machine and associated environment for code portability can be viewed as a layer added to the operating system within each platform (see section 4.4.3). As illustrated in figure 7.4, this new layer adds a uniform execution model and environment for distributed software applications. It can be viewed as a homogeneous layer that sits on top of existing heterogeneous platforms (like Windows, Mac OS, and different forms of UNIX). Further, there is no reason (other than inconvenience in provisioning and application composability) not to have two or more parallel virtual machine layers supporting different groups of applications.

A layer that hides the horizontal heterogeneity of the infrastructure below and is widely deployed and available to applications is called a *spanning layer*. The most

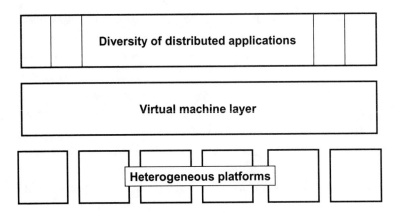

Figure 7.4
The widely deployed virtual machine can create a homogeneous spanning layer for applications that hides the heterogeneity of platforms.

important spanning layer today, the internet protocol, was specifically designed to hide heterogeneous networking technologies below. The virtual machine is another example of a spanning layer, arguably not yet widespread enough to deserve this appellation. One way to view the relation between these spanning layers was illustrated earlier in the "hourglass" of figure 4.6.

A second driver for layering is the trend toward applications that integrate processing, storage, and communication and mix data, audio, and video (see section 3.1). In contrast to the stovepipe, each horizontal layer (and indeed the entire infrastructure) supports a variety of technologies, applications, and media.

Example   Within the communication infrastructure, the IP layer has been extended to support data by the addition of the TCP layer and extended to support streaming audio media by the addition of an RTP layer on top of UDP (see figure 7.3). A given application can mix these media by accessing the TCP layer for data and the RTP layer for audio and video.

A third and related driver for layering is value added to infrastructure that can support the composability of different applications (see section 3.2.12), which is one of the most important roles of infrastructure. By binding different applications to different infrastructures, a stovepipe architecture is inherently constrained in its ability to support composability, but a layered architecture is not.

A fourth driver for layering is its allowance for incremental extension and elaboration while continuing to support existing applications. This reduces the barrier to entry for applications that require new infrastructure capabilities, since most of the supporting infrastructure does not need to be acquired or provisioned. Looking at it from the computer industry perspective (infrastructure first, applications later), this allows incremental investments in infrastructure for both supplier and customer.

Modularity introduces inefficiency, and layering is no exception. Compared to a monolithic stovepipe, layering tends to add overhead, no small matter in a shared infrastructure where performance and cost are often important. The processes described by Moore's law are thus an important enabler for layering (see section 2.3).

Layering fundamentally shifts the structure of industry competition. Each layer depends on the layers below (they are complementary), and an application requires the provisioning and operation of all layers upon which it depends. This creates complementary infrastructure suppliers, and a burden on infrastructure provisioning to integrate layers. Competition in the infrastructure is no longer focused on segmentation of the market for applications but rather on competition at each layer, each supplier attempting to provide capabilities at that layer for a wide range of applications. The integration of layers requires coordination among suppliers (see section 7.2), and functionality and interfaces are fairly constrained if alternative suppliers are to be accommodated.

Layering fundamentally changes the core expertise of industry players. Expertise about particular application segments no longer resides with infrastructure suppliers but primarily within application suppliers. Market forces encourage infrastructure suppliers to extend the capabilities they supply to serve all (or at least a broader range of) applications because this increases market size. This increases their needed range of expertise, and if this proves too daunting, they may narrow their focus vertically by specializing in only one or two layers. Startup companies especially face a challenge in this industry structure because of the generality and hence high development costs and wide-ranging expertise required. Thus, startup companies tend to focus either at the top (applications) or bottom (technology) of the layering architecture, where diverse solutions thrive and there are fewer constraints and less need to coordinate with others (see section 7.1.5.).

Example The physical layer of communication (transporting a stream of bits via a communication link) is a ripe area for startup companies, especially in light of the variety of media available (optical fiber, radio, free-space optical, coaxial cable, and wirepair). As long as they interface to standard solutions for the layers above, innovation is relatively unconstrained. The analogous opportunity in processing is the microprocessor, so one might expect a similar diversity of startups. In fact, microprocessor startups are rare because the instruction set is deeply intertwined with the software layers above, greatly limiting the opportunity for differentiation. The emulation or virtual machine idea is one way to address this, but this reduces performance, one of the prime means of differentiation. An interesting attempt at combining the virtual machine and the custom microprocessor concepts is Transmeta's Crusoe, a small, energy-efficient processor with a proprietary instruction set complemented by a software layer that translates standard Intel instruction sequences into Crusoe instructions.

It is useful to examine the appropriate modularity of layering in more detail. It is striking that no single organization has responsibility for consciously designing the overall layered architecture. Rather, it is determined by research and company initiatives, collaborations among companies, and standardization bodies. The result is "creative chaos" that introduces strengths and weaknesses. On the plus side, innovations are welcome from many quarters, and good ideas have a reasonable chance of affecting the industry. On the negative side, application suppliers and provisioners must deal with a lot of uncertainty, with competing approaches to consider and no clear indication as to which ones will be successful in the long term.

Example   The first successful attempt at enabling cross-platform middleware as a spanning layer was the Object Management Group's common object request broker architecture (CORBA), a suite of standards to enable distributed object-oriented applications. CORBA has been successful in intraenterprise integration, where platform variety arises out of acquisitions and mergers and yet cross-platform integration is required. CORBA did not achieve similar success in interenterprise integration, where heterogeneous platforms are even more prevalent. A later approach to cross-platform integration was Java, now usually used in conjunction with CORBA in enterprise solutions. Again, interenterprise integration remains beyond reach for technical reasons. The latest attempt at global integration is Web services based on XML (extended markup language) and other Web standards (see section 7.3.7). With Web services emerging as the most likely universal spanning layer, competition in the layer immediately below heats up: Microsoft's .NET Common Language Runtime and its support for Web services compete against the Java virtual machine and its emerging support for Web services.

Historically, the approach was very different in the telecommunications industry. This arguably resulted in less change and innovation (but still a remarkable amount) but in a more reliable and stable infrastructure.

Example   Until about two decades ago, each country had a monopoly national telephone service provider (often combined with the post office). In the United States this was the Bell System, with its own research, equipment, software development, and manufacturing. Suppliers and providers coordinated through standardization bodies in Geneva, predominantly the International Telecommunication Union (ITU), formerly called Comité Consultatif International Téléphonique et Télégraphique (CCITT). Through these processes, the national networks and their interconnection were carefully planned top-down, and changes (such as direct distance dialing) were carefully planned, staged, and coordinated. This resulted in greater reliability and stability but also fewer competitive options or diversity of choice.

Since the networked computing infrastructure has not followed a top-down process, beyond the core idea of layering there is no overall architectural vision that guides the industry. Rather than pointing to a guiding architecture, we must resort to an analysis of the current state of the industry. An attempt at this analysis is shown in figure 7.5 (Messerschmitt 1999b). It illustrates three stovepipes of lower layers, one specific to each technology (processing, storage, and connectivity). Distributed applications (as well as nondistributed applications that combine processing and mass storage) want a homogeneous infrastructure that combines these three technologies in different ways, and thus the top layers are common to all three (see table 7.1).

The essential idea behind figure 7.5 is illustrated in figure 7.6. The intermediate layers provide a common set of services and information representations widely used

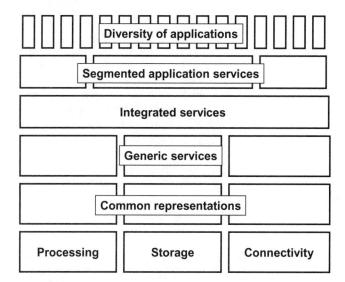

Figure 7.5
A layered architecture for distributed applications and the supporting infrastructure.

Table 7.1
Description of Layers Shown in Figure 7.5

Layer	Description	Examples
Applications	A diversity of applications provide direct and specific functionality to users.	
Segmented application services	Captures functionality useful to a narrower group of applications, so that those functions need not be reimplemented for each application. This layer has horizontal heterogeneity because each value-added infrastructure element is not intended to serve all applications.	Message-oriented middleware emphasizes work flow applications; information brokering serves as an intermediary between applications or users and a variety of information sources.
Integrated services layer	Provides capabilities that integrate the functions of processing, storage, and connectivity for the benefit of applications.	Directory services use stored information to capture and identify the location of various entities— essential to virtually all distributed applications.
Generic services layer	Provides services that integrate processing, storage, and connectivity in different ways.	The reliable and ordered delivery of data (connectivity); the structured storage and retrieval of data (storage); and the execution of a program in an environment including a user interface (processing and display).
Common representations layer	Provides abstract representations for information in different media (like processing instructions, numerical data, text, pictures, audio, and video) for purposes of processing, storage, and communication. They are deliberately separated from specific technologies and can be implemented on a variety of underlying technologies.	A virtual machine representing an abstract processing engine (even across different microprocessors and operating systems); a relational table representing the structure of stored data (even across different platforms); and a stream of bytes (eight-bit data) that are delivered reliably in order (even across different networking technologies).
Processing, storage, and connectivity	Provide the core underlying technology-dependent services.	Microprocessors, disk drives, and local-area networking.

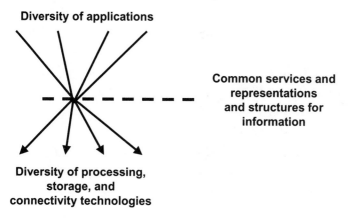

Diversity of applications

Common services and representations and structures for information

Diversity of processing, storage, and connectivity technologies

Figure 7.6
Layering provides separation of a diversity of technologies from a diversity of applications.

by applications. The goal is to allow a diversity of technologies to coexist with a diversity of applications without imposing the resulting chaos on applications—applications and technologies can evolve independently without much effect on each other. Providing a reimplementation of the common representation and services layers for each distinct technology accommodates this.

Of particular importance is the spanning layer. Assuming it is not bypassed—all layers above make use of its services but do not interact directly with layers below—a well-designed spanning layer can eliminate the dependence of layers above from layers below, allowing each to evolve independently. Successfully establishing a spanning layer creates a large market for solutions (application and infrastructure) that build upon it, both above and below. The spanning layer brings to bear the positive feedback of network effects without stifling technical or competitive diversity of layers below. It illustrates the desirability of separating not only application from infrastructure but also infrastructure from infrastructure.

Example The internet protocol can be viewed as a spanning layer, although it is limited to the connectivity stovepipe. As illustrated by the hourglass of figure 4.6, the IP layer does effectively separate applications from underlying networking technologies and has become virtually ubiquitous. Suppliers creating new communication and networking technologies assume they must support an IP layer above, and application suppliers assume they can rely on IP layers below for connectivity. Applications need not be redesigned or reconfigured when a different networking technology (e.g., Ethernet local-area network, wireless local-area network, fiber-optic wide-area network, wireless wide-area network, or satellite network) is substituted. The existence of IP also creates a ready and large market for middleware products building on internet protocols.

There are, however, limitations to layering. Mentioned earlier is the added overhead necessary to implement any strong modularity, including layering. In addition, intermediate layers can hide functionality but not performance characteristics of the underlying technology from applications.

Example   When the user substitutes a slow network access link for a faster one, the delay in packet delivery due to transmission time will be increased. Nothing in the intermediate layers can reverse this.

The preferred approach today to dealing with performance variations is to make applications robust and adaptive to the actual performance characteristics.[4] Applications should be able to take advantage of higher-performance infrastructure and offer the best quality they can subject to infrastructure limitations.

Example   A Web browser-server combination will display requested pages with low delay when there is ample processing power and communication bandwidth. When the bandwidth is much lower (say a voiceband data modem), the browser and server should adjust by trading off functionality and resolution for added delay in a perceptually pleasing way. For example, the browser may stop displaying high-resolution graphics, or ask the server to send those graphics at a lower resolution, because the resulting diminution in delay more than compensates perceptually for lost resolution.

Many current industry standardization and commercialization efforts would support the layered model (see figure 7.7 for examples). For each standard illustrated, there are standards competing for adoption. At the common representation layer, the Java virtual machine, the relational table, and the Internet's TCP are widely adopted. At the generic services layer are shown three standards that support object-oriented programming (OOP), a standard programming technique that emphasizes and supports modularity (see section 4.3). Programs constructed according to this model consist of interacting modules called objects, and the generic services layer can support execution, storage, and communication among objects. Java supports their execution, the object-relational database management system (ORDBMS) supports the storage of objects, and IIOP allows objects to interact over the network in much the same way as they would interact within a single host.

At the integrative services layer, CORBA attempts to identify and standardize a set of common services that integrate processing and connectivity (by incorporat-

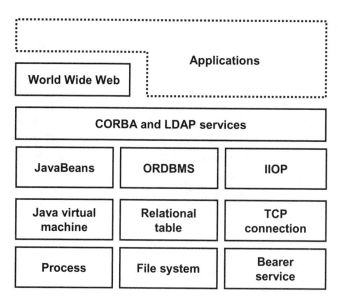

Figure 7.7
Examples of industry standards fitting the layered model of figure 7.5.

ing Java mobile code capabilities) and processing and storage (by providing for the storage of objects). Examples include the creation or storage of objects on demand, and directories that discover and locate objects and services on the network to make distributed applications easier to develop. The Web was mentioned earlier as an application that "grew up" to become an infrastructure supporting applications that access and update information over the network. On the other hand, the Web does not support all applications (e.g., those not based on a client-server architecture). Thus, the Web-as-infrastructure falls at the segmented application services layer.

7.1.4   Core Competencies
Earlier, the historical approaches of the telecommunications and computer industries were contrasted. This contrast raises an important issue for industrial organization: Who is responsible for provisioning and operation? As described in section 6.2, there are three primary options: an independent service provider (the historical telecommunications industry model), the application or infrastructure supplier (rare), or the user (the historical computer industry model). Of course there are other options, such as splitting responsibility for provisioning and operation, application and infrastructure, or different parts of the infrastructure.

The increasing role of application service providers in the software industry, and the trend in the telecommunications industry to focus on the provisioning and operation of infrastructure and not applications (particularly in the Internet segment of their market) suggests that radical change in industry structure may be occurring. This change can be traced to at least three undercurrents. One is the ubiquity and performance of the Internet, which opens up the option of operations shifted to a service provider while making application functionality available over the wide-area network. From the user perspective it makes no difference where the operations reside, except for important factors like performance, availability, and customer service. A second undercurrent leading to organizational change is the growing specialization and diversity of applications, and the resulting importance of application suppliers' focusing their efforts on satisfying user needs and requirements. Infrastructure suppliers and service providers have not proven as effective at this as more specialized application suppliers; this suggests an organizational separation of applications and infrastructure.

These observations provide hints as to how the industrial organization may evolve in the future. Like good software architecture (see section 4.3), market forces encourage an industrial organization with weak coupling of functions and expertise across different companies and strong cohesion within companies. These properties can be interpreted in different ways, such as transaction costs and coupling of expertise. In the long term, it seems that market forces reward firms that specialize in certain responsibilities but share core competencies, because many managerial approaches, such as compensation and organizational structures and processes, are tied to these competencies. Of course, there are many other considerations of importance, such as the desire of customers for a complete product portfolio or turn-key solution, or opportunities to gain competitive advantage by synergies among complementary responsibilities.

This suggests a fresh look at the software value chain (see section 6.2), not in terms of responsibilities but in terms of core competencies. Seven core competencies can be identified (see table 7.2).

To the extent that industrial organization is presaged by natural groupings of core competencies, the independent service provider (as embodied in the application service provider model) seems a likely outcome, because the core competencies resident there are quite distinct from those of the other roles. Telecommunications service providers should not try to be exclusive application suppliers; rather, they should focus on making their infrastructure services suitable for a wide range of applications and encourage a diversity of applications from many sources. They may

Table 7.2
Core Competencies Relating to the Software Industry

Competency	Description
Business function	An end-user organization should understand its business functions, which in most cases are not directly related to software or technology or software-based services.
User needs and requirements	Industry consultants should understand end-user needs, which increasingly requires specialized knowledge of an industry segment or specific organizational needs, in order to help organizations revamp business models, organization, and processes to take maximum advantage of software technology.
Application needs	Infrastructure suppliers should understand needs common to a wide variety of applications and application developers, and also market forces that strongly influence the success or failure of new infrastructure solutions.
Software development	Both application and infrastructure software suppliers need software development and project management skills, with technical, organizational, and management challenges. Application suppliers must also be competent at human-centered considerations such as user interfaces.
Provisioning	Constrained by the built-in flexibility and configurability of the application, the system integrator and business consultant must understand unique organizational needs and be skilled at choosing and integrating software from different firms.
Operation	Operators must be competent at the technical aspects of achieving availability and security, administrative functions like trust and access, and customer service functions such as monitoring, billing, and helpdesk.

exploit their core competency in operations by extending it from today's narrow range of applications (telephony, video distribution) to a wider range acquired from independent application suppliers, increasing the diversity of application service providers' offerings.

The increasing diversity and specialization of applications, and the need to consider the organizational and process elements of information technology and the interface between organization and technology, have profound implications for application software suppliers. As these core competencies differ sharply from software development, these enterprise and commerce software suppliers should look more and more to industry consultants to assist in needs and requirements definition.

For end-user organizations, focusing on core competencies would imply out-sourcing application development to application software suppliers, and provisioning and operation to system integrators, consultants, and service providers. In fact, this is becoming prevalent.

7.1.5 Horizontal Heterogeneity

From a technical perspective, an infrastructure layer that is horizontally homogeneous is advantageous (see section 7.1.3). This is an important property of a spanning layer because it creates a large market for layers above and below that can evolve independently. However, as shown in figure 7.5, it is entirely appropriate for horizontal heterogeneity to creep into the layers near the top and the bottom. Near the top, this segments the market for infrastructure to specialize in narrower classes of applications. With platforms supporting applications, one size does not fit all.

Example Distributed applications benefit from an infrastructure that hides the underlying host network structure, but this is unnecessary overhead for applications executing on a single host. Work flow applications benefit from a message and queuing infrastructure, and online transaction processing applications benefit from a database management system.

Near the bottom, it is desirable to support a diversity of technologies. This diversity arises out of, as well as encourages, technological innovation.

Example Innovation in microprocessor architecture has accompanied Moore's law as an important enabler for improving performance. Sometimes these architectural innovations can be accomplished without changing the instruction set—which clearly contributes to horizontal heterogeneity—but innovations in instruction sets enable greater advances. An example is the idea of a reduced instruction set computer (RISC), which traded simplicity in the instruction set for higher instruction execution rates. Numerous technological innovations have spawned heterogeneity in storage (e.g., recordable optical disks) and communication (e.g., wireless) as well. As underlying technology changes, so does the implementation of the lower layer infrastructure.

History and legacy technologies are another reason for heterogeneity.

Example Many historical operating system platforms remain, and several remain vibrant, evolving, and attracting new applications. The Internet brought with it distributed applications and network effects that place a premium on interoperability across platforms, e.g., a Web server running on a UNIX server and a Web browser running on a Macintosh desktop platform. The Internet has also brought with it a need for composability of different applications running on different hosts. For example, MIME[5] is a standard that allows a wide variety of applications on different platforms to agree on content types and the underlying data formats and encodings (it originated to support e-mail attachments but is now used more broadly).

It was argued earlier that unconditional software portability is neither a practical nor a desirable goal (see section 4.4.3), and for the same reason evolving toward a single platform is not desirable. There is no predetermined definition of which functionalities belong in applications and which in infrastructure, but rather capabilities that many applications find valuable (or that keep appearing in multiple applications) work their way into the underlying platform. The commonality inherent in ever-expanding platforms enables greater diversity of applications and especially supports their interoperability and composability. That this can occur in multiple platforms speeds the diversity of ideas that can be explored, and offers application developers some choice among differentiated platforms. At the same time, industry must deal with the reality of heterogeneous platforms, especially for distributed applications that would otherwise become Balkanized, confined to one platform and a subset of users, with the resulting network effect diminution of value. Fortunately, the owners of individual platforms—especially those with a smaller market share and especially with the rising popularity of distributed applications—have a strong incentive to ensure that their platforms can participate in distributed applications with other platforms. But specifically what can they do about it? Adding a layer with the hope that it becomes widespread enough to be considered a spanning layer is one approach.

Example Sun's Java effort, including the Java programming language, runtime environments (including virtual machines), libraries, and interfacing standards, created such a candidate for spanning layer, abstracting from underlying platforms, software, and hardware. Other examples include the CORBA standards and Microsoft's COM and .NET.

However, given the difficulties of establishing a totally new layer that achieves a high enough market penetration to attract a significant number of applications, new layers can arise out of an existing application or infrastructure.

Example The Web migration from application to infrastructure resulted from two factors. First, it had become ubiquitous enough to attract application developers, who were not ceding much market potential by adopting it as a foundation. Second, the Web provided open APIs and documented internal interfaces that made it relatively straightforward to exploit as an infrastructure. This illustrates that an application that is more open or less proprietary is more likely to be adopted as the basis for other applications, that is, as infrastructure.

Another response to heterogeneous platforms is to design an application to be relatively easy to port to different platforms. This places special requirements on interfaces between the application and its underlying platform; if they are designed in a relatively platform-independent and open way, the porting becomes easier (but exploiting the strengths of specific platforms becomes harder).

Example The Web is a good illustration of this. As a distributed application, the Web had to deal with two primary challenges. First, if the Web was to be more than simply a vehicle for displaying static stored pages (its original purpose), it had to allow other applications to display information via the Web browser and server. For example, dynamic Web pages based on volatile information stored in a database management system required an intermediary program (encompassing what is usually called the application logic) that requested the appropriate information from the database and displayed it in the proper formats in the browser. For this purpose, an open and relatively platform-independent API called the common gateway interchange (CGI) was standardized. The second challenge was the interoperability between browser and server running on different platforms. Fortunately, this problem was already partially solved by IP, which provided a communication spanning layer that allowed one host to communicate data to another using a standard packet representation, and a TCP that provided reliable and ordered transport of a stream of bytes. The Web simply had to standardize an application-layer transfer protocol (HTTP). These open standards made the Web relatively platform-independent, although different versions of the browser and server still had to be developed for the different platforms. Later, these open interfaces were an important factor in the evolution of the Web into infrastructure. For example, other applications could make use of HTTP to compose the entire browser or server into an application, or could even use HTTP independently (e.g., Groove, an application that uses HTTP as a foundation to share files and other information among collaborating users).[6] The latest generation of standardization focuses on Web services, and one of the core protocols in this space (SOAP: simple object access protocol) usually operates on top of HTTP (see section 7.3.7).

Another approach is to embrace horizontal heterogeneity but arrange the infrastructure so that interoperability and even composability are achieved across different platforms by appropriate industry standards or by platform-specific translators.

Example Different platforms for both servers and desktop computers tend to use different protocols and representations for file storage and print services. Users, on the other hand, would like uniform access to their files across all platforms (including Mac OS, the different forms of UNIX, and Windows), for example, to access files or print services on a UNIX server from a desktop (Linux or Mac OS or Windows) platform. Various open source solutions (e.g., Samba) and commercial solutions (e.g., Netware, NFS, Appletalk, Banyan Vines, and Decnet) provide this capability. See section 7.3 for additional examples in the context of software components and Web services.

Instead of tackling protocols (which specify how information gets from one platform to another) other industry standards focus on providing a common, flexible representation for information (without addressing how that information gets from one platform or application to another). These are complementary, since information must be transferred and must be understandable once it has been transferred.

Example XML is a flexible and extensible language for describing documents. It allows standardized tags that identify specific types of information to be identified. A particular industry can standardize these tags for its own context, and this allows different firms to exchange business documents and then extract the desired information from those documents automatically. For example, one industry might define an XML-based standard for describing purchase orders, and then each company can implement translators to and from this common representation for purchase orders within its (otherwise incompatible) internal systems. Unlike HTML, XML separates the formatting of a document from its content. Thus, workers can display XML purchase orders in presentations specific to their internal needs or practices.

A fourth approach to dealing with heterogeneous platforms is to add a service provider who either acts as an intermediary or centralizes the application.

Example Some companies have created a common intermediary exchange as a place to procure products and services from a set of suppliers. Sometimes this is done on an industry basis, as in the automotive industry (Covisint 2000). Considering the latter case, the exchange does not directly overcome platform and application incompatibilities among the participating organizations, but it does make the challenges considerably more manageable. To see this, suppose there are n distinct firms involved in the exchange. The intermediary has to deal with these n firms separately. Without the intermediary, each firm would have to work out similar interoperability issues with each of the $n - 1$ other firms, or in total there would be $n \cdot (n - 1)$. such relationships to manage, a much greater total burden. Interestingly, intermediaries tend to compete as well, leading to k intermediaries and thus $k - n$ relationships. For $k = 1$, the single intermediary can gain substantial market control, and the desire of the coordinated firms to retain agility tends to encourage formation of a competing intermediary. As k approaches n, the benefit of having intermediaries disappears. Market forces thus tend to keep the number of competing intermediaries low.

Distinct types of infrastructure can be identified in the layered architecture of figure 7.5. In classifying a particular type of infrastructure, it is important at minimum to ask two basic questions. First, does this infrastructure support a broad range of applications (in the extreme, all applications), or is it specialized to one segment of the application market? Second, is the infrastructure technology-specific, or does it not matter what underlying technologies are used? Neither of these distinctions is black-and-white; there are many nuances. The answers can also change over time because new infrastructure typically must start with only one or a few applications and then grow to more universal acceptance later. Table 7.3 gives examples of infrastructure categorized by application and technology dependence. Each category in the table suggests a distinct business model. As a result, infrastructure

Table 7.3
Examples of infrastructure Defined by Application and Technology Dependence

	Not Application-Dependent	Particular to One Application Market Segment
Not technology-dependent	The Internet TCP transport layer is widely used by applications desiring reliable, ordered delivery of data. The specific networking technologies present are hidden from TCP and layers above by the Internet IP spanning layer.	Message-oriented middleware supports work flow applications, and the Web supports information access and presentation. Each emphasizes distributed applications across heterogeneous platforms.
Particular to one technology platform	Operating systems are specific to a computer platform, although some (like Linux, Solaris, Windows NT, and Windows CE) have been ported to several. Each is designed to support a wide variety of applications on that platform.	Information appliances typically support a single application, and build that application on a single infrastructure technology platform.

suppliers tend to specialize in one (with a couple of notable exceptions): infrastructure suppliers at the lower layers focus on technology-dependent infrastructure, and those at the higher layers on application-dependent infrastructure. In the extreme of application dependence, some infrastructure may support a specific application but offer open APIs in the hope that other applications come later. In the extreme of technology dependence, an infrastructure may be embedded software bundled with hardware and sold as equipment or an appliance. In this case, the software is viewed as a cost of development, with no expectation of selling it independently.

Application- and technology-independent infrastructure clearly has the greatest market potential as measured by adoptions or unit sales. However, this type offers little opportunity for differentiation as to functions or features. To actually achieve universality, it must be highly standardized and hence commoditized. If it is well differentiated from other options, it is likely struggling for acceptance. Thus, this type of infrastructure probably represents the least opportunity for profit but is nevertheless quite important and beneficial. The current trend is therefore to use community-based development methodologies to create and maintain this type of software (as illustrated by the Samba example earlier; also see section 4.2.4), although not exclusively. Its universal appeal and wide use lend themselves to community-based development. This is leading to new types of software licensing approaches that mix the benefits of community-based development such as open source with commercial considerations such as deriving revenue and profit (see chapter 8).

Example Sun Microsystems has been a leading proponent of community-based development of infrastructure, examples being its Java middleware layer for portable execution (see section 4.4.3) and Jini, a platform for plug-and-play interoperability among information appliances (Sun microsystems 1999b). Other firms, such as Apple Computer (Mac OS X) and Netscape (Mozilla browser) have followed this approach. Several firms (e.g., IBM and Hewlett-Packard) have chosen open source Linux as an operating system platform.

At the other extreme, application- and technology-dependent infrastructure is characteristic of the stovepipe architecture (see section 7.1.3), and for the reasons discussed earlier is disappearing because of shrinking market opportunity. Most commercial infrastructure differentiates itself in the application or technology space, but not both.

7.1.6   Competition and Architecture

This section has enumerated some global architectural alternatives and their relation to industry structure. Architecture, because it defines the boundaries of competition and complementarity, is an important strategic issue for software suppliers (see section 6.1), and successfully defining and promulgating an architectural model is an important element of long-term success (Ferguson and Morris 1994). In contrast, suppliers who provide point solutions or who must plug solutions into an architecture defined elsewhere lose some control over their own destiny and have less strategic maneuvering room. Doubtless because of its significance, architectural control has also been a source of industry controversy and even government antitrust complaints (see chapter 8).

Within a given architecture, competition exists at the module level, and where a supply chain is created by hierarchical decomposition, at the submodule level as well. On the other hand, interacting modules are complementary. Suppliers naturally try to avoid direct competition in modules, particularly because high creation costs and low replication and distribution costs for software make competitive pricing of substitutes problematic (see chapter 9). Generally, open standardized interfaces (see section 7.2.3) make head-on competition more difficult to avoid, and for this reason industry standards are increasingly defined with a goal of enabling competitive suppliers to differentiate themselves with custom features or extensions while maintaining interoperability. In contrast, if suppliers choose not to offer complementary modules themselves, they encourage competitive options for those modules so that customers have a wider range of options with attractive prices and features and so that the overall system pricing is more attractive.

The architectural options and evolution discussed here have considerable implications for competition. Applications and infrastructure are complementary, and thus suppliers of each generally encourage competitive options in the other. While the expansion of infrastructure capabilities is a way to improve economic efficiency through sharing (see chapter 9) and to improve performance and quality, it also changes the competitive landscape by shrinking some application markets or at least introducing new competition.

No architectural issue has had more effect than the evolution from stovepipe toward layering architecture. This shifts the landscape from horizontal market segmentation, with an inclination toward vertical integration within each segment, to a vertical segmentation of functions where multiple complementary suppliers must cooperate to realize a full system solution.

The spanning layer is a key element of a layered architecture. Because it allows greater independence of evolution in the layers below and above, it is another form of common intermediary that makes practical a larger diversity of interoperable options below and above. Even if not initially defined with open interfaces, the ubiquity of a spanning layer implies that its interfaces below and above become de facto standards. In order for the entire infrastructure to evolve, a spanning layer and its interfaces must also evolve over time, insofar as possible through extensions rather than changes. While the spanning layer offers compelling advantages, commercial control of such a layer raises complaints of undue influence over other layers and overall system evolution. One response is government-imposed limits on the business practices of the owner of a spanning layer (see chapter 8). Another is to abandon the spanning layer in a way that preserves most advantages, such as horizontal heterogeneity within a layer, while maintaining interoperability or portability (see sections 7.1.5 and 7.3). Another is to promulgate a spanning layer in the public domain (through community-based development or similar methodologies, as in the Samba example).

7.2   Cooperation in the Software Industry

Just as participants in the software value chain (including nonsoftware companies) maintain ongoing business relationships (see section 6.3), so do participants within the software creation industry. Monolithic software solutions are today the exception rather than the rule; in most cases, a total solution of value to users integrates content from a number of software companies.

Example   A single desktop computer with a standard suite of office software might serve the needs of some users, and the software on such a platform might come from a single supplier like Apple Computer, Microsoft, or Sun Microsystems. Even in this simple case there will likely be contributions from other suppliers. For example, Microsoft Word XP includes modules and content acquired from other suppliers, like the equation editor, the document version comparer, parts of the spelling correction system, thesaurus, hyphenators, and dictionaries for many different languages, as well as some templates and fonts. Further, when the user browses the Web, the Web server may well be open source software (like Apache) or proprietary Web server software from another supplier (like IBM WebSphere or BEA WebLogic).

A pervasive issue is the coordination of software suppliers so that their solutions are either automatically composable or can at least be purposefully integrated. This creates a conspicuous need and opportunity for different software companies to coordinate through business or cooperative arrangements. As in other industries, coordination can take many forms, the extremes being proprietary bilateral business relationships on the one hand, and cooperative standards processes open to all interested parties on the other.

7.2.1 Supplier-Consumer Relationships

Some business relationships within the software industry take the traditional supplier-consumer form, although this does not evoke standard images of warehouses, shipping, and inventory. Since software can be freely replicated, a supplier need only provide a single copy to the customer together with the appropriate authorization, in the form of a licensing agreement (see chapter 8) spelling out the terms and conditions, for the customer to replicate the software in its products or to provision within its environment.

Where one software supplier is incorporating modules supplied by others, those modules must be integrated. This system integration step frequently requires modification of the purchased modules. The license permitting, changes to acquired modules may be made by the integrator (this requires source code). More often, the supplier makes these changes, and these repairs or refinements benefit all customers. Generally, the process and issues to be addressed are similar to end-user acquisition of software (see section 6.3.4). Differences do arise if the customer passes this software through to its own customers rather than provisioning it internally. Thus, the revenue stream expected from its customers, rather than its internal value proposition, becomes an element of price negotiation. Further, there is the issue of customer support: How do operators and users obtain support for modules acquired rather than developed by their immediate supplier? Is this a two-step process, or should the supplier directly support operators and users? Of course, customers generally prefer an integrated customer support solution. A common form of licensing agreement refers to the indirect suppliers as original equipment manufacturers (OEMs) and leaves all customer support with the immediate supplier of a product. Internally, that supplier will draw on technical support from the OEM.

Example   Comparable OEM agreements exist between manufacturers of personal computers and the suppliers of preinstalled operating systems and applications. Customers receive integrated support from the computer manufacturer, who may in turn depend on the OEM when it cannot deal with an issue.

7.2.2 Application Program Interface

Recall that the API is an interface designed to support a broad class of extensions (see section 4.3.4). The open API allows one software supplier to extend or incorporate software from another supplier without establishing a formal business relationship. The owner of the open API exports services through an interface that is documented and where the software license allows for the unfettered use of this interface unconstrained by intellectual property restrictions and without payment. Technically, it is possible for a module from another supplier to invoke actions at this interface, which requires that it be accessible through mechanisms embodied in industry-standard infrastructure. One of the roles of infrastructure is to enable the composability of modules from different suppliers, and the API is one of the key constructs made possible.

Example   An application may offer an API that allows other suppliers to add value to that application, for instance, in the common gateway interface to a Web server that allows other applications to display their content via a Web browser. This API is technically feasible because the operating system provides mechanisms for one program to interact with another program executing on the same host.

It should be emphasized that not all interfaces in a software product are APIs. Most interfaces are proprietary, designed for internal interaction of modules and neither documented nor made available through technical means to software from other suppliers. Other interfaces may be documented and technically available, but because they are designed for a specific and narrow purpose, they fail to quality as an API. Further, suppliers reserve the right to change internal interfaces but implicitly or explicitly commit to extending but not changing an API (so as not to break other modules depending on it). Choosing to include an API in a software product is a serious business decision. Besides potential benefits, there are significant costs. Future versions of the product will either have to maintain compatibility, thus possibly requiring substantial engineering effort, or abandon existing clients using the API, thus risking dissatisfied customers and opening an opportunity for competitors.

If future extensions can be anticipated and are of broad interest, the supplier may wish to create and market these extensions itself, rather than ceding this opportunity to other suppliers, by building in an API. Infrastructure software's value is through the applications supported, and the API is the enabler. To the application software supplier, the API may be a vehicle by which other suppliers or even customers may customize that application to more specific (company or vertical industry) needs, increasing its value.

An alternative to the API is to offer contract development services to customize software. The supplier may maintain a services organization that contracts for customizations or extensions to meet specific customer needs.

The API is a software interface for software executing within a single host. A similar idea can be achieved over the network, where software from one supplier can interface with software from another supplier using the network. In this case, the API is replaced by a network protocol with similar business issues and characteristics.

7.2.3 Open Standards

An *industry standard* is a specification that is commonly agreed upon, precisely and completely defined, and well documented so that any supplier is free to implement and use it. Of course, it may or may not be widely adopted or uniformly implemented. In the software industry, the most common targets for standardization are architectural decomposition and the interfaces or network protocols defining the interactions of modules within that architecture. This type of standard seeks interoperability among modules, either within the same host or across the network (see section 4.5).

Example   The USB (universal serial bus) port is a standard interface to personal computer peripherals that includes physical (plug geometry, functions of the different pins) and electrical (voltage and waveform) characteristics, as well as the formats of bit streams that allow messages to be passed between a CPU and a peripheral. Like most standards, it does not address the complementarity of function in the computer and the peripheral, such as printing a page or communicating over a telephone line.

Another common target for standardization is the representation used for specific types of information, so that information can be exchanged among different applications or within an application.

Example   JPEG and MPEG are popular industry-standard compressed representations for pictures and audio/video, respectively. They allow one application to capture music in a file and another application to access that file and recreate the music. MP3 is a popular standard for sharing compressed music based on the audio portion of MPEG.

Programming languages are often standardized as well.

Example   The International Standards Organization (ISO) has standardized COBOL, FORTRAN, PL/1; the American National Standards Institute (ANSI) has standardized C and C++; the European Computer Manufacturers Association (ECMA) has standardized ECMAscript (also known as JavaScript or JScript) and C#.

An *open standard* is available for anybody to implement, well documented, and unencumbered by intellectual property restrictions, so any supplier is free to implement the standard without making prior business arrangements.

Example Many open standards are created by independent standardization bodies in which a number of companies collaborate in finding a mutually satisfactory solution. The body that creates the open Internet standards (including IP, UDP, and TCP) is the Internet Engineering Task Force (IETF). The World Wide Web Consortium (W3C) defines open standards for the evolution of the Web.

"Openness" is not an absolute because some of these properties can be relaxed, making the standard less open but still not closed or proprietary.

Example Sometimes a standard encumbered by intellectual property rights may be considered open if a promise has been made to exercise those rights in a measured fashion. In the most common arrangement, in return for inclusion in the standard the owner promises that a license will be granted to any and all under terms that are reasonable (moderate in cost) and nondiscriminatory (the same terms for all). For instance, the MP3 audio compression standard is an ISO/IEC standard, but is still covered by patents held by Fraunhofer IIS-A and Thomson multimedia that require licensing and fee payment for any but private and small-scale use.[7]

Other interfaces, protocols, or representations may carry more restrictions and still be labeled an industry standard, even if not considered an open standard.

Example Java is promulgated as a programming language, associated virtual machine for supporting portable execution, and an environment for portable and mobile code (see section 4.4). The specifications and associated tools were first developed by Sun Microsystems, which maintained licensing terms intended to prevent variants. Sun imbued Java with the characteristics of a standard (widely promulgated and used) while retaining control through intellectual property laws (see chapter 8). Among those provisions, any implementations that use the Java trademark must meet certain acceptance tests.

7.2.4 Why Standards?

The industry standard helps coordinate suppliers of complementary products, but it is not the only such mechanism. The supplier-customer business relationship allows a supplier to buy rather than make some portion of its software product.

The API enables a one-to-many relationship, where one software supplier deliberately creates an opportunity for all other suppliers to extend or exploit its product without the need for a formal business relationship. The industry standard excels at supporting a multilateral relationship among suppliers. The typical approach is to define and document an interface or a network protocol that can be exploited by many companies. In contrast to the API, where one supplier maintains a proprietary implementation of one side of an interface and allows other suppliers to define products on the other side of that interface, a standardized interface allows companies to define products that support the interface from either side.

From the customer and societal perspectives, open standards allow competition at the subsystem level: suppliers can create competitive substitutes for subsystems and know that the customer will have available the necessary complementary subsystems from other suppliers to forge a complete solution. Similarly, customers can mix and match subsystems from different suppliers if they feel this results in a better overall solution in dimensions such as price, features, performance, and quality. Modules can be replaced without replacing the entire system, reducing switching costs and lock-in. The disadvantage is that the customer must integrate subsystems from different vendors. In spite of standards, this additional integration takes time and effort, and sometimes introduces problems.

Example The PC offers open standards for serial and parallel connections between CPU and peripherals, including modems, printers, and display, so customers can mix and match PCs and peripherals from different manufacturers. Apple Computer pursued a more monolithic approach with the original Macintosh, which had the advantage that the system was operational out of the box. As the PC platform has matured, plug-and-play technology has made integration more seamless, and vendors like Dell accept customized system orders and perform the integration for the customer. Meanwhile, the Macintosh has moved toward an open standards approach (supporting open industry standards such as the universal serial bus). Today this distinction between the two platforms is minimal.

Network effects sometimes drive standardization (see section 3.2.3) in a multi-vendor solution. The incentive for standardization in this case is to avoid the proliferation of multiple networks, with the resulting fragmentation and reduced value to users and the benefits of positive feedback.

Example The peer-to-peer architecture for distributed applications creates a need for standards to support interoperability among peers (see section 4.5.3). Without such a standard, users could only participate in the application with users who have adopted that same vendor's solution. This is illustrated by instant messaging, where several firms offer services (AOL, Microsoft, and Yahoo, among others) that are currently incompatible, creating fragmented networks. The DVD illustrates the benefit of a standardized information representation that tames indirect network effects. Two industrial consortiums proposed incompatible standards for video playback but ultimately negotiated a single standard, driven by concern about the market dampening effect of network effects and consumer confusion if two or more standards were marketed, and by pressure from content suppliers, who were concerned about these issues.

7.2.5 How Standards Arise

An industry standard is the outcome of a process, sometimes a long and messy one. Influences on the eventual standard may be user needs, market forces, the interests of or strategy pursued by individual suppliers, and occasionally government laws or regulations. The possibilities range from a *de facto standard* to a *de jure standard*. The de facto standard begins life as a proprietary interface or protocol, but through market forces becomes so commonly adopted by many companies that it is an industry standard in fact (Shapiro and Varian 1999a). In the case of interfaces, some de facto standards begin life as APIs. Undocumented proprietary interfaces are less likely to become de facto standards because they prohibit (using intellectual property laws) or discourage participation by other suppliers.

Example The Hayes command set started as an API chosen by a leading voiceband modem manufacturer and was initially offered by most suppliers of telecommunications software to control the Hayes modem. Since this API was widely supported by software, other modem manufacturers began to implement the same API, and it became a de facto standard. Later, Hayes attempted to force other modem manufacturers to pay royalties based on patented technology it had incorporated into the implementation. Another example is the operating system APIs, allowing programs to send a packet over the network or save a file to disk. The primary purpose is encouraging application software suppliers to build on the operating system; a diversity of applications provides greater value to users. A side effect is to potentially enable an alternative infrastructure software supplier to independently implement and sell a direct substitute operating system, except to the extent that the API may be protected by intellectual property restrictions (see chapter 8.) Such independent reimplementation is unlikely for an operating system, however, because of the large investment and unappealing prospect of head-to-head competition with an entrenched supplier with substantial economies of scale (see chapter 9).

In the case of both interfaces and protocols, de facto standards often begin as an experimental prototype from the research community.

Example   The protocol and data format used to interact between client and server in the Web (HTTP and HTML) allows a Web browser and server to compose regardless of who supplies the client and server. It began as a way to share documents within a research community. Later, it was popularized by the innovative Mosaic Web browser from the University of Illinois, which provided a general graphical user interface. Today, there are more than a half-dozen suppliers of servers and browsers, and within the limits of the imprecise definitions of HTML, any server can interoperate with any browser using these standards (and their successors). Similarly, the socket is an operating system API that allows applications to communicate over the network. It has become a de facto standard resident in several operating systems, but it started as an API for the Berkeley UNIX operating system from the University of California.

At the other end of the spectrum, the de jure standard is sanctioned by a legal or regulatory entity.

Example   Regulatory forces are most likely to impose themselves when some public resource like the radio spectrum is required. In most countries there is a single legally sanctioned standard for radio and television broadcasting, as for wireless telephony. In the latter case the United States is an exception; the Federal Communications Commission specifically encouraged the promulgation of several standards. These standards deal with the representation and transmission of voice only across the wireless access link, and admit the conversions that allow for end-to-end voice conversations; direct network effects do not intervene. Another example is the Ada programming language, defined by the U.S. Department of Defense and imposed on its contractors until the late 1990s.

There are many cases intermediate to de facto and de jure, some of which are discussed later in conjunction with standards processes.

As applied to interfaces and network protocols, an essential first step in defining such standards is to locate interfaces or protocols that are candidates for standardization. This is an architectural design issue for purposes of standardization as well as implementation. There are several approaches to determining where there should be an interface or protocol to standardize. The first is to explicitly define the location of an interface as part of the standardization process. Such decomposition is called a *reference model*, a partial software architecture covering aspects of the architecture relevant to the standard. A reference model need not be a complete architecture; for example, modules within an implementation may be hierarchically decomposed from a single reference-model module, an implementation choice not directly affecting compliance with the standard.

Example   CORBA is a standard for a middleware infrastructure supporting object-oriented distributed systems promulgated by the Object Management Group. One of its primary contributions is a reference model for a number of common services that support such distributed applications.

A second approach to defining the location of a standardized interface is creating an interface and putting it into the public domain as a standard or letting it grow into a de facto standard.

Example   Desktop computer vendors (both IBM and Apple) defined a number of interfaces that grew into industry standards, including interfaces to monitor and peripherals, an API for application programs, and standards for the bus that supports expansion cards.

Third, the location of an open interface might be defined by market dynamics or be a side effect of the preexisting industrial organization. These types of interfaces typically follow the lines of core competencies, such as integrated circuit manufacture and infrastructure or application software.

Example   When IBM designed its first PC, it made decisions on outside suppliers that predefined some interfaces within the design, and those interfaces later evolved into de facto standards. By choosing an Intel microprocessor rather than developing its own, IBM implicitly chose an instruction set for program execution. By deciding to license its operating system (MS-DOS) from Microsoft (which importantly targeted this instruction set) rather than develop its own, IBM adopted operating system APIs that were later used by alternative operating systems (for example, Linux uses a FAT32 file system adopted from DOS, and Novell marketed a version of DOS). These choices reduced the time to market but also created an opportunity for other suppliers, including the PC clone manufacturers (Compaq was an early example) and AMD (which manufactures microprocessor chips compatible with Intel's).

Standards also address a serious problem in software engineering. In principle, a new interface could be designed whenever any two modules need to compose. However, the number of different interfaces must be limited to contain the development and maintenance costs arising from a proliferation of interfaces. Besides this combinatorial problem, there is the open-world problem. The open-world assumption in systems allows new modules to be added that weren't known or in existence when the base system was created—this is the motivation for APIs. It is impractical (indeed impossible) to have a complete set of special-case or proprietary interfaces to connect a full range of modules that may arise over time. A practical alternative is to define a limited set of standardized interfaces permitting interoperability over a wide range of functionality and complementarity.

Example   The CORBA standards standardize IIOP, a network protocol layered on top of TCP, which allows modules (in this case, the most limited case of objects) to interface with one another in a similar way whether they reside on the same host or different hosts. In effect, IIOP hides the details of the underlying network protocols (potentially multiple) and multiple platform implementations of those protocols behind a familiar interface. While individual applications would be free to develop a similar capability on a proprietary basis, an industry-standard solution reduces the number of implementations that are developed and maintained.

7.2.6   The Evolution of Standards Processes

Interfaces, the functionality related to these interfaces, the preferred decomposition of systems, and the representations used for sharing information can all be standardized to enable interoperability. For needs that are well understood and can be anticipated by standardization bodies (such as industrial consortiums or governmental standardization institutions) standards can be forged in advance of needs and later implemented by multiple vendors. This process has unfortunately not worked well in the software industry because of the rapid advances made possible by software's inherent flexibility and rapid distribution mechanisms, with the result that new products are often exploring new technology and applications territory. Thus, this industry has relied heavily on de facto standardization.

   Another approach has been to emphasize future extensibility in standards that are developed. This is a natural inclination for software, which emphasizes elaboration and specialization of what already exists (e.g., through layering; see section 7.1.3). For example, it is often feasible to elaborate an existing API rather than to define a new one. This can be accomplished by following the *open-closed principle*, which requires that interfaces be open to extension but closed to change. As long as existing actions are unchanged, the interface can be elaborated by adding new actions without affecting modules previously using the interface.

Example   Successive generations of an operating system try to maintain compatibility with existing applications by not changing the actions available in its API.

The new version may be new or improved "under the hood," for example, improving its stability or performance without changing the API. The new version may add new capabilities (added actions) to benefit future applications without changing those aspects of the API used by old applications.

The Internet has increased the importance of standards because of the new dependence (and direct network effects) it creates across different platforms. In an attempt to satisfy this thirst for standards, but without introducing untoward delay and friction in the market, industry has experimented with more facile and rapid standardization processes.

One trend is standardization processes well integrated with a research or experimental endeavor, in which the standard is deliberately allowed to evolve and expand in scope over time based on continual feedback from research outcomes and real-world experience. In fact, this type of standardization activity shares important characteristics (like flexibility and user involvement) with agile software development processes (see section 4.2.5).

Example   IETF has always recognized that its standards are a work in progress. The mechanism is to publish standards but to allow newer versions to make older ones obsolete. Most IETF standards arise directly from a research activity, and there is a requirement that any additions to the suite of standards be based on working experimental code. One approach used by the IETF and others is to rely initially on a single implementation that offers open-world extension hooks. Once it is better understood, a standard may be lifted off the initial implementation, enabling a wider variety of interoperable implementations.

In contrast to this continual refinement, a traditional top-down process is less chaotic and allows greater reflection on the overall structure and goals. It attempts to provide a lasting solution to the whole problem, all at once. A refinement process acknowledges that technologies are dynamic; whereas a reference architecture must be reasonably well defined to begin with, the details of functionality and interfaces can evolve over time.

Much depends on the maturity of an industry. For the time being, the de facto and continual refinement standardization processes are appropriate for many aspects of software because they allow innovation and evolution of solutions, reflecting market realities. When a stage of maturity is reached where functionality is better defined and stable, traditional top-down standardization processes can take over.

Layering is important because it allows standards to be built up incrementally rather than defined all at once (see section 7.1.3). The bottom layer (called wiring or plumbing standards) is concerned with simple connection-level standards.

Functionality can then be extended one layer at a time, establishing ever more elaborate rules of interoperation and composability.

Example   The early Internet research, as more recently the IETF, used layering. The bottom layer consisted of existing local-area networking technologies and displayed horizontal heterogeneity because there were numerous local-area and access networking technologies. The Internet standard added an IP layer interconnecting these existing technologies, and it provides today a spanning layer supporting a number of layering alternatives above. The IETF has systematically added layers above for various specific purposes. Sometimes lower layers need to be modified. For example, version four of the IP layer is widely deployed today, and the next version (version six) has been standardized. Because IP is widely used, any new version should satisfy two key constraints if at all possible. First, it should coexist with the older version, since it is impractical to upgrade the entire network at once. Second, it should support existing layer implementations above while offering new services or capabilities to new implementations of those layers or to newly defined layers.

Another trend is standardization processes that mimic the benefits of de facto standards but reduce or eliminate the time required for the marketplace to sort out a preferred solution. A popular approach is for a group of companies to form a consortium (often called a forum) that tries to arrive at good technical solutions by pooling expertise; the resulting solutions do not have the weight of a formal standard but rather serve as recommendations to the industry. Often such a consortium will request proposals from participants and then choose a preferred solution or combine the best features of different submissions or ask that contributors work to combine their submissions. Member companies follow these standards voluntarily, but the existence of these recommendations allow the market to arrive at a de facto standard more quickly.

Example   The Object Management Group, the developer of the CORBA standards, was formed to develop voluntary standards or best practices for infrastructure software supporting distributed object-oriented programs. It now has about 800 member organizations. W3C was formed by member companies at the Massachusetts Institute of Technology to develop voluntary standards for the Web; it now has more than 500 member organizations. ECMA was formed to reach de facto standards among European companies but has evolved into a standards body that offers a fast track to the International Organization for Standardization.

7.2.7 Minimizing the Role of Standards

While standardization has many benefits, they have disadvantages as well. In an industry that is changing rapidly with robust innovation, the existence of standards and the standardization process can impede technical progress. Sometimes standards come along too late to be useful.

Example The Open Systems Interconnect (OSI) model was a layered network protocol providing similar capabilities to the Internet technologies. It was an outgrowth of a slow international standardization process and, because it attempted to develop a complete standard all at once, was expensive and slow to be implemented as well. By the time it arrived, the Internet had been widely deployed and was benefiting from positive feedback from network effects. OSI was never able to gain traction in the market.

Where standards are widely adopted, they can become a barrier to progress. This is an example of lock-in of the entire industry resulting from the difficulty and expense of widely deploying a new solution.

Example Version six of IP has been much slower to deploy than expected. While it will likely gain acceptance eventually, version four has been incrementally upgraded to provide many of the capabilities emphasized in version six, and the substantial trouble and expense of deploying version six is an obstacle.

Another disadvantage of standards is that they may inhibit suppliers from differentiating themselves in the market. A way to mitigate this, as well as to allow greater innovation and faster evolution of the technology, is to define flexible or extensible standards.

Example XML is a W3C standard for representing documents. Originally defined as a replacement for HTML in the Web, XML is gaining momentum as a basis for exchanging information of various types among departmental, enterprise, and commerce applications, and is one underpinning of Web services (see section 7.3.7). One advantage is that unlike HTML, it separates the document meaning from screen formatting, making it useful to exchange meaningful business documents whose content can be automatically extracted and displayed according to local formatting conventions. Another advantage is its extensibility, allowing new industry- or context-specific representations to be defined. XML and its associated tools support a variety of context-specific standards or proprietary representations.

Where reasonable to do so, it is appropriate to minimize or eliminate the role of standards altogether. Although standards are always necessary at some level, modern software technologies and programmability offer opportunities to reduce their role, especially within applications (as opposed to infrastructure).

Example   The device driver shown in figure 7.8 is used in connecting a peripheral (like a printer) to a personal computer. The idea is to exploit the programmability of the computer to install a program that communicates with the printer, with complementary embedded software in the printer. This allows the operating system to focus on defining standard high-level representations for printed documents (such as Postscript), while the device driver encapsulates low-level protocols for interoperation between the computer and the printer. Since the device driver is supplied by the printer manufacturer, it can do whatever it chooses (like differentiating one printer from another) without requiring an inter-operability standard. Of course, the device driver and printer build on a standard for exchanging content-blind messages, such as the computer serial or parallel port.

Mobile code can realize the same idea dynamically (see figure 7.9). Interoperability issues suggest the need for standardization when two modules on different

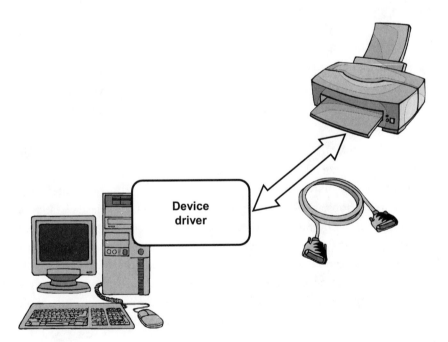

Figure 7.8
The device driver can allow interoperability while moving standardizations to a higher abstraction.

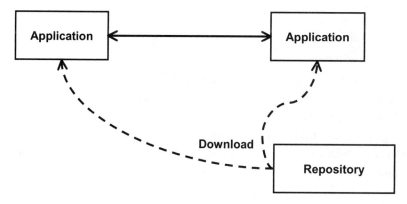

Figure 7.9
Direct network effects can be eliminated by mobile code.

hosts may originate with different suppliers. However, if both modules originate with the same supplier, they may be interoperable by construction with no need for standardization. Their interfaces can even be changed in new versions, as long as both modules are upgraded simultaneously.

Example Real Networks supplies complementary streaming audio-video RealServer and a RealPlayer for the client desktop. Over time, Real has been relatively free to upgrade its RealServer capabilities, even at the expense of compatibility with the RealPlayer, because it is reasonable to expect users to upgrade the client to the latest available version over the network. (Users with no Internet connection would not be candidates to use streaming audio-video.)

Downloaded software or mobile code is a particularly powerful way to bypass direct network effects, as evident in a peer-to-peer architecture.

Example Successful peer-to-peer applications like Napster (music file sharing) and Groove (file sharing and collaborative tools) have benefited from the ability to download the peer software from a central server. To join the network, a new user can easily download and install the necessary software (or with mobile code it can even be made transparent). Were it necessary to purchase equipment or software in a store, these sorts of applications would find it dramatically more difficult to reach critical mass and benefit from positive feedback.

Another approach to mitigating some problems with standardization is to standardize languages that can describe application elements, such as the interaction between modules, the functionality of modules, or the representation of information elements. We call this a meta-standard because it standardizes a way of describing something rather than standardizing that something directly. This can substantially increase the ability of suppliers to innovate and differentiate.

Example For communicating images from one host to another, a representation that includes a way of digitizing the image and compressing it must be shared by the transmitter and receiver. To avoid standardization, a meta-standard might take the form of a language capable of describing a large collection of decompression algorithms. A typical description of a compression algorithm would be something like "use an n by n discrete cosine transform with $n = 8$ followed by a quantization algorithm of the following form. . . ." Constrained only by the linguistic expressiveness of the meta-standard language, a transmitter is free to choose any compression algorithm and convey it (this is a form of mobile code) along with the image representation to the receiver. An early example is self-extracting archives, which are compressed collections of computer files arriving as an executable bundle that, upon execution, unpacks itself, yielding the collection of files.

Rudimentary forms of meta-standards already exist.

Example The interface definition language (IDL) of CORBA allows modules to disclose their capabilities by describing the actions that are available. XML for documents provides a language for describing, in effect, new markup languages.

7.3   Component Software

Most new software is constructed on a base of existing software (see section 4.2). There are a number of possibilities as to where the existing software comes from, whether it is modified or used without modification, and how it is incorporated into the new software. Just as end-users face the choice of making, buying, licensing, or subscribing to software, so do software suppliers. This is an area where the future industry may look very different (Szyperski 1998).

7.3.1   Make vs. License Decisions

Understanding the possible sources of an existing base of software leads to insights into the inner workings of the software creation industry. Although the possibilities form a continuum, the three distinct points listed in table 7.4 illustrate the range of possibilities. In this table, a software development project supports the entire life cycle of one coherent system or program through multiple versions (see section 5.1.2).

The handcrafting methodology was described in section 4.2. In its purest form, all the source code for the initial version is created from scratch for the specific

Table 7.4
Methodologies for Building Software on an Existing Code Base

Development Methodology	Description
Handcrafting	Source code from an earlier stage of the project is modified and upgraded to repair defects and add new features.
Software reuse	In the course of one project, modules are developed while anticipating their reuse in future projects. In those future projects, source code of existing modules from different projects is modified and integrated.
Component assembly	A system is assembled by configuring and integrating preexisting components. These components are modules (typically available only in object code) that cannot be modified except in accordance with built-in configuration options, often purchased from another firm.

needs of the project and is later updated through multiple maintenance and version cycles. Thus, the requirements for all the modules in such a handcrafted code base are derived by decomposition of a specific set of system requirements.

In the intermediate case, software reuse (Frakes and Gandel 1990; Gaffney and Durek 1989), source code is consciously shared among different projects with the goal of increasing both organizational and project productivity (recall the distinction made in section 4.2.3). Thus, both the architecture and requirements for at least some individual modules on one project anticipate the reuse of those modules in other projects. A typical example is a *product line architecture* (Bosch 2000; Jacobson, Griss, and Jönsson 1997), where a common architecture with some reusable modules or components is explicitly shared (variants of the same product are an obvious case; see section 5.1.2). To make it more likely that the code will be suitable in other projects, source code is made available to the other projects, and modifications to that source code to fit distinctive needs of the other project are normally allowed. Because it is uncommon to share source code outside an organization, reuse normally occurs within one development organization. A notable exception is contract custom development, where one firm contracts to another firm the development of modules for specific equirements and maintains ownership in and source code from that development outcome.

Example A hypothetical example illustrates software reuse. The development organization of Friendly Bank may need a module that supports the acquisition, maintenance, and accessing of information relative to one customer. This need is first encountered during a project that is developing and maintaining Friendly's checking account application. However, Friendly anticipates future projects to develop applications to manage a money market account and later a brokerage account. The requirements of the three applications have much in common with respect to customer information, so the first project specifically designs the customer module, trying to meet the needs of all three applications. Later, the source code is reused in the second and third projects. In the course of those projects, new requirements are identified that make it necessary to modify the code to meet specific needs, so there are now two or three variants of this customer module to maintain.

Reused modules can be used in multiple contexts, even simultaneously. This is very different from the material world, where reuse carries connotations of recycling, and simultaneous uses of the same entity are generally impossible. The difference between handcrafted and reusable software is mostly one of likelihood or adequateness. If a particular module has been developed with a special purpose in mind, and that purpose is highly specialized or the module is of substantial but context-specific complexity, then it is unlikely to be reusable in another context. Providing a broad set of configuration options that anticipates other contexts is a way to encourage reuse.

The third option in table 7.4 is component assembly (Hopkins 2000; Pour 1998; Szyperski 1998). In this extreme, during the course of a project there is no need to implement modules. Rather, the system is developed by taking existing modules (called components), configuring them, and integrating them. These components cannot be modified but are used as is; typically, they are acquired from a supplier rather than from another project within the same organization. To enhance its applicability to multiple projects without modification, each component will typically have many built-in configuration options.

Example The needs of Friendly Bank for a customer information module are hardly unique to Friendly. Thus, a supplier software firm, Banking Components Inc., has identified the opportunity to develop a customer information component that is designed to be general and configurable; in fact, it hopes this component can meet the needs of any bank. It licenses this component (in object code format) to any bank wishing to avoid developing this function itself. A licensing bank assembles this component into any future account applications it may create.

Although the software community has seen many technologies, methodologies, and processes aimed at increasing productivity and software quality, the consensus today is that component software is the most promising approach. It creates a supply chain for software, in which one supplier assembles components acquired from other suppliers into its software products. Competition is shifted from the system level to the component level, resulting in improved quality and cost options.

It would be rare to find any of these three options used exclusively; most often, they are combined. One organization may find that available components can partly meet the needs of a particular project, so it supplements them with handcrafted modules and modules reused from other projects.

7.3.2 What Is a Component?

Roughly speaking, a *software component* is a reusable module suitable for composition into multiple applications. The difference between software reuse and component assembly is subtle but important. There is no universal agreement in the industry or literature as to precisely what the term *component* means (Brown et al. 1998; Heinemann and Councill 2001). However, the benefits of components are potentially so great that it is worthwhile to strictly distinguish components from other modules and to base the definition on the needs of stakeholders (provisioners, operators, and users) and the workings of the marketplace rather than on the characteristics of the current technology (Szyperski 1998). This leads us to the properties listed in table 7.5. Although some may still call a module that fails to satisfy one or more of these properties a component, important benefits would be lost.

One of the important implications of the properties listed in table 7.5 is that components are created and licensed to be used as is. All five properties contribute to this, and indeed encapsulation enforces it. Unlike a monolithic application (which is also purchased and used as is), a component is not intended to be useful in isolation; rather its utility depends on its composition with other components (or possibly other modules that are not components). A component supplier has an incentive to reduce context dependence in order to increase the size of the market, balancing that property against the need for the component to add value to the specific context. An additional implication is that in a system using components (unlike a noncomponentized system) it should be possible during provisioning to mix and match components from different vendors so as to move competition from the system level down to the subsystem (component) level. It should also be possible to replace or upgrade a single component independently of the remainder of a system, even during the operation phase, thus reducing lock-in (see chapter 9) and giving greater flexibility to evolve the system to match changing or expanding requirements.[8] In theory, the system can be gracefully evolved after deployment by incrementally upgrading, replacing, and adding components.

Table 7.5
Properties That Distinguish a Component

Property	Description	Rationale
Multiple-use	Able to be used in multiple projects.	Share development costs over multiple uses.
Non-context-specific	Designed independently of any specific project and system context.	By removing dependence on system context, more likely to be general and broadly usable.
Composable	Able to be composed with other components.	High development productivity achieved through assembly of components.
Encapsulated	Only the interfaces are visible and the implementation cannot be modified.	Avoids multiple variations; all uses of a component benefit from a common maintenance and upgrade effort.
Unit of independent deployment and versioning	Can be deployed and installed as an independent atomic unit and later upgraded independently of the remainder of the system[a]	Allows customers to perform assembly and to mix and match components even during the operational phase, thus moving competition from the system to the component level.

a. Traditionally, deployment and installation have been pretty much the same thing. However, Sun Microsystem's EJB (a component platform for enterprise applications) began distinguishing deployment and installation, and other component technologies are following. Deployment consists of readying a software subsystem for a particular infrastructure or platform, whereas installation readies a subsystem for a specific set of machines. See Szyperski (2002a) for more discussion of this subtle but important distinction.

While a given software development organization can and should develop and use its own components, a rather simplistic but conceptually useful way to distinguish the three options in table 7.4 is by industrial context (see table 7.6). This table distinguishes modules used within a single project (handcrafted), within multiple projects in the same organization (reusable), and within multiple organizations (component).

Component assembly should be thought of as *hierarchical composition* (much like hierarchical decomposition except moving bottom-up rather than top-down).[9] Even though a component as deployed is atomic (encapsulated and displaying no visible internal structure), it may itself have been assembled from components by its supplier, those components having been available internally or purchased from other suppliers.[10] During provisioning, a component may be purchased as is, configured for the specific platform and environment (see section 4.4.2), and assembled and integrated with other components. As part of the systems management func-

Table 7.6
Industrial Contexts for Development Methodologies

Methodology Type	Industrial Context	Exceptions
Handcrafted	Programmed and maintained in the context of a single project.	Development and maintenance may be outsourced to a contract development firm.
Reusable	Programmed anticipating the needs of multiple projects within a single organization; typically several versions are maintained within each project.	A common module may be reused within different contexts of a single project. Development and maintenance of reusable modules may be outsourced.
Component	Purchased and used as is from an outside software supplier.	Components may be developed within an organization and used in multiple projects.

tion during operation, the component may be upgraded or replaced, or new components may be added and assembled with existing components to evolve the system.

A component methodology requires considerably more discipline than reuse. In fact, it is currently fair to say that not all the properties listed in table 7.5 have been achieved in practice, at least on the widespread and reproducible basis. Components are certainly more costly to develop and maintain than handcrafted or reusable modules. A common rule of thumb states that reusable software requires roughly several times as much effort as similar handcrafted software, and components much more. As a corollary, a reusable module needs to be used in a few separate projects to break even, components even more.

If their use is well executed, the compensatory benefits of components can be substantial. From an economic perspective, the primary benefit is the discipline of maintenance and upgrade of a single component implementation even as it is used in many projects and organizations. Upgrades of the component to match the expanding needs of one user can benefit other users as well.[11] Multiple use, with the implicit experience and testing that result, and concentrated maintenance can minimize defects and improve quality. Components also offer a promising route to more flexible deployed systems that can evolve to match changing or expanding needs.

Economic incentives strongly suggest that purely in economic terms (neglecting technical and organizational considerations) components are more promising than reuse as a way to increase software development productivity, and that components will more likely be purchased from the outside than developed inside an organization. Project managers operate under strict budget and schedule constraints, and developing either reusable or multiuse modules is likely to compromise those constraints. Compensatory incentives are very difficult to create within a given development organization. While organizations have tried various approaches to requiring or encouraging managers to consider reuse or multiple uses, their effectiveness is the exception rather than the rule.

On the other hand, components are quite consistent with organizational separation. A separate economic entity looks to maximize its revenue and profits and to maximize the market potential of software products it develops. It thus has an economic incentive to seek the maximum number of uses, and the extra development cost is expected to be amortized over increased sales. Where reuse allows the forking of different variations on a reused module to meet the specific needs of future projects, many of the economies of scale and quality advantages inherent in components are lost. It is hardly surprising that software reuse has been disappointing in practice, while many hold out great hope for component software.

There is some commonality between the ideas of component and infrastructure. Like components, infrastructure is intended for multiple uses, is typically licensed from another company, is typically used as is, and is typically encapsulated. Infrastructure (as seen by the application developer and operator) is large-grain, whereas components are typically smaller-grain. The primary distinction between the components and infrastructure lies in composability. Infrastructure is intended to be extended by adding applications. This is a weak form of composability, because it requires that the infrastructure precede the applications, and the applications are developed specifically to match the capabilities of an existing infrastructure. Similarly, an application is typically designed for a specific infrastructure context and thus lacks the non-context-specific property. Components, on the other hand, embody a strong form of composability in that the goal is to enable the composability of two (or more) components that are developed completely independently, neither with prior knowledge of the other. Achieving this is a difficult technical challenge.

7.3.3 Component Portability

The issue of portability arises with components as well as other software (see figure 7.10). A portable component can be deployed and installed on more than one platform. But it is also possible for distributed components to compose even though they are executing on different platforms. These are essentially independent prop-

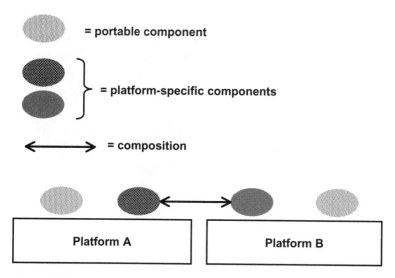

Figure 7.10
Components can be portable, or they can compose across platforms, or both.

erties; a component technology can support one or the other or both of these properties, often limited to specific platforms and environments. Almost all component technologies today support distributed components that execute on the same type of platform.

Insisting on unconditional portability undesirably limits innovation in platforms (see section 4.4.3) but also desirably increases the market for a portable component or eliminates the cost of developing variants for different platforms. Cross-platform distributed component composition offers the advantages of portability (components can participate in applications predominately executing on different platforms) without its limitations (each component can take full advantage of platform-specific capabilities). Here the trade-off is one of efficiency: performance suffers when crossing software and hardware platform boundaries. Of course, this issue also interacts with provisioning and operation (see section 7.3.7).

7.3.4 Component Evolution

There is a fundamental tension in the component methodology relating to the inherent evolution of user requirements (Lehman and Ramil 2000). Recall the distinction between specification-driven and satisfaction-driven software (see section 3.2.11). Particularly if a component is to be licensed rather than developed, it is simpler contractually to view it as specification-driven. It can then be objectively evaluated by laboratory testing, and the contractual relationship between licensee and licensor is easier to formulate in terms of objective acceptance criteria. The tension comes from the reality that applications as a whole are decidedly satisfaction-driven programs. Can such applications be assembled wholly from specification-driven components? Likely not. In practice, some components (especially those destined for applications) may be judged by satisfaction-driven criteria, greatly complicating issues surrounding maintenance, upgrade, and acceptance criteria. Worse, a successful component is assembled into multiple satisfaction-driven programs, each with distinct stakeholders and potentially distinct or even incompatible criteria for satisfaction of those stakeholders. This tension may limit the range of applicability of components, or reduce the satisfaction with componentized systems, or both. It tends to encourage small-grain components, which are less susceptible to these problems but also incur greater performance overhead. It may also encourage the development of multiple variants on a component, which undercuts important advantages.

A related problem is that a project that relies on available components may limit the available functionality or the opportunity to differentiate from competitors, who have the same components available. This can be mitigated by the ability to mix components with handcrafted or reusable modules and by incorporating a broad set of configuration options into a component.

7.3.5 An Industrial Revolution of Software?

Software components are reminiscent of the Industrial Revolution's innovation of standard reusable parts. In this sense, components can yield an industrial revolution in software, shifting the emphasis from handcrafting to assembly in the development of new software, especially applications. This is especially compelling as a way to reduce the time and cost of developing applications, much needed in light of the increasing specialization and diversity of applications (see section 3.1). It may even be feasible to enable end-users to assemble their own applications. This industrial revolution is unlikely to occur precipitously, but fortunately this is not a case of "all or nothing" because developed or acquired modules can be mixed.

This picture of a software industrial revolution is imperfect. For one thing, the analogy between a software program and a material product is flawed (Szyperski 2002a). If a program were like a material product or machine, it would consist of a predefined set of modules (analogous to the parts of a machine) interacting to achieve a higher purpose (like the interworking of parts in a machine). This was, in fact, the view implied in our discussion of architecture (see section 4.3), but in practice it is oversimplified. While software is composed from a set of interacting modules, many aspects of the dynamic configuration of an application's architecture are determined at the time of execution, not at the time the software is created. During execution, a large set of modules is created dynamically and opportunistically based on specific needs that can be identified only at that time.

Example A word processor creates many modules (often literally millions) at execution time tied to the specific content of the document being processed. For example, each individual drawing in a document, and indeed each individual element from which that drawing is composed (lines, circles, labels) is associated with a software module created specifically to manage that element. The implementers provide the set of *available* kinds of modules, and also specify a detailed plan by which modules are created dynamically at execution time[12] and interact to achieve higher purposes.

Implementing a modern software program is analogous not to a static configuration of interacting parts but to creating a plan for a very flexible factory in the industrial economy. At the time of execution, programs are universal factories that, by following specific plans, manufacture a wide variety of immaterial artifacts on demand and then compose them to achieve higher purposes. Therefore, in its manner of production, a program—the product of development—is not comparable to a hardware product but is more like a very flexible factory for hardware components. The supply of raw materials of such a factory corresponds to the reusable resources of information technology: instruction cycles, storage capacity, and communication bandwidth. The units of production in this factory are dynamically assembled modules dynamically derived from modules originally handcrafted or licensed as components.

There is a widespread belief that software engineering is an immature discipline that has yet to catch up with more mature engineering disciplines, because there remains such a deep reliance on handcrafting as a means of production. In light of the nature of software, this belief is exaggerated. Other engineering disciplines struggle similarly when aiming to systematically create new factories, especially flexible ones (Upton 1992). Indeed, other engineering disciplines, when faced with the problem of creating such factories, sometimes look to software engineering for insights. It is an inherently difficult problem, one unlikely to yield to simple solutions. Nevertheless, progress will be made, and the market for components will expand.

A second obstacle to achieving an industrial revolution of software is the availability of a rich and varied set of components for licensing. It was argued earlier that purchasing components in a marketplace is more promising than using internally developed components because the former offers higher scale and significant economic benefit to the developer/supplier. Such a *component marketplace* is beginning to come together.

Example Component technologies are emerging based on Microsoft Windows (COM+ and CLR) and Sun Microsystems' Java (JavaBeans and Enterprise JavaBeans). Several fast-growing markets now exist (Garone and Cusack 1999), and a number of companies have formed to fill the need for merchant, broker, and triage roles, including ComponentSource and FlashLine. These firms provide an online marketplace where buyers and sellers of components can come together.

One recognized benefit of the Industrial Revolution was the containment of complexity. By separating parts suppliers and offering each a larger market, economic incentives encouraged suppliers to go to great lengths to make their components easier to use by abstracting interfaces, hiding and encapsulating the complexities. New components will also tend to use existing standardized interfaces where feasible rather than creating new ones (so as to maximize the market), reducing the proliferation of interfaces. Thus, a component marketplace may ultimately be of considerable help in containing software complexity, as it has for material goods and services.

Another obstacle to an industrial revolution of software, one that is largely unresolved, is trust and risk management. When software is assembled from components purchased from external suppliers, warranty and insurance models are required to mitigate the risk of exposure and liability. Because of the complexity and characteristics of software, traditional warranty, liability laws, and insurance require rethinking in the context of the software industry, an issue as important as the technical challenges.

Another interesting parallel to component software may be biological evolution, which can be modeled as a set of integrative levels (such as molecules, cells, organisms, and families) where self-contained entities at each level (except the bottom) consist mainly of innovative composition of entities from the level below (Petterersson 1996).[13] Like new business relationships in an industrial economy, nature seems to evolve ever more complex entities in part by this innovative composition of existing entities, and optimistically components may unleash a similar wave of innovation in software technology.

It should be emphasized that these parallels to the industrial economy and to biological evolution depend upon the behavioral nature of software (which distinguishes it from the passive nature of information), leading directly to the emergence of new behaviors through module composition.

7.3.6   Component Standards and Technology

Assembling components designed and developed largely independently requires standardization of ways for components to interact. This addresses interoperability, although not necessarily the complementarity also required for the composition of components (see section 4.3.6). Achieving complementary, which is more context-specific, is more difficult. Complementarily is addressed at the level of standardization through bodies that form domain-specific reference models and, building on those, reference architectures. Reference architectures devise a standard way to divide and conquer a particular problem domain, predefining roles that contributing technologies can play. Components that cover such specified roles are then naturally complementary.

Example   The Object Management Group, an industrial standardization consortium, maintains many task force groups that establish reference models and architectures for domains such as manufacturing, the health industry, or the natural sciences.

Reusability or multiple use can focus on two levels of design: architecture and individual modules. In software, a multiuse architecture is called a *reference architecture*, a multiuse architecture cast to use specific technology is called a *framework*, and a multiuse module is called a component. In all cases, the target of use is typically a narrowed range of applications, not all applications. One reason is that, in practice, both the architecture and the complementarity required for component composition requires some narrowing of application domain. In contrast, infrastructure software targets multiple-use opportunities for a wide range of applications.

Example   Enterprise resource planning (ERP) is a class of application that targets standard business processes in large corporations. Vendors of ERP, such as SAP, Baan, Peoplesoft, and Oracle, use a framework and component methodology to provide some flexibility to meet varying end-user needs. Organizations can choose a subset of available components, and mix and match components within an overall framework defined by the supplier. (In this particular case, the customization process tends to be so complex that it is commonly outsourced to business consultants.)

The closest analogy to a framework in the physical world is called a platform (leading to possible confusion, since that term is used differently in software; see section 4.4.2).

Example   An automobile platform is a standardized architecture and associated components and manufacturing processes that can be used as the basis of multiple products. Those products are designed by customizing elements fitting into the architecture, like the external sheet metal.

In essence a framework is a preliminary plan for the decomposition of (parts of) an application, including interface specifications. A framework can be customized by substituting different functionality in constituent modules and extended by adding additional modules through defined gateways. As discussed in section 7.3.5, a framework may be highly dynamic, subject to wide variations in configuration at execution time. The application scope of a framework is necessarily limited: no single architecture will be suitable for a wide range of applications. Thus, frameworks typically address either a narrower application domain or a particular vertical industry.

Component methodologies require discipline and a supporting infrastructure to be successful. Some earlier software methodologies have touted similar advantages but have incorporated insufficient discipline.

Example   Object-oriented programming is a widely used methodology that emphasizes modularity, with supporting languages and tools that enforce and aid modularity (e.g., by enforcing encapsulation). While OOP does result in an increase in software reuse in development organizations, it has proved largely unable to achieve component assembly. The discipline as enforced by compilers and runtime environment is insufficient, standardization to enable interoperability is inadequate, and the supporting infrastructure is also inadequate.

From a development perspective, component assembly is quite distinctive. Instead of viewing source code as a collection of textual artifacts, it is viewed as a collection of units that separately yield components. Instead of arbitrarily modifying and evolving an ever-growing source base, components are individually and independently evolved (often by outside suppliers) and then composed into a multitude of software programs. Instead of assuming an environment with many other specific modules present, a component provides documented connection points that allow it to be configured for a particular context. Components can retain their separate identity in a deployed program, allowing that program to be updated and extended by replacing or adding components. In contrast, other programming methodologies deploy a collection of executable or dynamically loadable modules whose configuration and context details are hard-wired and cannot be updated without being replaced as a monolithic whole.

Even an ideal component will depend on a platform's providing an execution model to build on. The development of a component marketplace depends on the availability of one or more standard platforms to support component software development, each such platform providing a largely independent market to support its component suppliers.

Example There are currently two primary platforms for component software, the Java universe, including Java 2 Enterprise Edition (J2EE) from Sun Microsystems, and the Windows .NET universe from Microsoft. Figure 7.11 illustrates the general architecture of Enterprise JavaBeans (EJB), part of J2EE, based on the client-server model. The infrastructure foundation is a set of (possibly distributed) servers and (typically) a much larger set of clients, both of which can be based on heterogeneous underlying platforms. EJB then adds a middleware layer to the servers, called an *application server*. This layer is actually a mixture of two ideas discussed earlier. First, it is value-added infrastructure that provides a number of common services for many applications. These include directory and naming services, database access, remote component interaction, and messaging services. Second, it provides an environment for components, which are called Beans in EJB. One key aspect of this environment is the component container illustrated in figure 7.12. All interactions

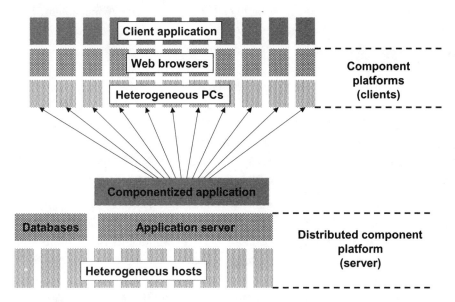

Figure 7.11
An architecture for client-server applications supporting a component methodology.

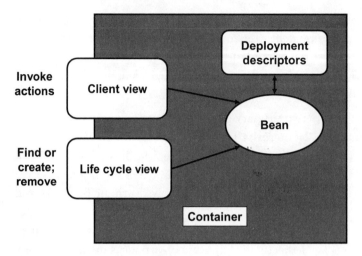

Figure 7.12
A component container in JavaBeans.

with a given component are actually directed at its container, which in turn interacts with the component itself. This allows many additional value-added services to be transparently provided on behalf of the component, such as supporting multiple clients sharing a single component, state management, life cycle management, and security. The deployment descriptors allow components to be highly configurable, with their characteristics changeable according to the specific context. In addition, J2EE provides an environment for other Java components in the Web server (servlets) and client Web browser (applets) based on a Java browser plug-in, as well as for client-side applications. In the .NET architecture, the role of application server and EJBs is played by COM+ and the .NET Framework. The role of Web server and Web service host is played by ASP.NET and the .NET Framework. Clients are covered by client-side applications, including Web browsers with their extensions.

Component-based architectures should be modular, particularly with respect to weak coupling of components, which eases their independent development and composability (see section 4.3.3). Strong cohesion within components is less important because components can themselves be hierarchically decomposed for purposes of implementation. Market forces often intervene to influence the granularity of components, and in particular sometimes encourage course-grain components with considerable functionality bundled in to reduce the burden on component users and to help encapsulate implementation details and preserve trade secrets (see chapter 8).

In some cases, it is sheer performance objectives that encourage course-grained components because there is an unavoidable overhead involved in interacting with other
components through fixed interfaces.

Constructing an application from components by configuring them all against one
another, called a *peer-to-peer architecture*, does not scale beyond simple configurations because of the combinatorial explosion of created dependencies, all of which
may need to be managed during the application evolution. A framework can be
used to bundle all relevant component connections and partial configurations, hierarchically creating a coarser-grain module. A component may plug into multiple
places in a component framework, if that component is relevant to multiple aspects
of the system. Figure 7.13 illustrates how a framework can decouple disjoint dimensions.[14] This is similar to the argument for layering (see figure 7.6), standards (see
section 7.2), and commercial intermediaries, all of which are in part measures to
prevent a similar combinatorial explosion.

Example   An operating system is a framework, accepting device driver modules
that enable progress below (although these are not components because they can't
compose with one another) and accepting application components to enable
progress above (assuming that applications allow composability). Allowing component frameworks to be components themselves creates a component hierarchy.

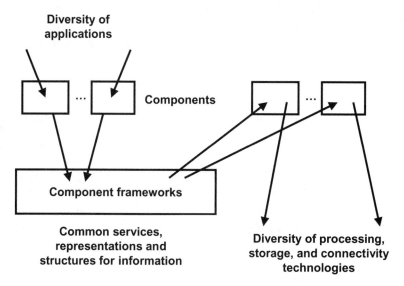

Figure 7.13
Component frameworks to separate dimensions of evolution.

For example, an OS-hosted application can be turned into a framework by accepting add-ins (a synonym for components).

7.3.7 Web Services

The provisioning and operation of an entire application can be outsourced to a service provider (see section 6.2). Just as an application can be assembled from components, so too can an application be assembled from the offerings of not one but two or more service providers. Another possibility is to allow end-users to assemble applications on a peer-to-peer basis by offering services to one another directly, perhaps mixed with services provided by third-party providers. This is the idea behind *Web services*, in which services from various service providers can be considered components to be assembled. The only essential technical difference is that these components interact over the network; among other things, this strongly enforces the encapsulation property. Of course, each component Web service can internally be hierarchically decomposed from other software components. Services do differ from components significantly in operational and business terms in that a service is backed by a service provider who provisions and operates it (Szyperski 2001), leading to different classes of legal contracts and notions of recompense (Szyperski 2002b). The idea that components can be opportunistically composed even after deployment is consistent with the Web service idea.

Distributed component composition was considered from the perspective of features and functionality (see section 7.3.3). Web services address the same issue from the perspective of provisioning and operation. They allow component composition across heterogeneous platforms, with the additional advantage that deployment, installation, and operation for specific components can be outsourced to a service provider. They also offer the component supplier the option of selling components as a service rather than licensing the software. Web services shift competition in the application service provider model from the level of applications to components.

If the features and capabilities of a specific component are needed in an application, there are three options. The component can be deployed and installed on the same platform (perhaps even the same host) as the application. If the component is not available for that platform (it is not portable), it can be deployed and installed on a different host with the appropriate platform. Finally, it can be composed into the application as a Web service, avoiding the deployment, installation, and operation entirely but instead taking an ongoing dependence on the Web service provider.

A Web service architecture can be hierarchical, in which one Web service can utilize services from others. In this case, the "customer" of one service is another piece of software rather than the user directly. Alternatively, one Web service can be considered an intermediary between the user and another Web service, adding value by customization, aggregation, filtering, consolidation, and similar functions.

Example A large digital library could be assembled from a collection of independently managed specialized digital libraries using Web services (Gardner 2001). Each library would provide its own library services, such as searching, authentication and access control, payments, copy request, and format translations. When a user accesses its home digital library and requests a document not resident there, the library could automatically discover other library services and search them, eventually requesting a document copy in a prescribed format wherever it is found and passing it to the user.

An important element of Web services is the dynamic and flexible means of assembling different services without prior arrangement or planning, as illustrated in this example. Each service can advertise its existence and capabilities so that it can be automatically discovered and those capabilities invoked. It is not realistic, given the current state of technology, to discover an entirely new type of service and automatically interact with it in a complex manner. Thus, Web services currently focus on enabling different implementations of previously known services to be discovered and accessed (Gardner 2001).

Web services could be built on a middleware platform similar to the application server in figure 7.11, where the platform supports the interoperability of components across service providers. However, this adds another level of coordination, requiring the choice of a common platform or alternatively the interoperability of different platforms. A different solution is emerging, standards for the representation of content-rich messages across platforms.

Example XML (see section 7.1.5) is emerging as a common standardized representation of business documents on the Web, one in which the meaning of the document can be extracted automatically. The interoperability of Web services can be realized without detailed plumbing standards by basing it on the passage of XML-represented messages. This high-overhead approach is suitable for interactions where there are relatively few messages, each containing considerable information.[15] It also requires additional standardization for the meaning of messages expressed in XML within different vertical industry segments. For example, there will be a standard for expressing invoices and another standard for expressing digital library search and copy requests.

The dynamic discovery and assembling of services are much more valuable if they are vendor- and technology-neutral. Assembling networked services rather than software components is a useful step in this direction, since services implemented on different platforms can be made to appear identical across the network, assuming the appropriate standards are in place.

Example   Recognizing the value of platform-neutral standards for Web services, several major vendors hoping to participate in the Web services market (including Hewlett-Packard, IBM, Microsoft, Oracle, and Sun) work together to choose a common set of standards. SOAP (simple object access protocol) is an interoperability standard for exchanging XML messages with a Web service, UDDI (universal description, discovery, and integration) specifies a distributed registry or catalog of available Web services, and WSDL (Web services description language) can describe a particular Web service (actions and parameters). Each supplier is developing a complete Web services environment (interoperable with others because of common standards) that includes a platform for Web services and a set of development tools.[16] UDDI and Web services work together as illustrated in figure 7.14,

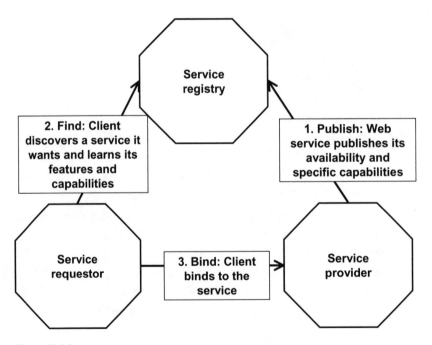

Figure 7.14
The Web services reference model, now on its way toward adoption as a standard, shows how UDDI supports service discovery (Gardner 2001).

with three primitive operations: publish, find, and bind. First, each service provider advertises the availability of its Web services in a common service registry. A service requestor discovers a needed service in the registry, connects to the service (including functions like authentication and arranging for payment), and finally starts using it.

7.4   Research and Discussion Issues

1. One recurring theme is the indirect network effect of applications and infrastructure: applications seek widely deployed infrastructure, and infrastructure seeks a diversity of applications. What are some specific ways in which the market can overcome this chicken-and-egg conundrum? Can you give examples of these? What are their relative merits? Which are most likely to be commercially viable?

2. Consider in specific terms what properties an infrastructure must have to enable new applications to arise without the knowledge or participation of the infrastructure supplier or service provider.

3. Give some additional examples of how the tendency of the market to add to infrastructure rather than change it leads to later difficulties. Can you identify some examples and specific methodologies in which infrastructure can be changed rather than merely expanded?

4. What are the best areas of the software industry for venture-funded companies? for large established companies? Why?

5. Because of the substantial economies of scale, it is wise to avoid direct undifferentiated competition in the software industry. What are some specific strategies that suppliers use to differentiate themselves in applications? in infrastructure?

6. A dogmatic view of layering requires that layers be homogeneous and interact only with the layers directly above and below. What are some advantages and disadvantages of relaxing this dogma, as in the example of figure 7.3?

7. What are some differences in the strategic challenges of firms competing in a stovepipe and in a layered structure in the industry?

8. Consider how the properties of good software modularity (see section 4.3.3) apply more or less strongly to industrial organization.

9. Discuss in some depth whether an infrastructure service provider should also bundle applications, and whether it should develop or acquire those applications.

10. Discuss in some depth the relation between standardization and industrial organization, specifically different types of standardization (e.g., de facto vs. an industry standards body).

11. What strategies do software suppliers use to maintain control over an architecture and in taking advantage of that architectural control?

12. What are the considerations in choosing to offer an API or not?

13. What are all the elements that make up an open standard, and when these elements are modified or eliminated, when does the standard cease to be open? This question is best considered in the context of what kind of benefits an open standard confers, and when those benefits are compromised.

14. Consider the process by which a de facto standard develops in the marketplace. Is a de facto standard always an open standard? When is encouragement of a de facto standard in the best interest of a supplier? Do different types of de facto standards (e.g., interfaces, APIs, data representations) arise in similar ways?

15. Discuss the relation between an agile software development process (see section 4.2.5) and an agile standardization process (one that is flexible and adaptive). Under what conditions is a standardization process essentially (or at least part of) a collective development process?

16. Composability of modules requires interoperability and complementarity (see section 4.3.6). What is the proper role of standardization in these two aspects? What else is required besides standardization?

17. Consider mechanisms and incentives that could be used to encourage software reuse in a development organization. Do you think this can be effective? What disadvantages might there be?

18. For each property of a component listed in table 7.5, discuss the business considerations and possibilities that arise from that property. What are the implications to component supplier, component customer (e.g., system integrator or system developer), and end-user?

19. Discuss how component software differs from infrastructure software, since both concepts emphasize multiple uses. How do the challenges and strategies of component suppliers differ from those of application and infrastructure suppliers?

20. Reflect further on the challenges of satisfaction-based requirements for a component supplier-customer relationship. Also consider the issues of risk and trust, and how these relate to satisfaction.

21. Imagine that you are in the business of producing and selling plans for a flexible factory. What kind of business challenges would you face?

22. Discuss the possible parallels and differences between component assembly as a model of emergence in software and business relationships as a model of emergence in the industrial economy. What can be learned from these parallels?

23. Repeat the last question, substituting innovative composition of entities as a model for emergence in biological evolution.

24. How does the philosophy of Web services (assembling applications from component services) differ from that of the application service provider (accessing fully integrated applications over a wide-area network)? What are the differences in terms of business models, opportunities, and challenges?

25. Discuss the business issues that surround the assembly of applications from two or more Web services. These include the necessary coordination and issues of trust and responsibility that arise from outsourcing component services.

7.5 Further Reading

Mowery and Nelson (1999), Mowery and Langlois (1994), and Torrisi (1998) describe the general structure of the software industry, particularly from a historic perspective. Ferguson and Morris (1994) give a useful introduction to the computer industry, with an emphasis on hardware and the importance of architecture. While there are a number of books on software reuse, the Jacobson, Griss, and Jönsson (1997) book is one of the best. Szyperski (2002a) has the most comprehensive treatment of software components, including both economics and business issues. The state-of-the-art collection of edited articles in Heineman and Councill (2001) provides a wealth of additional information on most related issues.

8
Government

All technologies can be used for good or for ill. They can be used to serve society or harm it. . . . Public policy will determine in large measure . . . how much benefit will be derived from constructive uses of this remarkable technology.
National Research Council

In the epigraph quotation, the National Research Council (1996) speaks specifically of cryptography, but this observation applies to software technology and its effects as well as to other technologies. Today's market-based approach to information technology (IT) and its applications is effective in promulgating wide use and commercial exploitation. It still leaves many essential roles for government. These include grants and protections of property rights, a legal basis for the licensing of software, regulating some aspects of the market economy, ensuring the continued rapid advance in technology, and limiting some possible injurious effects of IT. In this chapter we discuss these roles of government, focusing on details that most directly relate to software technology.

8.1 Intellectual Property

Ownership confers the right to control the dissemination and use of information and software, or the ideas incorporated therein, and is an essential underpinning of the commercial relationships described in chapter 6. Information and software present some special challenges, because they are nonrival in use and easily replicated and distributed at low cost. Thus, ownership in this context assumes a different form from ownership of material goods. Distributing information or software for use intrinsically provides the buyer with a replica that can be further copied or replicated and passed on to third parties, although digital rights management technologies can interfere with this. Government laws on intellectual property protection and their enforcement play an essential role in preserving ownership rights in software (Dam 1995), and therefore in preserving incentives for investments in software research and development (R&D). The four forms of intellectual property protection—trade secret, patent, copyright, and trademark—are complementary.

8.1.1   Trade Secrets and Patents

The *trade secret* laws protect proprietary information. If the holder of a trade secret can prove that proprietary information (the trade secret) was obtained by others through an act of malfeasance, it can obtain a court injunction against the use of the trade secret and possibly compensatory and punitive monetary damages. The trade secret does not prevent others from exploiting the same information or ideas developed independently. In the software industry, it is especially common for workers to switch employers, and trade secret laws are a primary protection for firms in preventing proprietary knowledge gained in one firm from being exploited in another.

A *patent* grants the limited-term (roughly two decades) exclusive right to make, use, or sell products incorporating an *invention*, a practically useful idea that is both novel and nonobvious. Unlike the holder of a trade secret, the patent owner can preclude others from using an invention even if others later discover the invention independently.

Software is implicitly divulged as it is used—or at least its possibilities are revealed—and it is nonrival in use, making it a poor investment without property rights that preclude others from simply appropriating and exploiting ideas or techniques embodied in the software code. Patents encourage investment in R&D by promising a period of exclusivity but also divulge inventions (rather than keeping them secret), allowing others to improve upon them whether they are used or not.

The theoretical interchangeability of hardware and software was the original basis of software patents. Prior to the 1980s, software inventions were not patentable because they were deemed to be expressions of a mathematical algorithm and scientific principles, and mathematical formulas were specifically not eligible for patenting. This restriction broke down because if it is reasonable to allow hardware inventions to be patented, then it should be equally reasonable to allow patents for functionally equivalent inventions embodied in software. Patents have also recently been permitted on business processes, which underlie some software applications, particularly enterprise and e-commerce applications.

Example In the first major business process patent case, the courts upheld the right of Signature Financial Group to exclude other firms from using a patent on "hub and spoke" structure for mutual funds. Later, Amazon successfully kept Barnes and Noble Booksellers from adopting its "one-click" checkout scheme. Priceline.com patented its reverse-auction business model in which customers bid a price they are willing to pay and sellers take it or leave it. The latter two patents dealt directly with software systems, and can be considered a hybrid between a software and business process patent.

Software and business process patents are controversial. Some argue that the software industry changes much faster than the patent system can accommodate (both the time to issue a patent and the lifetime of the patent). The main difficulty is that the state of the art has not been captured through the five decades of the software industry, reducing the completeness and accuracy of the patent office reviews of prior art and obviousness. It is important to evaluate software and business process patents in terms of the original justification for the patent system—encouraging investments in R&D and discouraging trade secrets. It has been argued that software and business process inventions (unlike implementation) require far smaller investments than other areas of technology (like electronics and pharmaceuticals) and thus necessitate milder incentives, and also that trade secrets make less sense because to use these types of inventions is to reveal them, and therefore the fundamental justification for patenting these types of inventions is weaker.

Firms must make difficult tactical choices between employing the trade secret, the patent, or neither for each individual innovation (Shapiro 2001b). While the trade secret excludes others, there is the danger that another firm may file a patent, which the trade secret would then infringe. A patent filing is expensive and reveals the innovation but also opens the possibility of excluding competitors or extracting license royalties. Publication of an innovation (placing it clearly in the prior art) may forestall others from filing a patent but precludes any form of exclusivity. Important considerations include how fundamental the innovation is, how difficult it would be to circumvent it, whether there would likely be license royalties, how important the innovation is to future business plans, and how easy it would be to detect infringement. Compared to some other areas of technology (such as biotechnology or semiconductors), software patents tend to be less fundamental and more easily circumvented. Nevertheless, there are circumstances where they are considered crucial.

Example   A patent for a specific encryption/decryption algorithm may be difficult to circumvent in that it is difficult to perform a compatible encryption or decryption without infringement. However, it is easy to circumvent by choosing (or inventing) an alternative and incompatible encryption algorithm. Encryption per se would be considered today a prior art. A patent is an important element of a standardized system for rights management (see section 8.1.5), because an adversary who pirates information by reverse-engineering and copying the system can likely be sued for patent infringement (Traw 2001). This adversary cannot use an alternative encryption algorithm and still be standards-compatible.

The general approach to patents is also an important strategic decision for software firms. An offensive strategy is to extract royalties for use of the invention or gain competitive advantage by excluding others. A defensive strategy is to build a large patent portfolio to defend against a competitor who sues for patent infringement, since an infringement countersuit may be possible based on other patents held by the defendant. Large software firms are increasingly aggressive in building a patent portfolio, largely for defensive purposes. With this portfolio in hand, it makes sense to avoid litigation by negotiating blanket cross-licensing agreements with other large firms. In terms of social policy, this has the desirable outcome of discouraging trade secrets without creating monopoly positions in particular technologies. Overall, the exclusionary use of patents is less common in software than in some other industries, like biotechnology or pharmaceuticals, in part because patents offer less fundamental protection.

Patent infringement suits from individuals, universities, or small firms without significant revenues are to be feared more because infringement countersuits are unlikely to be effective and blanket cross-licensing agreements make little sense in these cases. Small firms, especially startup companies, consider patents an important asset that can exclude large competitors or derive royalty revenue. Patents are an important enabler for venture capital investments to the extent that they can preclude or slow down competition. Defensive patent strategies thus predominate for large firms and offensive strategies for individuals and small firms.

8.1.2 Copyrights
Historically, inventions were thought to be embodied in physical processes but not in information. A different form of intellectual property right—the copyright—was created for information goods, and patents were reserved for physical processes. The *copyright* protects an original collection of information (called a work) by granting the creator exclusive control of the work (including the right to sell or license) and precluding others from appropriating, replicating, or selling the work without permission. Because it protects the *expression* of facts or ideas, not those facts or ideas themselves, a copyright (like a trade secret) does not prevent others

from independently developing a similar work based on the same ideas or intended purposes.

Example   Software, especially application software, reveals its capabilities when it is used, and in the case of a standard or an application programming interface (API) is associated with a detailed specification. Another organization can legally reproduce the same capabilities or specification unless there is also patent protection. This is often done in a *cleanroom*, a project team isolated from all knowledge of or access to the original code. Careful documentation is kept of who worked on the project and what information they had available as a defense against future claims of copyright or trade secret infringement.

Before software patents, the law recognized software as an economic good similar to information, and the copyright was a primary grant of property rights in a collection of software code. Thus, the copyright can exclude others from replicating and distributing code but cannot prevent someone from independently developing software with similar or even identical capabilities. The copyright also grants the original creator the exclusive right to control derivative works, which in the case of software includes reuse of the code in other projects (possibly after modification) or modification of the code in new versions. Although the copyright expires after a fixed period of time (much longer than the lifetime of a patent), lifetime is less an issue for software because of the rapid changes in the industry and the necessary maintenance and upgrade cycle.

With the advent of software patents, more fundamental exclusionary property rights may be granted an invention embodied in software, allowing the patent holder to prevent others from using that invention even if their embodiment is created and developed independently. With the software patent, the law recognizes software as an economic good distinct from information, the distinction being that software embodies behaviors rather than insights or knowledge (see chapter 9 for further consideration of the differences between information and software). Other provisions of copyright law, such as second-copy and fair use, limit the rights of the copyright holder. Fair use is particularly significant, since it may grant users the right to make replicas of information or software for their own use.

As with information, exact replicas of software are easily created, and these replicas are nonrival in use. Security schemes can discourage unauthorized replication and distribution, but they inhibit usability and are thus unpopular with users. They also cannot deter well-funded attacks (see section 8.1.4). Only social constructs such as established ethics, legal restrictions, and active law enforcement can prevent *piracy*—large-scale unauthorized manufacture and sale of software—and, it is argued, thereby encourage substantial investments in the creation of software. The community-based software development movement demonstrates that it is possible to develop software without financial incentives but only in limited circumstances (see section 4.2.4).

8.1.3   Software Licensing

Software is normally licensed to whoever provisions and operates it. The *license* allows a holder (licensor) of intellectual property rights (any of the four forms) to grant to a second party (the licensee) the right to use. The license usually specifies the conditions under which the software can be used or disseminated to third parties, payments to the licensor, whether modifications of the software are allowed, the risks and liability each party assumes, representations and warranties, and promises of support and maintenance (Chavez, Tornabene, and Wiederhold 1998). Many other types of terms and conditions are possible (Katz and Shapiro 1986a), such as who owns the source code if the licensor goes out of business.

Although copyrights can protect the property rights for either source code or object code, in practice both are copyrighted, but it is usually object code that is distributed and licensed (see section 4.4). This is a form of encapsulation that allows the licensee to execute the code without easily examining its design or modifying it. Object code constitutes an obstacle (not insurmountable) to reverse engineering, which can uncover ideas and techniques, increasing the expense of a rival wishing to reproduce similar capabilities. Object code also inhibits passing unauthorized copies of software to others because it will usually fail after a while to run on upgraded platforms or to interoperate with complementary software. Ongoing releases resulting from continued maintenance and upgrade are thus a practical deterrent to illegal copying and piracy. Another is the common practice of offering substantial discounts on upgrades, provided a proof of payment for the original version can be presented. Most important, object code is much more difficult to modify: customer modifications would effectively invalidate warranties and preclude customer support. Source code is sometimes licensed (at a much higher price than object code) in instances where a customer may want or need the right to modify or at least to inspect for security reasons. In this case, the licensor's support and maintenance obligations must be appropriately limited. In other cases, the source code copyright may be sold outright, as is common for outsourced development.

Because replication and distribution costs are low, some unusual licensing terms become economically viable. *Freeware* involves no payment and allows the user to replicate and distribute the software freely. While this provides no revenue, neither does it represent a financial burden as long as the license absolves the licensor of liability and offers no warranties. *Shareware* is provided free, but a voluntary payment is requested if the user puts the software to productive use.

Source code licenses, those that grant access to source code to the licensee, are a particularly interesting case because many more things can be done with source code and licenses could vary depending on the objectives and business model of the licensor. The term *open source license* usually refers to a specific set of terms and conditions that meet the requirements for certification by the Open Source Initiative (OSI), including the right to read, modify, redistribute, and freely use the source code. Some examples of source code software licenses are listed in table 8.1. The primary issues in choosing license terms and conditions are whether the licensor wants license revenues, whether it wants to allow the source code to be used for proprietary purposes, whether it wants to allow modifications to the source code and whether it allows the source code to be "forked" into different versions or requires that all modifications of the code be arbitrated by the licensor or some third party to maintain a single version.

While source code licensing was once restricted to software created and maintained outside the commercial environment, there is increasing commercial interest in this type of license. The *copyleft license* essentially precludes the ability to gain revenues from the code itself but still admits other business models, such as paid training, support, and consulting services for users. This type of license seems especially appropriate for technology- and application-independent infrastructure software (see section 7.1.1), where there is a collective interest in providing a common reliable and secure technological underpinning for other commercial software. The *community license* and *examination license* approaches are interesting for paid software licenses as a way of garnering customer or community assistance in improving software and encouraging complementary research activities (particularly in academe).

Example The Sun Community Source License has been adopted by Sun in promulgating its Java technology, such as Jini, its platform that allows appliances to interoperate opportunistically (Sun Microsystems 1996). This license follows the community model, and its license specifies three levels of participation: research use (examination and evaluation of the source code), internal deployment (right to manipulate the code during development and testing), and commercial use (use of the code in a commercial product triggering royalties back to Sun). Licensees must contribute maintenance improvements to the community but are free to make proprietary improvements or extensions as long as they have open interfaces. Sun's

Table 8.1
Generic Types of Source Code Software Licenses

License Type	General Terms and Conditions	Motivation
Public	Source code may be freely modified and/or incorporated into proprietary products. No attribution of original creator is required.	Licensor desires no interest in (or liability for) the source code's creation; this is a no-strings-attached contribution of source code to the community.
University	Source code may be freely modified and/or incorporated into proprietary products as long as the original copyright notice and attribution remain attached.	Licensor wants to encourage technology transfer through incorporation into commercial products but also wants to be credited for its contribution.
Copyleft	Source code can be freely modified but cannot be incorporated into proprietary products. Any derivative software must retain the original copyright terms and conditions.	Licensor wants to ensure that its software is not used for commercial gain but also to encourage improvements or modifications for specific environments.
Community	Right to improve code is conditional on passing a set of compliance tests and contributing the modifications to the community, proprietary extensions are allowed, and commercial deployment triggers royalties to the licensor.	Licensor wants to remain the primary developing organization that manages the project, maintain control over compatibility of different versions through compliance test suites, and ultimately derive royalties but also invites others to join in the development and contribute improvements and extensions to the collective benefit.
Examination	Source code can be examined but not modified. Suggested improvements may be donated to the licensor, who has the option to incorporate them into future versions.	Licensor wants to maintain control over a single source code distribution but encourage others to examine the code for flaws or to encourage extensions. This form of license has been called shared source when the licensees include select customers of a commercial project.

motivation is to gain wide participation in advancing and promulgating the plat-form, while still maintaining a degree of control and achieving revenues. Similarly, Microsoft offers a shared source license for the .NET Common Language Infra-structure and associated C# compiler (now also adopted as ECMA standards).

8.1.4   Trademarks

The *trademark* is a visible sign or device used to identify goods and distinguish them from those made or carried by others. The trademark helps a business build a brand identity. The societal interest is in encouraging firms to invest in high-quality prod-ucts by allowing them to benefit from a positive reputation based on past products. In software, given the nature of copyright protection, the trademark can also pre-serve a single unified distribution by preventing copying of capabilities and features.

Example   The ability to recreate the functionality of software in a cleanroom or the ability to modify source code in a copyleft license can result in "forks"—inde-pendent but distinctive versions of what is essentially the same software. This hap-pened with the UNIX operating system, which was promulgated by AT&T and also through several derivatives of university versions, resulting in fragmentation of the UNIX market and ultimately stifling that market (especially on the desktop) through the negative feedback of network effects. Learning from this example, Sun Microsys-tems utilized the Java trademark to establish name recognition for Java and prevent others from creating incompatible versions. Of course, firms would be free to inde-pendently create similar functionality to the extent they did not infringe on Sun patents; however, these alternatives could not legally carry the Java trademark. Compliance tests were defined that had to be passed by implementations claiming to be Java.

All four forms of intellectual property can be invoked in complementary ways depending on the particular circumstances. A public, university, or copyleft licensed software project is the most complex situation because of the possibility of many people's modifying source code for various purposes.

Example   The originator of a hypothetical copyleft project OpenCode, Soft-ware4U, establishes the ground rules through the original copyright license. Anybody examining or modifying the OpenCode source must adhere to the license terms and conditions set by Software4U. Others may independently create the same capabilities and features, but confusion is avoided since they cannot attach the name OpenCode, which was trademarked by Software4U. Software4U also obtained a patent for an invention it incorporated into OpenCode. Anybody who bases a commercial product on OpenCode under the terms of the copyright license must also license this patent and pay royalties to Software4U, unless they manage to change the capabilities or implementation in a way that avoids infringement. Others creating an independent product must do the same. OpenCode also created a commercial package based on OpenCode and incorporated some proprietary ways to improve its performance (thus distinguishing it from other versions) that it maintains as a trade secret.

8.1.5   Rights Management

The challenge in rights management is to enforce the terms and conditions of a license for information or software. For example, the terms of the license may prohibit the licensee from making a replica and giving that replica to a third party or from going into business producing many replicas and selling them. These terms and conditions are limited by any fair use provisions of the copyright law, which may grant limited rights to licensees to create replicas exclusively for their own benefit.

There are two complementary ways to enforce a copyright: through technology and through legal mechanisms. Considering first technology, from a security perspective rights management is a twofold problem: the first part is *conditional access control* (see section 5.4), where the objective is to allow a licensee to access information or run software but prevent a nonlicensee from doing the same. Conditional access can be accomplished by standard authentication and conditional access techniques. The second part is *copy protection*, which prevents a licensee from replicating and disseminating to others the information or software it legally possesses and uses. Without copy protection, the licensor is dependent on the honesty and good will of the licensee to avoid further distribution. Unfortunately, copy protection can never be fully effective, because legitimate access and use of information or software inherently makes it susceptible to copying or replication.

Example   Once a picture or document reaches the eyes, it is possible to capture it with a camera, and once audio reaches the ears it is possible to capture it with a microphone. In order to run a software program, its instructions must be available to the computer in an executable form, and that same executable form could in principle be replicated and run on another identical computer.[1]

Copy protection can never prevent the copying of information on the screen or through a speaker, so it focuses instead on preventing replication of the original digital representation of the information or software (see section 2.1.2). Encryption, such as is used in confidentiality, is a useful tool (see section 5.4.5), although copy protection is fundamentally different from confidentiality. In confidentiality, each party trusts that the other will reveal neither secret keys nor plaintext to third parties; the two parties have a mutual interest in preventing disclosure of the information. Copy protection is appropriate when the licensor does not trust the licensee to keep secrets or worries that the licensee will reveal plaintext to others.

Example If a content provider encrypts a digital representation and simply provides the decryption key to the user (as in a confidentiality protocol), the user could provide a replica of the plaintext, or alternatively both the ciphertext and decryption key, to a friend.

Some common approaches to copy protection are described in table 8.2. None is foolproof, and each has its disadvantages (Wallach 2001). The *incompatibility* approach can be annoying to users, including those wanting to exercise legitimate fair use rights. The *service provider* approach is most applicable to a specific model for selling software, and the *license server* approach requires full-time Internet access. The *trusted system* approach introduces the additional cost of an information appliance but is attractive where that appliance is required anyway.

In general, copy protection schemes that rely on special hardware are more secure than software-only solutions. By its very nature, software (including object code) can be reverse-engineered and modified by a sophisticated individual. On the other hand, there are techniques for encapsulating information within hardware (such as unique identifiers or secrets) that make it difficult and expensive to extract. For example, such information can be hard-wired into integrated circuits so that an attempt to extract the information (by removing the protective casing) will destoy it. Thus, most trusted system approaches are at least partly hardware-based. However, it is important to realize that an adversary willing to expend sufficient resources can defeat even such a scheme.

Software has always been digitally represented, but the trend is toward end-to-end digital representations of information as well because this preserves high quality and is efficient in its use of resources. This has brought information into the same league as software in terms of the importance attached to copy protection.

Example Satellite and increasingly over-the-air and cable television use compressed digital representations, principally because the compression can increase the number of TV channels available within a given communication channel (such as radio spectrum). Similarly, the analog VCR is being displaced rapidly by the digital DVD as a recording medium. In order to preserve quality, this digital representation is increasingly preserved all the way to the television monitor.

Table 8.2
Approaches to Copy Protection

Approach	Description	Scope and Limitation	Example
Incompatibility	Replication of digital information or software is deterred because of incompatibility with standard tools for replication (such as copying the contents of one disk to another).	Useful for the distribution of information or software on recordable media; however, sophisticated users (such as those capable of programming) can easily circumvent.	The Sony PlayStation has its games stored on standard CDs, but in a way that is incompatible with widely available CD-ROM burner software on personal computers (Wallach 2001).
Service provider	The user accesses information or makes use of software through a trusted service provider. Information content is made available only by query or streaming, not by replication.	Useful for making the capabilities of software available to the user without access to source or object code. Allowing the user to query a database to extract specific information makes it difficult to replicate the entire database, and providing video or audio by streaming avoids giving the user an entire replica at once.	The application service provides (ASP) model avoids making software code available to the user. Many Web pages are generated dynamically using information extracted from a database. Many audio/video content suppliers provide only streaming media.
License server	Software execution is made conditional on permission of a remote license server.	Useful where the platform has a full-time network connection and unique identifier.	Microsoft Windows XP generates a platform signature based on hardware configuration, and requires a network registration procedure called Product Activation.

Table 8.2 (continued)

Approach	Description	Scope and Limitation	Example
Trusted system	Information can only be accessed using a licensed information appliance that can be trusted to enforce license terms and conditions.	Useful for information, where only the trusted system can decrypt the digital representation, and for software, where the source or object code is encapsulated within the system.	The signal sent to satellite TV receivers is encrypted; only licensed receivers possess an encapsulated secret decryption key; they output only an analog representation.

Content providers are reluctant to make their copyrighted material available in this increasingly digital environment without strong copy protection. The trusted system approach is attractive, particularly where information appliances are the norm anyway (as in consumer audio or video). Since users are accustomed to exchanging information among different appliances, and making copies for their own use, copy protection relies on coordination of the industry through standardization (see section 7.2).

Example In the TV example, a user will typically have a satellite TV receiver or set-top box, a recording appliance, and a monitor. The user and the industry want to preserve the ability for the consumer to mix and match options from different manufacturers. If these are all digital, the content provider wants to ensure that the digital signal cannot be captured and replicated as it passes from one appliance to another. The content supplier will thus require that each licensed appliance be a trusted system compliant with a copy protection scheme, and that each makes content available digitally only to other compliant appliances. Further, the license will specify connections to other licensed appliances use encryption on all open interfaces. To thwart the capture, replication, and playback of the encrypted signal, the encryption keys used on these open interfaces must be changed often. This can be accomplished by using the certificate infrastructure and session key approach described in section 5.4.7, for example. Two standard open interfaces for this purpose are illustrated in figure 8.1, one between a satellite TV receiver and a digital recorder, and the second between the recorder and a digital TV. The first two are interfaced with the IEEE 1394 (Firewire) using Digital Transmission Copy

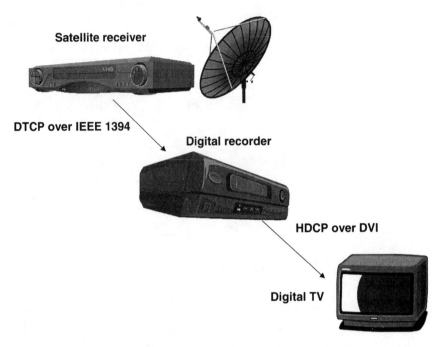

Figure 8.1
A chain of copy protection between information appliances.

Protection (DTCP) and the second Digital Video Interface (DVI) with High-Bandwidth Digital Copy Protection (HDCP). In each case, the license requires a compliant device to interoperate with another device only after determining that it is also compliant and establishing a one-time session encryption key.

Because a recording medium is passive, and a recording and playback appliance can communicate only through information stored on the medium, challenge-response authentication as described in this example is not possible for recordable media. Thus, more complicated copy protection mechanisms are necessary to prevent the unauthorized replication of digital recordings. An objective in this case is to prevent bit-by-bit copies of information on one medium being recorded on another medium and then played back. This implies that each instance of a copy-protected recording medium must have a unique identifier, and the recording must ensure that changing the identifier prevents playback.

Example The Copy Protection for Removable Media (CPRM) standard allows users to make recordings of digital content, but without allowing copies of those recordings to be made (Traw 2001). The standard is licensed to manufacturers of both removable media and recording and playback appliances. Licensees are issued the information illustrated in figure 8.2. Each compliant appliance is issued device-specific secrets that must be encapsulated within the appliance (usually in hardware) so that they cannot be easily extracted by a cracker. Each compliant recording medium has a read-only section that cannot be modified, and that section includes an identifier (like manufacturer identifier and a serial number) unique for each medium (tape or disk). If content is bit-by-bit copied from one medium to another, the different identifier will preclude playback in a compliant appliance. The medium also includes a large readable table of values called the Media Key Blocks (MKB) containing public corroboration information for the secrets within the appliances (similar to the public key in an asymmetric encryption system; see section 5.4). The MKB is actually a large table of data covering all present and future compliant appliances. The copy protection scheme then works as shown in figure 8.3. Each appliance calculates a Media Key (MK) based on its own secrets, the MKB, and the medium identifier. Because (and only because) both appliances use the same medium identifier, the MKs they calculate are identical. A random Title Key (TK) is generated, encrypted using MK, stored in encrypted form on the writable portion of the disk, and later decrypted on the playback device. TK is also used to encrypt the content, which is stored on the writable portion and decrypted in the playback device. Crackers, lacking access to the device-specific secrets, cannot determine MK and hence TK.

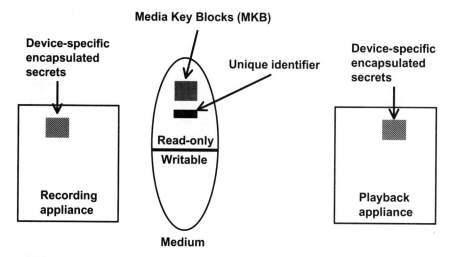

Figure 8.2
The appliance- and media-specific information supporting CPRM.

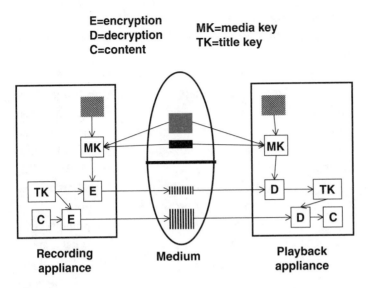

Figure 8.3
The CPRM copy protection scheme supports renewability.

Another capability of the most modern copy protection schemes is renewability. Most such schemes are eventually cracked, so they have a finite lifetime. Renewability extends the lifetime by allowing revocation or upgrading. Revocation means that the privilege of a specific compliant appliance to participate in copy protection can be revoked, and upgrading means its internal software can be upgraded to change the scheme even after it is in the hands of the user. Revocation without upgrading requires the user to return the appliance for replacement.

Example   The privileges of either the recording or playback appliances in figure 8.3 can be revoked by deliberately introducing errors in MKB for all future manufactured media. Previously manufactured recordable media will continue to work, but all media manufactured post-revocation will not work with the revoked appliances. Of course, it is a difficult step in the marketplace to revoke the privileges of an appliance in the hands of the user through no fault of their own. Thus, upgradeability is a better approach, one that is available to appliances that routinely have phone or Internet access, like satellite TV receivers.

Copy protection schemes are effective against casual infringers or users who may not be cognizant of the relevant laws; this is exactly the situation where legal remedies are not effective. On the other hand, copy protection can never be effective against a well-funded adversary who is willing to reverse-engineer and manufacture clones; fortunately, these are the adversaries who are more susceptible to legal action and law enforcement. Thus, copy protection and legal remedies are complementary, and both are considered essential by content providers (Traw 2001).

Example An adversary could clone recordable media as shown in figure 8.2 by simply capturing the public information on the disk. By manufacturing cloned disks all with the same (supposedly) unique identifier, mass reproduction of digital content that would play on compliant devices would be possible. However, such an adversary would either have no license to CPRM or would be violating the license terms, and could be pursued by legal means.

While popular with content providers, copy protection is not popular with consumers (Shy and Thisse 1999), and software suppliers (in contrast to content providers) have been relatively inactive in strengthening the laws against piracy (Garcia 1998). Copy protection is controversial among civil libertarians for a couple of reasons. First, copy protection as a means of enforcing a copyright may be more restrictive than the copyright laws and hence interfere with legally sanctioned rights of the user.

Example Under the fair use provisions of copyright law, users may have a right to make copies of information content to access it on different devices and appliances that they own. Thus, the law may align fair use rights with a person or a household rather than with a device. A copy protection scheme that is clearly person-based (recalling that approaches like passwords are not suitable because they could be given away along with content) is biometric authentication, but this is difficult in practice because it requires a trusted system to collect and report the biometric data on all devices, an infrastructure that does not exist at present. A viable alternative is the smartcard, in which authentication is based on possession of a hard-to-forge artifact, although this still requires a trusted system authentication mechanism.

Second, recognizing that copy protection is imperfect and can always be circumvented given sufficient time and effort, content providers may seek to criminalize efforts to undercut copy protection, and this may in turn limit civil liberties.

Example In the United States, the Digital Millennium Copyright Act (DMCA) of 1998 includes an *anticircumvention provision* that prohibits "any technology, product, service, device, component, or part thereof, that . . . is primarily designed or produced for the purpose of circumventing protection afforded by a technological measure that effectively protects a right of a copyright owner." Many civil libertarians object to this law because it may outlaw various activities that have no relation to copyright infringement and are protected under other laws (Samuelson 1999). For example, a researcher who examines a copyright mechanism, finds a flaw, demonstrates that flaw with a software program, and publicly divulges that program may run afoul of the DMCA even if the intent is not to enable copyright infringement or if the intent is to enable allowable replication of information under fair use. This activity is also desirable because strength of security measures is enhanced by public scrutiny, useful knowledge about strong security may be gained, and this researcher may be exercising her right to free speech guaranteed under the U.S. Constitution. Proponents of the DMCA argue that it is necessary to protect the rights of copyright holders to prevent widespread copyright infringement in ways that are not easily countered by other legal means.

Even effective copy protection is at best a partial solution for information (in contrast to software) because it cannot prevent analog copies of works from being captured from video screens or speaker jacks. A secondary technological protection for copyright holders is the watermark (Lanqelaar, Setyawan, and Laqendijk 2000; Macker, Park, and Corson 2001; Podilchuk and Delp 2001). A *watermark* is information that is imperceptibly embedded in an information representation that may specify the copyright ownership of that work or identity of the party to whom the work has been licensed. An ideal watermark would be imperceptible to the user (so that it doesn't interfere with legitimate uses), would be robust to legitimate operations like analog-to-digital-to-analog conversion and digital compression (so it would be preserved in all representations, including analog), and would be difficult to remove deliberately. Watermarking technologies utilize signal-processing techniques similar to military communication techniques (e.g., spread spectrum) that are difficult to detect and do not interfere with other communication. However, like other forms of technological rights management, watermarks today fall short of meeting all these objectives. Worse, there is a simple technique that is likely to eliminate watermarks, assuming access to multiple legitimate copies, each with their own watermark. By simply taking the signal average (sum of all copies' signals divided by number of copies), the original content prevails while the watermarks are averaged out. There are sophisticated watermarking approaches that require access to an immense number of legitimate copies, but these are in early research stages only.

8.2 Regulation

While the marketplace works for most purposes, there are situations where government regulations can and should intervene in ways that place requirements or constraints on the software industry. These include situations where larger societal interests such as law enforcement and national security intervene, or where the market may fail to provide sufficient protections to users (such as security and privacy), where the rights of some citizens may need to be preserved, or where vibrant competition in the marketplace may be at stake.

8.2.1 Law Enforcement and National Security

Like other aspects of our society, software has considerable impact on law enforcement and national security. This has three facets. First, IT creates new challenges for law enforcement, including new laws to enforce and new ways for lawbreakers or national enemies to coordinate themselves or hide their activities. Second, the new tools in the hands of lawbreakers requires law enforcement agencies to adopt new countermeasures. Third, like other institutions, information technologies provide law enforcement and intelligence agencies with some tools to improve organizational effectiveness and productivity.

As IT is increasingly woven into the social fabric, governments have increasing concern that the benefits be maximized while avoiding possible negative implications. Nowhere is this tension more evident than in the area of computer security. On the one hand, it is important to promulgate strong technological security measures to limit the potential for computer crime so as to contain the losses and limit the resources devoted to law enforcement ("an ounce of prevention is worth a pound of cure"). There is even increasing concern about sophisticated attacks by terrorists or enemies. To counter these threats, the many authentication- and encryption-based tools and technologies discussed in section 5.4 should be in common use, and operators and users should be well trained and vigilant. On the other hand, similar security tools and technologies can be utilized by criminals and terrorists to hide their activities. This has led governments to attempt to limit the use of encryption technologies, or to limit the "strength" of encryption technologies that are used, even though that might reduce our collective security (Dam and Lin 1996; 1997).

Example   For much of the past decade, the U.S. government has classified encryption as a "defense article" on the Munitions List, making it subject to the Arms Control Export Act (Levin 1999; NRC 1996). An export license from the Department of State (and later Commerce) was required to sell products incorporating encryption. Regulations limited the number of bits in encryption keys to 40 (or 56 in some cases). This "weak" encryption was sufficient to thwart casual attacks but was also susceptible to sustained cryptanalysis attacks given sufficient resources (e.g., government intelligence services). The motivation was to allow strong encryption to be used within the United States (where no restrictions were placed) but limit its availability outside the United States. Opponents of this policy argued that overseas companies could develop the same technologies, creating new competitors for U.S. companies. Civil libertarians argued that this violated free expression by limiting the right of researchers or commercial firms to publish their encryption knowledge, and also the privacy and security of individuals by exposing their encrypted information to possible scrutiny. These export restrictions were incrementally relaxed (but not eliminated) in 1998 and 2000.

As a rule, attempts to ban the civilian use of new software technologies are likely to be ineffective, except in the unlikely event that they are globally banned, because many countries have the capability to develop them.

Escrowed encryption is a more direct way to address these conflicting concerns, enabling strong encryption and legitimate access by authorities at the same time (NRC 1996). It creates three classes of entities: *users*, who have unconditional access to the plaintext; *adversaries*, who never have access, and *authorities*, who are allowed access under exceptional circumstances strictly defined by laws or policies. The first two classes are recognized by ordinary confidentiality protocols (see section 5.4.5): users have access to the secret decryption key and adversaries don't. The class of authorities can be supported by *key escrow agents*, one or more disinterested entities who have access to a decryption key but are legally bound to release this key to specified authorities under a set of prescribed policies and bear legal responsibility for malfeasance or mistakes.

Escrowed encryption can solve a number of problems in law enforcement and national security. For example, it can be used to allow law enforcement authorities exceptional access to encrypted information under court order (similar to a search warrant) or to allow intelligence authorities access to encrypted information while still preventing access by adversaries. However, escrowed encryption requires the cooperation of users, either voluntarily or because they are legally bound. Escrowed encryption has other applications as well. For example, an organization may routinely keep vital information assets in encrypted form to prevent inadvertent disclosure or theft, but then the loss or corruption of the decryption key means loss of the information. Escrowed encryption provides a mechanism to recover lost keys.

A number of escrowed encryption protocols are possible, depending on the precise social needs (Denning and Branstad 1996). An important design parameter is the granularity with which a key is used and susceptible to being revealed.

Example   The public key infrastructure provides a natural mechanism for escrowed encryption; since the certificate authority (CA) creates the secret key and distributes it to individuals or organizations, the CA could also retain a copy of these keys and provide one to an authority under exceptional circumstances. However, this potentially gives the authority access to *all* confidential communications directed at the user with this secret key. Access can be limited to a specific session by using a one-time randomly generated session key (see section 5.4.7). An escrowed encryption protocol using a session key would communicate the session key confidentially to the key escrow agent (for example using its authenticated public key).

An additional level of trust and protection can be introduced by using two or more key escrow agents, requiring them to work in concert to reconstruct a secret key. This reduces the possibilities of both malfeasance (requiring collusion) and mistakes (requiring all agents to make a mistake). Most practical applications of key escrowing have other detailed requirements that make the required protocols considerably more intricate than those described.

Example   In 1994 the U.S. government proposed the Escrowed Encryption Standard (EES) for use in confidential telephone conversations (Denning 1994). (This was more popularly known as the clipper chip initiative.) EES uses a one-time random session key for each telephone call, two key escrow agents who must collaborate to allow a law enforcement authority to decrypt a conversation, and sufficient information carried with the encrypted telephone signal itself to allow this. Each telephone encryption device has a unique secret and encapsulated device key split into two pieces, each of those pieces supplied to one of the escrow agents. The encryption device attaches a law enforcement access field (LEAF) to each communication. The LEAF includes sufficient information to uniquely identify the encryption device and, with coordinated information obtained from both escrow agents, obtain the session key and decrypt the conversation. EES was proposed for widespread use but never gained traction because it received a poor reception from civil libertarians. Today, EES is a voluntary standard for federal agency communication.

Authentication is another illustration of a tough balancing act for governments. On the one hand, biometric authentication is a powerful evidentiary tool in law enforcement, and is also the most effective form of access control in computer applications or at national borders. However, it also raises numerous issues relating to personal privacy and civil liberties.

Example   In the United States a national identity smartcard containing biometric information has occasionally been proposed. This smartcard could encapsulate a secret establishing its authenticity, and that secret could be verified using a challenge-response protocol. Further, the identity and biometric information provided by the smartcard could be digitally signed by an authority, establishing its integrity, and could be compared with biometric information gathered at border crossings, airport gates, and so on. Even though this security system would not require a central database nor require the storage of information on the whereabouts of individuals as they traveled, there would be strong motivation to capture and store this information for possible investigative or evidentiary purposes. There is considerable opposition to this system on the basis of privacy and civil liberties.

One of the greatest challenges for law enforcement arises from the global nature of the Internet compared to the geography-based jurisdictions of most agencies and courts. Without firewalls placed at national boundaries, the Internet is transparent across geographic and jurisdictional boundaries. Where a jurisdiction might attempt to ban offensive software (such as strong encryption) or information (such as pornography), this can be circumvented by making it available on a server in another jurisdiction.

On the opportunity side, software-based information management techniques are essential tools in crime detection and investigation. A big opportunity is the *federation* of information repositories held by different agencies, a term applied to building a layer of middleware above a set of separately administered databases that gives them the appearance of being merged. This is a natural way to share the information stored in fragmented databases among agencies. Another opportunity is *data mining*, a term applied to extracting unexpected patterns from masses of information. A current research topic—one that raises many privacy and civil liberties issues—is the dispersal of many tiny sensors with wireless networking or the mass surveillance of public spaces using miniature video cameras. Such sensors can be used for monitoring the location of individuals (like parolees), intrusion detection, and the detection of chemical or biological attacks.

8.2.2 Security

Government interest and involvement in security issues (see section 5.3.1) has increased markedly in recent years, for several reasons. As the use of computers and the Internet in commercial activities has become widespread, the vulnerability to attacks has increased. Not only are there direct monetary losses to worry about, but consumer confidence and hence national economic performance can potentially be affected. The global Internet has opened everyone to organized and sophisticated attacks by foreign governments and terrorists. There have been some well-publicized successful attacks wrought by individual crackers that illustrate our vulnerability.

Example   A worm (allegedly unleashed by a graduate student at Cornell University) caused a major collapse of servers on the Internet in November 1988 by exploiting several vulnerabilities in UNIX programs and continually replicating itself. As these types of operating system vulnerabilities have increasingly been plugged, recent worms have focused on e-mail attachments. In February 2000 a denial-of-service attack (allegedly launched by a Canadian teenager using tools readily available on the Internet) brought to a halt several major e-commerce sites (including eBay, Schwab, and Amazon).

The primary defense against attacks is the actions taken by provisioning and operation personnel to protect themselves and users. However, there are a number of reasons why these measures may, by themselves, be inadequate. Operators only have control over their own vulnerabilities, and many techniques to reduce these vulnerabilities are both expensive and invasive—they typically interfere with usability. Good security does nothing to increase revenue for either operators or suppliers; it simply combats losses, often of an unknown or unspecified nature. Thus, operators have mixed incentives and may underinvest in security measures. Very specialized expertise is required to achieve security, expertise that is expensive and difficult to develop in individual organizations, the latter because it benefits directly from the learning curve of dealing with many incidents. Operators have no control whatsoever over the other side of security, the threats, and have great difficulty assessing risks. Further, there are externalities: inadequate measures taken by one user may increase the threat to other users.

Example   A distributed denial-of-service attack is typically mounted by cracking multiple hosts and installing attack programs on all of them. Thus, an attack on one host is assisted by the weak security of other hosts anywhere on the Internet. From the perspective of the site being attacked, it is difficult to detect the difference between legitimate use and a denial-of-service attack (although tools are being developed by some startup companies, such as Arbor Networks, Asta Networks, Lancope Technologies, and Mazu Technologies, to detect and thwart such attacks). The spread of viruses is interrupted by users' installing viral protection software, and worms can be defeated by installing the latest security patches; in this manner, each user is affected by the collective actions of others.

Perhaps most important, security is ultimately a systems issue; to a large extent, good security can be achieved only by software suppliers working together and with provisioning and operation personnel across all organizations. In this sense, security has a lot in common with public health, where individuals must take responsibility for their own health but also depend on a whole infrastructure to assess risks, monitor the system, coordinate actions, and take speedy and collective remedial measures when problems occur.

All these issues, and especially the public health analogy, suggest a role for government laws and regulation in increasing the collective level of security. The level of threat can be reduced by laws that impose criminal penalties for certain types of cracking activities, especially where there is a resulting direct harm or economic loss.

Example   In the United States the 1986 Computer Fraud and Abuse Act made it a federal crime to gain unauthorized access to certain types of hosts, such as those of financial institutions and those involved in interstate commerce. It was amended by the National Information Infrastructure Protection Act of 1996.[2] To conduct a felony prosecution, the attacked organization must maintain comprehensive audit trails to prove that the penetration occurred and that losses where suffered.

Laws may also outlaw the creation or dissemination of software tools that assist crackers, although these raise significant issues of free speech (similar to copy protection circumvention; see section 8.1.5).

On the demand side, the primary mechanism for ensuring good security is customer evaluation of security features as one important criterion for choosing one supplier over another. Unfortunately, there are limits to the sophistication of most customers, and they may also lack adequate information to make an informed decision. Additional economic incentives for suppliers flow from product liability laws that penalize suppliers for security breaches within their control, and insurance underwriters who price in accordance with a professional assessment of risk. To supplement these economic forces, an argument can be made for laws that mandate measures (such as incorporating virus protection software in every operating system) that reduce threats to other users. There may be measures that can be introduced into the infrastructure at extra expense to improve collective security but that may have to be mandated by government because the market provides insufficient or even adverse economic incentives (analogous to automotive seatbelts, which were not common until mandated by government). Another useful government tool is policies for procurement of equipment and software for its internal use: if those policies mandate strong security features, this will stimulate vendors to develop the requisite technology and then amortize the resulting costs over commercial as well as government sales. Or government could simply mandate full disclosure of available information on security features and defects, giving customers all available information so that they can exercise market power.

As in public health, a simple and uncontroversial measure that governments can undertake is a campaign to educate users about the nature of threats and measures they can take to counter them. It can also fund organizations to conduct research, monitor, and respond to security threats (like the U.S. Centers for Disease Control).

Example After a major security incident in 1988 brought to a halt a substantial portion of the Internet, the U.S. government funded the CERT Coordination Center at Carnegie Mellon University, which by its own description "studies Internet security vulnerabilities, handles computer security incidents, publishes security alerts, researches long-term changes in networked systems, and develops information and training to help you improve security at your site." The government also operates a Federal Computer Incident Response Center (FedCIRC) to provide operational support to federal civilian agencies.

8.2.3 Privacy

Privacy (see section 5.3.2) is similar to intellectual property rights protection in that no completely satisfactory technological solution is possible, and ultimately users must rely to some extent on government regulation or voluntary action on the part of companies gathering personal information. When personal information is disclosed to a company for legitimate business purposes, the user is dependent on that company to appropriately limit the disclosure of personal information to others. There is no technological or other measure the user could directly employ that would guarantee that. Of course, many of the security technologies described in section 5.4 are available to assist the company in exercising its responsibilities.

While there is no doubt that privacy is an area of great concern for users of the Internet, there is considerable debate over the appropriate role for government regulation. Generally, the European Union has imposed a stronger regulatory regime, whereas the United States has relied more on voluntary action. Since the Internet is global, and users may be in different countries from companies that collect their private information, regulatory regimes in single countries or regions have global ramifications.

Example In the United States the Federal Trade Commission has a systematic privacy initiative that monitors Web sites to see if they disclose privacy policies, and initiates actions against sites that violate their own policies under existing consumer fraud legislation.[3] There are no specific laws on consumer privacy, except for those governing financial institutions (the Gramm-Leach-Bliley Act). The European Union, on the other hand, has enacted comprehensive privacy legislation (the Directive on Data Protection) that requires creation of government data protection agencies, registration of databases with those agencies, and in some instances prior approval of disclosure of personal information. These European laws apply to U.S. companies dealing with European citizens, so the United States and Europe negotiated a set of safe harbor principles that when adhered to, will protect U.S. companies from disruption of business and from legal action.[4]

The most fundamental disagreement is over whether the market provides adequate incentives to preserve the right balance between the interests of companies and individual users. A problem with government regulation is that it cannot distinguish the widely varying concerns of different users, whereas voluntary action can. Laws can establish a framework under which privacy policies are disclosed and those disclosed policies are enforced. With adequate disclosure, users can exercise market power by not dealing with companies they feel do not sufficiently respect their personal information. Another approach that accommodates users' varying degrees of concern is conditional policies that allow users to either opt in (the default is no disclosure of personal information to others) or opt out (the default is disclosure). Companies can provide monetary incentives (such as discounts) to users who choose to opt in. A third technological approach is to automate the choice of opt in or opt out transparently to the user.

Example   The Platform for Privacy Preferences (P3P) is a standard of the World Wide Web Consortium (W3C). Each user configures her browser to incorporate preferences as to the circumstances under which personal information is to be disclosed, and the P3P standardizes a way for a server to describe its privacy policies to the browser, where those policies are compared to the user preferences. P3P acts as a gatekeeper to allow personal information to be supplied only under circumstances acceptable to the user. However, by itself, such an automated scheme cannot confirm that the described policies are actually adhered to.

Proponents of stronger government regulation in the United States argue that companies are biased toward the dissemination of personal information in light of the revenues they can derive from selling that information, and that any voluntary policies may be arbitrarily abandoned if a company is sold or goes bankrupt. They also argue that concern over privacy is stifling Internet commerce, and thus government regulation that restored confidence would help the economy. Industry has responded to consumer concerns not only through voluntary policies but also through voluntary certification efforts.

Example   TRUSTe is a nonprofit initiative financed by a group of major corporations. It licenses the right to display the TRUSTe branded trademark on Web sites that adhere to its rules for a privacy policy that is adequately disclosed, allows an adequate range of consumer choice, and is enforced by adequate security measures. TRUSTe also implements procedures for oversight and complaint resolution. Licensees are required to post a verification seal that allows consumers to authenticate that site as TRUSTe-certified using a secure server. (This can be implemented by giving each licensee a secret, knowledge of which can be verified by a challenge-response authentication protocol from the TRUSTe server.)

It is clear that informing users about the use of their personal information is necessary, whether by voluntary or government-mandated means, since providing personal information is necessary for legitimate business purposes but its unauthorized disclosure may not otherwise be visible to the consumer and can bring harm. It is clear that consensus has not yet been reached in this debate in the United States.

8.2.4   Access and Free Speech

The balance between free speech (the unconditional right of individuals to freely provide information of their choosing) and legitimate restrictions on those rights has been debated for centuries. (In this context, *speech* is synonymous with information in all media, not just the spoken word.) The reality is that many governments place legal restrictions on free speech, limiting either what can be published (for example, the literature of certain hate groups is banned in some countries) or limiting access to certain types of information (for example, access to pornography by children is banned in most countries). The Internet poses some special challenges in trying to enforce limits on the publication of or access to speech. The fundamental issue is one of authentication: the Internet includes no internal foolproof mechanism to authenticate either the source or the destination of information transmitted over it. This problem manifests itself in several ways, depending on what limitations on speech a government wants to impose.

Limitations on acceptable speech can be circumvented by moving the source of the offending speech outside jurisdictional boundaries and exploiting the global nature of the network. A government might respond by imposing access control either locally or remotely.

Example   The governments of Singapore and China have attempted to censor the Internet by blocking access to certain foreign sites and by proscribing regulations on speech on the Internet within their borders (Augaud Nadarajan 1996; Hartford 2000). China did this by maintaining control over all foreign links and blocking certain IP addresses, and Singapore by requiring all Web accesses through a sanctioned "proxy server" that refused to connect to certain sites.

Since such censorship was not a design requirement in the original Internet, technological measures can usually be defeated by sophisticated users. Censorship can be bypassed by frequently moving the offending information around or replicating it in many places. Alternatively, a government may attempt to impose its laws on the information source, requiring it to authenticate and block access to its citizens, though the basic design of the Internet includes no technical provision to identify the country from which a user is accessing the network.

Example   France has outlawed literature from Nazi organizations, but such literature is protected free speech under the Constitution and laws of the U.S. A French court attempted in 2001 to enforce its law against Yahoo (which had Nazi paraphernalia for sale in its auctioning site). Yahoo argued that there was no feasible way to restrict access to French citizens alone, and a U.S. court refused to enforce French law in the United States.

Any limits to access of speech imposed by law require the authentication of at least the minimum identifying information for the user attempting access. Implementing this requires authentication, which in turn requires an infrastructure of third-party authorities who certify identity or identifying characteristics (see section 5.4.3).

Example   Placing a lower age limit on access to pornographic literature in the physical economy is relatively easy, because sales clerks interact directly with the buyer and can estimate their age or ask for proof of identity in questionable cases. On the network there is no comparable physical identifying characteristic to rely on, and in no country is there a suitable authentication infrastructure. Indeed, in some countries (like the United States) there is considerable opposition to such an infrastructure based on privacy concerns. In the United States this issue has been addressed by two (at best only partially effective) means—parental control through firewall software in a home computer, and authentication of users at pornographic sites by possession of a valid credit card (it being assumed that a child would not possess such a card).

Legal limits to the publication of or access to speech would be considerably easier to enforce if there were a universal infrastructure for authentication of users. The most effective infrastructure would be a universal requirement for users to obtain authoritative digital certificates containing biometric data and mechanisms to check this biometric data (see section 5.4.3). The certificates could include information on country of citizenship, age, and other relevant personal information, and servers could then implement authentication and access control that implemented jurisdiction-specific policies. This is unlikely to happen soon, in part because of the serious privacy and "Big Brother" concerns that it would raise.

An interesting and important question is whether software is protected free speech, or whether it is inherently distinct from information. This is a difficult issue because of the dual purpose of software code, first, as a means of directly controlling a machine (the computer) in the case of object code, and second, as a means programmers use to document and modify a program (especially source code). This question comes up specifically in the copyright protection anticircumvention restrictions, since software running on a personal computer can be an anticircumvention device (see section 8.1.5). Civil libertarians argue that banning the publication and dissemination of such code is a prior restraint of speech, something prohibited by the U.S. constitution. Copyright owners argue that such code constitutes an anticircumvention device and can therefore be banned under the Digital Millennium Copyright Act. This issue is greatly complicated by compilation (see section 4.4.4): while the source code is primarily for the eyes of programmers, which can be viewed as protected free expression, it can also be automatically translated (compiled) into object code, which is primarily for execution on a computer. Civil libertarians and programmers generally argue that a clear distinction should be made between publication, viewing, and modification of software code (which is purely an expression of ideas) and the act of compiling and executing such code. They also point out, rightly, that source code is an important mechanism for distributing new results in computer science, both conceptually and in terms of implementation, and that it serves as the basis for community-based software development (see sections 4.4.4 and 4.2.4). Some copyright owners have argued that no legal distinction should be made between source and object code, and between the publication and execution of either source or object code, and that the publication of offending object and source anticircumvention code should be banned as the most practical way to prevent its illegal use. This argument also has validity, in that legally enforcing a ban on the execution of published code against individual users is difficult at best. In light of these ambiguities, the banning of such code is an issue still awaiting a definitive ruling from the U.S. Supreme Court.

Example   DeCSS is a small program that allows DVD video files encrypted using the DVD Content Scrambling System to be stored on a computer's disk and played back by unlicensed software-based DVD players on that or another computer. Its origins are in creating an open source DVD player for the Linux platform. DeCSS can be used by a user to move DVD playback to a different platform, but it can also be used as the first step in illegally distributing DVD video in unprotected form. The U.S. District Court issued an injunction in January 2000 against *2600 Magazine*, barring it from posting DeCSS source code on the Web or even linking to other Web sites that posted the code (Touretzky 2001). Programmers who believed this ruling improperly put a prior restraint on speech pointed out that the algorithms embodied in the source code could be expressed in many essentially equivalent ways, such as in English or an alternative source language for which no compiler exists. To buttress this point, many equivalent but nonexecutable expressions of the algorithms embodied in DeCSS have been created (some of them humorous), including the hardware description language Verilog, songs, and printing on T-shirts (Touretzky 2002).

8.2.5   Antitrust and Competition

The antitrust laws are intended to preserve competition in the industry (the emphasis in Europe) or to protect the interests of consumers (the emphasis in the United States) by regulating certain business activities. Antitrust laws affect several aspects of the software industry, including mergers and acquisitions, cooperation among firms, and business strategies (Katz and Shapiro 1999a; 1999b; Kovacic and Shapiro 1999).

When two firms merge, or one acquires the other, there is generally a regulatory review focused on the harm to consumers due to a reduction of choice, increased prices, and so on. This is a judgment call, because this harm has to be balanced against potential efficiencies and other benefits that might accrue to companies and consumers.

Example   A proposed merger of Worldcom and Sprint was abandoned in July 2000 in the face of an antitrust lawsuit filed by the U.S. Department of Justice largely because of the concentration in business data services this would create. While there were a number of competitors for these services, most of them could not provide the geographic coverage of Worldcom, Sprint, and AT&T. In another case, Microsoft tried to acquire Intuit, a software supplier specializing in personal finance and tax preparation software but abandoned the deal in 1995 after encountering regulatory opposition because of the market concentration in personal finance software (Microsoft Money and Intuit Quicken).

Mergers come in three primary forms (Farreel and Shapiro 2000). Horizontal mergers involve direct competitors, vertical mergers involve suppliers and customers, and complementary mergers allow firms to broaden their product base to offer a larger product portfolio or a more complete system. Horizontal mergers raise the most regulatory questions because they reduce consumer choice and increase market share, but they can also have significant benefits such as eliminating duplicated costs or achieving synergies. In the software industry, manufacturing and distribution costs are small, so efficiency arguments are largely limited to the development costs for maintenance and upgrades and the costs of customer service. Thus, the arguments in favor of horizontal mergers are arguably weaker than in some other industries.

Example   Horizontal mergers are regulated in the United States by the Clayton and Sherman Antitrust Acts and the Federal Trade Commission Act. The U.S. Department of Justice and the Federal Trade Commission have issued standard guidelines for evaluating horizontal mergers in light of these laws.[5] One of the key criteria is the Herfindahl-Hirschman index (HHI) of market concentration, defined as the sum of the squares of the market shares (in percent) of all participants. For example, if there are four firms with market shares of 30, 30, 20 and 20 percent, the HHI = $30^2 + 30^2 + 20^2 + 20^2 = 2600$. The HHI is divided into three ranges of market concentration, unconcentrated (between 0 and 1000), moderately concentrated (between 1000 and 1800), and highly concentrated (between 1800 and 10,000). Mergers that move the HHI above 1800 receive special scrutiny.

Of course, there are many possible definitions of market share. One special challenge with software is that revenue, unit sales, and actual use of a software application may diverge significantly. For example, users may purchase and install software just to have it available for occasional use (like sharing files with colleagues), or site license arrangements may offer significant unit discounts. The resulting difficulty of accurate market sizing is combined with an equal difficulty of share attribution, given that no measurable physical resource, territory, or similar metric is involved and that revenues are split across the actual software and many associated services, including consultancy, help desks, and provisioning, all of which vary widely among software makers. Market share analysis is thus fraught with complications.

Antitrust laws also place limits on collaboration and standard-setting activities in the industry (Shapiro 2000) when those activities cross the line into conspiracies among competitors to limit competition or raise prices to the detriment of consumers.[6] Thus far there have been no major accusations of such conspiracies in the software industry, but since collaboration among firms and standard setting are important dynamics in the software industry, caution is in order.

Example   A standardization activity that would clearly not be anticompetitive is the agreement on standards for Web services or for component interoperability, since those standards are focused on moving competition from the level of whole applications down to the level of component services that can be mixed and matched (see section 7.3.7). As the intended effect is to offer customers more choices and lower the barriers for entry of suppliers, they cannot be construed as anti-competitive. On the other hand, an explicit agreement with a competitor for a specific application to divide up the market—each competitor focusing on a different platform—may be illegal.

The antitrust laws also deal with issues of monopolization, when one firm has sufficient market share to allow it substantial control over pricing or the ability to exclude competition. In the United States such monopolies are not illegal per se if they arise from normal market forces such as network effects or a patent (Povtero-Sánchez 1999; Shapiro 2001a) or simply competing on the merits. Monopolization by other means or unfair business practices can be illegal. Once a monopoly is created, it places special regulatory constraints on business practices, such as using market power to coerce other firms into exclusive deals or leveraging one monopoly to create a second (a strategy known as tying).

Example In 1982 the U.S. government dropped an antitrust complaint filed in 1969 against IBM alleging that it had illegally monopolized mainframe computers (Levy and Welzer 1985). With the benefit of hindsight, this illustrates the effect of rapid technological change on winners and losers in the industry, since IBM's computer industry market share is much lower today. In 1998 the U.S. government filed an antitrust complaint against Microsoft alleging illegal monopolization of the market for "Intel-compatible PC operating systems" and Web browsers and the illegal tying of the Internet Explorer browser to the operating system (U.S. Dept. of Justice 1998; Furse 1998; 1999; Liebowitz and Margolis 1999). The tying complaint was later dropped, but the findings of fact in the case (U.S. Dept. of Justice 1999) supported the illegal monopolization complaint. As of this writing, the final settlement and remedy are not completed.

Compared to other industries and products, the software products of different companies tend to be more dependent on complements (e.g., application and infrastructure). Also, software suppliers strive to differentiate their products for valid business and economic reasons, in part because of the large economies of scale that make head-to-head competition problematic (see chapter 9). Putting these two observations together, antitrust laws become an important consideration in some business decisions.

Example The decision to offer an API that enables extensions to a software product by other suppliers is an important business decision, as is opening up internal interfaces within a product as APIs (see section 4.3.4). On the plus side, such APIs add value to customers by offering them more choice and the ability to mix and match solutions from different suppliers. Although this added value aids suppliers by making their products more valuable to customers, this needs to be balanced against the competition it enables, especially if the suppliers plan to offer products on the other side of the interface being considered as an API. Since failure to provide a fully documented API can constitute illegal tying in some circumstances, antitrust laws need to be taken into account in such business decisions.

8.3 Research and Education

The government plays an important role in the software industry through the public funding of education and research, supplementing private investments in both arenas.

8.3.1 Workforce

The success of individual software suppliers and the ability of end-user organizations to successfully provision and use software crucially depend on an educated workforce that can capture user requirements, develop software, and provision and operate the infrastructure and applications (NRC 2001). Government and industry share responsibility in ensuring an adequately educated and adequately large workforce to maintain a healthy software industry.

The workforce in IT can be divided into two major categories: those who are primarily engaged in hands-on activities in the technology itself, such as specification, design, testing, and maintenance of software (the technology category; see section 4.2), and those who are primarily engaged in the uses and applications of technologies developed by others, such as conceptualization and analysis, provisioning, and operation (the user category; see section 5.1). The characteristics of these two categories are quite different.

Example In the United States it is estimated that about 5 million out of a total workforce of 140 million are in IT occupations, about equally divided between the two categories (NRC 2001). Estimates of the user category are the more difficult because there is no clear definition or distinction between these IT workers and the users of IT.

Two essential requirements of the workforce are education and training. Working in IT requires conceptual abilities, knowledge of theoretical IT constructs and frameworks, and applied technical skills. Conceptual and theoretical knowledge is usually acquired in a formal educational setting, whereas many skills can be acquired in vocational training programs or through on-the-job experience. Even the general population of IT users, which includes a large fraction of the population, requires some level of literacy or fluency in IT (NRC 1999a; 2002), a need generally unsatisfied in today's general education curricula in secondary schools and colleges.

The software industry has grown rapidly, and technologies change rapidly. Both growth and change raise concerns about the availability of appropriately educated workers. Many have argued that there is a shortage of appropriately educated workers, although this is difficult to substantiate. Clearly the labor market is tight, with salaries rising more quickly and with more job turnover compared to the general labor market. (The market for IT professionals is cyclical, however, and dropped off considerably in the recession of 2001–2002.)

Example   In the United States the Current Population Study finds that salaries of IT workers in the technology category are rising between 3.8 and 4.5 percent annually (exclusive of noncash forms of compensation, such as stock options) as compared with 3.2 percent for workers as a whole (NRC 2001). This more rapid rise signals a general tightness in the labor market. This workforce has also expanded rapidly, growing by 60 to 75 percent in an eight-year period starting in 1991. This rapid growth suggests that many are entering the workforce through on-the-job experience rather than formal education, and thus raises questions about the qualifications of the workforce.

There are two ways to acquire an educated workforce in a particular country like the United States: educate your own populace or import workers educated elsewhere. Both mechanisms have been important to the United States, and government initiatives are crucial to both. Foreign educated workers have been a significant and growing source of labor in the United States.

Example   In the United States the H-1B visa has allowed an increasing number of foreigners to work temporarily for up to six years. Foreign-born individuals represent about 17 percent of IT workers in the technology category (compared with about 10 percent of the U.S. population), and as much as 10 out of the 17 percent may be temporary workers under the H-1B visa program. Under considerable pressure from IT employers, but also taking into account the effect on opportunities and wages of American workers, the American Competitiveness and Workforce Improvement Act of 1998 increased the annual quota of H-1B visas from 65,000 to 115,000 per year, and established an IT technical training grant program using fees collected in issuing the visas. Some other developed countries, notably Germany, have discussed importing more foreign workers.

Of course, foreign workers can be utilized in place rather than brought into another country, and this is also a growing trend.

Example India has developed a multibillion dollar software industry, over half its revenues based on exports ("Software in India" 1996). A major enabler is substantial investment in education (India is also a major source of H-1B visa applicants in the United States), together with a large expatriate population working overseas that can shuttle business to India or return in managerial roles, and good English-speaking skills in the educated populace. Relatively little revenue is based on original software applications, in part because of the lack of a large domestic market for software (Balasubramanyam and Balasubramanyam 1997). Rather, the dominant activity is "body shopping," where well-specified modules are outsourced to Indian companies for implementation, and another revenue source is customizing software to specific end-user needs (Abraham, Ahlawat, and Ahlawat 1998).

With a rapidly improving infrastructure supporting international development efforts in software, a globalization of the software industry appears inevitable. That infrastructure includes not only networking but also increasingly sophisticated software collaboration and project management tools. As IT expands in many countries, they will develop an indigenous software industry to support local needs, and that will lead to export markets as well. Concurrent development of software—splitting project teams into different time zones so that the development can proceed twenty-four hours a day and reduce completion times accordingly—is also a major opportunity. A growing market for components should also assist the international market.

The characteristics of the IT workforce differ substantially from the general population in both racial and ethnic diversity, gender, and age distribution, and this is of considerable concern. White and Asian males are overrepresented, as are younger age groups, and clearly redressing this diversity would increase the supply of workers. This is an area where greater government involvement in training could be helpful.

8.3.2 Technology Transfer

Research in software is a good investment if it results in fundamental understanding that aids the education of current or future generations of students, or if it results in outcomes that are ultimately applied to commercial uses. Over the long term, investments in research as well as education are an important predictor of success in the software industry.

Technology transfer—moving research outcomes to commercial realization—is an integral part of research planning and investments. A book by Donald Stokes (1997) has galvanized a lot of thinking, both helping to explain some of the recent trends in industrial research and stimulating further changes. Before Stokes, thinking was dominated by the linear model (see figure 8.4). The development, provisioning, and operation phases were previously discussed in section 5.1. In the linear model, research is a separate activity that precedes development, one that is divided into basic and applied. Basic research embarks on the unknown, enlarging the realm of the possible, and applied research elaborates and applies the known in new ways. Thus, basic research focuses on the expansion of human knowledge, and applied research attempts to find new uses for existing knowledge. Development, on the other hand, directly adapts research findings into commercial products.

Research policy in the United States has been dominated for five decades by the linear model as promulgated by Vannevar Bush (the government's science adviser in the 1940s). Bush asserted that "applied research invariably drives out pure" and therefore basic research must be completely isolated from considerations of use. The two-dimensional Stokes model, on the other hand, recognizes a third category of research in addition to pure (Bohr's quadrant) and applied (Edison's quadrant),

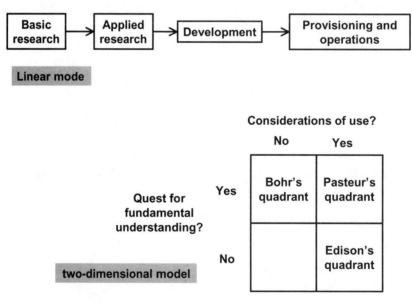

Figure 8.4
Two models of technology transfer.

which he calls Pasteur's quadrant. In this quadrant, considerations of use are a motivator, but the acquisition of new fundamental knowledge in pursuit of these new uses is also appreciated and encouraged.

Example It is an oversimplification to attribute any research purely to one quadrant, yet most research activities can be identified predominantly with one of Stokes's quadrants. The pursuit of mathematical models for computational complexity and fundamental limits to our ability to compute certain algorithms (major topics of computer science theory) have the flavor of Bohr's quadrant. As predicted by the linear model, such research finds useful application; for example, it has proven fundamental to the understanding of cryptography, which is based on hard computational problems. The UNIX operating system is arguably an outcome of Edison's quadrant research, since it was first prototyped by researchers at Bell Laboratories to serve as a platform for their other software research and not as a research objective in itself. An example of Pasteur's quadrant research is the seeking of stronger security protocols, which has also led directly to fundamental insights into protocols and algorithms (such as zero-knowledge proofs and protocol design and verification schemes).

The observation of the existence and importance of Pasteur's quadrant research leads to a revised dynamic model of technology transfer (see figure 8.5).

Example Investigations into the use of speech in user interfaces are an example of use-inspired basic research in software. While this research is inspired by the promise

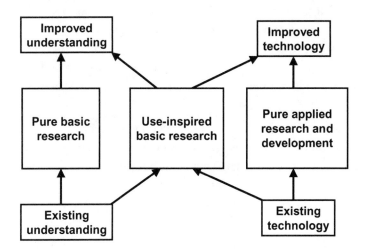

Figure 8.5
A dynamic model of technology transfer based on the Stokes (1997) two-dimensional model.

of more intuitive and natural interfaces that mimic they way people interact with one another, it also results in numerous basic insights into speech. Improved accuracy in speech recognition has led to better understanding of the physiology of speech production and new statistical techniques (so-called hidden Markov models). Automated understanding (not just recognition) of speech has led to many linguistic insights. Research into the interactions between humans and complex software systems has led to new insights in cognitive psychology.

While many top industrial research laboratories once believed in the linear model, today the trend is toward Pasteur's quadrant research, which has proven an effective way to enhance the returns on research investment to the sponsoring organizations. This increasingly leaves a gap in Bohr's quadrant research, a gap that can and should be filled with publicly funded research.

Today industrial researchers are usually encouraged to keep in close touch with product business units, and sometimes even forced to obtain a portion of their funding directly from these units. It is also common for researchers to switch from research to development organizations and back, an effective means of technology transfer and also an effective way to sensitize researchers to the opportunities and challenges of use.

Example IBM Research has been a leader in connecting its researchers directly with customers, with the objective of forming a more direct connection between research directions and market opportunities and challenges.[7] Its First-of-a-Kind program creates direct partnerships between promising technologies and customers who may be able to benefit. It has created three Industry Solutions Laboratories in the United States, Europe, and Japan to display research outcomes to visiting customers and enhance the dialogue between customers and researchers. Another example is the IBM Institute for Advanced Commerce, which sponsors conferences and university partnerships to initiate new interdisciplinary research on the effect of IT on commerce.

While direct contributions to corporate success are a major motivation for funding research, there are other benefits as well. The top-notch scientists and engineers that a research laboratory can attract benefit a corporation in many ways, such as reviewing development projects, providing new product ideas, and providing advice on the direction of technology to top executives. Also, internal researchers will maintain contacts with the broader industrial and public research activities and bring them into the company.

8.3.3 Publicly Supported Research

While industrial research expenditures are large and growing, publicly supported research (largely in universities and government laboratories) plays an essential role in the software industry. This is not primarily a result of industrial research laboratories' emphasis on use-inspired research, because a great deal of publicly funded research on software is use-inspired as well. Rather, it is primarily a matter of time horizon, where industrially funded research emphasizes outcomes that can enhance revenues in the relatively short term, and publicly funded research can pursue long-term objectives.

Industry expenditures are generally reported for the aggregate of research and development, and it is important to note that most of these expenditures are directly in support of product development, not research (although the demarcation is fuzzy, particularly in Pasteur's quadrant).

Example Annual federal spending in the United States on research in computing was estimated at about $1 billion as of the mid-1990s, compared to industry research (not including development) expenditures of about $1 billion to $1.5 billion (NRC 1999a). Government funding has grown steadily over past decades, whereas industrial funding is quite volatile and in fact decreased dramatically during the 1990s' presumably because of an increasingly competitive industry environment. Government funded about 70 percent of total university research on computing.

Government support of research is crucial to the development of a highly educated work force in computing, directly supporting research assistantships for over half the graduate students at the best universities (NRC 1999b). Economists have also identified reasons why competitive markets and price mechanisms are not as effective in producing and distributing knowledge (a primary outcome of research) as they are for tangible goods, primarily because knowledge has many characteristics of public goods (NRC 1999b). Particularly important in the case of computing research is that the payoffs ascribed to major technology shifts (in contrast to ongoing incremental change) are uncertain and far in the future.

Example A study in 1995 examined the effect of major government-funded research in the 1960s over the intervening years (NRC 1995). In a number of cases, research led to $1 billion or greater commercial revenues, but the delay between the early research and major commercial application was in every case one to three decades. These cases included time-sharing (leading to minicomputers and today's client-server computing), computer graphics, the Internet, desktop workstations, graphical user interfaces, reduced instruction set computer architectures, computer-aided design of integrated circuits, parallel disk arrays, and parallel computing. A more recent study confirmed a continuation of this phenomenon, examples including relational databases, artificial intelligence, and virtual reality (NRC 1999b).

Historically, government-sponsored research has played an important role in the evolution of the computing industry. The long time horizon of commercial exploitation of many fundamental advances makes it difficult to justify these types of research by a return-on-investment analysis, even though intuition suggests (and history confirms) that some portion of such research eventually has major commercial payoffs. Patents are not fully effective in protecting research outcomes, and their two decades of protection is ineffective for these long-term benefits. With the rapid turnover of workers, and the disclosure of an invention's possibilities through the act of using it, trade secrets are difficult to preserve in the long term. Thus, long-time horizon research outcomes are relatively easily appropriated by those who did not contribute to the research (other companies or venture capitalists). Where effective, patents create a monopoly and trade secrets limit wide availability of knowledge, whereas publicly supported research can be widely disseminated and used and thus maximizes the benefit of research expenditures to society as a whole.

8.4   Research and Discussion Issues

1. Should software share identical property rights (e.g., term) with other types of inventions? Or should software be subject to special rules, taking into account the characteristics of this industry? If so, how would the rules be modified? Perhaps the protection period should be variable with associated fees?

2. What constitutes fair use of copyrighted information in the digital age? Should this definition be adjusted in light of special challenges of digital representations and the limitations of technology?

3. What new licensing terms and conditions may be possible (or desirable) in light of new technologies like network monitoring of usage, Web services, components, or software portability?

4. What is the tension between maintaining control over software technology through intellectual property laws and maintaining control through standardization? What are trade-offs between maintaining individual firm control and collective industry control?

5. With traditional literary goods protected by copyright it is possible to change ownership (e.g., used in-book stores), temporarily lend works to others, and so on.

What modifications to rights management systems would be required to support such traditional (and arguably acceptable) forms of use?

6. Discuss the controversy between those who assert that copy protection can never work and therefore information and software suppliers should define new business models, and those who advocate copy protection as a way to preserve traditional business models.

7. Discuss the usability effect of copy protection and the restrictions it may impose on legitimate uses protected under the copyright laws. Are these issues damaging to copy protection as an antipiracy measure?

8. Consider the differences between willful but incidental sharing of copyrighted material and wide-scale piracy. What is the appropriate role of copy protection and other legal protections for these two cases?

9. Suppose that watermarking were completely effective, secure, and foolproof. What would be its appropriate uses in deterring or punishing the infringement of copyright rights? Would copy protection and other measures still be necessary?

10. Considering different types of market failure mechanisms, such as direct network effects or the indirect network effect of applications and infrastructure (see section 7.4), what are some legitimate government roles in ensuring a vibrant software industry?

11. Discuss the complementary roles of end-users and operators, insurers, software suppliers, and government in ensuring effective security. Repeat for privacy.

12. Debate both sides of the issue: Should software be protected speech, or not?

13. Thus far the antitrust laws have not been adjusted to special conditions in the software industry. Is this appropriate, or should this industry operate under different rules?

14. Software research outside large corporations is increasingly affected by the size and complexity of today's systems. Learning from other engineering disciplines, new models may need to be found to encourage deeper interaction between research and education at universities and industrial R&D. What would be the software equivalent of the common approach in electronics, where students design chips that can be prototyped in industrial facilities?

8.5 Further Reading

Studies conducted by the National Research Council advise the government on technology-related issues and are an excellent resource for technology policy and government initiatives. All are available online. Some concern social issues in networked communities and cryptography policy (NRC 1994; 1996), intellectual property in the digital age (NRC 2000a), education (NRC 1999a; 2002), workforce issues (NRC 2001), and government support of research (NRC 1999b). The discussion of the types of research and technology transfer is based largely on *Pasteur's Quadrant* (Stokes 1997), a book that has had considerable impact on the conduct of research in industrial laboratories. Shapiro and Varian (1999b) have an excellent discussion of intellectual property portfolios and rights management, especially as they relate to strategy and to economics.

9

Economics

Ignore basic economic principles at your own risk.
Carl Shapiro and Hal Varian

Economics offers a number of useful insights on management and on business relationships and strategies in the software industry, insights that can and should affect the strategies of the major players, as Shapiro and Varian (1999b) point out. Many economics issues have already been discussed in earlier chapters. This chapter develops some additional understanding of the economic properties of software, gives additional depth to some issues already mentioned, and raises new ones.

Most prior work on the economics of software—performed by practitioners of software engineering, who are technologists at heart—has focused on serving software developers, where the emphasis is on cost estimation and justification of investments, and to a lesser extent, estimation of demand (Boehm 1981, 1984; Boehm and Sullivan 1999, 2000; Clark and Levy 1993; Gulledge and Hutzler 1993; Kang and Levy 1989; Kemerer 1998; Levy 1987; Thebaut and Shen 1984; and Veryard 1991). As mentioned, software shares some characteristics with information, and thus many concepts of information economics (Shapiro and Varian 1999b), such as network effects and lock-in, apply to software as well as information, albeit with occasional modifications. Considerable accumulated understanding of the economics of standardization (David and Greenstein 1990)—a process that applies to many industries besides software—applies directly to software, again appropriately modified and interpreted.

One goal is to expand the definition of "software economics" beyond its focus on software investments and software development that dominates the use of this term in the literature. A more precise name for the latter is "software engineering economics." The "software industries" include not only developers and suppliers but also various types of consultants, system integrators, service providers, and end-user organizations (see chapters 5 and 6).

This chapter looks at software from the demand and supply perspectives, followed by a discussion of pricing. Most interesting, perhaps, is consideration of the overall economic properties of software compared to many other goods and services, drawing on the perspectives of earlier chapters. At the end of this chapter we summarize the primary similarities and differences between software and other goods and services.

9.1 Demand

Much of the literature on software engineering economics focuses on the supply side, but the demand side is important as well because it provides insights into the value proposition for software and heavily influences pricing (see section 9.3). There are three distinct customer groups for software: those who provision, those who operate, and those who use. Sometimes two or three of these groups are in the same organization, or all three may be in different organizations. The value derived by users was discussed in chapter 3, and the considerations of provisioning and operations were taken up in chapter 5. Overall, suppliers must take into account the need of all these groups, trying to maximize the value while minimizing the costs incurred in provisioning and operations. The software industry is relatively immature, and doubtless many new ways will be found to add value and minimize costs in the future (see chapter 10).

Two influences on demand worthy of further discussion from an economic perspective are network effects and lock-in. First we delve more deeply into the idea of market penetration.

9.1.1 Market Share

Network effects (see section 3.2.3) apply when demand for a good is affected by the size of the network. Antitrust law and policy are concerned with market concentration (see section 8.2.5). Both of these concepts bear on market share. Reasonable indicators of market share for a given software product category include the fraction of unit sales, the fraction of total revenue from sales, or the fraction of total usage. Arguably usage would be the most direct indicator of the effect on or value to the total community, but direct network effects would be most directly affected by unit sales (related to the number of adopters ready and able to participate in the network), and revenue from sales would be the best predictor of future business prospects (related to profits and the ability to invest in maintenance and upgrades). For many goods and services, these different indicators might yield similar conclusions for a given product category, but they can diverge dramatically for software. Unlike most goods (e.g., hardware) software is not subject to material or resource limitations: it can be replicated, distributed, stored, and executed at very low marginal cost. Thus, there is low cost to both supplier and user associated with multiple adoptions by the same user, even where the adoptions are almost direct substitutes or are rarely used.

Example   In the interest of sharing documents with others, a user might install a second word-processing program and use it infrequently. The supplier can encourage this by making available free or at a discount a version of its word processor that only installs when another vendor's program is already installed. Especially this discount is common practice under so-called competitive upgrade schemes. There is little cost penalty to the supplier, and it can help to tilt network effects in its favor. Of course, this would not apply to complex distributed or organizational applications, where there may be significant provisioning and operational costs.

Unit sales and usage can differ radically. Revenue and usage can also differ radically for software sold at a fixed price rather than priced according to some usage metric. Usage itself is difficult to define. In human terms, it might be defined as "face time" (or "eyeballs"), but software can be autonomous, operating independently of human involvement. In conclusion, the concept of market share should be treated with caution.

9.1.2   Direct and Indirect Network Effects
The discussion of network effects in section 3.2.3 distinguishes between two types of network effects: direct and indirect. It is helpful to clarify the difference between these using simple models and also to appreciate some influences of network effects on the dynamics of software markets.

Network effects predict that demand for a good is affected by the actions of other users. What is the appropriate determinant of value from network-effects in light of the alternative measures of market share discussed in section 9.1.1? For direct network effects, the best metric is usually the total size of the network (those able to use the product), and for indirect network effects the aggregate usage (those who regularly use the product, and how much they use it). To model network effects, we use network size (alternative definitions are easily substituted). Let n be the network size out of a total population of N. Assume that the demand in the absence of network effects is represented by $d(n)$, interpreted as the nth consumer's willingness to pay (consumers are ordered from highest to lowest willingness to pay), or equivalently, the price at which the product will be sold to n consumers.

Example   If the consumers are uniformly dispersed in their willingness to pay, and the first consumer is willing to pay p, then $d(n) = p \cdot (N - n)/(N - 1)$. The first adopter is willing to pay p, the last is not willing to pay anything, and approximately half the consumers are willing to pay $p/2$ or more.

Network effects can be introduced by adding a second argument to the demand function, which is the total network size expected or anticipated by the nth consumer. Denote this second argument by n' and the refined demand function by $d(n, n')$. The reason for using *expected* (not actual) network size is that there may be some divergence: the consumer lacks accurate information on the actual network size and may adopt on the basis of expected future growth in the network, and the supplier can manipulate expectations through effective marketing campaigns. With some loss of generality, this function can be factored: $d(n, n') = d(n) \cdot e(n')$, $0 \le e(n') \le 1$, where the first factor is the demand in the absence of network effects and the second factor is the multiplier by which demand is reduced because all the consumers expect the network size to be n'. The simplification is that all consumers have the same expectation n' on network size, and their willingness to pay is influenced in the same way. When everybody is expected to become an adopter, assume that $d(n, N) = d(n)$ and hence $e(N) = 1$.

Example   A widely cited estimate for direct network effects is *Metcalfe's law* (named after Ethernet pioneer Robert Metcalfe), which assumes that the willingness to pay of each consumer is proportional to the network size. If the boundary conditions are $e(1) = 0$ (a single adopter derives no value) and $e(N) = 1$, then $e(n') = (n' - 1)/(N - 1)$. Metcalfe's law is usually stated as a function of the value of an entire network, which is the product of the value to each adopter and the network size, proportional to the square of the network size. Metcalfe's law is pessimistic in that it is likely each adopter has a natural community of interest and limited interest in connecting outside this community. In that case, the value of the product to an adopter would depend on adoptions within that community rather than on total network size.

The point at which consumer expectations are aligned with reality is a candidate for market equilibrium. This occurs at $n = n'$ with demand $d(n, n) = d(n) \cdot e(n)$. The distinctive characteristic of a market with direct network effects is that $d(1, 1) = 0$ (because $e(1) = 0$, a single adopter derives no value). Demand actually increases with adoptions (because of the increasing $e(n)$ actor) and ultimately starts decreasing again (because of the decreasing $d(n)$ factor).

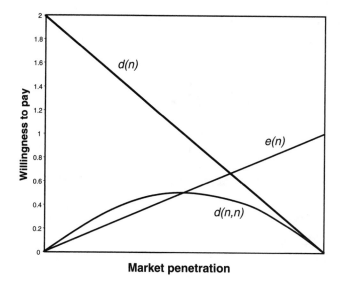

Figure 9.1
Demand function for uniformly dispersed willingness to pay and Metcalf's law for the direct network effect.

Example   Total demand is plotted against market penetration (n/N) in figure 9.1 for a market obeying Metcalfe's law with uniformly dispersed willingness to pay and maximum willingness to pay $p = 2$. Notice that the maximum willingness to pay is considerably reduced by network effects (to 0.5).

The distinguishing characteristic of a market with an indirect network effect is $e(0) > 0$, because the supplier can ensure that there is some supply of the complementary commodity available to the first adopter.

Example   Assume the supplier makes an initial investment in supplying the complementary commodity and then increases its investment in proportion to revenue, which is likely in turn to be proportional to the network size (assuming no usage component to pricing). Thus, assume that $e(n')$ is linear between $e(1) = g$ and $e(N) = 1$, $0 < g < 1$, or $e(n') = ((1 - g)n' + Ng - 1)/(N - 1)$. This model for the indirect network effect is plotted for $g = 0.25$ in figure 9.2, again for uniformly dispersed intrinsic demand. Note the larger demand at low network sizes. In fact, if $g > 0.5$ (the supplier is willing to make half or more of its full market penetration investment up front), demand is decreasing for all n.

In summary, where direct network effects reign, the supplier has to make a full investment to develop a product but faces a severe challenge in gaining initial

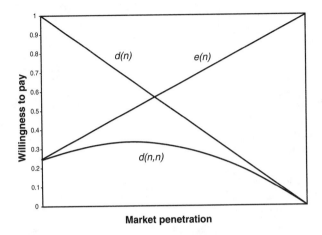

Figure 9.2
Demand for a uniform dispersion in willingness to pay and a model of indirect network effects, with g = 0.25.

adoptions because the initial demand is low regardless of the intrinsic merits of the product. With indirect network effects, the supplier of the primary product must make sure the complementary commodity is initially in good supply, an easier-to-address challenge.

The dynamics of the market are also of interest, as illustrated in figure 9.3 (Economides 1996). The supply curve (the unit costs assumed by the supplier) intersects the demand curve twice (if at all) for direct network effects, creating three equilibrium points (where supply equals demand). One is the unfortunate case where both supply and demand are zero; this equilibrium is stable because of negative feedback (a slight decrease in market share causes a reduction in demand resulting from network effects, further dampening demand). All products begin at this equilibrium, and it is difficult to circumvent. The next equilibrium is critical mass, where demand reaches supply and the supplier can price to recover costs. This equilibrium is unstable because market forces drive market share away, either up or down. In the up direction, the market experiences the virtuous cycle of positive feedback in which increasing market share stimulates greater demand, and the supplier can price the product to increase the size of the network while deriving a profit. Finally, the market reaches the third (stable) equilibrium, beyond which the consumers' willingness to pay doesn't offset costs.

Indirect network effects have a similar market dynamic, where demand is initially increasing, but with the important distinction that the supplier has a ready way to

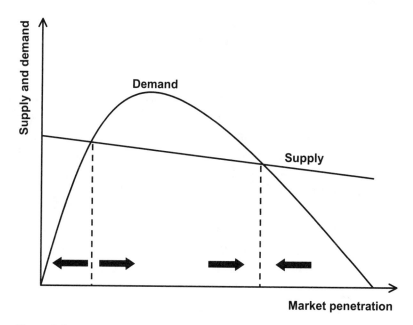

Figure 9.3
Market dynamics with direct network effects.

stimulate initial demand by investing in the complementary asset (equivalently increasing *g*). For direct network effects it may be necessary initially to subsidize purchases to seed demand.

Network effects have a strong influence on the software industry, but with considerable differences among different types of software. Considering first infrastructure, before the Internet enabled communication among computers, different platforms could coexist and compete for the same customers. The primary source of value related to network size was success in attracting application developers to the platform, that is, indirect network effects. The platforms tended to segment the market: mainframes for back-office business applications, the personal computers for home productivity applications, and UNIX servers and workstations for the scientific and technical market and for departmental business applications. After the Internet attracted many users, the platform for distributed applications became collectively all types of computer platforms, the network, and any middleware (the middle layers in figure 7.5). Virtually all infrastructure suppliers need to consider prominently their role in an ecosystem of complementary as well as competitive suppliers.[1]

Prospective infrastructure solutions (hardware, operating systems, and middleware) today face two related forms of network effects. First, they must achieve a sufficiently large penetration to attract a reasonable suite of applications. Second, there is the chicken-and-egg obstacle that infrastructure offers value only to the extent that it attracts applications, but application developers are only interested in layering on infrastructure with a significant market penetration (see section 7.1 for a discussion of strategies to overcome this).

Some categories of applications also experience significant network effects. Most distributed applications today follow the client-server architecture, in part because this model experiences weaker indirect network effects: the first client of a new server-based application derives considerable value if information content is initially available (see section 4.5). If a server-based application depends on information content suppliers, its users may benefit significantly as the market penetration increases and more content is attracted. An advantage of the application service provider model is that installing software on many clients is not needed. On the other hand, applications that adopt the peer-to-peer architecture encounter stronger direct network effects. Examples include video conferencing, facsimile, and instant messaging. Nevertheless, since the Internet became operational, this model has enjoyed some significant successes because of the relative ease of distributing the necessary software over the network and (often) a willingness to make per-peer software available free.

Example In the peer-to-peer category are Napster (Sullivan 1999), which allowed users to share music files directly between home computers, and the Groove Transceiver (Bulkeley 2000), a collaboration application. In part because it offered free downloads, Napster was very successful until it ran into difficulties with the copyright law. If an application is sufficiently compelling, users will download peer software over the network as long as they feel it is benign (comes from a trusted source, and especially if signed; see section 5.4.6).

The peer software could be automatically shared with another user intending to participate in a peer-to-peer application, avoiding installation using mobile code (see section 4.4.3).

Example A software vendor could market a remote-conferencing application using a peer-to-peer architecture. To counter any initial dampening of demand due to direct network effects, the application might be licensed (for a price) to users with the condition that participating with another user without a paid license is permitted by creating a temporary free license for the other user and sharing the necessary software using mobile code. This has been demonstrated as an adjunct to a Java-enabled Web browser (Chang and Messerschmitt 1996).

9.1.3 Lock-in

Customers often have considerable *switching costs* in replacing one product with another, and this adds an impediment to competitive suppliers trying to attract customers (Farrell and Shapiro 1988; Shapiro and Varian 1999b). A complete provisioned application is composed of and depends on a number of complementary elements, including different application components and infrastructure equipment and software. There are also less tangible complementary investments, such as the training of workers and the costs of reworking the administration and operation of the software (see capter 5). Suppose the customer considers changing the supplier of one application or infrastructure element. There are likely to be switching costs.

Example Customers choose an infrastructure platform on the basis of available applications and intrinsic attributes (e.g., price, quality). Suppose a customer wants to adopt an attractive new application. This may require changing the platform—new equipment, new infrastructure software, retraining system administrators—and possibly replacing administrative and management tools. In turn, this might require replacing other applications with ones that utilize the same platform, unless those applications are portable (see section 4.4). Even a portable application may have to be relicensed. Any replacement application will incur acquisition and user training costs. If an application composes with other applications, it may be necessary to replace other applications or acquire or write new translation software. Simply adding a new platform will incur significant provisioning and operational costs. Because of these costs, many organizations are predisposed to supporting only a small number of platforms.

There are two distinct types of costs in acquiring a new software product. The direct acquisition costs are all the costs (equipment, software licensing, provisioning, training) associated with that product—these costs are largely under control of the supplier through pricing strategies. Other costs in excess of direct acquisition costs are collectively known as switching costs. Many switching costs are not under direct control of a new supplier, and to some degree they can be manipulated by an existing supplier.

Example An infrastructure supplier can increase switching costs for its existing customers by failing to directly support portability of application software. Then application suppliers are less likely to make their applications portable. The motivation for the infrastructure supplier is the added costs of replacing many applications if the customer contemplates switching to a new platform. Of course, the downside is reduced application availability, reducing the value of the platform to new adopters.

Any discussion of lock-in should not focus exclusively on equipment, provisioning, and operations. The most significant source of switching costs is often user training and redesign of associated business processes. If moving to a new supplier requires reengineering processes, reorganizing and training workers, and disrupting business during deployment, the switching costs can be very high.

If a monetary value is attached to switching costs, some simple modeling illustrates the opportunities and challenges presented by lock-in. Assume two suppliers are available to the customer that offer competitive products: existing supplier A and new supplier B. Let the total switching costs to move from supplier A to B be $S_{A \to B}$, and let the value (as measured by willingness to pay) for the two products be V_A and V_B (so that they are substitutes but not necessarily direct substitutes). Both the suppliers and the customer should ignore any sunk costs incurred in the past, and focus on all present and future costs. Assume the two suppliers have costs C_A and C_B, and they choose to charge prices P_A and P_B. If the costs (including switching costs) and the revenues are spread over time, these should be interpreted as present values; that is, all future prices/revenues and costs are discounted according to the time value of money.[2]

The consumer's total cost is the sum of the price paid to the supplier and the switching costs, $P + S_{A \to B}$. The customer will be indifferent between the two suppliers when its consumer surplus (excess of value over price) is equal for the two suppliers, $V_A - P_A = V_B - (P_B + S_{A \to B})$. Similarly, the two suppliers have producer surpluses (excess of revenue over cost), $P_A - C_A$ and $P_B - C_B$. Finally, one or the other of the suppliers will be at a competitive advantage if three conditions are simultaneously satisfied: (1) the consumer is indifferent between the two suppliers, (2) the price can be set so that the advantaged supplier's surplus is positive (there is a profit opportunity), and (3) the disadvantaged supplier's surplus is zero or negative (there is no profit opportunity). Applying these three conditions, the competitive advantage can be gauged by comparing supplier A's value advantage, $V_A - V_B$, to supplier B's switching-cost-adjusted cost advantage, $C_A - (C_B + S_{A \to B})$. If (and only if) the former is larger than the latter, supplier A enjoys a competitive advantage and has a surplus equal to the difference, $P_A - C_A = (V_A - V_B) - (C_A - C_B) + S_{A \to B}$.

This producer surplus is essentially the asset value (present value of all present and future revenue minus cost) to supplier A of a locked-in customer. To reiterate, this price (and resulting surplus) forces supplier B's surplus to zero when the customer is indifferent, and supplier B would be unlikely to make a sale to the customer. The point to note is that supplier A has the benefit of a "headwind" facing supplier B that is equal to the switching costs; even where supplier B offers more value or has a lower cost, supplier A will still enjoy a competitive advantage if the switching costs are sufficiently large. Supplier B has two ways to gain competitive advantage—offer more value or experience lower costs—but must overcome the customer's switching costs: it must subsidize these costs with a lower price in order to render the customer indifferent. For the case of a perfect substitute product and equal costs, supplier A's surplus (the asset value of the customer) equals the switching costs.

The typical situation for the most common business model of selling periodic software upgrades is where the alternative supplier is offering its product as an alternative to an upgrade. The original supplier may have a marginal cost advantage because it has amortized a portion of its fixed costs in the original sale. The original supplier may offer an attractive upgrade price, both to compete against its own installed base (older versions) and the alternative supplier. There are a number of ways the original supplier can increase the switching costs, further adding to its competitive advantage. These include proprietary APIs, forcing composability with other applications to be reimplemented with any replacement supplier, and utilizing proprietary data representations that make it difficult to move information content to a replacement supplier. The original supplier must temper these tactics with the realization that they reduce the application's value to new (rather than upgrading) customers, who appreciate the significance of switching costs, too.

An alternative supplier can overcome lock-in by subsidizing the customer's switching costs, thereby reducing its own revenue. An alternative that is fairly unique to software is to reduce the customer's switching costs, for example, by incorporating one-way or two-way compatibility with the first supplier's product or offering API or data representation translators (Shapiro and Varian 1999b), but this is at the expense of added development costs.

Example Most individual productivity applications, including virtually all office suites, include import/export tools to read and write document formats defined by competing products. In addition, open standard formats such as XML and HTML are increasingly defusing the proprietary format lock-in. Many productivity applications also include user-selectable emulation modes to behave just like some competing product, for instance, by reassigning command keys to allow users familiar with the competing product to continue their keyboard habits, reducing their retraining overhead.

As discussed in section 8.1.1, software products can generally be operated side-by-side, allowing alternative suppliers to supply their products at a significant discount to their competitors' existing customers without having to convince customers to immediately substitute. Finally, as discussed in section 9.2.5, in a rapidly expanding market (as is often the case with software) acquiring new customers is as or more important than stealing them away from other suppliers, and thus lock-in is a less important consideration.

In infrastructure, layering significantly reduces switching costs, since new infrastructure capabilities can be added without abandoning the old (see section 7.1.3). In the operational environment, existing applications can continue to utilize lower layers directly even while new applications depend on added upper layers. Added layers are often utilized as a location for translations needed for application composability. This further explains an attraction of layering as a means of advancing the infrastructure. In fact, layering is a natural outcome of market forces in both the material and immaterial worlds, in part because it deals gracefully with switching cost issues.

9.1.4 Open Systems vs. Proprietary Solutions

Lock-in is an important (but not the only) consideration in the trade-off between open systems and closed proprietary solutions (see section 5.1.3). Open systems—systems that are modular with open standard interfaces and APIs—are attractive to customers because they readily allow competition in individual modules rather than at the system level, at least to the extent that suppliers actually use them. When the customer can mix and match modules from different suppliers, it allows the customer to replace one component with minimal switching costs. The competition at the component level rather than at the system level also increases competition (ideally improving price, quality, and performance parameters) for each component. On the other hand, there is the acquisition cost and time required to integrate components from different vendors or switching costs associated with integration of a replacement component.

At the other extreme, a proprietary monolithic solution offers a complete system solution to the customer, with no opportunity to choose different vendors for different modules. Advantageously, this shifts the burden of system integration costs from the customer to the supplier, where they are amortized over all customers, and the risk assumed by the customer is reduced. Monolithic products tend to be more manageable and usable because everything was designed to work together from the beginning. They also provide clearer accountability for problems, as there are fewer opportunities for "finger-pointing" among suppliers in system integration, which is important from a risk management point of view (section 6.6.3). However, monolithic solutions cannot be replaced in piecemeal fashion, and thus the switching costs associated with moving to a competitive supplier are high.

Example   The divergent strategies of Apple Computer and IBM illustrate this. Apple offered the Macintosh as an integrated "as is" solution, including CPU, monitor, peripherals, hardware, and infrastructure software. Partly as a result, the Mac was easier to configure and extend in its early years. The IBM PC, on the other hand, followed an open systems approach, encouraging competition from vendors of peripherals and separating hardware and software vendors. This places more of a burden on both owners and suppliers to deal with many interoperability issues that arise when peripheral and software products from different vendors are integrated. It also resulted in attractive competitive options, attractive prices, and growing market share. Over time, the approaches have converged somewhat. Apple has encouraged more competition in peripherals, and industry initiatives in the Windows space like plug-and-play have made integration more seamless. Dell Computer has been successful in building desktop computers to customer specifications, taking on more integration responsibility itself.

The *information appliance* is a product offering an application as is in a package, including both application software and infrastructure software and hardware. Packaged appliances are more affordable because of reductions in hardware costs, and they are generally praised for ease of use. But consumers dislike having to own multiple appliances for multiple applications, each with a different user interface to learn. Appliances have also been criticized as inflexible, but this has been partly addressed by software upgrades. Appliances can internally bundle and utilize open system solutions from other vendors, even open source software.

Example   TiVo is an information appliance providing a personal digital receiver capability for television. A TiVo offers many TV schedule search and navigation features, and allows the user to schedule programs for later recording and interactive viewing. It requires a phone connection so that it can download TV schedules and software upgrades, and features can be upgraded. It uses the open source Linux operating system and a commercial database management system, together with custom hardware and software.

Both open systems and monolithic approaches have strong advantages, and customers must simply evaluate which factors are most important to them. In practice, there is fertile middle ground, and most suppliers attempt to strike a balance. For example, products with monolithic solutions often provide open APIs that allow extensions by other vendors.

Example An office suite like Microsoft Office tends toward the monolithic approach, offering a collection of integrated applications that can easily share information. However, Microsoft may also provide APIs that allow applications to be extended and integrated into the Office other applications. In Office, the two primary avenues for extensions are ActiveX controls, which can be added to toolbars or embedded into documents to achieve new functionality, and Visual Basic for Applications (VBA), which can be used to build on Office as a platform for new applications. (The same APIs that Office applications provide to VBA are available for externally developed extensions.) In combination, these mechanisms are used to build industry-specific applications that require core Office capabilities, such as solutions for medical or accounting practices.

Similarly, the suppliers of products utilizing open systems try to gain advantage by two techniques. First, they encourage competition in complementary components—reducing cost and improving quality for their customers' integrated systems solution—while trying to differentiate themselves from competitors in their own space. Second, they often attempt to increase the switching costs incurred by customers considering replacing their components with competitive solutions. Sometimes these two strategies are at cross-purposes.

Example Operating system suppliers actively encourage applications for their platform, to benefit from the positive feedback of indirect network effects. They also try to encourage competitive options in each application category to improve price, quality, and performance of complementary products available to their customers. Besides applications competing above the operating systems, they try to encourage competition below, at the level of supported hardware extensions and matching device drivers. Similarly, they may increase competition in the complementary equipment by porting their operating system to more than one microprocessor. In so doing, however, they potentially reduce the switching costs of customers, giving them more opportunity to replace the operating system without replacing the equipment.

9.2 Supply

Many supply side characteristics of software have been discussed in previous chapters. Since it shares a digital representation with information, software has high fixed costs, is inexpensively replicated, and is nonrival in use (see section 2.1). In many other respects, the economics of supply for software differs from that for information. One substantial difference is in the supply chain (see section 5.1), where the value added by provisioning and operation differs substantially from value added in information industries. It is also important to keep in mind that software and information go hand-in-hand. Information content is an essential element of most software applications, and software is commonly used to facilitate access to information. Content and software may be supplied by the same or different firms.

9.2.1 Economies of Scale

The creation of software is a major undertaking (see chapter 4). High creation costs coupled with low replication and distribution costs result in large supply economies of scale. Similarly, software maintenance costs are relatively independent of the size of the user population and usage, while customer support costs are more dependent on these factors. Other supply costs typically not borne by the supplier, but nevertheless very real, include provisioning and operation and typically increase with the user base (see chapter 5).

The economies of scale permit a supplier with a larger market share to price more attractively. Like network effects, this is a form of positive feedback that contributes to further increases in market share. Scale economies (Silvestre 1987) also do not allow a market to approach pure competition (Marshall 1890), an amorphous state of the market in which no seller can alter the market price by varying output and no buyer can alter it by varying purchases. Since competition drives prices toward marginal costs, which are below average costs, it is important for suppliers to differentiate their products from the competitors' to avoid ruinous price competition. It is much easier to differentiate application software (which by its nature is specific to a user context) than infrastructure software. The latter must address the lowest-common-denominator needs of many applications, and thus there is less opportunity for one supplier to differentiate its products from anothers. Infrastructure products that err on the side of either application or technology dependence offer more opportunity for differentiation (see section 7.1.5). On the other hand, provisioning and operation, not benefiting from substantial economies of scale, encourage competition on more conventional terms, such as efficiency, effectiveness, worker productivity, and quality of outcomes.

9.2.2   Risk

The development costs of software are largely sunk, particularly for software constructed to meet a very specific need (an extreme case is software developed by an organization for its internal needs). The payoff can be very small (zero, if the software isn't used) or very large (in monetary terms for software that sells well, or in other terms for software that pays dividends in quality or productivity). There is thus considerable risk to investing in the creation of new software. To mitigate risk, suppliers use a portfolio diversification strategy, investing in multiple products with overlapping product lifetimes—the occasional big winners can make up for losses. (This strategy can also deal with some issues in project management in development organizations; see section 4.2.3.) Sometimes this portfolio is accumulated by a single large company, and sometimes it is accumulated by venture capitalists that split an investment pool over a number of smaller companies.

Once a software product is well established, during most of its life cycle the maintenance and upgrade costs are predicated on fairly predictable revenues from reselling to existing customers; in this case, there is less risk.

Reuse and multiple uses can mitigate risk to some extent (see section 7.3). The development costs for reusable modules are less likely to be sunk: if they aren't used in the present project, they may be usable in another. Acquiring components rather than developing similar capabilities from scratch will reduce development costs and make them more predictable, and often licensing arrangements will be less risky if fees are required only if the software is used. Of course, if certain components are also available to competitors, then the opportunities to differentiate on the basis of features and capabilities are reduced.

A surprisingly large number of large software developments are failures in the sense that the software is never deployed. Many of these failures occur in internal developments in end-user organizations. There are many sources of failure, even for a single project, but common ones are excessive compliance with changing requirements or inadequate experience and expertise to undertake the project. This form of risk can also be mitigated by leveraging frameworks and components to the extent possible.

9.2.3   Complementarity

Suppliers commonly offer a portfolio of complementary software products. This reduces risk (see section 9.2.2), makes sales and marketing more efficient, and can be attractive to customers by shifting system integration problems and costs to the supplier and offering a single point of contact for sales, support, billing, and payment.

Nevertheless, most software suppliers depend heavily on complementary products from other suppliers for a complete customer solution. Each supplier wants to differentiate its own products and minimize its competition, but desires strong competition among its complementors so its customers can enjoy overall price and quality advantages and so that it can extract more of the value of the total solution for itself and increase its sales. This is an important motivator for defining open APIs (see section 4.3.4), encouraging other suppliers (often multiple other suppliers) to invest in complementary projects.

9.2.4   Dynamic Supply Chains

For material goods, suppliers and customers can have long-term contractual relationships, or procurement can occur dynamically in a marketplace (electronic or otherwise). For software, similar means are common, but there are other possibilities that leverage the special characteristics of software, including network distribution and portable code. While these means are perfectly adequate, customers may circumvent a download and share code directly with one another.[3] To deal with this eventuality while still getting paid, it is possible to make software supply chains fully self-aware—this is a unique opportunity for software.

Example   The shareware software licensing model depends on free distribution of software (exploiting low replication and distribution costs) and voluntary payments. In the *superdistribution* model (Cox 1996) for software components, when a component is executed, whether it originated directly from the supplier or was obtained from another customer, encapsulated usage monitors initiate and enforce a fair compensation to the original supplier using an enabling microbilling infrastructure. From the supplier perspective, the component is a trusted system that enforces usage-based payment (see section 9.3).

9.2.5   Rapidly Expanding Markets

Software markets often expand very rapidly, especially in light of the low replication and distribution costs and the low delay in distribution.

Example   In spite of the obstacles of a peer-to-peer model, Napster was a music-sharing application that accumulated 20 million users in less than a year (Cartwright 2000). This can be attributed to the compelling interest in the service, the fact that it was free, and the networked software distribution model: each user downloaded and installed the application before joining the network.

Rapidly growing markets engender special challenges and require special strategies. A simple theory of lock-in (see section 9.1.3) does not apply in a rapid-growth situation because capturing a significant fraction of current customer adoptions does not by itself suffice to gain a longer-term advantage. While growth is rapid and network effects are not strong, new competitors can enter and attract a significant share of new customers entering the market, for example, by aiming at a more attractive price-value point or set of features, offering a more attractive bundle, or offering other advantages such as better integration with other applications. Leveraging the first- (or early-) mover advantage requires rapid and continuing innovation, despite any lock-in advantage a supplier may gain with the initial customer base.

9.2.6 Whence Competitive Advantage?

The best way to derive revenue from software is by maximizing the value to the customer and differentiating from competitors' products. However, it is difficult to prevent competitors from imitating application features once the software is released. Compared to patents in some other industries (such as biotechnology) software patents are often less fundamental and relatively easy to circumvent by accomplishing the same or similar ends in a noninfringing way (see section 8.1). Copyrights are even less effective at deterring legitimate competition. They provide no protection for ideas or techniques, and have proven ineffective at preventing the copying of the features and "look-and-feel" of applications. Reproducing the same features and specifications independently in a cleanroom environment can circumvent copyrights while reducing development costs, if feature differentiation is not an objective.

What, then, are the fundamental deterrents to competitors, aside from intellectual property protections? There are several. First, enlightened competitors attempt to differentiate themselves because they know that profits are otherwise difficult to obtain, particularly with substantial economies of scale (see section 9.2.1). Competitors tempted to copy have the second-mover disadvantage of beginning with a smaller market share. Second, a supplier who has achieved significant market share and economies of scale can employ *limit pricing*, which takes into account the high creation costs faced by a new entrant (Gaskins 1971). The objective of limit pricing is to extend the period of time a competitor requires to recover development costs by offering a lower price. Even a credible threat of competitive price reductions can be a deterrent. Third, network effects can be enhanced by emphasizing features that create a network, like sharing of information among users of the software. An established product may then benefit from positive feedback (see section 9.1.2). Fourth, switching costs can be advantageous to the supplier with the largest market share by requiring a competitor to subsidize a customers' switching costs (see section 9.1.3). Original suppliers may work to maximize their customers' switching costs, for example, by adding proprietary features or enhancing their application's interoperability with complementary products. On the other hand, competitors can employ many strategies to reduce those switching costs, such as offering automated translations of data representations or backward compatibility (Shapiro and Varian 1999b), many of these measures specific to software.

9.3 Pricing

Pricing is an important issue in any supplier-customer relationship, and one where economics offers many useful insights. Software is most frequently licensed rather than sold outright (see section 8.1.3), resulting in licensing revenue but not precluding licensing to other customers or charging again for future upgrades. The large supply economies of scale make pricing a particular challenge for software suppliers—unit costs offer minimum guidance, since they decrease rapidly with market size (Shy 2001). This and many other considerations admit a wide range of pricing strategies with an equally wide range of consequences. Some considerations are how revenue is spread over time, how different customers are treated, terms and conditions, who pays, and bundling.

Some commonly used pricing options for software are listed in table 9.1. All options shown are available whether software is sold as a service (its features accessed over the network) or code-licensed (provisioned and operated by the user or end-user organization). Although subscription or usage pricing are most often associated with the service model, these options are available with code licensing as well. Software is different from material and information goods in that it can be self-aware and can thus self-enforce (through monitoring and billing) the terms and conditions of sale (see section 9.2.4).

9.3.1 Spreading Revenue over Time

As outlined in section 5.1, creation of software entails not only initial development but also ongoing maintenance (repairing defects), upgrade (providing increasing capabilities or meeting changing needs), and customer support. If software is sold

Table 9.1
Examples of Pricing Options for Software Applications

Option	Description
Individual license	Fixed price for one individual to install and use an application; may or may not allow installation on two or more computers. Typical of consumer applications.
Site license	For a fixed price, unlimited right to install and use within a given organization. The price is usually based on organization size, is often individually negotiated, and is predicated on the organization's taking responsibility for provisioning and operation.
Seat or host license	For a fixed price, unlimited right to install and use on a specific computer without regard to who accesses that computer. Often a pricing schedule offers a volume discount for larger number of seats. Pricing can be predicated on the capacity of the host, based on measures such as the number and speed of processors.
Floating license	For a fixed price, right for a certain maximum number of users to be using the application concurrently. Typically installation on a larger number of computers is permitted, and a license server monitors and limits the number of concurrent users.
Subscription	Similar to a site, seat, or floating license, except that there are fixed recurring payments as long as the application is used and all version releases are included.
Usage- or transaction-based license	Similar to site, seat, or floating license, except that the payments are based on some direct objective metrics of usage, such as number of user hours or number of e-commerce transactions successfully conducted.

as a service, there are also costs associated with provisioning and operation. How is the revenue from an individual customer to be spread over the life cycle of the software, recovering these costs and making a profit? Is the strategy to front-load the revenue, even it out over time, or offer the initial product as a loss-leader, recovering the costs late in the life cycle? The total revenue will depend on the revenue from an individual customer and from a growing customer base.

The three example approaches shown in figure 9.4 illustrate how revenue accumulates with time. In the individual, site, seat, and floating licenses users are charged explicitly for upgraded versions, so that revenue arrives at discrete points (see section 5.1.2). Typically a new version has improved features, quality, and performance, and is offered at a discount to the initial purchaser. This discount recognizes that the biggest competition for a new version is the installed base of older versions, that

Accumulated revenue

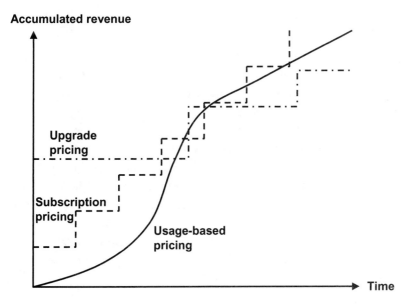

Time

Figure 9.4
Several ways to spread revenue from a single customer over time. Note that the supplier cost structures for these pricing options may be distinctly different, particularly as provisioning and operation move from customer to provider responsibility.

the new version may offer a lower incremental value than the initial acquisition, and that the new version may have been cheaper to create. This pricing strategy front-loads the revenue from each customer and depends on a growing customer base to expand total revenue. New versions bring in revenue from existing customers and help make the software more attractive to new customers. Any switching costs expected when the customer moves to an alternative supplier can be taken into account in setting the upgrade price.

In the subscription option (see figure 9.4), the customer makes regular payments, spreading revenue more evenly over time. Some customers appreciate knowing costs in advance (which helps budgeting) and recognize the time value of money. The subscription is particularly appropriate where provisioning and operation are bundled with the software (as in the application service provider model; see section 6.2) because operational costs spread out more evenly than development costs. (Note that when the supplier handles provisioning and operation, its costs may be considerably higher, so revenue is not the total picture.) The upgrade and subscription models can be combined, for example, by offering maintenance and operation by subscription while licensing the software separately through charging for upgrades.

The usage-based option (see figure 9.4) may be attractive to customers who consider value to be directly related to usage and to a confident supplier who is sure the software will be used a lot. A disadvantage to the supplier is that revenue may be slower to develop—it tends to be back-loaded—or may never materialize. The individual, seat, and floating licenses are crude approximations to usage, tending to increase revenue from a given customer as usage grows.

Late in a software product's life cycle, it may become a financial burden to its supplier. The user community can dwindle to the point that revenues do not justify upgrades, or the supplier may want to replace the software with an innovative new variant. Unfortunately, terminating these investments in upgrades will alienate existing customers by stranding them with deteriorating (and eventually unusable) software, or by stranding investments they have made in complementary software.

Example Stranding existing customers has been an issue in operating systems. Customers typically make major investments in applications, so offering a more modern or more widely accepted operating system often means the supplier assumes the financial burden of supporting two operating systems with considerable costs but with little compensating advantage. Examples include Digital VMS and Ultrix (a kind of UNIX); Hewlett-Packard, HP-UX (a kind of UNIX) and Windows; IBM (MVS, OS-400, OS-2, AIX (a kind of UNIX), Windows, and Linux; and Apple, classic MacOS and new MacOS X). Microsoft, although not a computer supplier, is another example: the initial market split between Windows 95 and Windows NT remained intact until the introduction of Windows XP; a separate Windows CE line continues as well.

Component technologies (see section 7.3) offer a smoother transition strategy, provided old and new versions of a component can be installed side-by-side.[4] Then older versions can be phased out slowly, without forcing users of the older versions to move precipitously to the new version. Replacing layers in an infrastructure while allowing older versions to remain is a variation on this strategy.

9.3.2 Different Prices for Different Customers
A second general issue in pricing is how different customers may be treated differently. Pricing is considered nondiscriminatory when the prices charged to different customers are based wholly on the marginal costs they create for the supplier; that is, the difference between price and marginal cost is the same for each customer.[5] In

this case, the supplier is expected to make up for the large fixed costs of software creation and maintenance in this fixed difference. For software, this issue is complicated by the presence of provisioning and operation intermediaries: the customers may be these service-provider intermediaries or users or end-user organizations. The issue is also complicated by group sales; particularly for sociotechnical applications, software is often sold to an organization for the benefit of its internal users.

Some major sources of marginal costs in all stages of the supply chain for software (see section 5.1) are listed in table 9.2. Other important business functions like marketing, sales, and administrative overhead that are not specific to software are not listed. The implications of these marginal costs to pricing depend on the industrial organization. For example, the costs of customer support and how they are reflected in pricing depend on who the customer is—customer support of a service provider doing provisioning and operation is a much different from customer support of individual users.

A strong competitive market may force nondiscriminatory pricing and very low margins (excess of price over marginal cost), but this creates a problem in recovering fixed costs, principally the creation costs of analysis and development, maintenance and upgrade. These are substantial costs for software not reflected in nondiscriminatory pricing that must be recovered entirely in the margins. Suppliers thus try hard to minimize direct competition and increase margins by differentiating their software products and by exploiting market mechanisms like switching costs and network effects.

Another way to help recover the high fixed costs of software creation and maintenance is through *price discrimination*, pricing that is somehow decoupled from marginal costs (Varian 1992). Assuming the supplier is able to substantially differentiate a product, its most extreme manifestation is *value pricing*, where prices are based entirely on customer willingness to pay rather than on costs (Shapiro and Varian 1999b), sometimes referred to by customers as "charging what the traffic will bear". Value pricing is complicated by a wide range in willingness to pay among different consumers and thus requires price discrimination.

Forms of price discrimination include *individualized pricing*, based on customers' value or willingness to pay, *customer segmentation pricing*, based on different groups of customers with different willingness to pay (e.g., educational pricing), and *versioning*, in which customers self-select their most attractive price-quality trade-off from among alternative versions of the product (Shapiro and Varian 1999b). Price discrimination may mean that customers operate under (or self-select) different pricing schedules but not necessarily.

Table 9.2
Costs in Supplying Software to the End-User

Function	Marginal Costs
Analysis	Generally these are fixed costs; however, meeting the needs of a new type or category of users can create marginal costs in understanding their distinctive needs and capturing them in requirements.
Development	Generally these are fixed costs; however, as with analysis, expanding the requirements to satisfy new types of users can create marginal costs.
Maintenance	These are largely fixed costs related to identified defects in the software itself and thus largely independent of the market size; however, more adopters may uncover more defects earlier, creating added marginal costs.
Upgrade	Costs of creating upgraded versions have similar characteristics to costs for analysis and development. If the upgrade expands the market by accommodating a new type or category of users, then marginal costs may be assigned to those new users.
Customer support	Some types of customer support costs (e.g., telephone agent salaries) may increase with the number of adopters. For that reason, it is important to minimize these marginal costs through rapid service releases, online problem databases, and other means.
Provisioning	Typically, a provisioning organization serves groups of users. The recurring costs (salaries and professional services) will largely be fixed for each group but will grow with the number of groups. Capital facilities costs (network, server) will be related to the number of users and their usage. Viewed in the large, these are predominately marginal costs.
Operation	Similar to costs for provisioning. Viewed in the large, predominately marginal costs, but it is important to contain them through good customer support and administrative software tools. The cost of security tends to grow with the user population, in part because a more popular application attracts more crackers.

Example A pricing schedule may include a usage-based component. If the customer is doing its own provisioning and operation, then the software supplier's costs are, to first order, independent of usage. The usage component is therefore related to the customer's value rather than to the supplier's marginal cost. On the other hand, usage-based pricing for an application service provider may (at least to first order) reflect that provider's marginal costs of provisioning and operation.

The user's willingness to pay depends on many factors (see section 3.2). Some of these, such as usage, quality, and fidelity, can vary over time for the same user. While the common pricing strategies shown in table 9.1 certainly offer opportunities to price-discriminate, this is predominately based on crude usage metrics. Other value factors that may differ significantly from one user to another may be reflected in prices determined through individualized license negotiation or selective discounting from catalog prices.

The business model and pricing strategy can have a significant effect on supplier incentives and targets for investment. For example, usage-based pricing provides an ongoing revenue stream even without new versions and puts the emphasis on maximizing usage.

In the versioning approach to price discrimination, a portfolio of software variants is created that offers different levels of value (e.g., features, quality, performance) (Shapiro and Varian 1998; Varian 2001). (The meaning of *version* differs in economics and in the software field; see section 5.1.2.)[6] Customers will select a variant with the most attractive combination of value and price, and this can increase total revenue. The voluntary nature of this discrimination is relatively popular with customers and with suppliers, who avoid having to conduct individualized price negotiations. Frequently, a basic variant is offered free, either for a limited-time trial or indefinitely, while more capable variants are sold. The free offering bears little marginal cost to the supplier and serves to familiarize customers with the product in the hope that they will move to a paid variant.

Example The business model of many suppliers of software for the Web has been to offer the client viewer for free download and sell the server software to information and service providers. Examples include Adobe Acrobat and Real Network's RealPlayer. Adobe and Real Networks also offer for sale a variant of the client with added features.

The key to success in versioning is pricing higher-value variants so that customers with a higher willingness to pay will not be tempted to save money and opt for a lower-value variant. This is done by adjusting the consumer surplus (willingness to pay minus price) to be equal or higher for the higher-value variant. For example, with two variants, the difference in value (willingness to pay) must exceed the difference in price. In the absence of versioning, typically the higher-value variant is the biggest revenue opportunity, and adding a lower-value variant reduces the price that can be charged for the higher-value variant but increases total revenue and makes the product available to a larger audience. Economic theory further suggests that the value of the lowest-price variant should be set lower than even price-sensitive consumers would be willing to pay in order to encourage less price-sensitive consumers to opt for the higher-value variant.[7] It is common to offer a third, even higher-value, variant, because experience suggests that consumers are psychologically biased toward a middle-of-the-road choice.

Versioning is particularly appropriate for software because the marginal development cost of offering variants is low—it is a matter of developing the highest-value variant while building in the flexibility to turn off certain features or degrade performance. This does, however, have to be anticipated early in the development. At the architectural design, modularity should ensure that modules can be added or removed, resulting in a coherent addition or removal of features. During development, configuration options can be included that allow certain capabilities to be substituted or bypassed. As these options are difficult to retrofit, the business model and pricing strategies should be established early, and developers should take into account pricing strategies as well as the needs of users.

9.3.3 Bundling

Another issue related to pricing is what is bundled in the sale. Beyond the software code itself, options include future service releases, future new versions, customer support, and even provisioning and operation. The several common business models discussed in chapter 6 amount to different bundles.

While different bundles are often associated with specific pricing strategies, presupposing pricing options is not a good way to differentiate bundling options because software pricing is so flexible (see section 9.3.1). A better approach is to consider the range of skills required to supply the bundle, the effect on transaction costs, and the advantages or disadvantages from a customer perspective.

Example While code licensing and customer installation are usually associated with site, seat, or floating licensing, networked software can communicate with a license server to offer subscription or per-transaction pricing. Software sold as a service is usually associated with subscription pricing but can also be sold at a fixed price. A more important consideration in comparing these bundling options is whether it is the supplier or the customer that bears the burden of provisioning and operation.

Suppliers often bundle complementary pieces of software, or software and hardware, in order to offer a full systems solution to the customer.

Example Historically, the manufacturers of voiceband data modems (such as Hayes) bundle the hardware with a communication application, such as terminal emulation. One reason is that the modem is useless without the communication application and vice versa. Bundling removes the burden of having to choose and purchase two products. A similar approach is followed now by suppliers of full-featured sound cards and DVD drives, who bundle software to make the added value of these products more evident to the customer or more demonstrable in the retail store.

Bundling can help deal with the dispersion of customer demand (Shapiro and Varian 1999b), which makes it challenging to set a revenue-maximizing price.

Example The office suite (usually including a bundle of word processor, spreadsheet, presentation, e-mail, and database) is a good example. Some users may want the word processor badly but have only occasional need for a spreadsheet, and others may use a spreadsheet intensively but only occasionally use a word processor. The supplier can set the individual prices of the word processor and spreadsheet high enough to derive maximum revenue from the intensive users while disenfranchising the light users, or set the price low enough to attract the light users while forgoing the higher price the intensive users would be willing to pay.

The dispersion in demand is often lower for a bundle than for its constituents, increasing total revenue when the supplier is forced to set a single price.

Example Suppose there are 100 customers, half of them willing to pay $1 for product A and $3 for product B, and the other half willing to pay $2 for product A and $1 for product B. If product A and B are sold separately, the revenue-maximizing price for product A is $1 (revenue $100) and for product B is $3 (revenue $150), for a total revenue of $250. However, if A and B are sold as a bundle at a single price, then half the customers are willing to pay $4 and the other half $3, and the revenue-maximizing price is $3, for a total revenue of $300. The bundle has less dispersion in willingness to pay ($1 versus $3).

Bundling is particularly natural for software, where the incremental cost of bundling other pieces of software is very low. Since costs are not much of an issue, the objective of bundling is to maximize revenue (as in the example). There is an opportunity cost for not selling that software separately, but often it is just the oppo-site: greater value can be derived by adjusting the price for the bundle rather than by selling the constituents separately, as the example illustrates. Another way to view bundling is as a strategy to derive some incremental revenue from a product that the customer is unlikely to buy separately by bundling it with a product the customer does value greatly.

The value of a bundle can be increased through the composability of the constituents (see section 3.2.12).

Example   Suppliers of office suites enhance the capabilities of the constituent appli-cations to share information, such as directly translating a spreadsheet into a word-processing table. They carry this further by allowing one application to manage objects embedded in a document managed by another application, e.g., the presen-tation application managing a figure in a word-processing document.

To reiterate, the variants of a piece of software are almost direct substitutes but offer different baskets of capabilities, features, and performance. The customer is expected to want only one variant, the one that maximizes his consumer surplus. Bundled pieces of software are not substitutes and may even be highly comple-mentary—the expectation is that the customer wants them all. Both versioning and bundling address dispersion in demand using different techniques in different circumstances.

9.3.4   Terms and Conditions

Another issue surrounding pricing is the terms and conditions of sale. As with other goods and services, there is typically a coupling between these terms and conditions and the price that can be charged. One set of conditions relates to how payments are spread over time and the future obligations for payment (see in section 9.3.1). Terms and conditions also include any warranties on correct functioning and any commitments to provide support and future maintenance, possibly associated with payments.

Another important issue is the upgrade policy. Is the supplier obligated to provide future versions as well as to maintain the software in the future? Is the customer obligated to purchase later versions? If customers are not required to use the latest version, how long does the supplier agree to maintain and support older versions? A common (but not necessary) provision of the service provider model is automatic upgrades to the latest version, but this may be problematic for some users who have to change versions at times not under their control. By maintaining a range of supported versions (sometimes called a *window*), customers are not forced to upgrade in lock step.

Another issue is performance and availability parameters. Sometimes an agreement is entered to achieve specified performance and availability characteristics, called a *service level agreement* (SLA) (Hiles 1993; Koch 1998). An SLA for licensed software in isolation doesn't make sense: very few if any service qualities are a property of software alone. Rather, these are system properties affected by software, the operational environment that includes infrastructure software and equipment, and the skill level of the operating organization. Thus, SLAs are most common for the service provider model, including networking and application hosting. SLAs for customer-operated software are possible but need conditional clauses that require the customer to obey rules, such as dedicating a server to the software.

Other terms and conditions relate to standard business relationships not unique to software. For example, how often is the customer billed, and how fast is payment expected? Software does offer more options for billing and payment (as illustrated by superdistribution; see section 9.2.4) than material goods or many other services.

9.3.5 Who Pays?

Another set of pricing issues relates to who pays. As is typical of many information suppliers, software suppliers (or more often service providers) are supported by third-party payments in return for advertising made possible by the low marginal costs of software distribution. For the application service provider subscription model, advertising can be tailored based on user profile, taking into account the application context and the specific user activity. For this revenue model, the determinant of value to the advertiser is user attention rather than the direct value of software features and capabilities to the user. Unlike traditional media, advertisements in networked media can be tailored to the user and updated dynamically, and can include hyperlinks to the advertiser's Web site, where unlimited information can be offered. This revenue model is one source of dispute over privacy policies, particularly where personal information is shared with advertisers or marketers (see section 5.3.2).

All the dimensions of pricing previously discussed are often interdependent. Usage-based or per-use pricing inherently requires periodic billing, a prepayment and debit system, or a pay-before-use infrastructure (such as digital cash). A supplier should not promise new versions (with the attendant ongoing development costs) unless they are purchased separately or there is ongoing subscription revenue.

Similarly, an application service provider should expect subscription revenues to offset operational costs.

9.4 Rationale for Infrastructure

The distinction between infrastructure and application has been emphasized repeatedly in earlier chapters. As elsewhere in the economy, infrastructure is an important economic enabler for the software industry. Economics can provide some important insights into the role of infrastructure and help clarify its value.

The definition of infrastructure used earlier was "everything that supports a number of applications and is specific to none." Here we use an expansive interpretation that includes capabilities directly assisting the execution of an application and also the development of applications and the provisioning and administration of applications. These latter elements are economically significant, given that development, provisioning, and operation are significant contributors to the total cost of ownership (see section 5.2). A capable infrastructure makes it quicker and cheaper to develop, provision, and operate software. This lowers the barrier to entry for individual applications and enables a greater diversity of applications serving more special needs. A significant trend is toward more diverse and specialized applications (see section 3.1), and infrastructure is a significant enabler.

Infrastructure is an essential underpinning of many industries, but there are three particularly important economic foundations for infrastructure supporting software: the *sharing* of resources, the *reuse* of designs, and productivity-enhancing *tools*.

9.4.1 Sharing
A classic purpose for infrastructure (not only software) is resource sharing. An important economic benefit of this is lowered marginal costs for provisioning and operating a new application based on an infrastructure already operational in the customer's environment.

Another economic motivation for sharing is benefiting from economies of scale. If, as a resource is provisioned in larger quantities the unit cost decreases, it becomes attractive to provision and share larger quantities. The motivation for sharing in the case of software is, however, more complex than this. Software, like information, is freely replicated and nonrival in use (see section 2.1). Thus, there is no economic motivation to share software code itself—it can be freely replicated and executed in as many places as make sense. However, software also requires a material infrastructure to support its execution, and sharing that material infrastructure can exhibit economies of scale. There are two primary examples of this. The first is sharing a single host over two or more users or over two or more applications. In fact, this is the central idea of both the mainframe and time-sharing computing (see table 2.3) and is also a motivation for the client-server architecture (see section 4.4). The second is the sharing of the network by many hosts. The economic justification for these two instances of sharing is somewhat different.

A primary motivation for host sharing is the convenience and efficiency of administration of information that is common to users and applications. A secondary motivation is sharing of the processor resource. There are economies of scale in processing, because equipment costs increase more slowly than performance (at least up to whatever technological limits are in place). A bigger factor is the locality of data access: if a common repository of data is accessed, then as shared data are split over two or more hosts, efficiency is lost and the administrative costs of maintaining the data increase substantially.

These considerations are different for the network, where resource sharing is much more common; in fact, it is almost universal. Higher-bandwidth switches and communication links exhibit economies of scale like processors. A much bigger consideration is the sharing of real estate and radio spectrum: in a wide-area network, it is necessary to use either the radio spectrum (typically licensed from the government) or else accumulate the geographic right-of-way to run fiber optic cables. There are large economies of scale in the latter because the cost of acquiring right-of-way and the cost of laying trenches and cable conduits is substantial, whereas the aggregate bandwidth capability is effectively unlimited for a given right-of-way.

Relieving congestion is another motivation for sharing. Congestion occurs when the load on a resource (either processing or network) is irregular and variable with time (see section 2.3.1). The variable load results in the arrival of work (tasks to processor or packets to communicate) temporarily exceeding capacity, and the excess work has to be deferred until there is an opportunity to complete it, creating an excess congestion-induced delay. Performance considerations or service-level agreements typically limit the acceptable delay (congestion-induced or otherwise) and hence place a limit on the resource utilization. When a single source is shared over multiple workloads, it turns out that a higher utilization can be accommodated for the same congestion-induced delay. The reason is simple: the service time of a higher-performing resource is reduced, and congestion delay is proportional to the service time. This is called a *statistical multiplexing* advantage and is another source of scale economy.

Example   If irregular automobile traffic arrives at a bridge, occasionally the traffic arrival rate will exceed the bridge capacity, and there will be a backup in front of the bridge. To limit the average congestion delay, the average incoming traffic rate has to be limited. If the same traffic is divided into two equal pieces, each crossing two parallel bridges with half the speed limit and hence half the capacity, then the total incoming traffic will have to be further limited to maintain the same average congestion delay.

Because of a statistical multiplexing advantage, provisioning and sharing a larger resource (processor or communication link) instead of a number of smaller resources with the same total capacity increases the average utilization for the same average congestion delay.

Example   Assuming the simplest model for irregular loads described in section 2.3.1, the total average delay D is related to the average service time D_s and the average utilization u by

$$D = \frac{1}{1-u} D_s.$$

Now compare two situations: N identical servers have the same utilization u_N and service time D_s, and a single high-capacity server has N times the capacity, utilization u_1, and the same average delay D. The higher-capacity server, because it completes tasks by a factor N faster, has a smaller service time by the same factor D_s/N. This is the source of the statistical multiplexing advantage. These two situations will yield the same average congestion delay when

$$\frac{1}{1-u_n} D_s = \frac{1}{1-u_1} \frac{D_s}{N}.$$

This increasing return to scale is *in addition to* any capital cost advantage of a single server over multiple lower-capacity servers and any reduction in administrative costs from operating a single server.

Example   Suppose we have 100 identical servers operating at a 75 percent utilization, and assume the simple congestion model of the last example. This utilization was chosen to achieve an acceptable average delay (four times as large as the average service time). If these 100 servers are replaced by a single server that is 100 times faster, then the utilization can be increased to $1 - (1 - 0.75)/100 = 0.9975$, or 99.75 percent. At the same overall average delay, the result of sharing this single server is the accommodation of a 33 percent higher throughput (by increasing utilization from 75 percent to 99.75 percent) for the same total capacity. The relation is plotted in figure 9.5 for two through five slower servers replaced by a single faster server.

There are also disadvantages to gaining efficiency by this *scale-up* (replacement of servers by fewer faster ones) rather than *scale-out* (adding additional slower

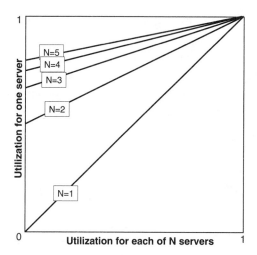

Figure 9.5
The utilization that can be achieved for a single faster server (*y*-axis) in comparison to *N* slower servers (*x*-axis) for the same average delay.

servers). For example, availability may be adversely affected, since single outages affect more users and can be more disruptive. Also, and important for organizations facing unpredictable growth, it is easier as demand increases to scale out an existing installation (by adding more servers) than it is to scale up (by replacing servers with faster ones).

Another challenge with resource sharing is that one user's increasing resource consumption causes increased congestion experienced by other users. If there is no compensating payment, this is a negative congestion externality. Another way to state this: How do we maintain control over the utilization, thereby controlling the congestion delay? There are a number of forms of congestion control. One is *admission control*, which is just another form of access control (see section 5.4.2) based on the current level of congestion rather than access privileges.

Another approach often advocated by technologists is *overprovisioning*, which is simply provisioning an adequate resource that throughput fluctuations can never credibly overwhelm it. An advantage often cited so that hardware and communication resources are cheap (and getting cheaper, per Moore's law), whereas congestion control increases complexity and cost. Often lost in this argument is the value that congestion control may bring to users: the cost of congestion control can only be evaluated in relation to any added value that it may bring. Of course, overprovisioning adds costs, too, and it is not clear what economic incentives service providers have to expend these costs. Unlike congestion control, overprovisioning also leaves resources vulnerable to abusive use. One security hole is the denial-of-service attack, in which a vandal generates many spurious requests on a resource with the goal of creating artificial congestion and denying that resource to legitimate users. Once such an attack is identified, some form of admission control can be invoked to block these abusive requests. A more sophisticated attack is mounted simultaneously from various locations, making defense more difficult. The recent incidents of Internet *worms* (rogue programs that replicate across vast numbers of machines) demonstrate the vulnerability of any shared resources made available on the Internet, and the difficulty of mounting defenses. Overprovisioning is an ineffective defense for any but the largest-capacity operations, whereas other congestion control mechanisms can help.

Economists have their own prescription (seldom seen in practice today) for congestion control through *congestion pricing*. Each user is charged a fluctuating price based on the current congestion and reflecting the cost imposed by that use on other users. Accurately implemented, congestion pricing allows a resource to be allocated optimally based on the user's willingness to pay, taking into account both the benefit of resource utilized and the impairment of congestion-induced delay. Congestion pricing has two important advantages. First, users who have genuine need to use more of the resource (and corresponding willingness to pay) are able to get it. This is not a capability of involuntary admission control. Second, the revenue from congestion pricing increases as congestion increases, and this extra revenue is available to the service provider to add capacity and relieve congestion. Of course, a skeptic would assert that the provider might just pocket this revenue. In fact the economic theory indicates not. If the congestion price is high enough, the provider can increase profits by adding capacity. This price threshold is identical to the condition under which there is a collective social benefit to users and providers in adding capacity (MacKie-Mason and Varian 1995). Congestion pricing does require an especially complex infrastructure, although it can make use of billing and payment mechanisms shared by usage-based pricing. Weaker forms of congestion pricing, such as pricing based on time-of-day (where statistically predictable congestion exists) are easier (but also less effective).

9.4.2 Reuse and Multiple Use

While the sharing of software code considered as a resource is not advantageous, using the same software code in multiple designs is of intense interest. This reuse or multiple use sense of infrastructure is shared with many products in the material world (e.g., automobile platforms share common components over multiple models). Reusable modules, components and frameworks seek to contain one of the most important costs, that of development (see section 7.3). On the other hand, designing and developing reusable software modules, components, and frameworks invariably take considerably more time, effort, and expense than single-purpose designs. Thus, there must be a compelling expectation of multiple uses before this becomes economically feasible.

Reuse and multiple use apply in other contexts as well. Much of operation and administration involves setting up organization-specific processes and partly automating those processes through various programs and scripts. If those processes and scripts can be shared with other administrators, as they often are, this constitutes reuse.

9.4.3   Tools

Tools are another form of software infrastructure that reduce the time and effort required to develop, provision, and operate applications (see section 4.4.7). By automating many tasks that would otherwise have to be performed manually, tools reduce time, effort, and expense, and contribute to quality. Integrated development environments include rich toolkits for software development (see section 7.3.6). Tools are crucial to operation as well as development.

Example   *Network management* is a category of software tool that allows system and network administrators to keep track of and configure various equipment resources (e.g., computers, network switches) from a central location as well as signal and trace the causes of problems that may arise. Not only can such tools increase worker productivity, but they also contribute to effectiveness by allowing each worker to encounter and deal with more problems and challenges.

9.5   Software as an Economic Good

In the economics profession, software is often described as a special type of information good. Is this a valid characterization? Certainly, in looking through the previous chapters, the discussion of both technology and the industry would be very different if information and the information industries were the topic. Are these differences merely window dressing from an economics perspective? Or is software fundamentally different? In fact, software shares economic characteristics with not only information but also material goods as well as with services, combining their characteristics in unique ways. Our thesis is that software is different, and software is unique.

Of course, any similarly between software and information depends on the definition of information. Software consists of a set of instructions that are executed sequentially on a processor. Like information, software is represented by data, in part so it can share the same storage and communication technology infrastructure with information.[8] If we were to define information as "anything that can be represented by data," then software would be a particular case of information. However, this definition is flawed.

Example   The sentence "On planet Earth, the sky is always green" could be represented by data, like any other sentence, but would hardly be considered informative. The essence of the economic value of information is its informative nature, affecting behavior or emotions of the recipient or contributing to the recipient's knowledge in ways that are beneficial. There are also examples of data that are not misinformation, like the "green sky" example but simply have no value to a user. Cryptography and communication systems, for example, frequently internally generate and utilize sequences of bits designed to be as completely random as practicable; that is, containing no discernible pattern or information.

Its actual or possible representaion by data is not a definition of information but rather a technical property of information and only as it is represented within the limited domain of information technology. Information appears in many other forms, including ways that cannot currently be digitally represented (like smell or touch). The definition of information (see section 2.1) as "recognizable patterns that inform or influence people" brings in the important element of beneficial usefulness or influence on people. By this definition, software would be information for some people, but not most people.

Example   Software source code is informative to a programmer but likely not to a layperson. Object code itself (see section 4.4.4) would not be too informative (even to programmers) short of expending extraordinary effort, although it can be very useful to people as it is executed on a processor.

While software does inform programmers, its primary utility is in instructing computers on what to do on the behalf of people, and its primary value is in the actions and behavior of the program as executed on that computer. Programming is an intermediate step to extracting this value but decidedly not an end in itself.

9.5.1 Demand Side: Software as a Material Product or Service
On the demand side, any economic good is characterized principally by its value to the consumer. From this perspective, software's ultimate utility to people is embodied in what it does, with the aid of the computer (see section 3.1). Software is valued

for its execution, and the behavior that execution engenders, rather than for the insights it offers. This is the primary reason that the patent law recognizes that software, but not information, can encompass an invention (see section 8.1). The law on copyright management also outlaws anticircumvention devices, some of which may be implemented partly or wholly in software (see section 8.1.5). This appears to place such software in the position of not being protected by the principles of free speech in the United States, as most forms of information are (see section 8.2.4). Thus, the laws increasingly recognize software as distinct from information. Of course, one common function of software is manipulating and presenting information content; in this context, software is valued in part for how it finds and manipulates information. Certain quality and usage attributes also contribute to value (see section 3.2).

Information is valued for how it informs or teaches. As a rule, the more unique or surprising an insight communicated by information, the more valuable it becomes.[9] Thus, information thrives on diversity and uniqueness. On the other hand, surprise or uniqueness is not usually a valued characteristic of software. Predictability (the absence of surprise) is a hallmark of high-quality software. In fact, in the presence of network effects, software that is so unique as to not be interoperable or that imposes major training costs suffers in terms of its value (see section 9.1.2).

Many material goods are also valued for what they do (e.g., the automobile, which takes us places, or scissors, which cut paper), so the question arises, is software perhaps closer in its characteristics to many material products (traditional engineering artifacts) than to information? From the perspective of the user (the demand side), it is. This assertion is supported by numerous instances in which software, supported by its execution platform and environment, directly substitutes for physical products.

Example   The typewriter can be replaced by a deskstop computer, printer, and word-processing application; a game board by a game application; an abacus by a spreadsheet application; and a telephone by a computer with microphone, audio card, Internet connection, and telephony application.

Services are also valued primarily for what they do. Often software is directly substituted for the services provided by people.

Example   A calendar and scheduling application can substitute for the services of an administrative assistant in scheduling a meeting. A word-processing application can substitute for many of the services of a typing pool. An e-mail application can substitute for some services of the post office.

In summary, we conclude that in terms of value, software most closely resembles material products and human-provided services rather than information. Of course, the demand side involves considerations other than value. Software shares some characteristics with information, some of those characteristics being dissimilar to those of material products and services, and some being similar. Like information, software is often an experience good—it must be experienced to be appreciated—and sometimes less so. Some services and material products are experience goods, and some are not.

Example   Once a user has used a particular spreadsheet application, he can probably appreciate other spreadsheets. Once spreadsheets become a standard tool in a business education, and the application area has matured to the extent that different spreadsheet products are little differentiated, then a spreadsheet can no longer be considered an experience good. However, the user has to use at least one spreadsheet to appreciate its capabilities. Commodities like oil and flour, and services like oil changes or bank account withdrawals, have obvious uses and need not be experienced. Unique goods and services like the Frisbee or palm reading probably need to be experienced before they can be fully appreciated. Similar observations can be made for information, but more on the basis of the type of information than the ubiquity or maturity of the information. For example, stock price quotes probably don't have to be experienced to be appreciated, but creative writing does.

9.5.2   Supply Side: Software as a Plan and Factory

The supply side is characterized principally by the costs of production and distribution. In this regard, software shares with information high creation and provisioning costs and low replication and distribution costs. Software invariably incurs substantial recurring maintenance and upgrade costs, a characteristic it shares with some volatile forms of information (see section 5.1). It also incurs recurring operational costs, something usually not associated with information (but with the software facilitating access to the information). Unlike information, software can be self-aware, reporting defects or usage back to the supplier even as it is used. Like information, but unlike most other goods and services, software is easily replicated and nonrival in use. Thus it shares with information many characteristics in distribution and rights management (see section 8.1). The most important distinction between hardware (and other material goods) and software (cited in section 2.2.4) is the inherent flexibility of software, which can be transparently added to, repaired, and upgraded at any time, even as it is used. Information can similarly be repaired and upgraded, typically as facilitated by software.

From an economic perspective, a major supply-side issue is the means of production. As discussed in section 7.3.5, the Industrial Revolution was characterized in part by a shift from finished goods handcrafted from raw materials to assembly of standard multiuse parts purchased from multiple specialized suppliers. The question arises whether, even if component assembly of software becomes widespread, software will resemble material goods in this means of production. The answer is largely no; software is quite different in this respect because in a very real sense it is much more dynamic and self-constructing (see section 7.3.5). It most closely resembles the plans for a flexible factory.

It is worth summarizing the relation of software to other economic goods and services. Software resembles information in its supply cost structure but most closely resembles a plan for a very flexible factory in the material world in its means of production. On the demand side it resembles a material product (created by that factory) or a service in the user's value proposition. The computer serves as an intermediary, acting as the generic factory that executes specific factory plans (software) to produce the working product, dynamically and on demand in response to specific user needs. Like a factory, the executing program requires human workers to provision and operate it; that is, getting things installed and keeping them running. The software code plan is a form of information, one that shares many characteristics of information like high creation costs and low reproduction costs, but it informs the computer rather than the user.

The following is a rather good analogy to the software industry and its customers from an economic perspective: (1) a planning organization creates and continually maintains and updates a plan for a flexible factory (an activity that does exist in the material economy); (2) multiple instances of a factory based on that plan, each constructed, operated, and upgraded by human workers, churns out very flexible material products; and (3) consumers (often organizations) use and benefit from those products. What this analogy fails to capture is the ongoing and complex interaction between the user and the factory's products, which is more extreme for software than for material products.

9.6   Research and Discussion Issues

1. Develop guidance for a software supplier facing the issue of pricing of new versions of its software (see table 5.2).

2. What is the relation between software pricing and patent or copyright licensing terms and conditions (see section 8.1.3)?

3. Metcalfe's law is clearly simplistic in that for any given user some adopters are clearly more important than others. Given that the actual effect on demand is probably product-dependent, what would be a good methodology for estimating the diminution of demand in any specific case?

4. What are some specific strategies for reaching critical mass in software products, where the demand exceeds supply, in the presence of network effects? Do these strategies differ markedly for different types of software?

5. How is the notion of market share affected by various forms of software use, licensing, and pricing? What might be suitable measures of market share?

6. What are some ways that alternative software suppliers try to overcome switching costs for a prospective customer? Do these strategies differ across different types of software? How does software differ from other goods and services?

7. What is the relation between lock-in and innovation? How can even existing suppliers be constrained from introducing innovative technologies by their customers' switching costs?

8. This chapter has emphasized customer lock-in, but consider also supplier lock-in. Do suppliers become constrained by their own switching costs, or does the software industry as a whole become locked into existing technologies (e.g., through standardization)? What strategies can be employed to counter these effects?

9. Consider the issue of open versus proprietary systems. How do the strategies differ, and how does this interact with pricing, network effects, and lock-in?

10. How can the self-awareness property of software be used to aid suppliers or customers? Detail some ways, if exploited, it may affect the economic properties of software.

11. Discuss in some depth the advantages of subscription pricing, usage-based pricing, and pricing for periodic upgrades. Which is in the best interest of the supplier? the customer?

12. Considering the sources of competitive advantage as well as their limitations, has software proven to be a good business overall (relative to other products and services)? Have existing firms fully exploited their opportunities, or are there significant improvements in strategy that they could effect?

13. What are some ways that software pricing should and could take into account network effects?

14. Qualitatively, what do you believe is the relative importance of the sources of value (as reflected in willingness to pay) for software (see section 3.2)? How important are these generic factors in relation to specific capabilities and functionality?

15. Consider the triumvirate of software supplier, operator, and user, with revenues flowing from user to operator to supplier. What are the most appropriate pricing mechanisms for operator and supplier? What is the relation between these two pricing strategies?

16. Consider the relation of bundling and composability (see section 3.2.13). Does composability of the products within a bundle enhance the value of the bundle as a whole, and is this enhancement different than if the products were not bundled?

17. Congestion in the presence of statistical multiplexing displays the characteristic that throughput can be increased at the expense of latency, and vice versa. How do the relative values of throughput and latency differ across different types of software? To whom (user or operator) do these have primary value? How can this trade-off be used to maximize revenue?

9.7   Further Reading

Economides (1996) has an excellent tutorial on network effects. Shapiro and Varian (1999b) discuss strategic issues related to the economic properties of information and software. Shy (2001) offers a rigorous survey of the economics surrounding networked industries, including but not limited to software, which details the economics of pricing, including complementarities and competition.

10
The Future

You can never plan the future by the past.
Edmund Burke

More so than most technologies and markets, software is in a constant state of flux. Presumably this is due in part to the inherent flexibility of software and in part to its immaturity as a technology and industry. The merging of communication with storage and processing (as represented by the Internet) represents a major maturation of the technology: with a full complement of nearly ubiquitous mass storage and communication together with computing, there are no remaining major technological gaps of note. However, the market implications of this limited technological maturation have only begun to be felt. In addition, there are other technological and market trends that are easily anticipated because they have already begun. These are essentially an extension of the computing phases shown in table 2.3.

10.1 Slowing Technological Advance

The exponential advance of all the underlying technologies noted by Moore's law cannot continue indefinitely. Nevertheless, dire predictions for the end of this advance in electronics have consistently been wrong because they have underestimated the continuing technological innovation and the rapid market expansion, fueled by declining prices and innovative new applications, that continue to pay for that innovation and for increasingly expensive fabrication factories. What is clear, however, is that continued scaling of existing technologies will someday run out of gas, perhaps in a decade or two. The limitations may be physical (the number of atoms per device gets small enough so that the devices no longer work properly) or economic (the costs of technological innovation or capital expenditures become excessive).

The end of scaling for existing technologies is probably not the end of technological advance because radically new technologies may be possible. Nanoscale technologies and quantum electronics are currently being pursued in research laboratories. These technologies directly exploit the quantum properties of individual atoms and thus work very differently than current electronic technologies. While conceptually possible and consistent with the laws of physics, they are unproven in practice. If they can be made to work, they will yield dramatic advances over current technologies, creating a discontinuity in performance characteristics, although cost is more of a question mark. They, too, will experience physical limitations and will thus postpone but not eliminate the day when the advance noted by Moore's law comes to an end.

When technological advance does slow down, the effect on the software industry may or may not be dramatic. A lot depends on when it happens. If it were to happen today, the effect would be felt strongly, reversing some industry trends such as increasingly centralized server functionality, fueled largely by lower recurring costs. Examples of this include client-server computing (section 4.5.3), the application server platform (section 7.3.6), and Web services (section 7.3.7). Exponential advance of technology is a significant enabler of this trend because it (along with increasing parallelism enabled by faster networks) enables this architectural model to keep up with the mainstream demanding applications. A slowing of technological advance today would require a rethinking of this architecture and likely encourage more decentralization of processing requirements to clients.

Today technology has largely outstripped the needs of desktop computers for standard business applications, although many other types of engineering and scientific applications have an insatiable demand for processing power. Technological advances could eventually outstrip even the needs of the most demanding commercial applications (as happened in commercial aerospace with the commercial failure of supersonic transport), which would remove one important economic driver for further advances. In any application area, further advances have diminishing returns in terms of benefits to users, and at this point their economic underpinning is diminished.

In summary, there are three possible causes for slowing technological advance: physical limitations, increasing and unaffordable development and fabrication costs, and outstripping the performance needs of the mainstream applications that finance it. It is difficult to predict the outcome, but it is the balancing of supply and demand reflected in the last two factors that will most likely determine the point of slowing advance, not insurmountable physical barriers.

10.2 Information Appliances

Instead of installing specialized applications on general computers, software can be bundled with hardware to focus on a narrower purpose. *Information appliances* bundle and sell encapsulated software applications with dedicated hardware (Heer and Maher 1995).

Example Bundling an inexpensive and encapsulated computer with Web browsing and e-mail software (such as the IOpener) results in an appliance that is arguably easier to set up, administer, and use than the desktop computer but also less flexible. The personal digital assistant (PDA), such as the Palm or PocketPC, targets personal information management, and similar capabilities are increasingly bundled in the cellular phone. The game console (sold by Microsoft, Nintendo, and Sony) and the personal video recorder (sold by Microsoft, SonicBlue, and Tivo) provide personal entertainment. All these products are essentially specialized computers but unlike the desktop computer all except the PDA offer dedicated applications with limited provision to add other applications.

Information appliances exploit the decreasing cost of hardware to create devices that are more portable and ergonomic, and have enhanced usability. The usability point is the least clear, however, because information appliances also spawn multiple, inconsistent user interfaces, compounding the learning and training issues. Furthermore, they introduce a barrier to application composition, a capability offered by the desktop computer with considerable value through the indirect network effects it engenders. Partly as a result, the most successful appliances have been conceived and designed as an adjunct and complement to the computer, not as a replacement.

Example Most personal information manager, audio player, and digital camera appliances have a docking cradle or serial interface to the desktop computer. This allows information to be stored in the desktop for use by other applications and peripherals, while still allowing the portability and usability advantages of the appliance. Examples of information appliances not interoperable with desktops include digital television set-top boxes and personal video recorders; however, this may be an interim step because interesting options (like configuration and programming) could be accomplished by accessing these products through the Internet. Content suppliers may be opposed to Internet connection because of rights management issues (see section 8.1.5).

In this architecture, the computer essentially acts as a server to the appliances, which are its clients. A viable alternative is peer-to-peer networking of appliances, an approach that can also enable information sharing and application composition (see section 10.3) and may bypass one current limitation of appliances.

Historically, three phases of information product design, driven by the declining cost and increasing complexity of hardware, can be observed. First, the high cost of hardware dictates a single-use appliance, because the technology is barely able to meet the functional and performance requirements, and programmability would be infeasible or too expensive. In this phase, requirements tend to be satisfied with special-purpose hardware rather than through programmability.

Example Stand-alone word processors and programmable calculators were information appliances predating the personal computer that have largely been displaced by computer applications. The microprocessor was invented (by Ted Hoff of Intel) in the context of a calculator implementation that would allow more applications to share common hardware through the addition of programmability. However, this development depended on technological advances' outstripping the needs of the specific applications, leaving significant room for new forms of flexibility.

In the second phase, the hardware is sufficiently capable to allow cost-effective programmability, adding flexibility and allowing upgrades and new applications added after manufacture. Factors that make this approach attractive include the sharing of a single piece of (relatively expensive) equipment over multiple applications, the value of being able to add additional applications later, and the relatively easy composition of applications. In the third phase, the cost of hardware declines sufficiently to make the limited-purpose appliance affordable if portability and usability are sufficiently advantageous.

Looking forward, the declining cost and increasing performance of hardware implies that user decisions over the right mix of generality and specialization will be driven less by hardware cost considerations and more by considerations of functionality and usability. This is a happy situation for both the software industry and its customers.

Software in the appliance domain assumes characteristics closer to traditional industrial products. The software is more often bundled with the hardware at the time of manufacture, although later upgrades become possible if the appliance is networked. The embedded software is developed for a controlled platform and environment, with fewer configuration options and fewer challenges associated with expansion and peripherals. In most instances, maintenance and upgrade become steps within the appliance product development activity rather than a separable software-only process.

Since software is embedded at the time of manufacture, appliance manufacturers have traditionally viewed software as a cost of product development, not as a separate revenue opportunity. That is, they don't view themselves primarily as software suppliers and they view the software as a necessary price for market entry rather than as a separate revenue opportunity. In the future, as the software content becomes a greater source of value to users and consumes a larger share of development costs, appliance suppliers will view software as a separate revenue opportunity. This affects many things discussed previously, such as maintenance and support, pricing, versioning, and upgrades (see section 5.1). It also suggests a trend toward creating an open platform, one where other software suppliers are given an opportunity to add applications.

Example   The dividing line between the information appliance and the personal computer is fuzzy. The Palm Pilot, although originally marketed primarily as a personal organizer, was from the start created as an open platform for other applications, and today has over 11,000 available applications (Palm 2002).

10.3   Pervasive Computing

Information appliances are still predominantly software-based products whose primary purpose remains the capturing, manipulating, and accessing information. Another trend is embedding software-mediated capabilities within a variety of existing material products, products whose primary purpose may not be information-related but that benefit from enhanced information processing and control.

Example   An increasing number of products include significant embedded software content, including audio or video equipment, kitchen appliances, home security systems, and automobiles. Software has become a standard means of controlling many mechanical devices. Increasingly these products are networked, allowing them to interoperate for common purposes, allowing remote access, and enabling downloadable software upgrades.

The logical extension of this is the embedding of information technology (IT) (including networked connectivity, processing, and storage) in many everyday objects, which is called *pervasive computing* (Ciarletta and Dima 2000; *IBM Systems Journal* 1999; Makulowich 1999; Weiser 1991). Pervasive computing includes information appliances but also an added capability and functionality in the material objects around us, including many opportunities that arise when these objects can communicate and coordinate. Our everyday environment becomes a configurable and flexible mesh of communicating and computing nodes (largely hidden from view) that take care of information-processing needs in the control and coordination of the material world.

In pervasive computing, much more so than in information appliances, composability that is flexible, opportunistic, and almost universal is an important goal because one of the major added values of software content is new ways of communicating among and controlling devices in the material world.

Example The ideal home security system should automatically close the drapes and turn out the lights when you watch a movie on your home theater, and the toaster should disable the smoke alarm while it is operating. The microwave oven should shut down while the cordless phone is in use to avoid interference. The stop sign and traffic lights at intersections should be eliminated, replaced by signals or automatic braking mechanisms within each automobile so that actions can be based entirely on the presence of conflicting traffic. The automobile horn (another car's initiating an alert) should be replaced by a signal in the car being alerted. (Of course, these ideas ignore the reality of pedestrians, bicycles, and so on.)

Further, taking advantage of IT to increase the complementarity of many products in the material world becomes a new and challenging goal for product marketing and design. This is also a severe technical challenge because of the diversity of products and vendors potentially affected, and because composability is carried to a larger dimensions than just the IT (see section 4.3.6).

Example Jini, which is based on Java (Sun Microsystems 1999b), and Universal Plug-and-Play (Microsoft 2000), are examples of technical approaches to interoperability in pervasive computing based on internet protocols. These protocols focus on achieving interoperability among information appliances and pervasive computers using similar technology to Web services (see section 7.3.7), offering discovery services for devices to opportunistically find one another, and interoperability standards based on dynamically loading device drivers (see figure 7.8) using mobile code (see section 4.5.5). They do not address specifically the challenges of complementarity, which must be addressed by context-dependent and industry-specific standardization efforts.

Many challenges of embedded software in pervasive computing are similar to IT equipment, the other major environment for embedded software. The primary differences are the much greater emphasis on composability and a less sophisticated operator and user (the general consumer), implying that all maintenance and upgrade processes must be automated and foolproof. Pervasive computing also presents interesting challenges to firms who find it difficult to develop a sophisticated software development capability because their primary expertise is elsewhere, and who may therefore be more disposed to outsourcing. On the other hand, as software functionality and content grows, these suppliers face the challenge of transitioning into software suppliers, with the distinctive business models this implies.

Example Bernina, a maker of high-featured sewing machines, now derives significant revenue from selling unbundled embroidery software for its machines, and offers a computer interface and various patches and maintenance releases of its software.

10.4   Mobile and Nomadic IT

The Internet has had a profound impact on software, as reflected in many examples in this book. One current result is freeing users from place. While many users access the Internet from a single access point (at home or work), *nomadic users* connect to the network from different access points (as when they use laptops while traveling). There are two cases: an appliance or computer can be relocated (e.g., a laptop or personal digital assistant—PDA), or the user can move from one appliance or computer to another (e.g., using a Web browser in an Internet café while traveling).

The advent of wireless Internet access based on radio technology allows *mobility*: mobile users maintain continuous network access (and thus change their topological point of connection) even in the course of using an application (e.g., using a cell phone or handheld device on a bus or train) (Macker, Park, and Corson 2001). A practical limitation of wireless connections is reduced communication speeds, especially relative to fiber optics. It is also often the case that wireless connectivity performance attributes (like bit rate or error rate) change with time, for example, as geographic obstacles come and go.

Ideally, nomadic and mobile users would benefit from transparent access to applications; that is, their nomadic or mobile state would not be evident. In practice today, we fall far short of this ideal. Two sorts of technical challenge arise with nomadic or mobile uses, those within the infrastructure and those within applications. In the infrastructure, sometimes distributed computing capabilities (see section 4.5) must be made dynamically reconfigurable.

Example The service discovery mechanism in Web services (see section 7.3.7) may have to be upgraded to account for nomadic services. Fortunately, most services are based in servers at static locations, and it is primarily the clients accessing those services that are nomadic or mobile. However, there may also be nomadic services. For example, a collaboration application may be based in part on services provided by the user's client machine, which in turn may be nomadic or mobile.

The Internet was not originally designed to support nomadic and mobile uses, and upgrading it to these capabilities has proven a challenge.

Example   The domain name system and the communication among hosts assume a static Internet address. Mobile IP (Maes et al. 2000) was developed to bypass this restriction by routing all communications through the mobile user's home or office computer; a home agent on this host then forwards the communication to the user's actual network access point. This overlay approach has disadvantages (a native Internet approach would be better). It is not transparent to the user (who has to install and configure home agent software and make sure its host is always available), and it often involves very circuitous "triangular" routing (through the forwarding host rather than directly to the user network access point) with extra delay and resource consumption.

The underlying technology supporting transparent nomadic and mobile uses is usually based on some variation of *indirection* (see figure 10.1). A nomadic server stores and updates information about its location, and the client can find the current location of the server before communicating directly with it. This form of indirec-

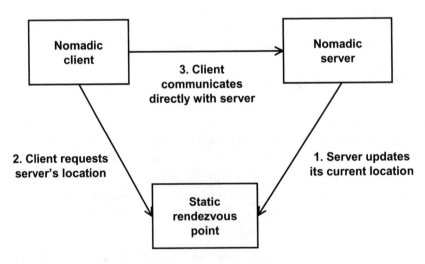

Figure 10.1
The rendezvous is a generic technique to allow a client to find a nomadic server.

tion doesnot support a mobile server; that requires the actual client-server communication to be routed through an indirection point (Mobile IP uses this approach).

There are also challenges for application developers. The application should recreate a consistent user environment wherever the user may move (different access points or different appliances or computers). Either applications need to be more cognizant of and adjust to wide variations in communication connectivity, or the infrastructure needs to perform appropriate translations on behalf of applications.

Example   The perceptual quality of video is affected by the bit rate and error rate on the lowest-quality link, and it is necessarily much lower on today's wireless access networks than in a fiber optics backbone network. An application utilizing video will have to adjust to available network resources, by depending on the network to perform translations from one video representation to another or by utilizing an end-to-end video service provided by the network. For mobile users, this adjustment must be dynamic, changing during one application session. Multipoint video services impose more severe requirements because end-points may have widely differing access rates.

It may be desirable to allow application code to reside within the network infrastructure to deal with some of the technical issues (see section 4.5.6). Mobile code is a way to achieve this flexibly and dynamically.

Example   A video or telephony session to an information appliance (like a video teleconference set or telephone) benefits from a translation between its predetermined representation and alternative representations used elsewhere in the network. The greatest flexibility is achieved when the translation is near the appliance; this suggests mobile code supplied by the application executing there.

Recognizing that the most cost-effective way to deal with these complicated issues is by upgrading the network infrastructure to directly offer nomadic and mobile services (data, audio, and video) rather than layering upon the current network to add these capabilities, the network will become increasingly sophisticated in this respect. While the technical challenges are daunting enough, some of the most interesting issues relate to the distributed ownership and management of the network (see section 5.4). Because of direct network effects, the user is best served if standardization is able to achieve interoperable management mechanisms across all network resources regardless of ownership and operational responsibilities. If this is not achieved, then network service providers who can offer global coverage and homogeneous end-to-end coordinated management of network resources will have a marked competitive advantage for end-user organizations who are able to outsource their network services to a single provider, and we can expect a rapid consolidation of the networking industry into a relatively few global providers. The increasingly sophisticated nomadic and mobile capabilities provided by the network in the future will also raise all sorts of issues relating to business models for service providers, including pricing and versioning (see section 9.3). With mobility, even a single application session may require dynamic pricing scenarios with settlements apportioning the revenue among different service providers.

10.5   Research and Discussion Issues

1. Is the demand for processing power, storage capacity, and communication bandwidth insatiable? Or do you believe that it will become increasingly difficult to justify the research, development, and capital costs of technological advances on the basis of commercial applications? If the latter, do you believe that governments will increasingly fund technological advances for the benefit of exotic military or intelligence applications?

2. Because of the ease with which information replication occurs in user-programmable platforms, content suppliers have largely avoided them in favor of information appliances with built-in rights management facilities (see section 8.1.5). Do you think this will be an impetus for information appliances? Or will rights management facilities be incorporated into programmable platforms?

3. Is the evolution from appliances to general-purpose platforms back to appliances observable in other (more mature) industries, or is software unique? Consider, for example, the electric motor.

4. What effect do you believe information appliances and pervasive computing will have on the fortunes of software companies? How will pricing and revenue models be different?

5. Issues like battery life and physical size have a considerable effect on mobile computing platforms. Because of these and other considerations, do you believe that the trend is toward a proliferation of appliances for different functions, or an integration of a standard set of functions in a single appliance?

10.6   Further Reading

The *IBM Systems Journal* (1999) is an excellent introduction to pervasive computing, and Weiser (1991), an early visionary of the concept, gives a worthwhile introduction.

Postscript

The best work is not what is most difficult for you; it is what you do best.
Jean-Paul Sartre

Software is one of the most interesting and exciting industries of our era. Starting from scratch with the first commercially available computer, the UNIVAC in 1951, it has grown to a major global industry in just five decades. The unparalleled flexibility, variety, and richness of software are countered by equally unparalleled societal, organizational, technical, financial, and economic challenges. Because of these factors—continually rocked by unremitting technological change—today's software industry and marketplace can surely be considered immature.

The software industry of the future will be much different than what we have seen. What is less clear is whether the changes can be accommodated by incremental new strategies and business models for existing players, or whether more fundamental restructuring of the software industry and its supporting industries (computing and telecommunications) will be the outcome.

A number of factors described in this book are driving industry change. The increasing ubiquity of high-performance networks opens up new possibilities. For example, they are the key enabler of new distribution and pricing models for software, for adopting a service provider model in software provisioning and operation, and for moving software into the multimedia and entertainment markets. The Internet also enables entirely new applications, including e-commerce and community collaboration, which raise many social and distributed management challenges. The infrastructure, including the network cloud, will add many capabilities transcending connectivity that were formerly in the domain of applications, and it is undergoing a major shift from a vertical to a layered architecture as driven by distributed and multimedia application needs. Mobility creates an endless variety of possible scenarios for the partitioned ownership and operation of the supporting infrastructure.

As the assembly of finer-grained software components replaces monolithic applications, and new value is created by the composition of applications or network services, even a single application may be composed from products of multiple suppliers. Application service providers, Web services, pervasive computing, and information appliances all push this trend to the extreme, as the goal is to allow composition of higher-level capabilities from different computing devices, often from different suppliers. This trend will be buttressed by new software development tools that automate much of drudgery, and together with component assembly and a richer value-added infrastructure, the skill required to prototype and develop new applications will be reduced, perhaps even enabling users to take a stronger role in developing or customizing their own applications.

Applications are becoming much more diverse and specialized in the enterprise (especially sociotechnical applications), in information appliances, and through pervasive computing. This drives application suppliers to find better ways to capture specialized needs and domain knowledge, and encourages a cadre of professionals and firms concerned with organizational needs and enhancing the user experience. These factors plus the increased need for an infrastructure with expanding capabilities is causing the industry to experiment with new development methodologies, such as agile and community-based development. The challenges of provisioning and operating applications become greater in a world with much more application diversity, with applications composed from multiple components and services, and with nomadic and mobile uses.

The special characteristics of software coupled with its rising importance have raised the awareness of many challenges for government policies and laws as well, including ensuring an adequately large and trained workforce, a competitive and vibrant industry, adequate long-term innovation, conquering the digital divide, and struggling with some special issues in intellectual property.

There are substantial opportunities to understand better the challenges and opportunities of investing in, developing, marketing, selling, provisioning, operating, and using software, and to use this understanding to conceptualize better strategies for the evolution of software technology as well as business models that better serve suppliers, operators, and users. We hope that this book makes a contribution toward realizing this vision by summarizing the current (unfortunately limited) state of understanding.

Software is subject to a foundation of laws similar to (and sometimes governed by) the laws of physics, including fundamental theories of information, computability, and communication. In practical terms these laws are hardly limiting at all, especially in light of remarkable advances in electronics and photonics that will continue for some time. Like information—that other immaterial good that requires a technological support infrastructure—software has unprecedented versatility. The only really important limit is our collective imaginations. That, plus the immaturity of the technology and its markets, virtually guarantees that this book has not captured the possibilities beyond a limited vision based on what is obvious or predictable today. The possibilities are vast and largely unknowable.

While the wealth of understanding developed for other goods and services certainly offers many useful insights, the fundamentals of software economics in particular are yet to be fully conceptualized. Competitive market mechanisms, valuation and pricing models, investment recovery, risk management, insurance models, value chains, and many other issues should be reconsidered from first principles to do full justice to this unique economic good. Similarly, many of the legal and policy issues associated with software are in a state of flux and even outright confusion, often associated with incomplete understanding and yet-to-be-formulated theories.

Much remains to be done. Without fanfare, let's move expeditiously forward to expand our understanding of software. Together, let's make the technology and industry the best it can be.

Notes

Chapter 2

1. The dictionary defines *transducer* as a device that converts energy from one form to another. Strictly speaking, a sensor is a transducer, too (it converts from mechanical or optical energy to electrical); however, engineers generally reserve *transducer* for the conversion from electrical energy. The specific case of a transducer that converts to mechanical energy is an *actuator*.

2. The usage of these terms is somewhat variable and inconsistent. For example, *data* is also commonly applied to information, such as that acquired in a scientific experiment, that has been subject to minimum interpretation.

3. Information conveyed through touch, taste, smell, and equilibrium may be difficult (although not impossible) to represent digitally. The observation that most information can be represented by data and an understanding of the implications of this are generally attributed to Claude Shannon, the originator of information theory. He developed a powerful mathematical theory on the number of bits required to represent information as well as the capability of communication channels to convey it (Shannon and Weaver 1949). One of the classic results of this theory is that a collection of bits can serve as a representation of information in common forms with an arbitrary accuracy (as more bits are used) and no loss of generality.

4. In contrast, the form of representation is necessarily much more variable in an analog medium. For example, with magnetic tape as an analog storage medium, the way in which audio and video are represented are necessarily quite different. The video requires special synchronization pulses to distinguish the start and end of individual images, something not required for audio.

5. This terminology is often applied loosely in practice. For example, in a computer system, replicating a file might be called copying. Digital representations of analog media (like audio or video) might be replicated (making a replica of the digital representation) or copied (converted to analog, copied in analog form, and reconverted to digital). These nuances become extremely important in digital rights management (see chapter 8).

6. The material world, especially in IT, involves more than just atoms. Nonatomic particles like electrons and photons play an essential role also. A more appropriate metaphor might be particles versus bits.

7. Occasionally *software* has been used to denote information content (Shy 2001). For example, the available DVD movies might be called the "software for consumer video

equipment." This is confusing and is avoided here. Fortunately it seems to be disappearing from common usage.

8. In the past IBM has had considerable ambitions in the area of communication but more recently has deemphasized this. Examples include its acquisition of Rolm and Satellite Data Services in the 1970s and its development of its Global Network, which it subsequently divested to AT&T.

9. The distinction among the three technologies is somewhat less sharp. In reality, storage cannot work without a little communication (the bits need to flow to the storage medium) and communication cannot work without a little storage (the bits cannot be communicated in zero time). Processing cannot work without both a little storage (creation of intermediate results) and a little communication (moving bits from communication or storage to processing units and back).

10. The details are less important than the overall trend that this model predicts. Nonetheless, we present them here (see Messerschmitt 1999c). D_c is average waiting time for a Poisson arrival of requests and an independent exponentially distributed time to service each request and average service time D_s. For example, $u = 0.5$ results in a congestion-induced delay equal to the average service time. Of course, this specific model would not always be an accurate reflection of reality in all instances of congestion.

11. The ability to improve capacity through the addition of hardware ("scaling out") depends on the proper architecture of an application and its underlying infrastructure. This is discussed further in chapter 4.

12. Up to the mid-1990s communication through fiber was limited by improvements in the electronics to transmit and receive the bits, and thus doubled about every eighteen months. The innovation that circumvented this bottleneck was wavelength-division multiplexing (WDM), which allowed multiple streams of bits to be transmitted simultaneously on different wavelengths. This has increased the rate of improvement dramatically because it bypasses the electronics bottleneck.

13. This is a fundamental consequence of the observation that the radio spectrum has vastly less bandwidth than the optical spectrum, even as the latter is limited by the material properties of the glass that makes up fiber.

14. For example, increasing the maximum load capacity of a train likely decreases both fuel economy and maximum velocity.

15. The advance of magnetic and optical storage focuses on decreasing the area required for storage of each bit, allowing more bits to be stored on a given disk and also, along with advances in electronics, enabling faster transfer of bits in and out. Advances in fiber optics focus on increasing the transfer rate of bits through the fiber, which is equivalent to reducing the length of fiber occupied by each bit, because the bits always travel at the same velocity (a fraction of the speed of light).

16. The time value of money dictates that a return R occurring n years in the future has present value $R/(1 + r)^n$ for prevailing interest rate r. The discount factor $(1 + r)^n$ is smaller for earlier returns (smaller n), increasing the present value of the return.

17. The specific risks to be concerned about are outright failure to achieve the goal, a need to increase the investment to achieve the goal, or a delay in achieving the goal.

18. These three businesses were once largely captive to large vertically integrated firms. Industry maturity and market forces have favored specialization, so now they are largely separate firms (with some notable exceptions). Many of the largest equipment manufacturers, like IBM, Nortel, Lucent, Siemens, Philips, NEC, Sony, and many others, retain internal integrated circuit manufacturing. However, they purchase many chips from specialized integrated circuit manufacturers like Intel and Texas Instruments. Meanwhile, most of the newer equipment manufacturers (like CISCO) outsource their integrated circuit manufacturing, even chips they design themselves.

Chapter 3

1. Performance is an important aspect of software composition (see section 3.2.12): two separately fast components, when combined, can be very slow—a bit like two motors working against each other when coupled. The exact effect of composed components on overall performance is hard to predict accurately for complex software systems.

2. Another common terminology is calling both groups hackers but distinguishing between "white-hat" and "black-hat" hackers. *Black-hat hacker* is synonymous with *cracker* as used here.

3. The literature refers to these as S-type and E-type programs (following the classification of music into serious and entertainment classes), but we substitute these more descriptive names here.

Chapter 4

1. There are published statistics on the failure rate, but they are not cited here because they mask major gradations of failure (ranging from time and budget overruns to outright cancellation to deployment followed by abandonment) and wide variation in the causes of failure. "Failed" projects can also yield useful outcomes like experience or fragments of code later used in other projects.

2. *Extreme programming* (Beck 1999) was probably the first widely acknowledged agile process. At its heart, extreme programming requests a close feedback loop with the customer of the software being developed, development in rapid cycles that maintain a working system throughout, the hand-in-hand development of increments and corresponding tests, and work in pairs to minimize mistakes caused by oversight.

3. This is essentially the same observation that underlies Metcalf's law of network effects (see chapter 9).

4. Where subsystem composition is guided by architecture, those system properties that were successfully considered by the architect are achieved by construction rather than by observing randomly emerging composition properties. For example, a security architecture may put reliable trust classifications in place that prevent critical subsystems from relying on arbitrary other subsystems. Otherwise, following this example, the security of an overall system often is only as strong as its weakest link.

5. Fully effective encapsulation mandates that implementation details not be observable from the outside. While this is a desirable goal, in the extreme it is unattainable. Simply by running

tests against a module, or in the course of debugging during a module integration phase, a module will reveal results that allow a programmer to conclude properties of the module's implementation not stated in its module's abstraction.

6. Interfaces are the flip side (technically the *dual*) of an architect's global view of system properties. An interface determines the range of possible interactions between two modules interacting through that interface and thus narrows the viewpoint to strictly local properties. Architecture balances the views of local interaction and global properties by establishing module boundaries and regulating interaction across those boundaries through specified interfaces.

7. Sometimes *emergence* is used to denote unexpected or unwelcome properties that arise from composition, especially in large-scale systems where very large numbers of modules are composed. Here we use the term to emphasize desired more than unexpected or unwanted behaviors.

8. Bits cannot be moved on their own. What is actually moved are photons or electrons that encode the values of bits.

9. This is a simplification of a real facsimile machine, which will attempt to negotiate with the far-end facsimile machine, and failing that will give up.

10. There are infrastructure extensions to the Mac OS that allow it to run Windows programs, such as Connectix's Virtual PC for Mac or Lismore's Blue Label PowerEmulator. Assume this is not present, so that the portability issue is more interesting. Alternatively, assume this is not sufficient, as it presents suboptimal integration of user interface behavior, look, and feel.

11. People can and do write object code. This used to be much more common, before Moore's law reduced the critical need for performance. However, object code (or a representation very close called assembly language) is still written in performance-critical situations, like for example in the kernel of an operating system or in signal processing.

12. C has long held primacy for system programming tasks (like operating systems). C++ is an extension of C using object-oriented programming, a methodology that supports modularity by decomposing a program into interacting modules called objects. Java was developed more recently, primarily to support mobile code. New languages are arising all the time. For example, C# is a new language (based on C++) designed for the Microsoft .NET initiative.

13. In some cases, source code as well as object code may be distributed (see section 4.2.4).

14. Interpretation introduces runtime overhead that reduces performance, whereas the one-time compilation before distribution is not of concern. Languages that are normally interpreted include built-in operations that perform complex tasks in a single step, allowing an interpreter to efficiently map these operations to an efficient implementation. Languages designed to be compiled avoid such built-in complex operations and instead assume that they could be programmed using only primitive built-in operations and operations already programmed.

15. By monitoring the performance, the online optimizer can dynamically optimize critical parts of the program. Based on usage profiling, an online optimizer can recompile critical parts of the software using optimization techniques that would be prohibitively expensive in terms of time and memory requirements when applied to all the software. Since such a process can draw on actually observed system behavior at use time, interpreters combined with online

optimizing compilation technology can exceed the performance achieved by traditional (ahead-of-time) compilation.

16. There is nothing special about intermediate object code: one machine's native code can be another machine's intermediate object code. For instance, Digital developed a Pentium virtual machine called FX!32 (*White Book* 2002) that ran on Alpha processors. FX!32 used a combination of interpretation, just-in-time compilation, and profile-based online optimization to achieve impressive performance. At the time, several Windows applications, compiled to Pentium object code, ran faster on top of FX!32 on top of Alpha than on their native Pentium platforms.

17. A generalization of this checking approach is now attracting attention: *proof-carrying code*. The idea is to add enough auxiliary information to an object code so that a receiving platform can check that the code meets certain requirements. Such checking is, by construction, much cheaper than constructing the original proof: the auxiliary information guides the checker in finding a proof. If the checker finds a proof, then the validity of the proof rests only on the correctness of the checker itself, not on the trustworthiness of either the supplied code or the supplied auxiliary information.

18. Of course, what we would really like is a trustworthy system. However, within the realm of cost-effective commercial systems, security systems are never foolproof. Thus, it is better to admit that a system may be trusted out of necessity but is never completely trustworthy. This distinction becomes especially important in rights management (see chapter 8).

19. A build system takes care of maintaining a graph of configurations (of varying release status), including all information required to build the actual deliverables as needed. Industrial-strength build systems tend to apply extensive consistency checks, including automated runs of test suites, on every check-in of new code.

20. Some competing networking technologies like Frame Relay and Asynchronous Transfer Mode required that a new LAN infrastructure be deployed. By the time they rolled out, the Internet had become strongly established and was benefiting from the positive feedback of direct network effects.

21. In fairness to those designers, providing more addresses requires more address bits in the header of each packet, reducing network efficiency. Four billion sounds sufficient in a world with a population of about six billion, but in fact the administrative realities of allocating blocks of addresses to organizations result in many unused addresses, and many Internet addresses are associated with unattended devices rather than people. The telephone network is experiencing a similar problem with block allocation of area codes to areas of widely varying populations.

22. Not too much significance should be attached to this razor blade analogy because of two major differences. Razor use does not experience significant network effects, and both razors and blades are sold to the same consumers. In fact, we have not been able to identify a close analogy to client-server complementarity in the material world.

23. There are difficult technical issues to overcome in peer-to-peer as well. For example, many hosts have dynamically assigned network addresses to aid in the administration of address resources. This is not a problem with clients, which normally initiate requests, but it is an obstacle for peers and servers, which must be contacted. Static address assignment is feasible for servers but likely not for (a large number of) peers.

24. The data generated by a program that summarizes its past execution and is necessary for its future execution is called its *state*. A mobile agent thus embodies both code and state.

25. The network cloud already has considerable processing and storage resources. However, these resources support embedded software that operates the network, and they are not made available to applications directly.

26. Communication links require right-of-way, so they are a natural target for the utility model. It is not practical for operators, even large corporations, to obtain their own right-of-way for communication facilities. The sharing of these links with the provisioning of switches is a natural extension. Thus, it is to be expected that networking would adopt the utility model first.

Chapter 5

1. The version is split into major version x and minor version y, with the informal intention that minor versions are largely backward-compatible, whereas major versions require adjustment when deployed to replace an older major version.

2. Although a user's deliberate or inadvertent revealing of a password is beyond the control of the software supplier, the software can include heuristics to check password quality (Is it long enough? Is it in the dictionary? Does it include numbers as well as alphabetic characters?). The software can also maintain a history of previously used passwords and prevent the reuse of old passwords within some (long) time window.

3. A firewall can also be realized as software running on commodity hosts or within standard network routing equipment. Firewall software is also available to run on a single host (like a home desktop computer) to isolate that host from the network.

4. The AT&T Privacy Bird (⟨http://privacybird.com/⟩) is an Internet Explorer plug-in that translates P3P documents into easily understood text and can issue privacy warnings to the user.

5. The usual explanation for this is that the Internet arose from an academic and scholarly environment that was trusting of all users. A more accurate, second explanation is that keeping the network simple while adding capability at the endpoints makes the technology more flexible (this is called the "end-to-end principle" (SalTzer, Reed, and Clark 1984). A third argument is economic: security features should be an add-on because not all users and applications desire them.

6. Some approaches based on the secure server can ensure that a password is not revealed outside a secure enclave. Also, it is possible to check a password using equivalent information without knowing that password directly. Thus, it is possible (but arguably not the norm) to build fairly secure authentication techniques around passwords.

7. Note that the secret is provided by and thus is known to the authority, which is responsible for destroying it or not divulging it to others. There are many complications not dealt with here, such as how to recover from the loss of a secret.

8. Practical and secure authentication protocols are considerably more complex than our description here, which tries to convey the essence of the idea without getting into details. There are many subtleties to consider, and desiging these protocols is best left to an expert.

Chapter 6

1. The acronym for infrastructure service provider, ISP, is the same as for an Internet service provider but not to be confused with it. The Internet service provider is both an infrastructure service provider (providing backbone network access) and an application service provider (providing application services like e-mail and Web hosting).

2. The telephone industry has traditionally called telephony a service, and additional features such as call waiting value-added service features. In fact, telephony is both an application (it provides specific capabilities to end-users) and a service (there has typically been a service provider, who does provisioning and operation). As telephony is licensed as a software application based on a generic Internet infrastructure, it becomes clearer that telephony is an application that may or may not be provided as a service.

3. Software suppliers are themselves major customers for software. They may license modules to be incorporated into their own products, or they certainly purchase development tools (such as build systems or compilers). They also incorporate many standard business functions like sales and accounting that are supported by applications acquired from other firms.

4. If a software supplier targets original equipment manufacturers or service providers as exclusive customers, there is an opportunity to reduce development and support costs because the number of customers is smaller and the execution environment is much better controlled.

5. In the case of both material and information goods, suppliers have found ways to approximate use-based pricing without direct usage reporting. A common approach is to lease rather than sell, and base the rental charges on the time of possession. An automobile logs its distance traveled (today using software), and that log can be captured when the car is returned. Utility meters are often read by sending a worker to the physical premises.

6. This example is based on the American Institute of Certified Public Accountants Statement of Position (SOP) No. 98-1 (Luecke, Meeting, and Klingshirn 1999).

Chapter 7

1. Within the limit of supporting a very specific application, this strategy is more accurately described as relying less on infrastructure and instead building more capability into the application. The telecommunications industry definitely follows an infrastructure strategy at the level of right-of-way and facilities, which are shared over voice, data, and video networks.

2. In contrast, the telephone network uses a different transport mechanism called circuit switching that does guarantee delay but also fixes the bit rate and does not achieve statistical multiplexing (see chapter 9).

3. The telecommunications industry developed new networking technologies such as asynchronous transfer mode and frame relay, whereas the Internet arose from the interconnection and interoperability of local-area networking technologies such as Ethernet. The Internet eventually dominated because of the positive feedback of direct network effects and because of decades of government investment in experimentation and refinement.

4. When high-performance infrastructure exceeding the needs of most applications becomes widely deployed, this issue largely goes away. An alternative approach that may become more

prevalent in the future is for applications to request and be allocated resources that guarantee certain performance characteristics.

5. MIME stands for multipurpose Internet mail extensions (Internet Engineering Task Force draft standard/best current practice RFCs 2045–2049).

6. The advantage of HTTP in this case is that it penetrates corporate firewalls because so many users want to browse the Web. Groove thus shares files among users by translating them into HTTP.

7. See ⟨http://www.mp3licensing.com/⟩ for a description of license terms and conditions.

8. Preserving proper system functioning with the replacement or upgrade of a component is difficult to achieve, and this goal significantly restricts the opportunities for evolving both the system and a component. There are a number of ways to address this. One is to constrain components to preserve existing functionality even as they add new capabilities. An even more flexible approach is to allow different versions or variations of a component to be installed side-by-side, so that existing interactions can focus on the old version or variation even as future added system capabilities can exploit the added capabilities of the new one.

9. See Ueda (2001) for more discussion of these methodologies of synthesis and development and how they are related. Similar ideas arise in the natural sciences, although in the context of analysis and modeling rather than synthesis. The top-down approach to modeling is reductionism (the emphasis is on breaking the system into smaller pieces and understanding them individually), and the bottom-up approach is emergence (the emphasis is on explaining complex behaviors as emerging from composition of elementary entities and interactions).

10. While superficially similar to the module integration that a supplier would traditionally do, it is substantively different in that the component's implementation cannot be modified, except perhaps by its original supplier in response to problems or limitations encountered during assembly by its customers. Rather, the assembler must restrict itself to choosing built-in configuration options.

11. As in any supplier-customer relationship in software, defects discovered during component assembly may be repaired in maintenance releases, but new needs or requirements will have to wait for a new version (see section 5.1.2). Problems arising during the composition of two components obtained independently are an interesting intermediate case. Are these defects, or mismatches with evolving requirements?

12. Technically, it is essential to carefully distinguish those modules that a programmer conceived (embodied in source code) from those created dynamically at execution time (embodied as executing native code). The former are called *classes* and the latter *objects*. Each class must capture various configuration options as well as mechanisms to dynamically create objects. This distinction is equally relevant to components.

13. By requiring each level (except the top) to meet a duality criterion—that entities exist both in a composition at the higher level and in independent form—nine integrative levels constituting the human condition can be identified from fundamental particles through nation-states. This model displays an interesting parallel to the infrastructure layers in software (see section 7.1.3).

14. Although component frameworks superficially look like layers as described in section 7.2, the situation is more complex because component frameworks (unlike traditional layers)

actively call components layered above them. Component frameworks are a recursive generalization of the idea of separating applications from infrastructure.

15. This inherently high cost plus the network communication overhead is one reason for the continued factoring of Web services into internal components, since components can be efficient at a much finer granularity.

16. These environments were initially called E-Speak (Hewlett-Packard), Web Services (IBM and Microsoft), and Dynamic Services (Oracle). The generic term *Web services* has now been adopted by all suppliers.

Chapter 8

1. While the challenge that anything that reaches the ears or eyes of a human could be recaptured digitally is fundamental because humans cannot be modified for technological or business convenience, the challenge of identical computers is not fundamental. For example, each piece of computer hardware could encapsulate a unique secret key and run only appropriately encrypted object code.

2. For detailed information on U.S. laws relating to computer security and crime, see ⟨http://www.cybercrime.gov/⟩.

3. The Federal Trade Commission's initiatives in consumer privacy are described in depth at ⟨http://www.ftc.gov/privacy⟩.

4. Full information on the safe harbor principles for the protection of privacy for European citizens in dealing with U.S. companies can be found at ⟨http://www.export.gov/safeharbor⟩.

5. Mergers are prohibited if their effect "may be substantially to lessen competition, or to tend to create a monopoly" (15 U.S.C. Section 18, 1988), if they constitute a "contract, combination or conspiracy in restraint of trade" (15 U.S.C. Section 1, 1988), or if they constitute an "unfair method of competition" (15 U.S.C. Section 45, 1988). The merger guidelines referred to are available at ⟨http://www.ftc.gov/bc/docs/horizmer.htm⟩.

6. The standard guidelines for acceptable collaboration among competitors from the U.S. Department of Justice and Federal Trade Commission are available at ⟨http://www.ftc.gov/os/2000/04/ftcdojguidelines.pdf⟩.

7. For further details on IBM Research's initiatives for working with customers, see ⟨http://*www.research.ibm.com/about/work_customers.shtml*⟩. The IBM Institute for Advanced Commerce is described at ⟨http://www.research.ibm.com/iac/⟩.

Chapter 9

1. A biological ecosystem is an oft-used and reasonably good analogy because its dynamics depend on a complex mix of complementary and competitive relationships among all organisms. Like the software industry, pairs of organisms often share complementary and competitive relationships at the same time. For example, a parasite depends on its host but also detracts from it.

2. If the prevailing interest rate is r per unit time, then revenue (or cost) incurred at a future time t is discounted by $\dfrac{1}{(1+r)^t}$.

3. From a security perspective, this is potentially a way to spread viruses. This can be prevented by attaching digital signatures from the original (trusted) supplier and always verifying those signatures before executing code obtained from any party (see section 5.4.6).

4. The NET Framework is an example of a platform that supports side-by-side installation of multiple versions of a component.

5. To be sensible, this definition of pricing nondiscrimination requires referencing "customer" to some common unit of use, like individual user or an e-commerce transaction. It wouldn't, for example, make sense to compare the gross margins of a sale to a large organization against an individual user.

6. The difference is that in the software field the whole point of versioning is for customers to select from among a set of product variants based on their willingness to pay. Typically, only one software version is sold at a time, although there may be older versions still in use.

7. This supplier strategy suggests that the complaints of airline customers about coach class are justified; in part, coach class must be unpleasant enough that less price-sensitive customers would not be tempted to fly coach.

8. This is a modern view of general-purpose computers. However, in the early days of computing, competing architectures were advocated that strongly separated programs from the data those programs manipulated. Once such "Harvard architecture" is still widely used in special-purpose computers, such as those for digital signal processing.

9. The information theory presented by Shannon and Weaver (1949) quantifies this statement. It asserts that the numerical "amount" of information is determined by its entropy. The entropy of unexpected outcomes is greater than the entropy of expected outcomes. For example, if you expect that a weighted coin when tossed will come up tails 99 percent of the time, then an actual outcome of a tail conveys little information, whereas a surprising outcome of a head conveys much more information.

Glossary

abstraction.   *See* **module.**

access control.   *See* **security.**

accountability.   In security, the means to impose penalties for violation of commitments. This requires a combination of technological mechanisms (such as the digital signature) to provide evidence of commitment and the legal means to enforce them. A *digital signature* attached to a piece of information, based on that information plus a secret, establishes that the signing entity possessed both the information and the secret, and that neither the information nor the signature was subsequently modified. An entity having created a digital signature is said to have *signed* that information.

action.   *See* **module.**

administration.   *See* **operations.**

admission control.   *See* **statistical multiplexing.**

agile development.   *See* **development.**

algorithm.   A finite sequence of steps that accomplishes some prescribed result or task. Software programs **implement** an algorithm.

analog.   *See* **information.**

analysis.   A set of activities in which the basic capabilities, functionality, and features and means of interaction between a software system and its users and other software systems are defined and refined based on user input, feedback, and experimentation. The outcome is a set of **requirements** (functional and performance) that are the starting point for **development.**

anonymous identity.   *See* **identity.**

anticircumvention.   See **rights management.**

antitrust.   A policy, regulations, and legal apparatus intended to ensure vigorous competition in an industry in the interest of consumers.

application.   *See* **software.**

application logic.   *See* **client-server.**

application programming interface (API).   An **interface** that is well documented and supports a broad class of **module** extensions. Despite its name, it does not apply exclusively to **applications.** An API (or other interface) is **open** when it is available for use without intellectual property restrictions or prior business arrangement.

application server.   **Infrastructure software** to host **components** that implement the **application logic** part of **distributed** *applications* such as **enterprise** or **e-commerce applications**. Other partitions of an application include the presentation logic hosted on a Web server, and the storage logic and actual data hosted on a database server (or *database management system*).

application service provider (ASP).   *See* **services**.

architecture.   An overall plan, as the first stage of implementation, for a software system. It includes a plan for *decomposition* (splitting up) into **modules**, a plan for the functionality of each module, and a plan for how those modules interact. The decomposition is often *hierarchical*, meaning modules are themselves decomposed. Notable examples include **client-server computing** and **layering**.

asymmetric encryption.   *See* **cryptography**.

atomic.   Cannot be subdivided; must be taken as a whole or not at all.

authentication.   Establishing and verifying the identity of some entity (e.g., **user** or **host**), especially over a **network**. Commonly based on knowledge of a secret (e.g., *password*, which is a secret created by the user), possession of a unique artifact (e.g., *smartcard*, a card containing a microprocessor and storage and, for this purpose, including an *encapsulated secret*), or physical characteristic like a fingerprint (*biometric authentication*). Authentication by secret can be accomplished without revealing the secret by challenging the entity to perform some task requiring knowledge of the secret (called a *challenge-response protocol*).

availability.   *See* **reliability**.

biometrics.   *See* **authentication**.

bundle.   A basket of goods and services packaged and sold as a unit.

business consultant.   *See* **consultant**.

business process.   *See* **process**.

capacity.   *See* **performance**.

capitalization accounting.   That portion of the cost of acquiring **software** that is treated as an asset to be depreciated over time rather than as an *immediate expense*.

challenge-response protocol.   *See* **authentication**.

ciphertext.   *See* **cryptography**.

class.   *See* **object-oriented programming**.

client.   *See* **client-server**.

client-server.   An **architecture** for distributed computing that mixes the best features of **time-sharing** and the personal computer. The application is partitioned onto a set of *clients* (each a desktop or personal computer dedicated to one **user**) and one or more **servers** (high-performance computers supporting many clients). The client emphasizes the *presentation* (that portion of an **application** that emphasizes presenting information to and gathering information from the user through a **user interface**), and the servers emphasize *application logic* (deciding what to do next). In a three-tier client-server architecture, the servers are further differentiated into those that support application logic and those that support data management. Client-server is distinguished from *peer-to-peer*, where peers (typically desktop computers) symmetrically interact with other peers. An example of client-server is the **Web; Web**

services utilize a hybrid architecture in which clients interact with servers, and servers assume a dual role as peers interacting with one another.

cloud. A term describing **infrastructure** that emphasizes what **services** are offered and ignores or deemphasizes the **implementation** detail. It is especially common to speak of a **network** cloud.

code. Any **digital representation** of **information** or **software** in terms of a discrete alphabet. In the case of information or software **object code**, the alphabet is typically bits or bytes (collections of eight bits), and in the case of software **source code**, it is usually the English alphabet and punctuation so as to be human-readable.

cohesion. *See* **module.**

common gateway interchange (CGI). *See* **Web.**

common object-request broker architecture (CORBA). *See* **object-request broker.**

communication. *See* **network.**

community development. *See* **development.**

compiler. *See* **processing.**

complementarity. *See* **composition.**

component. Module of *hardware* or **software** capability designed independently of any specific *system* context, intended to be used "as is" in many contexts, and supporting *composition* with other components. Components are typically purchased from a supplier and integrated into a design. Within a **development** organization, modules developed for one project may be *reused* in other projects, where modification is typically allowed. *Handcrafted* modules are implemented and used once for a single project.

composition. As an alternative to **decomposition** as a methodology for defining architecture, a system is assembled by the **integration** of existing **modules.** If these existing modules obey certain strong properties, they are called **components.** To be composable, two modules must be *interoperable* (able to successfully exchange meaningful messages to coordinate their interaction) and *complementary* (have functionality that allows meaningful and useful new properties to *emerge* from their integration).

computer. *Equipment* supporting the execution of **software** and storage of **data,** complemented by a **network** that allows computers to share data. Types of computers include a *mainframe* computer (a relatively expensive computer that emphasizes the high-performance processing of large amounts of information), a *time-sharing* computer, more recently called a *server* (a moderately priced computer shared by multiple users that allows them to interact with applications and collaborate with one another), and a *personal computer* (a relatively inexpensive computer normally dedicated to a single **user,** often participating as a **client** in a **client-server architecture**). A *host* is any computer that has Internet access and participates in **distributed** applications.

concurrent. Overlapped in time, usually applied to programs whose **execution** is overlapped in time while interacting among themselves.

confidentiality. *See* **security.**

configuration. Choosing from among a predefined set of parameters or options in a software **distribution** as part of software **deployment.**

congestion. *See* **statistical multiplexing.**

consultant. An outside individual or organization that provides advice or services related to the opportunities and needs of a vertical industry (*industry consultant*) or individual firm (*business consultant*).

copy protection. *See* **rights management.**

copyright. *See* **intellectual property.**

coupling. *See* **module.**

cracker. A person intent on evasion of **security policies** for personal gain or disruption. Distinguished from a *hacker*, who takes satisfaction in overcoming perceived limits through technical acumen.

cryptography. A body of techniques widely used in **security** based on the mathematics of hard-to-compute problems. *Encryption* is an *algorithm* that transforms a *plaintext* and an encryption *key* into a form (the *ciphertext*) that is meaningless without knowledge of a decryption key. There are two forms: *symmetric* (same key used for encryption and decryption) and *asymmetric* (different keys that are coordinated, but one cannot be inferred from the other). *Escrowed encryption* creates a class of **user** called an *authority* who has conditional access to encrypted information under exceptional conditions.

data. *See* **information.**

database management system (DBMS). **Infrastructure software** specializing in the capture, management, organization, and accessing of large amounts of related information.

de facto standard. *See* **standard.**

de jure standard. *See* **standard.**

decomposition. *See* **architecture.**

defect. *See* **reliability.**

delay. *See* **performance.**

denial-of-service attack. *See* **security.**

deployment. *See* **distribution.**

design. Starting with the results of analysis, creating a concrete plan for implementation. **Software design** is the first phase of **implementation,** including establishing an **architecture** and refinement of that architecture into a detailed plan and **requirements** for individual modules. In the course of designing, detailed scenario capture, requirement, and specification documents are developed to guide programming activities. The esthetic and interactive capabilities and features of the **software** in context must also be designed, including the *user interface* (encompassing details of how software captures inputs from and presents results to users), *interaction design* (how the user interacts with the software in complex ways to achieve higher-level purposes), *graphics design* (the pictorial and artistic presentation of information on a screen), and *industrial design* (the physical layout and properties of a material artifact such as an **information appliance**).

development. The set of organizational activities and processes surrounding the creation of a software artifact ready for **provisioning** and **operations.** The *waterfall* model decomposes development into a set of distinct activities. Development includes defining specific requirements (e.g., functionality, performance), defining an **architecture,** *implementation* (programming of *modules* to realize functionality promised at **interfaces**), *testing* (trying out in the intended **environment** to check for *fidelity* with requirements and for **defects**), and documentation. During provisioning and operations, developers continue to *maintain* the software (repair defects) and **upgrade** the software to improve it and accommodate changing requirements. The *spiral process* model defines how those activities can be performed iteratively, emphasizing how the complementary and conflicting needs of various stakeholders are satisfied. *Agile processes* emphasize ways in which evolving needs can be satisfied. In *community-based development*, a community of interested volunteer programmers has access to source code and governance mechanisms to choose and incorporate contributed improvements into a coherent software distribution. An example is *open-source* **software**, a specific set of licensing terms and conditions (defined and trademarked by the Open Source Initiative).

digital. *See* **information.**

digital certificate. A credential provided by a *certificate authority* to an entity (e.g., **host,** user) along with a secret to aid in that entity's **authentication.** The certificate includes identity information and corroboration **information** for the secret, and is **signed** by the certificate authority. Another party performing an authentication can use a certificate to validate the identity of the entity, assuming it trusts the authority, using a **challenge-response protocol.** An entire system of authentication based on certificates and certificate authorities is called a *public key infrastructure* (PKI).

digital signature. *See* **accountability.**

direct network effects. *See* **network effects.**

directory. *See* **location.**

distributed computing. A style of computing based on software that is partitioned across two or more **hosts** and having functionality based on interactions among those partitions involving communication across a network.

distribution. The act of conveying a **software** distribution to its eventual point of **provisioning** and **operations**, usually by download over a **network** or transport of a material **storage** medium. *Deployment* customizes a software distribution (an application or a component) for a particular platform (e.g., the configuration of a data-processing component to match a corporation's specific database schemas). *Installation* is the step of placing a deployed software distribution on a particular host, enabling its execution and use. If software is downloaded on demand, installation may be an automatic step performed after download and before use.

e-commerce applications. *See* **enterprise applications.**

economies of scale. In economics, on the supply side, describes a situation where the marginal unit cost of production is below average cost (strongly characteristic of **software**), and on the demand side, a situation when unit value increases with market share because of **network effects** (offset by declining demand).

embedded. *See* **software.**

emergence. *See* **composition.**

encapsulated. *See* **module.**

encryption. *See* **cryptography.**

enterprise applications. **Software applications** that serve end-to-end **business processes** in an organization. Major categories include enterprise resource planning (ERP), enterprise asset management (EAM), and customer relationship management (CRM). Increasingly, these are extended to suppliers and customers, creating *e-commerce applications.*

environment. *See* **release.**

equipment. A **bundle** of *hardware* and **software** that is manufactured and sold as a unit. Hardware includes those capabilities of **information technology** based on material devices, such as a **processor** (supports the execution of a program), **storage** (supports the shift of data from now to the future), or **network** (supports the shift of data from here to there).

escrowed encryption. *See* **cryptography.**

execution. *See* **processing.**

expense accounting. *See* **capitalization accounting.**

extranet. *See* **network.**

federation. Allowing heterogeneous and separately administered *systems* to be aggregated and giving them the appearance of homogeneity, often by deploying a **middleware layer.**

fidelity. *See* **reliability.**

firewall. **Equipment** placed in a **network** at boundaries of a protected enclave and aiding security by enforcing a set of **policies,** such as which **users** can access resources or which **applications** can communicate outside the enclave.

framework. Configurable and extensible **architecture** designed for multiple uses within a category of **applications. Components** and frameworks are complementary units of multiple use.

graphics. *See* **design.**

graphics design. *See* **design.**

hacker. *See* **cracker.**

handcrafted. *See* **component.**

hardware. *See* **equipment.**

hierarchy. *See* **architecture.**

host. *See* **computer.**

hypertext transfer protocol (HTTP). *See* **Web.**

identity. **Information** about a **user** (or other entity, like a **host** or **component**), including name and other personal information. **Authentication** allows an identity to be verified. An *anonymous identity* distinguishes an entity from all others without supplying any personal information and is useful in observing behavior without an invasion of **privacy.**

implementation. *See* **development.**

independent software vendor (ISV). A firm that is primarily a **supplier** that *licenses software* to others, as distinct from a **software developer** within an end-user organization or an **equipment** supplier that also develops its own **embedded** software.

indirect network effects. *See* **network effects.**

industrial design. *See* **design.**

industry consultant. *See* consultant.

information.   From a **user** perspective, recognizable patterns conveyed by a material medium (e.g., sound, light) that inform or influence us in some way, such as contributing to our knowledge or humor or emotion, or that influence us to take action. Within **information technology**, information comprises recognizable patterns represented by *data* (a finite collection of bits, each bit or binary digit assuming the value 0 or 1). *Digital information* is represented by a finite set of discrete values (usually, bits), whereas *analog information* is represented by continuous physical quantities (e.g., air pressure or voltage).

information appliance.   An **integrated bundle** of **hardware** and **software** that provides a single **application**.

information technology (IT).   *Technology* encompasses knowledge on changing nature to accommodate human needs and wants; human artifacts (not natural phenomena) that make use of these ideas and knowledge; processes and infrastructure for acquiring that knowledge; and designing, manufacturing, operating, and repairing those artifacts. Information technology is dedicated to capturing, manipulating, storing, communicating, and accessing **digital information**.

infrastructure. *See* **software**.

infrastructure service provider (ISP). *See* **services**.

installation. See **distribution**.

instruction set. See **processing**.

integrated development environment (IDE). *See* **tools**.

integration.   Making **modules** work together properly through **composition**, **testing**, and *refinement*. Within *software* **development**, integration turns a collection of module implementations into a *software* **release**. Integration of software from different **suppliers** is an important part of **provisioning**, and thus an independent firm that performs provisioning is sometimes called a *system integrator*.

intellectual property.   A set of government-sanctioned property rights granting ownership privileges to the creators of immaterial goods like **information** and **software**. Specific rights include the *trademark* (right to exclusive use of a name or symbol), *trade secret* (right to prevent the theft of proprietary information through malfeasance), *patent* (exclusive right to exploit a useful and novel idea), and *copyright* (right to control the replication and distribution of a creative work).

interaction design. *See* **design**.

interface. *See* **module**.

internet. *See* **network**.

internet inter-orb protocol (IIOP). *See* **object-request broker**.

internet protocol (IP). *See* **network**.

interoperability. *See* **composition**.

interpreter. *See* **processing**.

intranet. *See* **network**.

just-in-time compiler. *See* **portability**.

key.   *See* **cryptography.**

layering.   A specific **architecture** (usually represented diagrammatically as horizontal layers) in which **modules** are ordered and each module interacts primarily or exclusively with adjacent modules. As a layered industry organization for infrastructure (called a horizontal structure by economists), each firm supplies a layer of the infrastructure serving a comprehensive set of applications, depending on complementary layers from other suppliers for a total solution. This is distinct from a *stovepipe* (called a vertical structure by economists), in which each firm segments the market and provides a complete solution.

license.   A grant of the right to use **intellectual property,** accompanied by an agreement spelling out detailed terms and conditions (including payment).

local-area network (LAN).   *See* **network.**

location.   Where something **(host, module, object)** can be found preparatory to interacting with it. In **software,** location is usually specified in logical (host or topological connection point to a **network**) rather than geographic terms. Location **services** assist in locating things. One common location service is a *directory,* which provides the relations between names and locations. A *name* is a logical label that uniquely distinguishes one entity from another within a specified scope.

lock-in.   Competitive advantage of a **supplier,** when an existing customer will incur excess *switching costs* in choosing an alternative supplier.

loss.   *See* **performance.**

mainframe.   *See* **computer.**

maintenance.   *See* **development.**

management.   The set of processes and decision mechanisms required to bring *software* through the multiple stages from initial concept to use.

metastandard.   *See* **standard.**

middleware.   *Infrastructure* **software** layered on a **network** and **operating system** that provides *value-added services* to *applications.*

mobile code.   *See* **portability.**

mobility.   The ability of a *user* to make transparent use of an **application** while moving geographically. *Nomadicity* is transparent use of an application from any of a variety of fixed geographic locations.

module.   In an **architecture,** the basic unit of functionality, including an interface and an internal implementation. The *interface* specifies the *actions* (specific **atomic** and parameterized requests for something to be done) offered to other modules, and the **implementation** realizes those actions, including (if necessary) invoking actions of other modules. Interfaces also specify *protocols,* which are sequences of actions to accomplish higher-level nonatomic tasks. It is desirable for interfaces to be *abstract* (hiding unnecessary detail) and for the implementation to be *encapsulated* (making internal implementation details invisible and untouchable). Different modules should display weak *coupling* (their functions should be weakly related so they can be implemented largely independently) and strong *cohesion* (a module's distinct internal functions should be interrelated and dependent), although the latter is less important because its absence is an opportunity for **hierarchical decomposition.**

Moore's law.   The observation and expectation that several material **technologies** (**processing**, **storage**, and **communication**) will improve exponentially over time in performance per unit cost, often parameterized by the time required for a doubling of performance per unit cost.

name.   *See* **location.**

native object code.   *See* **processing.**

network.   Constructed from *communication* links and switches, it conveys packets from one node (**computer** or **information appliance**) to another. A *packet* is a collection of data that is conveyed as a unit through the network. A *switch* routes a packet from one incoming link to the appropriate outgoing link to get it closer to its destination. A *local-area network* (LAN) is a network designed to be used within a building or narrow geographic reach. An *internet* is a set of *open standards* and *equipment* and *software* complying with those standards that realizes a network composed of numerous underlying communication and networking technologies, distinguished by its ability to subsume existing and new LAN technologies for network access. Widely used internet standards define protocol *layers*, including the *internet protocol* (IP; conveys packets unreliably and without any particular order from one host to another) and the *transmission control protocol* (TCP; layered on IP, it reliably transports an ordered stream of bytes). The *Internet* is a large public network utilizing internet technologies; an *intranet* is a private restricted-access network based on internet technologies; and an *extranet* extends an intranet to suppliers and partners.

network effects.   Also called a *network externality*, an economic characteristic of goods or services for which the value (willingness to pay) to a user or adopter depends on the number of other users or adopters without a compensating payment. The effects may be positive (value increases with adopters, like a *network*) or negative (value decreases with adopters, like *congestion*). Network effects may be *direct* (value of each instance of the good or service is directly affected by other instances) or *indirect* (value is affected by the quantity of some complementary commodity).

networked computing.   *See* **distributed computing.**

nomadicity.   *See* **mobility.**

object.   *See* **object-oriented programming.**

object code.   *See* **processing.**

object-oriented programming (OOP).   A style of programming and set of languages and tools that emphasize and support **modularity.** (OOP has no particular relation to **object code.**) A program consists of a set of *objects* (another term for **module**) that invoke methods (another term for **actions**) on one another. Objects are instances of *classes*, which define the common properties among a set of similar objects. Classes form inheritance hierarchies. OOP is increasingly being subsumed by the more disciplined **component** methodologies.

object-request broker (ORB).   An **infrastructure layer** supporting **distributed object-oriented programs.** *Common object-request broker architecture* (CORBA) is a **reference model** and set of **interface** *standards* and **services** defining an ORB emanating from the Object Management Group (OMG). A particularly significant CORBA standard is the *internet inter-orb protocol* (IIOP), which allows **objects** to invoke *actions* on other objects across the network.

open standard.   *See* **standard; application programming interface.**

open-closed principle.   Open to extension, closed to change. With the goal of maintaining **composability** with other existing **modules** while also advancing, the principle attempts to ensure that any enhancements do not affect other modules currently using an **interface**.

open-source.   *See* **development.**

operating system.   *Infrastructure* **software** bundled with every **computer** (and other **equipment**, including an **information appliance**) that provides an **abstract environment** with a rich set of **services** to programs. It also supports multiple **concurrent** programs and dynamically allocates resources (e.g., **processing, memory, storage, network** *access*) to those programs.

operations.   Undertaken by a human organization, following **provisioning** and while **software** is employed by **users**; keeping the software and supporting **equipment** running in the face of evolving user and environmental needs (particularly **performance** and **security** threats); reporting *defects* and installation of new **releases**; maintaining vigilance for and responses to security threats; and supporting users. Includes functions typically called *system administration* (**installation, maintenance,** and **configuration**), helpdesk, and *systems management* (the operational parallel to provisioning).

overprovisioning.   *See* **statistical multiplexing.**

packet   *See* **network.**

password.   *See* **authentication.**

patch.   *See* **release.**

patent.   *See* **intellectual property.**

path-dependent effects.   In economics, the influence of accumulated past investments and management decisions on current circumstances, as distinct from a hypothetical situation that might result from starting from scratch.

peer-to-peer.   *See* **client-server.**

performance.   Metrics measuring aspects of speed for **software** and its **environment.** *Throughput* is a measure of what is accomplished per unit time, in terms of processing tasks or data stored, retrieved, or communicated. *Capacity* is the ideal throughput of a resource (**processing, storage,** or **communication**) if fully utilized at all times. *Utilization* is the actual throughput as a fraction of capacity (a number between 0 and 1). *Delay* is a measure of the time elapsing between when an action is requested and when it is completed in its entirety. An extreme form of delay is *loss*, when an action is not completed soon enough to be of use.

pervasive computing.   Computing and software embedded into many everyday products, scattered pervasively in our environment, and **networked** to enable those products to interact to provide new capabilities.

plaintext.   *See* **cryptography.**

platform.   A set of *infrastructure* **equipment** and **software** that is widely deployed and assumed available to support a given *software* **distribution** (possibly with complementary software that provides an **environment** for the distribution).

policy.   A plan or course of action guiding individuals, organizations, or governments. In computing, a prescribed set of actions or restrictions on actions that plays an important role in **security** and **system administration.**

portability. Describes a *software* **distribution** that can successfully execute with full functionality on different **platforms**. This requires portable *execution* (ability to run on processors with different instruction sets, enabled by a *virtual machine*) and an *environment* that appears to the program to be the same on each platform. The virtual machine is an **interpreter** (layered on the **operating system**) for the **object code** instruction set assumed within the distribution. It is also possible to **compile** that object code into the **native** *instruction set* of the **processor** the first time the software is executed using a *just-in-time compiler*. Alternatively, compilation can be performed at the time of **deployment** or **installation**. Portable software supports *mobile code*, in which software is **distributed** by dynamically downloading and executing without requiring a manual installation step.

presentation. *See* **client-server**.

price. In economics, what is charged for a product or service. *Price discrimination* occurs when the difference between price and marginal cost is different for different customers. One form of price discrimination is *versioning*, a strategy of providing distinct versions (or *variants*) of a product at different prices. *Value pricing* emphasizes willingness to pay rather than supplier cost, and requires price discrimination. A common approximation to value pricing is *usage-based pricing* (based on the number of users, the time they use the software, the payment per use, the number and performance of processors executing the software, and so on). Another distinction is between fixed payments for each **upgrade** or recurring *subscription* payments.

price discrimination. *See* **price**.

privacy. The ability of a user to share personal information for legitimate purposes while maintaining control over its dissemination to third parties.

process. A sequence of steps executed over and over to achieve some high-level ongoing need. A *business process* starts with material and various resources (e.g., workers, space) and ends with a product or service for customers. In an **operating system**, a process is an **abstract** *environment* for execution of a single **software** *program*.

processing. One of three supporting **information technologies**, it modifies **digital** *information* under control of **software** during the **execution** of that software. A *processor* has a defined *instruction set* (list of **atomic** *actions* the processor is prepared to execute on behalf of the program). A program expressed in terms of this instruction set is called **native object code**. **Source code** can be translated into this native object code in one stage or more than one stage (creating intermediate forms of object code using different instruction sets). A *compiler* does a one-time translation of source code to object code, or the source code (or intermediate object code) can be directly executed on the fly by an *interpreter*.

protocol. *See* **module**.

prototype. A *software* **implementation** that is not yet a **distribution**; that is, it demonstrates features and capabilities with sufficient **fidelity** for experimentation and feedback but is not ready for **provisioning** and **operations** in a production environment.

provisioning. Undertaken by a human organization after **development** and before **operations**, all the steps needed to acquire, integrate, and test software within its future operational context. Includes planning, training future operators and users, and taking into account human, organizational, and technological elements of the future operational context.

public key infrastructure (PKI). *See* **digital certificate**.

quality of service (QOS). For a **service provider, performance** *objectives* or guarantees that can be configured by appropriate resource allocations. A *service-level agreement* (SLA) between provider and customer lays out promises for QOS.

reference model. *See* **standard.**

release. A body of software tested and certified by the **developer** to be ready for **provisioning, operations,** and *use* within a specified **environment** (hardware and software assumed to be present, including a **platform** and any other complementary software). Typically, sequential *releases* are offered for a single software product, each repairing defects, adding functionality, and tracking changing needs. A *patch* provides urgent repair of defects, a *service release* provides a coherent collection of patches, and a new **version** (or *upgrade*) makes changes in intended functionality to add new features or improve old ones. Typically, only the latest release is **licensed** to new customers, but older releases may continue to be **maintained.**

reliability. A measure of how likely it is that software will be usable in the manner intended. System *reliability* refers to the proper operation of all elements of a system with one another (application and infrastructure software, equipment, network), and **software** *reliability* refers to the likelihood of *defects* (flaws in programming) interfering with the intended usage of the software only in its user context. Defects are distinguished from *fidelity*, or the correspondence of the intended functionality with the needs of users. A measure of system reliability is *availability*, the fraction of time the system is executing and can be used.

replication. Making another instance of **digital information** identical to the original in every way by copying the **representation** of that information. Distinct from *copying*, in which the original may not be preserved in all respects, as is characteristic of **analog information.** Copying and replication usually mean the same for digital information. However, there are "lossy" copying techniques that trade perfect reproduction for other properties, such as space or time savings: image encoding techniques such as JPEG are an example.

representation. A collection of **data** that takes the place of **information** within the **information technologies,** such that the information can later be recovered. A representation includes specific data formats for recognizable patterns in the information, and is a common target of **standards.**

requirements. A specific plan for capabilities and features of **software** based on the needs of **users** or **operators.** Requirements can be *satisfaction-driven* (emphasizing the perceptual needs and satisfaction of users or operators) or *specification-driven* (based on a set of objective metrics), or some combination. *See also* **analysis.**

research. Seeking new knowledge, understanding, or technology through thought, experiment, or theory. *Basic research* (*Bohr's quadrant*) emphasizes long-term or high-risk advances, fundamental understanding, and explanatory modeling and theory rather than complementarity to current technology or specific needs. *Applied research* (*Edison's quadrant*) emphasizes application and end-user needs and requirements, and defines, prototypes, and experiments with new opportunities in typical use contexts with complementarity to existing information technologies. *Pasteur's quadrant* combines the two by considering needs and uses in part as a stimulant for uncovering new knowledge or understanding.

reuse. *See* **component.**

rights management. Technology and processes to enforce the terms, conditions, and rights of ownership in **information** or **software** imparted by **license** agreements and **copyright** laws.

One technological mechanism is *copy protection*, which allows the user access to information or software while attempting to prevent **replication** and **distribution** to third parties, often making use of a **trusted system**. Since copy protection cannot be foolproof, *anticircumvention* regulations or laws prohibit the dissemination of devices and software that permit unauthorized replication. *Watermarks* attempt to identify the ownership or licensee for a replica by embedding within the *representation* imperceptible or inconsequential changes.

satisfaction-driven. *See* **requirements.**

scalability. A characteristic of a software architecture that the cost of the supporting equipment required to expand use increases linearly (or less than linearly) with that use.

security. A set of safeguards to prevent unauthorized or damaging attacks, such as theft, destruction, or modification of **information**, theft of **services**, denial of services to others by excessive use (**denial-of-service attack**), forgery, or mimicry. Security is based on the technological and operational enforcement of a defined set of *security* **policies.** These policies can take many forms, such as *access control* (right to use certain resources), *confidentiality* (the ability to use or communicate information without its being usable by others), and **privacy.** Regarding **users,** policies are typically based on social criteria such as organizational role and trust.

server. *See* **computer.**

service provider. *See* **services.**

service release. *See* **release.**

service-level agreement (SLA). *See* **quality of service (QOS).**

services. Software services are features and capabilities based on **equipment** and **software** accessed by invoking **actions** over a network or from locally executing software, often shared by multiple applications or multiple users. **Provisioning** and **operations** of the facilities, equipment, and software supporting services may by undertaken by an independent organization called a *service provider.* Like software itself, providers can be divided into *infrastructure service providers* (ISPs) and *application service providers* (ASPs).

signature. *See* **accountability.**

signing. *See* **accountability.**

smartcard. *See* **authentication.**

software. Comprises a set of instructions directing the actions of a *processor* and represented as either **source code** (most suitable for writing or reading by humans) or **object code** (suitable for direct processor execution). **Application** *software* meets the specialized needs of users, groups, or organizations in their domains of interest and activity, and **infrastructure** *software* provides common **services** utilized by a range of applications. *Embedded software* is bundled with equipment and controls an integral portion of its functionality, and **component** *software* is designed to be composed into a number of software programs.

software design. *See* **design.**

source code. *See* **processing.**

specification-driven. *See* **requirements.**

spiral model. *See* **development.**

standard. A well-documented and complete specification available to anybody to **implement.** A standard is *open* when available to all without need for a prior business relationship and unencumbered by **intellectual property** *restrictions*. Standards can be the outcome of an explicit standardization process, or arise from market forces (*de facto standard*), or be mandated by some governmental or regulatory authority (*de jure standard*). Common targets of standardization include **information representations**, a partial architecture (**reference model**), and **interfaces**. A *metastandard* defines a language to describe something rather than describing that something directly.

statistical multiplexing.   A rationale for the sharing of resources arising from the smoothing of load variation when a single resource (**processor** or **communication link**) is shared by many users. A side effect is *congestion*, or temporary oversubscription of the resource resulting in excess **loss** or **delay**. Congestion can be mitigated by many means, such as *congestion control* (controlling the load presented by its source), *admission control* (selectively denying new uses), *overprovisioning* (deliberately provisioning substantially more resources than needed), or *congestion* **pricing** (charging a premium price conditionally during periods of congestion).

storage.   One of three supporting information technologies, it conveys digital information from one time to another.

stovepipe.   *See* **layering**.

subscription.   *See* **price**.

superdistribution.   Exploiting the self-aware property of **software**, the ability to extract payments for its use regardless of how it is **distributed** (even user to user).

supplier.   A firm or other organization that **licenses** *a* **software distribution** or sells **equipment** or **information appliance** to others; generally divided into *application suppliers* and *infrastructure suppliers*.

switch.   *See* **network**.

switching costs.   *See* **lock-in**.

symmetric encryption.   *See* **cryptography**.

system.   An *integrated* set of interacting (typically heterogeneous) *modules* (which can themselves be **hardware, software**, and **equipment**) realizing higher purposes. An **open** *system* includes a rich set of *open* **interfaces** that enable the mixing and matching of modules from different **suppliers**.

system administration.   *See* **operations**.

system integrator.   *See* **integration**.

systems management.   *See* **operations**.

technology.   *See* **information technology**.

testing.   *See* **development**.

throughput.   *See* **performance**.

time-sharing.   *See* **computer**.

tools.   A category of **application software** that assists programmers in the **development** of new **applications** through the automation and optimization of common or tedious tasks. An *integrated development environment* is a complete suite of complementary tools supporting development.

total cost of ownership (TCO). The aggregate and comprehensive costs to a **user** or end-user organization to acquire, **provision, operate**, and use **software**, including user training and related administrative and managerial overhead.

trade secret. *See* intellectual property.

trademark. *See* intellectual property.

transmission control protocol (TCP). *See* **network**.

trust. *See* security.

trusted system. Equipment or **software** that is trusted (assumed to be trustworthy) to enforce a prescribed and delegated set of **policies**. Important applications are **authentication, rights management**, and firewalls.

upgrade. *See* distribution.

usage-based pricing. *See* price.

user interface. *See* design.

users. Persons, groups, organizations, or communities that use and benefit from a **software application** and supporting **infrastructure**.

utilization. *See* performance.

value chain. A sequence of complementary capabilities, functions, and services, each of which adds value to the previous, and all of which are required to serve the needs of **users**. For **software**, major ones include **analysis, development, provisioning**, and **operations**.

value pricing. *See* price.

variant. *See* versioning.

version. *See* release.

versioning. In economics, a form of **price discrimination** in which different versions of a product serving different price-quality-feature points are offered at distinct prices, and customers self-select based on their willingness to pay. In **software**, the term **variant** is used, because the term **version** has a different connotation (see **distribution**).

virtual machine. *See* portability.

waterfall. *See* development.

watermark. *See* rights management.

Web. Short for World Wide Web (WWW), an *information-access* **application** and set of **open standards** from the World Wide Web Consortium (W3C) employing a **client-server** architecture. It has more recently assumed a dual role as an **infrastructure** serving many other distributed applications. Important **open interfaces** in the Web are the *hypertext transfer protocol* (HTTP, governing the interaction between client and browser) and the *common gateway interchange* (CGI, an API governing interaction between Web server and other applications). The Web is being enhanced and expanded through *Web services*, which allow one Web server to make use of services provided by others.

Web services. A model for application **provisioning** based on offering and consuming packaged **services** over the Internet, analogous to **component** assembly. It allows capabilities currently offered by the **Web** to be extended.

References

Abraham, T., S. Ahlawat, and S. Ahlawat. 1998. The India option: Perceptions of Indian software solutions. *International Journal of Technology Management* 15 (6/7): 605–621.

Allen, M. W. 1971. History and applications of computers. In *Information, computers, machines, and man*, ed. A. E. Karbowiak and R. M. Huey. New York: Wiley.

Anderson, R. 2001. *Security engineering: A guide to building dependable distributed systems*. New York: Wiley.

Ang, P.-H., and B. Nadarajan. 1996. Censorship and the Internet: A Singapore perspective. *Communications of the ACM* 39 (6): 72–78.

Baker, A. L., and S. H. Zweben. 1979. The use of software science in evaluating modularity concepts. *IEEE Transactions on Software Engineering* TSE-5 (2): 110–120.

Balasubramanyam, V. N., and A. Balasubramanyam. 1997. International trade in services: The case of India's computer software. *World Economy* 20 (6): 829–843.

Baldwin, C. Y., and K. B. Clark. 1997. Managing in an age of modularity. *Harvard Business Review* 75 (5): 84–93.

Bass, L., P. Clements, and R. Kazman. 1998. *Software architecture in practice*. New York: Addison-Wesley.

Beck, K. 1999. *Extreme programming explained: Embrace change*. Reading, Mass.: Addison-Wesley.

Berztiss, A. 1996. *Software methods for business reengineering*. New York: Springer-Verlag.

Boehm, B.W. 1981. *Software engineering economics*. Englewood Cliffs, N.J.: Prentice-Hall.

———. 1984. Software engineering economics. *IEEE Transactions on Software Engineering* TSE-10 (1): 4–21.

———. 1988. A spiral model of software development and enhancement. *IEEE Computer* 21 (5): 61–72.

Boehm, B.W., and P. Bose. 1994. A collaborative spiral software process model based on theory W. In *Proceedings, 3d International IEEE Conference on the Software Process, Reston, Va.*

Boehm, B. W., A. Egyed, J. Kwan, D. Port, A. Shah, and R. Madachy. 1998. Using the WinWin spiral model: a case study. *IEEE Computer* 31 (7): 33–44.

Boehm, B. W., and K. Sullivan. 1999. Software economics: status and prospects. *Information and Software Technology* 41 (14): 937–946.

———. 2000. Software economics: A roadmap. In *The future of software engineering*, ed. A. Finkelstein. 22d International Conference on Software Engineering.

Bosch, J. 2000. *Design and use of software architectures.* Reading, Mass.: Addison-Wesley.

Brooks, F. Jr. 1975. *The mythical man-month.* Reading, Mass.: Addison-Wesley. Anniversary edition 1995.

Brown, W. J., R. C. Malveau, C. Raphael, W. H. Brown, W. H. McCormick, W. Hays III, and T. J. Mowbray. 1998. *Antipatterns: Refactoring software, architectures, and projects in crisis.* New York: Wiley.

Broy, M., A. Deimel, J. Henn, K. Koskimies, F. Plasil, G. Pomberger, W. Pree, M. Stal, C. Szyperski, and M. Broy. 1998. What characterizes a (software) component? *Software Concepts and Tools* 19 (no. 1): 49–59.

Bulkeley, W. M. 2000. Ozzie to unveil Napster-style networking. *Wall Street Journal Online*, October 24. ⟨http://www.zdnet.com/zdnn/stories/news/0,4586,2644020,00.html⟩.

Cartwright, S. D. 2000. Napster: A business in search of a viable model. *Journal of Business Strategy* 21 (5): 28–32.

Chang, W.-T., and D. Messerschmitt. 1996. Dynamic deployment of peer-to-peer networked applications to existing World-Wide Web browsers. In *Proceedings, Conference on Telecommunications Information Network Architecture (TINA), Heidelberg.*

Chavez, A., C. Tornabene, and G. Wiederhold. 1998. Software component licensing: a primer. *IEEE Software* 15 (5): 47–53.

Church, J., and N. Gandal. 1992. Network effects, software provision, and standardization. *Journal of Industrial Economics* 40 (1): 85–103.

Ciarletta, L. P., and A. A. Dima. 2000. A conceptual model for pervasive computing. In *Proceedings, 29th International Conference on Parallel Computing, Toronto.*

Clark, J. R., and L. S. Levy. 1993. Software economics: An application of price theory to the development of expert systems. *Journal of Applied Business Research* 9 (2): 14–18.

Conway, M. E. 1968. How do committees invent? *Datamation* 14 (4): 28–31, cited in Brooks 1975, *The mythical man-month*, anniversary edition (1995), 111.

Coplien, J. O. 1995. A generative development-process pattern language. In *Pattern Languages of Program Design*, ed. J. Coplien and D. Schmidt. Reading, Mass.: Addison-Wesley.

Covisint establishes corporate entity: Automotive e-business exchange becomes LLC. 2000. ⟨http://www.covisint.com/about/pressroom/pr/covisint_becomes.shtml⟩.

Cox, B. 1996. *Superdistribution: Objects as property on the electronic frontier.* ⟨http://virtualschool.edu/mon/TTEF.html⟩.

Dam, K. W. 1994. The economic underpinnings of patent law. *Journal of Legal Studies* 23 (1, pt. 1): 247–271.

———. 1995. Some economic considerations in the intellectual property protection of software. *Journal of Legal Studies* 24 (2): 321–377.

Dam, K. W., and H. S. Lin. 1996. National cryptography policy for the information age. *Issues in Science and Technology* 12 (4): 33.

————. 1997. Deciphering cryptography policy. *Issues in Science and Technology* 13 (4): 20.

David, P. A. 1990. The dynamo and the computer: An historical perspective on the modern productivity paradox. *American Economic Review* 80 (2): 355–361.

David, P. A., and S. Greenstein. 1990. The economics of compatibility standards: An introduction to recent research. *Economics of Innovation and New Technology* 1 (1/2): 3–41.

Denning, D. E. 1995. Key escrow encryption: the third paradigm. *Computer Security Journal* 11 (1): 43–52.

Denning, D. E., and D. K. Branstad. 1996. A taxonomy for key escrow encryption systems. *Communications of the ACM* 39 (3): 34–39.

Denning, D. E., and M. Smid. 1994. Key escrowing today. *IEEE Communications Magazine* 32 (9): 58–68.

Devanbu, P., P. Fong, and S. Stubblebine. 1998. Techniques for trusted software engineering. In *Proceedings, 20th International Conference on Software Engineering, Kyoto.* ⟨http://seclab.cs.ucdavis.edu/~devanbu/icse98.ps⟩.

ECMA. 1999. *ECMA-262: ECMAScript language specification.* ⟨http://www.ecma.ch/⟩.

————. 2001a. *ECMA-334: C# (C sharp) language specification.* ⟨http://www.ecma.ch/⟩.

————. 2001b. *ECMA-335: Common language infrastructure.* ⟨http://www.ecma.ch/⟩.

Economides, N. 1996. The economics of networks. *International Journal of Industrial Organization* 16 (4): 673–699. ⟨http://www.stern.nyu.edu/networks/top.html⟩.

Ellram, L. M. 1994. A taxonomy of total cost of ownership models. *Journal of Business Logistics* 15 (1): 171–191.

Ellram, L. M., and S. P. Siferd. 1998. Total cost of ownership: A key concept in strategic cost management decisions. *Journal of Business Logistics* 19 (1): 55–84.

Emigh, J. 1999. Total cost of ownership. *Computerworld* 33 (51): 52.

Farrell, J., and C. Shapiro. 1988. Dynamic competition with switching costs. *Rand Journal of Economics* 19 (1): 123–137.

————. 2000. Scale economies and synergies in horizontal merger analysis. ⟨http://www.haas.berkeley.edu/~shapiro/mergers.pdf⟩.

Ferguson, C. H., and C. R. Morris. 1994. *Computer wars: The fall of IBM and the future of global technology.* New York: Times Books.

Firesmith, D. G., and B. Henderson-Sellers. 2001. *The OPEN process framework: An introduction.* New York: Addison-Wesley. ⟨http://www.donald-firesmith.com/⟩.

Fowler, M., and J. Highsmith. 2001. The agile manifesto. *Software Development*, August. ⟨http://www.sdmagazine.com/documents/s=844/sdm0108a/0108.htm⟩.

Frakes, W. B., and P. B. Gandel. 1990. Representing reusable software. *Information and Software Technology* 32 (10): 653–664.

Frank, D. J., R. H. Dennard, E. Nowak, P. M. Solomon, Y. Taur, and H. P. Wong. 2001. Device scaling limits of Si MOSFETs and their application dependencies. *Proceedings of the IEEE* 89 (3): 259–288.

Frazier, T. P., and J. W. Bailey. 1996. The costs and benefits of domain-oriented software reuse: Evidence from the STARS demonstration projects. Paper P-3191. Institute for Defense Analysis.

Furse, M. 1998. United States vs. Microsoft: Ill-considered antitrust. *International Review of Law, Computers, and Technology* 12 (1): 99–120.

————. 1999. United States vs. Microsoft: High-tech antitrust. *International Review of Law, Computers, and Technology* 13 (2): 237–253.

Gaffney, J. E. Jr., and T. A. Durek. 1989. Software reuse—Key to enhanced productivity: Some quantitative models. *Information and Software Technology* 31 (5): 258–267.

Garcia, M. 1998. Institutional development in the software industry: Intellectual property protection. Ph.D. diss., University of Southern California, Los Angeles, CA 90089.

Gardner, T. 2001. An introduction to Web services. *Ariadne,* October 2 (no. 29). ⟨http://www.ariadne.ac.uk/issue29/gardner/⟩.

Garone, S., and S. Cusack. 1999. *Components, objects, and development environments: 1999 worldwide markets and trends.* International Data Corporation.

Gaskins, D. 1971. Dynamic limit pricing: Optimal pricing under threat of entry. *Journal of Economic Theory* (2): 306–322.

Gerlach, J. H., and F.-Y. Kuo. 1991. Understanding human-computer interaction for information systems design. *MIS Quarterly* 15 (4): 526–549.

Goertzel, B., and P. Pritchard. 2002. The Internet economy as a complex system. ⟨http://www.goertzel.org/papers/ecommerce.html⟩.

Gray, J., and P. Shenoy. 2000. Rules of thumb in data engineering. In *Proceedings, 16th IEEE International Conference on Data Engineering, San Diego.*

Great Books Online. 2002. ⟨http://www.bartleby.com/⟩.

Griffith, D. 1998. Total cost of ownership: The hidden margin-eating monster. *Computer Technology Review* 18 (6): 54–56.

Gulledge, T. R., and W. P. Hutzler, eds. 1993. *Analytical methods in software engineering economics.* New York: Springer-Verlag.

Hartford, K. 2000. Cyberspace with Chinese characteristics. *Current History,* September, 255. ⟨http://www.pollycyber.com/pubs/ch/home.htm⟩.

Heer, D. N., and D. P. Maher. 1995. The heart of the new information appliance. *IEEE Transactions on Consumer Electronics* 41 (3): 869–874.

Heineman, G. T., and W. T. Councill. 2001. *Component-based software engineering: Putting the pieces together.* New York: Addison-Wesley.

Hiles, A. 1993. *Service-level agreements: Managing cost and quality in service relationships.* London: Chapman and Hall.

Hopkins, J. 2000. Component primer. *Communications of the ACM* 43 (10): 27–30.

Howard, J. D. 1997. An analysis of security incidents on the Internet. Ph.D. diss., Carnegie Mellon University, Pittsburgh, PA 15213.
⟨http://www.cert.org/research/JHThesis/ Start.html⟩.

IBM Systems Journal. 1999. Vol. 38, no. 4. Special issue on pervasive computing. ⟨http://www.research.ibm.com/journal/sj38-4.html⟩.

International technology roadmap for semiconductors. 2002. Technology Working Groups of International SEMATECH. ⟨http://public.itrs.net/⟩.

Jacobson, I., M. Griss, and P. Jönsson. 1997. *Software reuse: Architecture, process and organization for business success*. Reading, Mass.: Addison-Wesley.

Jung, H.-W., and B. Choi. 1999. Optimization models for quality and cost of modular software systems. *European Journal of Operational Research* 112 (3): 613–619.

Kang, K. C., and L. S. Levy. 1989. Software methodology in the harsh light of economics. *Information and Software Technology* 31 (5): 239–250.

Katz, M. L., and C. Shapiro. 1985. Network externalities, competition, and compatibility. *American Economic Review* 75 (3): 424–440.

————. 1986a. How to license intangible property. *Quarterly Journal of Economics* 101 (3): 567–589.

————. 1986b. Technology adoption in the presence of network externalities. *Journal of Political Economy* 94 (4): 822–841.

————. 1999a. Antitrust in software markets. In *Competition, innovation and the Microsoft monopoly: Antitrust in the digital marketplace*, ed. J. A. Eisenach and T. M. Lenard, 29–81. Proceedings of a Conference of the Progress and Freedom Foundation, Washington, D.C. Boston: Kluwer. ⟨http://www.haas.berkeley.edu/~shapiro/software.pdf⟩.

————. 1999b. Competition policy in the information economy. ⟨http://www.haas.berkeley.edu/~shapiro/software.pdf⟩.

Keliher, M. J. 1980. Computer security and privacy: A systems approach is needed. *Vital Speeches* 46 (21): 662–666.

Kemerer, C. F. 1998. Progress, obstacles, and opportunities in software engineering economics. *Communications of the ACM* 41 (8): 63–66.

Keyes, R. W. 2001. Fundamental limits of silicon technology. *Proceedings of the IEEE* 89 (3): 227–239.

Koch, C. 1998. Service level agreements: put IT in writing. *CIO Magazine*, November 15. ⟨http://www.cio.com/archive/111598_sla.html⟩.

Kovacic, W., and C. Shapiro. 1999. Antitrust policy: A century of economic and legal thinking. ⟨http://www.haas.berkeley.edu/~shapiro/century.pdf⟩.

Kruchten, P. 2000. *The rational unified process: An introduction*. 2d ed. New York: Addison-Wesley.

Langelaar, G. C., I. Setyawan, and R. L. Lagendijk. 2000. Watermarking digital image and video data. A state-of-the-art overview. *IEEE Signal Processing Magazine* 17 (5): 20–46.

Langlois, R. N. 1992. External economies and economic progress: The case of the microcomputer industry. *Business History Review* 66 (1): 1–50.

————. 1999. Modularity in technology, organization, and society. University of Connecticut, Department of Economics, Working Paper 1999-05.

Langlois, R. N., and P. L. Robertson. 1992. Networks and innovation in a modular system: Lessons from the microcomputer and stereo component industries. *Research Policy* 21 (4): 297–313.

Laudon, K. C. and J. P. Laudon. 2001. *Management Information Systems: Managing the Digital Firm*. Englewood Cliffs, N.J.: Prentice Hall.

Lee, P., and M. Leone. 1996. Optimizing ML with run-time code generation. *ACM SIGPLAN Notices* 31 (5): 137–148.

Lehman, M. M., and J. F. Ramil. 2000. Software evolution in the age of component-based software engineering. *IEE Proceedings Software* 147 (6) 249–255.

Lehman, M. M., J. F. Ramil, P. D. Wernick, D. E. Perry, and W. M. Turski. 1997. Metrics and laws of software evolution: The nineties view. In *Proceedings, Fourth International Software Metrics Conference, Los Alamitos, Calif.*, 20–32.

Levin, S. I. 1999. Who are we protecting? A critical evaluation of United States encryption technology export controls. *Law and Policy in International Business* 30 (3): 529–552.

Levy, D., and S. Welzer. 1985. System error: How the IBM antitrust suit raised computer prices. *Regulation* 9 (5): 27–30.

Levy, L. S. 1987. *Taming the tiger: Software engineering and software economics.* New York: Springer-Verlag.

Lewis, T. 1997. *Friction-free economy: Strategies for success in a wired world.* New York: Harper Business.

Liebowitz, S., and S. Margolis. 1999. *Winners, losers and Microsoft: Competition and antitrust in high technology.* Oakland, Calif.: Independent Institute.

Lixin, T. 2001. Shifting paradigms with the application service provider model. *IEEE Computer* 34 (10): 32–39.

Luecke, R. W., D. T. Meeting, and R. G. Klingshirn. 1999. New AICPA standards aid accounting for the costs of internal-use software. *Healthcare Financial Management* 53 (5): 40–46.

Lyman, P., and H. R. Varian. 2000. How much information? ⟨http://www.sims.berkeley.edu/ how-much-info⟩.

Macker, J. P., V. D. Park, and M. S. Corson. 2001. Mobile and wireless Internet services: putting the pieces together. *IEEE Communications Magazine* 39 (6): 148–155.

MacKie-Mason, J. K., and H. R. Varian. 1995. Pricing congestible network resources. *IEEE Journal on Selected Areas in Communications* 13 (7): 1141–1149.

Maes, M., T. Kalker, J.-P. Linnartz, J. Talstra, F. G. Depovere, and J. Haitsma. 2000. Digital watermarking for DVD video copy protection. *IEEE Signal Processing Magazine* 17 (5): 47–57.

Makulowich, J. 1999. Pervasive computing: "The next big thing." *Washington Technology Online* 14 (8). ⟨http://www.wtonline.com/vol14_no8/cover/652-1.html⟩.

Markoff, J. 1999a. Growing compatibility issue: Computers and user privacy. *New York Times*, March 3.

———. 1999b. When privacy is more perilous than the lack of it. *New York Times*, April 4.

Marsh, G. 1987. Impacts of the new computer crime law on computer security operations. *CPA Journal* 57 (8): 106–107.

Marshall, A. 1890. *Principles of economics.* Reprinted: Prometheus Books, 1997.

Messerschmitt, D. 1999a. *Networked applications: A guide to the new computing infrastructure.* San Francisco: Morgan Kaufmann.

————. 1999b. The prospects for computing-communications convergence. In *Proceedings, MÜNCHNER KREIS, Conference VISION 21: Perspectives for Information and Communication Technology, Munich.*
⟨http://www.eecs.berkeley.edu/~messer/PAPERS/99/Munich. PDF⟩.

————. 1999c. *Understanding networked applications: A first course.* San Francisco: Morgan Kaufmann.

Messerschmitt, D., and C. Szyperski. 2001. Industrial and economic properties of software: Technology, processes, and value. University of California Berkeley Computer Science Division Technical Report UCB//CSD-01-1130 and Microsoft Corporation Technical Report MSR-TR-2001-11.

Meyers, J. 1993. A short history of the computer. ⟨http://ww.softlord.com/comp/⟩.

Microsoft Corporation. 2000. Universal plug and play device architecture.
⟨http://www.upnp.org/download/UPnPDA10_20000613.htm⟩.

Moore, G. E. 1965. Cramming more components onto integrated circuits. *Electronics* 38 (8): 114–117.

Mowery, D. C., and R. N. Langlois. 1994. Spinning off and spinning on: The federal government role in the development of the U.S. computer software industry. *Research Policy* 25: 947–966.

Mowery, D. C., and R. R. Nelson, eds. 1999. *Sources of industrial leadership: Studies of seven industries.* New York: Cambridge University Press.

Munter, P. 1999. Accounting for software development costs. *CPA Journal* 69 (2): 42–45.

NRC (National Research Council). 1994. *Rights and responsibilities of participants in networked communities.* Washington, D.C.: National Academies Press.

————. 1995. *Evolving the high performance computing and communications initiative to support the nation's information infrastructure.* Washington, D.C.: National Academies Press.

————. 1996. *Cryptography's role in securing the information society.* Washington, D.C.: National Academies Press.

————. 1999a. *Being fluent with information technology.* Washington, D.C.: National Academies Press.

————. 1999b. *Funding a revolution: Government support for computing research.* Washington, D.C.: National Academies Press.

————. 2000a. *The digital dilemma: Intellectual property rights in the digital age.* Washington, D.C.: National Academies Press.

————. 2000b. *Making IT better: Expanding information technology research to meet society's needs.* Washington, D.C.: National Academies Press.

————. 2001. *Building a workforce for the information rconomy.* Washington, D.C.: National Academies Press.

————. 2002. *Technically speaking: Why all Americans should know more about technology.* National Academies Press.

NSF (National Science Foundation). 2001. White paper on an NSF ANIR middleware initiative. CISE Advisory Committee, Subcommittee on the Middleware Infrastructure. ⟨http://www.cise.nsf.gov/anir/mwir_whiteppr.htm#1⟩.

Netpliance. ⟨http://www.netpliance.com/⟩.

Neumann, P. G. 1999. Robust open-source software. *Communications of the ACM* 42 (2): 128.

Nielsen, J. 1993. Noncommand user interfaces. *Communications of the ACM* 36 (4): 83–99. ⟨http://www.useit.com/papers/noncommand.html⟩.

———. 2000. *Designing Web usability: The practice of simplicity*. Indianapolis: New Riders Publishing.

Oberndorf, P. A. 1997. Facilitating component-based software engineering: COTS and open systems. In *Proceedings, Fifth International Symposium on Assessment of Software Tools and Technologies, Pittsburgh*.

Open Source Initiative. ⟨http://www.opensource.org/⟩.

O'Reilly, T. 1999. Lessons from open-source software development. *Communications of the ACM* 42 (4): 32–37.

Palm, Inc. 2002. The philosophy behind the Palm OS. ⟨http://www.palmos.com/platform/ philosophy.html⟩.

Parnas, D. L. 1972. On the criteria for decomposing systems into modules. *Communications of the ACM* 15 (12): 1053–1058.

Petreley, N. 1999. Total cost of ownership reduction may just be another impossible dream. *InfoWorld* 21 (40): 126.

Pettersson, M. 1996. *Complexity and evolution*. New York: Cambridge University Press.

Pfleeger, C. P. 1997. *Security in computing*. 2d ed. Englewood Cliffs, N.J.: Prentice-Hall.

Podilchuk, C. I., and E. J. Delp. 2001. Digital watermarking: algorithms and applications. *IEEE Signal Processing Magazine* 18 (4): 33–46.

Portero-Sánchez, L. M. 1999. Competition in the software industry: The interface between antitrust and intellectual property law. *Communications and Strategies* 35 (3d quarter): 45–79.

Pour, G. 1998. Moving toward the component-based software development approach. In *Proceedings, Conference on Technology of Object-Oriented Languages (TOOLS 27), Beijing*.

Pressman, R. S. 2000. *Software engineering: A practitioner's approach*. 5th ed. New York: McGraw-Hill.

Raymond, E. 1996. *The new hacker's dictionary*. 3d ed. Cambridge, Mass.: MIT Press.

Resnick, P., and H. R. Varian. 1997. Recommender systems. *Communications of the ACM* 40 (3).

Roberts, L. G. 1969. Data processing technology forecast. Advanced Research Projects Agency Internal Memorandum. ⟨http://www.ziplink.net/~lroberts/Forecast69.htm⟩.

———. 2000. Beyond Moore's law: Internet growth trends. *IEEE Computer* 33 (1): 117–119.

Robertson, P. L., and R. N. Langlois. 1995. Innovation, networks, and vertical integration. *Research Policy* 24 (4): 543–562.

Romero, S. 2001. Location devices' use rises, prompting privacy concerns. *New York Times*, March 4.

Royce, W. W. 1970. Managing the development of large software systems. In *Proceedings, IEEE WESCON.*

———. 1990. TRW's Ada process model for incremental development of large software systems. In *Proceedings, International Conference on Software Engineering, Nice, France.*

Saltzer, J. H., D. P. Reed, and D. Clark. 1984. End-to-end arguments in system design. *ACM Transactions on Computer Systems* 2 (4): 277–288. An earlier version appeared in *Proceedings, Second International Conference on Distributed Computing Systems* (April 1981), 509–512.

Samuelson, P. 1999. Why the anticircumvention regulations need revision. *Communications of the ACM* 42 (9): 17–21.

Sánchez, R., and J. T. Mahoney. 1996. Modularity, flexibility, and knowledge management in product and organization design. *Strategic Management Journal* (winter): 1763–1776.

Schaller, R. R. 1997. Moore's law: past, present and future. *IEEE Spectrum* 34 (6): 52–59.

Schattke, R. 1988. Accounting for computer software: The revenue side of the coin. *Journal of Accountancy* 165 (1): 58–70.

Shannon, C. E., and W. Weaver. 1949. *The mathematical theory of communication.* Urbana: University of Illinois Press.

Shapiro, C. 2000. Setting compatibility standards: Cooperation or collusion? ⟨http://www.haas.berkeley.edu/~shapiro/standards.pdf⟩.

———. 2001a. Antitrust limits to patent settlements. ⟨http://www.haas.berkeley.edu/ ~shapiro/settle.pdf⟩.

———. 2001b. Navigating the patent thicket: Cross licenses, patent pools, and standard setting. In *Innovation policy and the economy,* ed. A. Jaffe, J. Lerner, and S. Stern. ⟨http://www.haas.berkeley.edu/~shapiro/thicket.pdf⟩.

Shapiro, C., and H. R. Varian. 1998. Versioning: The smart way to sell information. *Harvard Business Review* 76 (6): 106–114.

———. 1999a. The art of standard wars. *California Management Review* 41 (2): 8–32.

———. 1999b. *Information rules: A strategic guide to the network economy.* Boston: Harvard Business School Press.

Shy, O. 2001. *The economics of network industries.* New York: Cambridge University Press.

Shy, O., and J. Thisse. 1999. A strategic approach to software protection. *Journal of Economics and Management Strategy* 8 (2): 163–190.

Silvestre, J. 1987. Economies and Diseconomies of scale. In *The new Palgrave: A dictionary of economics,* ed. J. Eatwell, M. Milgate, and P. Newman, 80–83. London: Macmillan.

Slaughter, S. A., D. E. Harter, and M. S. Krishnan. 1998. Evaluating the cost of software quality. *Communications of the ACM* 41 (8): 67–73.

Smith, R., B. Meyer, C. Szyperski, and G. Pour. 2000. Component-based development? Refining the blueprint. In *Proceedings, 34th International Conference on Technology of Object-Oriented Languages and Systems (TOOLS 34), Santa Barbara, Calif.*

Software in India: Bangalore bytes? 1996. *Economist,* March 23.

Software Productivity Consortium. 1994. Process Engineering with the Evolutionary Spiral Process Model SPC-93098-CMC, version 01.00.06. Herndon, Va.

Stawlings, W. 1999. *Cryptography and network security: Principles and practice.* 2d ed. New York: Prentice-Hall.

Stokes, D. E. 1997. *Pasteur's quadrant: Basic science and technological innovation.* Washington, D.C.: Brookings Institution Press.

Suganuma, T., T. Ogasawara, M. Takeuchi, T. Yasue, M. Kawahito, K. Ishizaki, H. Komatsu, and T. Nakatani. 2000. Overview of the IBM Java just-in-time compiler. *IBM Systems Journal* 39 (1): 175–193.

Sullivan, J. 1999. Napster: Music is for sharing. *Wired News,* November 1. ⟨http://www.wired.com/news/print/0,1294,32151,00.html⟩.

Sun Microsystems. 1999a. The Java Hotspot performance engine architecture: A white book about Sun's second-generation performance technology. ⟨http://java.sun.com/products/hotspot/whitebook.html⟩.

———. 1999b. Jini technology architectural overview. ⟨http://www.sun.com/jini/whitepapers/architecture.html⟩.

Szyperski, C. 1998. Emerging component software technologies: A strategic comparison. *Software Concepts and Tools* 19 (1): 2–10.

———. 2000. Rethinking our trade and science: From developing components to component-based development. *Modular Programming Languages. Joint Modular Languages Conference, JMLC 2000, Zurich.*

———. 2001. Components and Web services. *Software Development* 9 (8).

———. 2002a. *Component software: Beyond object-oriented programming.* 2d ed. New York: Addison-Wesley.

———. 2002b. Services rendered. *Software Development* 10 (1).

Thebaut, S. M., and V. Y. Shen. 1984. An analytic resource model for large-scale software development. *Information Processing and Management* 20 (1/2): 293–315.

Thompson, C., ed. 1998. Workshop Report. OMG DARPA Workshop on Compositional Software Architectures. ⟨http://www.objs.com/workshops/ws9801/report.html⟩.

Torrisi, S. 1998. *Industrial organization and innovation: An international study of the software industry.* London: Edward Elgar Publishers.

Touretzky, D. S. 2001. Free speech rights for programmers. *Communications of the ACM* 44 (8): 23–25.

———. 2002. Gallery of CSS descramblers. ⟨http://www.cs.cmu.edu/~dst/DeCSS/Gallery⟩.

Traw, C. B. S. 2001. Protecting digital content within the home. *IEEE Computer* 34 (10): 42–47.

Ueda, K. 2001. Synthesis and emergence: Research overview. *Artificial Intelligence in Engineering* 15 (4).

Upton, D. M. 1992. A flexible structure for computer-controlled manufacturing systems. *Manufacturing Review* 5 (1): 58–74. ⟨http://www.people.hbs.edu/dupton/papers/organic/ WorkingPaper.html⟩.

U.S. Department of Justice. 1998. *The United States of America vs. Microsoft Corporation.* Civil Action No. 98-1232. Complaint. May 18. ⟨http://www.usdoj.gov/atr/cases/ f1700/1763.htm⟩.

———. 1999. *The United States of America vs. Microsoft Corporation,* Civil Action No. 98-1232. Findings of Fact. November 5. ⟨http://www.usdoj.gov/atr/cases/f3800/msjudgex.htm⟩.

Usability Professionals Association. ⟨http://www.upassoc.org/⟩.

Vacca, J. 1993. Tapping a gold mine of software assets. *Software Magazine* 13 (16): 57–67.

Varian, H. R. 1992. *Microeconomic analysis.* 3d ed. New York: W.W. Norton.

———. 1993. Economic incentives in software design. *Computational Economics* 6 (3/4): 201–217.

———. 2001. Versioning information goods. In *Internet publishing and beyond: The economics of digital information and intellectual property,* ed. B. Kahin and H. R. Varian. Cambridge, Mass.: MIT Press.

Veryard, R., ed. 1991. *The economics of information systems and software.* Boston: Butterworth-Heinemann.

Wallach, D. S. 2001. Copy protection technology is doomed. *IEEE Computer* 34 (10): 48–49.

Ward, E. 2000. Viral marketing involves serendipity, not planning. *B to B* 85 (10): 26.

Weiser, M. 1991. The computer for the 21st century. *Scientific American* 265 (3): 94–104.

White book: How DIGITAL FX!32 works. 2002. ⟨http://www.support.compaq.com/ amt/fx32/fx-white.html⟩.

World Wide Web Consortium. 2002. A little history of the World Wide Web. ⟨http://www.w3.org/History.html⟩.

About the Authors

David G. Messerschmitt is the Roger A. Strauch Professor of Electrical Engineering and Computer Sciences (EECS) and the Acting Dean of the School of Information Management and Systems at the University of California at Berkeley. From 1993 to 1996 he served as chair of EECS, and prior to 1977 he was with AT&T Bell Laboratories in Holmdel, New Jersey. Current research interests include the future of wireless networks, the economics of networks and software, and more generally the interdependence of business and economics with computing and communication technology. He is active in developing new courses on information technology in business and information science programs, and introducing relevant economics and business concepts into the computer science and engineering curriculum. He is the author of a recent textbook, *Understanding Networked Applications: A First Course*, and the co-author of a widely used textbook, *Digital Communications*. He is a co-founder and former director of TCSI Corporation of Alameda, California. He is on the advisory board of the Fisher Center for Management and Information Technology in the Haas School of Business, the directorate for Computer and Information Sciences and Engineering at the National Science Foundation, and a member of the NSF Blue Ribbon Panel on Cyber-infrastructure, and he recently co-chaired a National Research Council study on the future of information technology research. He received a B.S. degree from the University of Colorado, and M.S. and Ph.D. degrees from the University of Michigan. He is a Fellow of the IEEE, a member of the National Academy of Engineering, and a recipient of the IEEE Alexander Graham Bell Medal recognizing "exceptional contributions to the advancement of communication sciences and engineering."

Clemens A. Szyperski is a software architect at Microsoft Research, where he furthers the principles, technologies, and methods supporting component software. He is the author of an award-winning book, *Component Software: Beyond Object-Oriented Programming*, and numerous other publications. He is the charter editor of the Addison-Wesley *Component Software* professional book series. He is a regular contributor to the *Beyond Objects* series of the widely read *Software Development* magazine. He is a frequent speaker, panelist, and committee member at international conferences and events, both academic and industrial. He is the originator and co-organizer of the series of Workshops on Component-Oriented Programming, held annually since 1996 in conjunction with the European Conference on Object-Oriented Programming. He served on review panels for major national funding boards in Australia, Canada, Ireland, and the United States. He is a frequent reviewer for learned journals on computer science and software engineering. He has served on the program committees of numerous conferences, including ECOOP, ICSE, and OOPSLA. He received an M.S. degree in electrical engineering from the Aachen Institute of Technology in Germany. He received a Ph.D. degree in computer science in 1992 from the Swiss Federal Institute of Technology (ETH) in Zurich under the guidance of Niklaus Wirth. In 1992–93 he held a postdoctoral scholarship at the International Computer Science Institute at the University of California, Berkeley. From 1994 to 1999 he was tenured as associate professor at the Queensland University of Technology, Brisbane, Australia, where he still holds an adjunct professorship with the School of Computing Science. In 1993 he co-founded Oberon Microsystems, Inc., Zurich, Switzerland, with its 1998 spin-off, esmertec inc., also Zurich.

Name Index

IBM, 22, 366n8
  AIX, 194
  antitrust and, 298
  bundling and, 203
  DBMS and, 136
  government and, 304
  layering and, 209–210
  open source and, 79, 321
  outsourcing and, 367n18
  platform issues and, 200
  System/360, 172
  Token Ring, 109–110
  WebSphere, 229
India, 301
Informix, 136
Inktomi, 116, 194
Intel, 22, 298
International Standards Organization (ISO),
  232–233
International Telecommunication Union
  (ITU), 215
Internet Engineering Task Force (IETF),
  233, 239–240

Kennedy, Jacqueline, 1
KPMG, 176

Lancope Technologies, 289
Liberty Alliance, 158
Lotus, 62
Lucent, 181, 190, 367n18

Massachusetts Institute of Technology, 240
Mazu Technologies, 289
Messerschmitt, David G., 403
Metcalfe, Robert, 312
Microsoft, xiii, 172
  antitrust and, 298
  CLR and, 99
  DBMS and, 136
  Excel, 82
  games and, 353
  Internet Explorer, 160
  MSN, 45
  NET, 99, 104, 117, 223, 258, 374n4
  Office, 62, 322

Passport, 158, 162
  platform issues and, 200
  program manager, 82
  shared source model and, 81
  Universal Plug-and-Play, 356–357
  Windows, 68, 104, 205, 225, 254
  Word, 19–20, 229
Moore, Gordon, 29
Motorola, 181

Napster, 186, 243–244, 316, 325
National Research Council, 13, 267
NEC, 367n18
Netpliance, 353
Netscape, 45, 160
Nintendo, 353
Nortel Networks, 181, 190, 367n18
Novell, 237

Object Management Group (OMG), 214,
  240, 255
Oracle, 136, 180

Pasteur, Louis, 303
PeopleSoft, 180
Perot Systems, 183
Philips, 367n18
Ploenzke, 180
Priceline.com, 269
Price Waterhouse Coopers, 176

Rational, 76
RealNetworks, 113, 186, 243, 333
Red Hat Software, 79
ReplayTV, 187
Rickover, Hyman G., 41
Roosevelt, Franklin Delano, 199

Sartre, Jean-Paul, 361
SBC, 181
Shapiro, Carl, 309
Siebel, 180
Siemens, 190, 367n18
Signature Financial Group, 268–269
Singapore, 293–294
Software4U, 275–276

Subject Index